Still
Unequal

Still
Unequal

The Shameful Truth About Women and Justice in America

Lorraine Dusky

CROWN PUBLISHERS, INC.
NEW YORK

Published by Crown Publishers, Inc., 201 East 50th Street, New York,
New York 10022. Member of the Crown Publishing Group.

Random House, Inc. New York, Toronto, London, Sydney, Auckland

http: //www.randomhouse.com/

CROWN is a trademark of Crown Publishers, Inc.

Printed in the United States of America

Design by Deborah Kerner

Library of Congress Cataloging-in-Publication Data
Dusky, Lorraine.
    Still unequal : the shameful truth about women and justice in America/
Lorraine Dusky. — 1st ed.
    Includes bibliographical references and index.
    1. Sex discrimination against women—Law and legislation—United
States.   2. Sexual harassment of women—Law and legislation—United
States.   3. Sex discrimination in justice administration—United States.
4. Sex Crimes—United States.   5. Women—Crimes against—
United States.   6. Women lawyers—United States.   I. Title.
KF4758.D87   1996
342.73'0878—dc20
[347.302878]   96-24410
                                                              CIP

ISBN 0-517-59389-0
10 9 8 7 6 5 4 3 2 1
First Edition

To Victoria Wrozek Dusky
and Anthony Brandt,
neither of whom tolerates injustice.

Acknowledgments

First and foremost, I would like to thank my husband, Anthony Brandt, for his unwavering support, financially and emotionally, for the three—or was it four?—years that this book took. His astute editing and guidance every step of the way helped me to realize the project as I saw it. Many people can't understand how two writers live and work together in the same not very large house. That we did it and survived is a testament to our bond, and I am truly grateful for his forbearance.

I would also like to mention those individuals who gave freely their time and expertise and were not put off by my incessant calls: Stephanie Goldberg, Jesselyn Brown, Joan Zorza, Dakila Divina, Jeryl Brunner, Madelyn Applebaum, Rachel Patrick, Marena McPhearson and all the people at the John Jermain Library in Sag Harbor, especially Patricia Brandt. The National Center for State Courts provided reams of data throughout the process and I am deeply grateful for their existence. I would also especially like to thank Lynn Hecht Schafran, who was first an inspiration, then a guide and, finally, a friend.

I thank my agent, Suzanne Gluck, for being exactly the kind of agent I needed and wanted—quick, tenacious and supportive—and Betty A. Prashker, for whom this book was always intended since that day in 1988 she sent me her card in the Grill Room at the Four Seasons and suggested that my next book be for Crown. The card—which I have kept—became my talisman as I wrote.

Last, I would like to thank my mother, Mrs. Victoria Wrozek Dusky, for providing the atmosphere where I learned as a girl that all people, rich and poor, female and male, are entitled to stand up for their rights and for seeing to it that I was able to attend college. Without her support at that critical juncture of my life, this book would never have been realized.

Contents

Contents

Introduction

The time to assert a right is the time when that right is denied.—ANGELINA
GRIMKÉ, IN AN 1837 LETTER TELLING WHY SHE AND HER SISTER WOULD NOT STOP MAKING AN ISSUE
OF WOMEN'S RIGHTS DURING THE ABOLITION MOVEMENT

SANDRA DAY O'CONNOR and Ruth Bader Ginsburg sit on the Supreme Court.
Janet Reno holds the top lawyer's job in America, that of attorney general. Her
deputy, Jamie Gorelick, is a woman. To date, women constitute more than 31
percent of President Clinton's federal judicial appointments, making the federal
bench more than 12 percent female. For the first time in its 117-year history,
a woman, Roberta Cooper Ramo, headed the American Bar Association (ABA),
in the 1995–96 term; and concurrently Martha Barnett chaired the powerful
House of Delegates. In 1987 the ABA convened a Commission on Women in
the Profession; Hillary Rodham Clinton was its first chair. The Association of
Trial Lawyers of America has had not one but two female presidents: Roxanne
Barton Conlin and Pam Anagnos Liapakis. Today it is not just men who are
high-profile lawyers: Marcia Clark and Leslie Abramson and Gloria Allred and
Linda Fairstein, not to mention Hillary Rodham Clinton, spring to mind. Today
nearly a quarter of all lawyers in private practice are women.

That number should grow, as women constitute approximately 43 percent
of law students. At some schools they even walk away with most of the prizes.
At the Ivy League Columbia University, from 1985 through 1995 women won
nine of the twelve awards for the highest grade-point averages.* At the Uni-

---

* One year two students had the same GPA.

versity of New Mexico in 1995, women constituted the majority of the top fifteen students in each of the three classes then at the school and more than half of the positions on law review, that singular badge of honor.

You would think that any problems vis-à-vis women in our legal system were solved. You would think that our nation had finally accepted women as full and equal partners in the pursuit of justice. You would think men and women were equal before the law.

You would be wrong.

The facts are these. At many if not most law schools, blatant discrimination against women is still the order of the day. Teachers don't call on women, won't listen to what they say, refuse to acknowledge that the law itself is written from the perspective of prosperous white males. Women experience law school as a gauntlet of sexism they must run, a searing initiation rite into a club only recently and reluctantly integrated. Not surprisingly, women do far worse at many schools than would be expected given their credentials when they enter. If they do well at Columbia, they do poorly at the University of Pennsylvania, where men walk away with the preponderance of the school's honors and lead most extracurricular activities. Are the men at Penn smarter than the men at Columbia? Are the women dumber? Don't you believe it. What is true at Penn is not the exception, it is the rule. Men find ways to keep women down.

So do law school curriculums. If the prevalence of rape in this country is a national disgrace, the way rape law is taught in law schools—if it is taught at all—is a national joke. In some law school textbooks rape victims are still presented as scarlet women preying on innocent boys and men, tricking them into having sex and then yelling rape. Some teachers are no less biased in their attitudes, and you can imagine how male students respond. At many schools, the best—Harvard, Yale, Penn—among them, if a woman takes a feminist point of view, she is labeled a "feminazi" or lesbian. Although women have been graduating from law schools in impressive numbers since the mid-1970s, you'll find precious few of them among the full professors at most schools, particularly the better ones. Women are traditionally clustered—call that "kept"—in the ranks of the untenured. In 1994, 67 percent of the lecturers/instructors and 52 percent of the assistant professors in law schools were women, but only 17 percent of the professors were. Somehow they're just not qualified for the top posts, right? Don't you believe it. Aging white males will do anything to maintain their hammer hold on positions of influence at the schools. Sexism in hiring and promotions is routine. Catharine MacKinnon, quite possibly the most in-fluential individual in American law living today, spent years moving from school to school because none would give tenure. The University of Michigan finally did in 1990.

Even the very books the law students read are rotten with bias. Most simply ignore the historical context of old judicial decisions that obviously discriminate against women and treat them as if they were still valid. Women appear in the stereotypical role of helpmate, or they are presented as either helpless vic-tims or scheming vixens. Their status as second-class citizens is taken for granted.

It's no better for women when they join the profession. Although women are hired in great numbers at law firms into entry-level positions, the process of becoming a partner winnows them out mercilessly. At most law firms, women are cut out of the circles of power, not mentored the same as men, not handed clients when somebody retires. If they gain too much power because they are responsible for so much business, men may try to steal their clients, and their clout. In major New York City law firms, only 5 percent of the women hired after 1981 were promoted to partner; 17 percent of the men were. Many law firms have created a partnership level below that of full partner. These individuals are called "partners," but they do not share in the profits of the firm. It is arguable that this new level was added to quiet many of the women who were eligible for partnership but in the male leadership's mind lacked that cer-tain something that made them one of the guys.

Given that there are too many lawyers in America in the first place, given the downturn of business in the late 1980s, competition among lawyers has become exceedingly keen, and the law has become a profession of nearly in-tolerable hours for anyone who wishes to succeed at most male-run law firms. This need not be so, because law is one profession that is perfectly suited to a workweek of however many hours one wishes to work. To work less, one need only take fewer clients. But law firms don't allow for this, and since women are still the primary caretaking parents of children, most law firms badly abuse those women who try to combine careers with children.

When women flee the steely sexism of most law firms for the more receptive shores of the legal departments of businesses, they are paid less than men. The Colorado Women's Bar Association surveyed in-house lawyers in that state a few years ago, and found that women who held the top job of general counsel averaged $152,000, while men averaged $205,000. The numbers possibly relate to the size of the company, but that only means that women are not getting the top jobs at large corporations. Only a few, a very few, are ever promoted to general counsel at Fortune 500 companies.

In court women lawyers are still demeaned, still sexually harassed, still made to prove that they can do the job, all of which places an extra and unnecessary burden on them. And it is not just the opposing counsel who is doing the harassing. There are still judges out there who haven't learned the first thing about how to treat women with respect. Who are, indeed, overt sexists. Who are, indeed, raping women in chambers and getting away with it.

The courts in America, for that matter, still do not guarantee women equal rights with men, regardless of the promises of the law. The laws were written as a body of rules by and for affluent white men, and to a degree so they remain. Although much has been made of the divorce reform that swept the country in the 1970s and 1980s, for example, women who have devoted their lives to making homes and raising children are routinely victimized by lawyers who want a quick resolution because they know the woman doesn't have any money to pay them well. All too many judges act as if a middle-aged or older housewife can be "rehabilitated" in a year or two and get a little job that will solve everything. The Rhode Island Supreme Court, in two decisions devastating to homemakers, one in late 1995, one in early 1996, refused to value women's contributions to the family assets when dividing the pot. In one case the woman gave up custody because she could not afford to care for her children adequately on the limited resources the court allotted her. In another the value of a chiropractor's "goodwill" in assessing the value of his practice—usually considered the major value of the practice when it is sold—could not be counted toward the wife's share of the assets. Instead she was awarded a mere 12 percent of the value of his practice, although she had sometimes worked in the office herself.

There is evidence that men who batter, either emotionally or physically, are the most likely to sue for custody. Although any hint of battering is supposed to prevent them from getting custody, this is often hidden from the courts, and in large enough numbers to be scary, they win. In Massachusetts men who fight for custody are awarded it 70 percent of the time. In Chapel Hill, North Carolina, they win it 84 percent of the time.

Although every state but Utah has some sort of rape shield law, lawyers find devious ways around them, so all kinds of extraneous "evidence" makes its way into court. The bra size of the retarded young woman who was molested by the Glen Ridge, N.J., high school boys was mentioned in court. Women are still being criticized for what they were wearing at the time of the rape and where they were when it occurred, and questioned why they were there in the first place—all of which would be unthinkable if the crime was, say, a mugging. As law professor Taunya Lovell Banks says, "No one ever questions if a person consents to other types of assault. Nonsexual victims don't have to say 'I didn't consent to be hit with that crowbar.' "

Only 2 percent of the victims of rape ever see their attacker caught, tried and imprisoned; more than half of all rape prosecutions are either dismissed before trial or result in an acquittal; almost a quarter of convicted rapists *never* go to prison; another quarter receive sentences in local jails, *where the average sentence is eleven months*. This means that almost *half* of all convicted rapists can expect to serve an average of *a year or less* behind bars.

In 1993 a judge convicted five men of raping an unconscious woman in a local bar and fined each of them $750. The following year a judge in Maryland sentenced a man to eighteen months of jail time for killing his wife after finding her in bed with another man. The judge said it was "understandable."

Incidents of injustice such as these are the reason that forty states and a number of the federal circuit courts have taken it upon themselves to examine the gender bias in their ranks. Gender bias reports that have been completed to date are full of data and incidents that would seem improbable—if they were not true. In North Carolina the courts decided they didn't need to look for the bias; the judges just assumed it existed and appointed a committee to effect some change. The women of North Carolina, particularly the women involved in custody disputes, are waiting. They should not hold their breath.

Regardless of how bad it is for white women, African American women, in each segment of the legal system, face the double burden of race and gender. White women lawyers, for instance, might be demeaned by opposing counsel; African American women lawyers will be asked to prove they are lawyers when they arrive at court in their silk suits.

The truth is that while some small progress has been made, our legal system is still the most backward, sexist, offensive set of institutions in the country, even after thirty years of the modern feminist movement and regardless of social commentators such as Rush Limbaugh who feel that women have achieved it all and asking for more makes you a "feminazi."

The shocking, aye, shameful, truth is that women still have not achieved anything like equality in the legal system. This book documents just how far the sexism penetrates, just how unequal is our justice, beginning in law school, continuing in the profession, and finally in the courts. While race of course is a great dividing factor in our legal system, so also is sex. There is the white man's justice; and there is second-class justice. That is the kind women get.

1

Legal Education

THE RISE OF A
MORALLY BANKRUPT SYSTEM

Learning to
"Think Like a Lawyer"

Any criticism of the Law School which suggests that change is desirable is likely to be met by two objections: the capacity to turn out highly successful professionals must not be endangered; and the current organization of the School maximizes the intellectual quality of the work done here.—DUNCAN KENNEDY

THE TROUBLE BEGINS in law school. Our institutions of legal learning are a microcosm of our legal system, with all its flaws and warts, and whatever problems women face in our legal system, they are compressed and played out in law school. Legal education not only reflects what is wrong in our justice system today, it also influences what it will be tomorrow. For it is law school that trains our next generation of leaders—not only the lawyers, good and bad, but also the judges and congressmen and senators and, yes, even presidents and their circles of advisers for whom law school is a kind of boot camp.

Although law school admissions have been down since *L.A. Law* went off the air and the job market for lawyers of the expansive 1980s dried up, there are still approximately 150,000 students in law school. The fact that law school is the ticket to so much in our culture is not lost on our young people. For the socially ambitious, law school promises financial reward and prestige; for the altruistic, the possibility of influencing social policy; and for some, perhaps a fortunate melding of both goals. Two-thirds of all our presidents have been lawyers. Since World War II six of the eleven U.S. presidents and nine of the twelve vice presidents have been lawyers. Because of the rich rewards law school offers, a large industry has grown up to fill the demand: our law schools are turning out more than forty thousand lawyers a year. In 1996 nearly 134,800 would-be lawyers are enrolled in the 178 schools accredited by the American

Bar Association. Add to that the thousands of students at the more than forty law schools in the country lacking the ABA stamp of approval. Women buy into the promise of law school in a major way: 43 percent of the candidates for a J.D. or an LL.B. are women. In the school year 1965–66, a mere thirty years ago, they were just over 4 percent of the student body.

But while women account for such a sizable chunk of the law school population today, they are still treated as second-class citizens at many schools. The same is true for the nearly 18 percent who are minorities. Minority women have the hardest time of all and face the double discrimination of race and gender. In some schools it is as if these groups of students barely existed except to pay their bills. While law schools welcome women and minorities to fill seats as well as to provide income—three years at a top-notch school can cost $100,000— far too many professors and administrators have been steadfastly unresponsive to this new crop of students' needs and desires, almost as if it were their God-given duty to withstand pressure to change and accommodate the diverse needs of their now diverse students. Like country clubs all over America, our system of legal education favors affluent white men.

Why? Why are law schools this way? One reason is that The Law and the institutions that do its work are designed to serve the elite and maintain the status quo. Laws are based on precedent. The well-to-do have always been the ones who had the money to carry their fights to courts, thereby establishing laws that the rest of us are bound by, thereby establishing, until very recently, that what a "reasonable man" might do in any given situation was the only appropriate response. But "reasonable men" do not include the poor, women, anyone who is less than big and strong and at least middle class, and most often that means white. Yes, the poor of all sexes and all colors can use the legal system, but their access to it is limited, limited by funds and an infinite sense of being outside the system. As Ralph Nader has observed: "How many share-croppers do you think sue Minute Maid?" At a conference on African American women and the law last year in Washington, D.C., a woman stood up when domestic violence was the topic and asked: "Do we want to put all our men in jail?" There ensued a discussion on whether calling the police was the proper course of action when you were battered by your man. Maybe what could happen if you called the cops was worse than being beaten up.

To assure that this caste system is passed on, law schools remain locked up in ivory towers, sometimes paying little heed to the real world outside its doors. And that they have managed to do exceedingly well. After a decade of civil rights, women's rights and antipoverty agitation, a study of the country's top law schools in 1970–72 found that a majority of the students not only came from upper-income families, *they represented a larger percentage of the student body at these elite schools than ten years earlier.* "Intellectual movements, large-scale political events, debates on social issues, theoretical musings, and ideology . . . apparently have no significant influence on the teaching of law at most schools," wrote legal historians Alfred S. Konefsky and John Henry Schlegel in 1982 in the *Harvard Law Review.* Like a medieval fortress, the walls of most law schools and the skulls of most professors of law are impenetrable. And when the issues of the day are discussed, they are kept in a narrow framework that prevents fundamental analysis and criticism. This is an efficient method, of course, for maintaining the status quo, for making sure that the real world and real-world problems and solutions are excluded. The dinosaur replicates itself.

Even Derek Bok, the past president of Harvard University and hardly an anti-Establishment spokesman, noted in 1982, "There is far too much law for those who can afford it and far too little for those who cannot." Bok laid much of the blame at the feet of law professors who fail to attack the basic flaws in our legal system, who emphasize instead training students "to think like a lawyer," a capacity that has produced many triumphs, but "has also helped to produce a legal system that is among the most expensive and least efficient in the world." Bok stated that Japan, a country half our size, has fewer than 15,000 lawyers, while it graduates 30 percent more engineers each year than we do. The American Bar Association has about 345,000 members. "As the Japanese put it, 'Engineers make the pie grow larger; lawyers only decide how to carve it up,' " Bok noted. The figures have changed since 1982, but not that much.

"[L]aw schools," he went on, "train their students more for conflict than for the gentler arts of reconciliation and accommodation . . . courses on the problems of the legal system are almost always relegated to elective slots where only a handful of students typically attend." But Bok's words have been taken to heart by far too few. It is not solely the fault of the academics: the students too share the blame for showing little commitment to the great social problems of the day. Unlike medicine, where young people decide to be doctors early in life, Bok commented, law has "traditionally been the refuge of able, ambitious college seniors who cannot think of anything else they want to do."

Another reason for the ivory tower atmosphere of law schools is the method of instruction. Law is taught as a science, one in which ideas become abstractions that are fitted onto a sort of mathematical grid. "The level of abstraction in most classrooms is both too theoretical and not theoretical enough; it neither probes the underlying foundations of legal doctrine nor offers practical assistance about how to use that doctrine in particular cases," Stanford law professor Deborah L. Rhode has commented. "In effect, students often get the legal analogue of 'geology without the rocks . . . dry, arid logic, divorced from society.'"

This law-as-science dictum emerged from the preeminent law school in the country, Harvard, nearly a century and a quarter ago. One of Harvard's early deans, Christopher Columbus Langdell, originated the idea, with motives that had more to do with commerce than altruism. He desired both to validate the teaching of law within the confines of a university and to elevate its faculties to the level of other disciplines taught there. Langdell postulated that "law is a science, and that all the available materials of that science are contained in printed books." By gaining acceptance for this point of view, Langdell was able to distance Harvard and other law schools from the way law was originally taught in the early republic, as an eminently practical course of apprenticeship conducted in the offices of those already practicing law. Langdell also popularized the idea that the only true method of learning law was the case method, which involves studying appellate cases relevant to the various subjects of the law: civil procedure, criminal law, the Constitution, the law of evidence, torts and so on. Originally the case method was taught as a way of getting at basic legal doctrines, which supposedly cut across state and perhaps national boundaries. But as later legal academics realized, law is complex and contradictory, and judicial decisions do not depend on unfailing logic in reaching their conclusions. Yet students learning with the case method still may spend hours trying to reconcile two legal decisions that have little more in common other than that they are both legal decisions. Even the most convoluted logic cannot reconcile all the decisions of a past Supreme Court with one in which the political leanings of the justices may be as different from those of the earlier court as day is from night.

So if they are not learning basic legal principles, what are these future lawyers learning? How to "think like a lawyer." They are learning the ability to dissect a legal problem as if they were cutting apart a frog in high school biology class, with no point of view holding more weight than the other, the heart versus the liver, except that a court has ruled in favor of one. Thinking like a lawyer means learning how to argue both sides of the question with nary a thought to the moral, political or economic issues involved. Thinking like a lawyer is learning how to think as a morally detached and distant individual, always coolly logical. How legal decisions actually affect people is left to the low-status clinical courses, where pro bono work in the community is done, or to possibly a single course in ethics, a subject that also gets no respect in law school. When Deborah Rhode looked at some 130 legal texts in 14 subjects, she found that the average amount of discussion devoted to ethical issues amounted to a meager 1.4 percent of total pages, and those mostly simply stated the relevant rules. To further distance ethical issues from legal questions, most professors spend little effort explaining the circumstances, the legal choices and the ultimate consequences of the decisions to the parties involved. In most course work it is as if real people didn't exist in the cases under discussion, that whatever the decision, it carries as much moral weight as the opposite one. Consequently Langdell's system of legal education is ultimately designed to train people how to be argumentative intellectuals but moral eunuchs.

THERE WERE WARNING SIGNS about the type of lawyer this method would produce. By the 1890s, the ABA's Committee of Legal Education was sounding alarms about the case method: "The student should not be so trained as to think he is to be a mere hired gladiator. . . . The result of this elaborate study of actual disputes, and ignoring of the settled doctrines that have grown out of past ones, is a class of graduates admirably calculated to argue any side of any controversy, or to make briefs for those who do so, but quite unable to advise a client when he is safe from litigation." But a pro-Harvard faction took control of the ABA soon after, Harvard became the most successful law school in the country, the norms that Langdell pioneered were copied almost universally, and he went down in history as the most influential figure in American legal education. At bottom, however, Langdell was a brilliant but myopic theoretician/businessman at whose grave the morally arid state of legal education in this country can be laid.

The case method early on became entangled with the so-called Socratic method of quizzing a student to push her thinking into the direction the professor wants it to go. While not all students can participate in the large classrooms of law school, ideally other students learn from listening to their peers arrive at the correct conclusions. Handled well, the Socratic method is a valuable teaching tool, and not just in law school; but under the stewardship of someone who is not aware of its pitfalls, it offers only enough "freedom to roam in an intellectual cage," as Ralph Nader has observed. Although it remains the

teaching method of choice in law school, it has come under heavy criticism for
favoring the quick and the witty. Many women are not comfortable with the
high-combat style of the Socratic method in its purest form. So many choose not
to engage. They react with silence. Male professors may not realize they are
failing to teach and test their female students as hard as they do their male
counterparts; in fact, they may fail to call on them at all.

In theory the Socratic method encourages careful preparation and rigorous
analysis; in practice it may substitute for both. In practice it may be the sadistic
approach of a Professor Kingsfield of the movie and television series *The Paper
Chase,* whose style was to intimidate his students with a volley of questions to
which there are no definite answers. Unlike a true Socratic dialogue, in which
a teacher and a few students explore philosophic questions, writes Carrie
Menkel-Meadow, a professor at the University of California at Los Angeles Law
School, "the law school dialogue occurs in so large a group that little reciproc-
ity, genuine communication, or exploration is possible. Students are often glad
that someone else is 'on the hook,' and while 'out there,' each student feels
alone, unsupported, alienated, fearful and grows increasingly apathetic." The
students may be terrified, but the professor will never be bored. Most male
professors are quite comfortable with this style of teaching; it's how they learned
how to be law professors themselves. The routine rarely varies. The professor
need not revise his course plan, the cases studied, anything but his exam questions. And as one law professor told a *New York Times* reporter, "The present
structure of law school is very congenial to us, it really is. We're not indifferent
to the fact that our students are bored, but that to one side, law school works
pretty well for us."

Moreover, the case cum Socratic method offers a trump card to law schools:
it is good business, a fact not lost on Langdell. One law professor can teach a
hundred students as well as twenty. And law school is a business—albeit a
declining business. The big name schools are somewhat impervious to market
influences, but the less than flattering image of Langdell-trained litigious lawyers
as an army of legal mercenaries and the already bloated population of attorneys
in the United States have led to a drop in the number of applicants to law schools
over the last few years. In the fall of 1995 more than 40 percent of ABA-
accredited law schools had smaller incoming classes. After years of spiraling
applications, the number of men and women applying to law schools has
dropped more than 15 percent, a trend that began in the 1992–93 academic
year. Most of the elite schools are hardly troubled by this—applications to

Harvard in 1994–95 were up 8 percent, while nationally the figure declined by over 6 percent—but it will change budgeting and staffing needs across the country. If this is the beginning of a long-term trend, as some believe, several schools will shrink and others will fold outright. But whether declining enrollment will mean that law schools will become more consumer-driven—and become friendlier places for women and minorities—is anybody's guess.

It won't happen easily. Women have always had to struggle for whatever beachhead they have been able to win in law schools.

THE HISTORY OF
WOMEN IN LAW SCHOOL

Portia at the Gates

October 7, 1869

Mrs. Belva A. Lockwood

Madam, the Faculty of Columbian College have considered your request to be admitted to the Law Department of this institution and after due consultation have considered that such admission would be not expedient as it would be likely to distract the attention of the young men.

Respectfully,

GEO. W. SAMSON, PRESIDENT

BEFORE THE TWENTIETH CENTURY, almost all avenues of advancement and achievement outside the home excluded women. The profession of law was no exception. While a few women argued cases in colonial courts, they did not open any doors for later generations. The Midwest and the West, however, were more receptive to the first women law students, perhaps because women had won some measure of acceptance as equals in settling the frontier. Eighteen hundred sixty-nine appears to have been a turning point for women entering law school, for at least three schools admitted women that year. One was a wealthy heiress from Brooklyn, Lemma Barkaloo. Turned down by both Columbia and Harvard Law Schools, she entered Washington University in St. Louis, Missouri. A classmate was Phoebe Couzins. After a year of study the remarkable Barkaloo, depicted as "an honor to her class," passed the Missouri bar. She tried a case that year and is thought to be the first woman to do so, but she died a few months later of typhoid. Biographers would later note that "mental overexertion" killed her. Couzins continued at law school to graduation, and at graduation she spoke of her warm reception from both faculty and students.

African American women were also opening the doors of legal education for themselves that same year. Charlotte E. Ray, who taught at Howard University, gained admission to the law department the same way Shannon Faulkner was admitted to The Citadel: by not signifying that she was female. When school administrators learned that C. E. Ray was a woman, they raised a ruckus but in the end did not keep her out. Later, the president of the university, wrote in his third annual report that "there was a colored woman who read us a thesis on corporations, not copied from the books but from her brain, a clear incisive analysis of one of the most delicate legal questions." Throughout Reconstruction, and up until 1900, white women attended law classes at Howard alongside black women and men. After the turn of the century, as more law schools opened up to white women, Howard became exclusively a school for African American men and women.

The University of Iowa also admitted women in 1869, but how welcome they were is a matter of conjecture. Society women accompanied young female students to classes to put them more at ease in those early years. At the University of Michigan, the president's wife protested admitting women to the law school, but to no avail, and the school graduated its first female law student in 1870. Twenty years later the school led the country in women law graduates.

Just as women faculty have lately had to sue to embarrass some law schools into hiring more than just a token few, so in the early years did women have to resort to the courts just to attend law school. Two who began classes in 1879 at the Hastings College of the Law in San Francisco were unceremoniously thrown out after the board of directors hastily decided that women would not be admitted. But Clara Foltz and Laura De Force Gordon were determined, and they took their case to court, arguing that since the school was a part of the University of California, and since the university accepted women, they should not be excluded from the law school. The press delighted in the uproar, but the accounts sound as if a fashion reporter had written them. Gordon "wore a stylish black dress with some suggestions of masculinity in the make." Foltz's braids fell "backward from the crown on her head like an alpine glacier lit by a setting sun." Nonetheless the women prevailed, and two years after they had been shown the door—by the school's janitor—they were back in school, more as a matter of principle than need. By then both had been admitted to the California bar and were quite skilled at litigation. Gordon later won a not guilty verdict in a scandalous murder trial. Foltz was an early public interest litigator, representing many indigent clients and never losing her feisty spirit. When an adversary suggested she might be better at home raising her children than opposing him in court, she coolly replied: "A woman had better be in almost any business than raising such men as you."

When Belva Lockwood was told in 1869 that she would "distract the attention of the young men" if she were to attend Columbian College in Washington, D.C., she replied this was hogwash, as she was nearly forty years old. She didn't get into Columbian, but she and fourteen other women were admitted to the National University Law School, also in the nation's capital. Only Lockwood and another woman withstood what must have been a fair amount of female bashing to complete their studies. But shortly before commencement, male students threatened to boycott graduation if they were required to share a stage with women. No problem, said the administration. The women's names were removed from the program. The women assumed they would get their degrees *after* commencement. Think again.

Now some of the men on the faculty balked, saying that the school's reputation would suffer if they gave women degrees. The matter seemed to be at an impasse. Even if they did get their degrees, they had to be signed by the president of the law school—who at the time was also the president of the United States, Ulysses S. Grant. Lockwood began practicing law where she could—police court, probate court, before justices of the peace—but decided in the fall of 1873 that she was fed up with waiting. She wrote a curt note to President Grant, stating that she had passed through the curriculum in the school "and am entitled to and demand my diploma." If Grant was not the school's president, she added, "then I ask that you take your name from its papers, and not hold out to the world to be what you are not." Two weeks later she got her signed diploma. Ten years later, in response to an inquiry, the school wrote that it was not admitting women.

Elsewhere women faced similar hostility. While Couzins in Missouri may have found a friendly environment, Clara Foltz in California did not. A whole classroom of men had coughing fits when she coughed—because of a bad cold—on her first day at Hastings. Lettie Burlingame, Michigan class of 1886, wrote in her diary that one professor would "arouse my indignation by picking out easy questions to ask us women." Newspaper accounts around the turn of the century trivialized women studying law, either commenting on their "feminine graces" (*New York Times*) or remarking, "Married women could better serve themselves and humanity than by becoming lawyers . . . the increasing newness of the 'new woman' may justly be viewed with alarm" (*Albany Express*).

But given the tenor of the times, none of this is all that unusual. What is surprising is that these shenanigans and humiliations are unhappily similar to what still goes on in some law school classrooms today.

Although they encountered resistance, at least these pioneers were attending law school. Not so at the elite schools. Harvard and Georgetown and Columbia, to name a few, spent their energies keeping women out. One woman, Alice Rufie Jordan, with a B.S. from the University of Michigan, actually attended Yale Law School before the turn of the century, receiving full credit for every examination; but she was denied a degree "in order to avoid any misunderstanding in the future." Yale did not graduate a woman until 1920. Columbia admitted women in 1927 only after Dean Harlan Fiske Stone had joined the U.S. Supreme Court. He had been known to promise that women would be admitted over his dead body.

Although women were breaking in here and there, the various indignities they endured were in keeping with the times: Libby Sacher was told in the 1920s in front of the class by a professor at New York University Law School that the only reason she was there was to get a husband. Sacher later became one of the first women judges in New Jersey. In the following decade Helen L. Buttenwieser created a stir at the same school when she became pregnant. As she told Karen Berger Morello, author of The Invisible Bar, she attended classes—horrors—while pregnant. "The professors had fits that whole semester whenever they saw me," she said. "They actually went so far as to hold a vote as to whether it was improper for a young man to be in contact with a pregnant woman and from what I understand, they agreed that it was." But they were apparently too chagrined to tell Buttenwieser about their vote. She heard about it after graduation. Evidently her "condition" did not hurt her ability, and she went on to become chairman of the board of directors of New York's Legal Aid Society.

African American women had the same prejudices directed against them and then some. In 1926 two black students—one woman, one man—were elected to the University of Pennsylvania Law Review. One of them was Sadie Tanner Mossell Alexander, and while the dean of the school did not make known any reservations he had about the black man's admission to law review, he attempted to deny Alexander membership. However, the editor of the law review threatened to resign unless the dean reversed his decision. He did. But Alexander was not the first woman elected to a law review at a predominately white school, for Clara Burrill Bruce had been elected editor in chief at Boston University a year earlier, in 1925. These accomplishments are nothing short of breathtaking, considering the prejudices that minority women still face in law school.

For setting up the path of most resistance the honor goes to Harvard and Dean Roscoe Pound, a formidable presence at the school after having served as its head for twenty years. A student recalls vividly one day in 1945 when Pound was presiding over a first-year property class. It was customary for students to invite friends to sit in on their classes, and one man brought his girlfriend with him. They sat at the back of the class, but Pound noticed her and stopped the class, ordering the couple out. Five years later women were finally admitted, but with this proviso: "Opportunities for women in the law still are limited . . . and the Faculty is well aware that many able men are turned away from our doors every year. It is our expectation that we will admit only a small number of unusually qualified women students, for the present, at least."

Indeed. They might let women in, but they weren't going to make them comfortable. When U.S. Supreme Court Justice Ruth Bader Ginsburg matriculated at Harvard Law in 1956 with nine other women, Dean Erwin Griswold—who led the fight against the Harvard corporation to admit women—asked each of them at a tea how they felt about taking places that had been earmarked for men. Not wanting to seem too assertive, Ginsburg recalls, she mumbled something about how studying law would help her understand her husband's work and could possibly lead to part-time employment for herself. The quizzing apparently went on for several years. These women were taking the places of worthy *men*. When a young woman named Hillary Rodham applied to law school in 1969, she was accepted at both Harvard and Yale. A second-year student, a male, naturally, took her to a cocktail reception and introduced her, as she puts it, "to one of the legendary Harvard Law professors" by saying, " 'Professor So-and-So, this is Hillary Rodham. She's trying to decide between us and our nearest competitor.' " The professor, she told Henry Louis Gates Jr. for *The New Yorker,* in his three-piece suit and bow tie, "looked at me and said, 'First of all, we have no nearest competitor, and second, we don't need any more women.' And that's how I decided to go to Yale." Which is where the future First Lady met another law student named William Jefferson Clinton.

Harvard women suffered innumerable indignities over the years, the most infamous of which was Ladies' Day, which was perhaps perfected—if that can be the word—at Harvard but was by no means limited to that school. New York University and Columbia also joined in the "fun." On Ladies' Day, which at some schools was on Valentine's Day, professors would order the women to the podium like performing bears, where they would be grilled. The infamous practice at Harvard did not come to an end until 1968. That year the women dressed all in black down to their briefcases, one of the women there recalled to Cynthia Fuchs Epstein, author of *Women in Law.* Since the professor who delighted in the practice, W. Barton Leach, a retired air force general, used the same case year after year—a case whose punch line involved women's underwear, a case designed to humiliate women—the women came prepared and knew all the answers. At the end he asked, as usual, "What was the *chose* in question?" (*Chose* in law means object or thing.) The women replied by announcing they had some samples and pulled out quantities of lacy lingerie from their briefcases and threw them at the boys. Leach almost had a stroke on the spot. Ladies' Day came to an end at Harvard.

But business is business. Although Harvard and the other Ivy League law schools rigorously limited the number of women, the situation did change in response to outside influences—regardless of the insularity law schools claim to maintain. Columbia's enrollment of women rose and fell in tandem with military draft calls during the Korean conflict. In 1953 the school graduated 4 percent women; in 1954, 8 percent; and in 1955, 10 percent; then, as the need for soldiers was drying up, the figure dipped back to 4 percent in 1957. But the greatest changes occurred in the late 1960s with the chance conjunction of two events: "a decline in law school applications as Lyndon Johnson began to draft law students and the first stirrings of a vocal, revitalized women's movement," according to historians Konefsky and Schlegel. As they point out, the subsequent interest in admitting women made "law schools look substantially more opportunistic than one might otherwise be led to believe." Opportunistic or simply businesslike. Suddenly they needed women to fill their seats. The explosion of women entering law school was just about to begin. Between 1972 and 1978 the number of women working toward their LL.B. or J.D. degree more than tripled, to 35,775, from 11,878. As far as the law was concerned, women were on their way. But the reception they received was nothing other than chilly. One woman who was considering applying to Harvard in 1973 visited the school one Friday and sat in on a class. Halfway through, the professor called on the man she had sat next to. " 'I see that Mr. X is starting the weekend early and has brought his girlfriend,' he said," the woman recalls. "Everybody turned around to look at us, and I realized that he was talking about me. I said, 'Excuse me, but I'm here to look over Harvard to see if I want to come to law school here, and you've just answered my question.' And I got up and walked out."

By 1973 the temperature hadn't changed all that much. And it still hasn't.

CLASSROOM ATMOSPHERE

What Is Wrong
with This Picture?

A lot of women talk about this—why do men turn into abhorrent pigs in law school when they weren't in college? The difference is that men are much more threatened by women now because we are encroaching on power that has been traditionally theirs. Anybody can get a B.A., but a professional degree, a J.D., that's different.

—STUDENT AT NEW YORK UNIVERSITY SCHOOL OF LAW

THE CLOSE TO seventy women students* interviewed for this book at twenty-eight randomly selected law schools around the country gave one depressing recital after another about their law school experience. To be sure, there were a few—three, in fact—who said they experienced no sex discrimination at all. One said that any discrimination she felt was indicative of the wider world, and her undergraduate engineering school in Detroit had been such a horrible experience, why even comment on the mild forms of bias she encountered at the University of Michigan Law School? But even students who began the interview saying they "loved" law school would then go on to recall a flagrantly discriminatory incident or two.

"I had a professor in Torts who is patronizing to women. We were talking about the 'reasonable' person, and he said in all seriousness, 'Is there any such thing as the *reasonable woman*?' And he just thought that was the funniest thing— 'Oh my God, it's an oxymoron.' " (Jill Morrison, Yale Law School)

"One day the teacher was drawing a bell curve on the board to show us an example of how to illustrate percentages of fraud. He said, 'Hey, this looks like a titty. Now all it needs is a nipple.' Everyone is too afraid to say anything, you

---

* *Students were interviewed from 1993 to 1995; many will have graduated by the time of publication but are referred to as they were when interviewed. Women who are members of minority groups are identified as such only when it is germane. Students not identified by name requested anonymity.*

don't want to antagonize him. You are sort of powerless when your education is in his hands." (Lisa Read, Birmingham School of Law)

"I had one professor who wouldn't call on women for three or four days at a time. Once I counted sixteen men before he called on a woman. When it was pointed out to him, he did call on women, but you felt he did it grudgingly. . . . When issues like this are raised with the administration there is no response, and that is almost as bad as the experience itself. I almost didn't come back after my first year even though my grades were good." (Elizabeth Wellinghoff, University of Chicago Law School)

"When I go to see male professors in their offices, you can tell they are uncomfortable. And they always make some remark about sex—even the younger professors do it. A number of us women talked about this, how this doesn't happen when you talk to a professor in a group, or with male students." (Student at Stanford Law School)

"If a white man is wrong, he's wrong, no big deal. But if I'm wrong—'Uh-huh, well, of course, *you're* wrong. . . .' I wish I could just feel comfortable if I did say something wrong." (Kim Robinson, an African American at Harvard Law School)

"Law school is debilitating for women. Part of it has to do with emotional issues being totally stifled. Law school is a stripping away of everything you once believed so that you can be remade into a lawyer, and that means being totally detached from what you are learning." (Lisa Ilka, University of Arizona College of Law)

"The way female professors are treated adds to the general atmosphere of male dominance. The male students challenge the women faculty in class, they are more likely to be disrespectful to them in class, they fidget and make noise, their attitude is one of 'I don't care because what you're saying can't be important.' And they talk about them badly outside of class. I heard one making a lewd sexual reference to a female professor." (Woman at Emory University School of Law)

"In my first year, if someone made a feminist point or discussed a gender issue, one student would hold up his arm as if he were going to shake hands and then curl back each finger slowly and methodically until he had the shape of a gun. Then he would make the muffled sound of it going off as it pointed at the woman. He was an asshole, but he wasn't alienated from the other guys. He was only ostracized by some of the women." (Milbrey Raney, University of Texas School of Law in Austin)

"I had a professor who ignored the women in his classes—except to have them give quick, short answers to questions such as 'Do you know the rule of law?' The guys would complain that the women had it easier, because he would have the men in the class standing for twenty minutes while they briefed a case. How could any woman expect to do well in a class like that? He simply wouldn't call on women. I would raise my hand for five minutes and he wouldn't call on me, so if I had a question that I wasn't sure someone else could explain to me, I would lean over to a guy and ask him to ask it. They were good about that. The guy would be called on and I would write the answer down." (Sonia Sanchez, John Marshall Law School)

"In a labor law class, the professor was going through a hypothetical [case] about a prenuptial agreement. Somebody was taping the class, but when he got ready to make a comment, he said, 'Shut that thing off.' Then he said something like 'Come on, guys, when you're writing an agreement like this, you are not thinking of each and every way the bitch is going to screw you.'" (Student at the University of Virginia School of Law)

This last incident was reported in the school paper, and male students came out in favor of the professor, added Mary Kostel, editor in chief of law review in 1992–93. "The administration didn't do anything," she said. "This kind of stuff just gets shoved under the rug, and if you say something about it, they say, 'Oh, it's just a rumor, he's a great guy,' and the criticism is totally discredited." Another student added: "If he had said 'nigger' all hell would have broken loose.'"

"There's a well-known professor who has been known to say at cocktail parties, 'Whenever I see a loopy handwriting, I know the person is stupid.'" (Sara Crovitz, University of Chicago Law School)

Do more women than men have "loopy" handwriting? Too bad. Professor Mary Becker, who teaches there, says that her own informal survey showed that when exams are handwritten the person grading them is likely to know the sex of the test taker, and "because of a general belief that men are better at law than women," this is likely to affect grading—to the detriment of women.

Make no mistake, law school can be a brutalizing, awful experience for many women. Not that it is a picnic for men. The pressure for grades is enormous, especially at the Ivy Leagues. Some professors do terrorize their students. The grilling of a student for twenty minutes or so in front of a classroom of one hundred or more students can unnerve anybody. The workload is overwhelming, the pressure to sound knowing and bright in class daunting, and the door-die atmosphere lethal. In the first year, students are thrown into the big sections and are somehow supposed to know something about the law the first time they speak. When they stick out their necks and say something, their heads are as likely to get chopped off as not. It's all part of the process of "learning to think like a lawyer."

THE SILENCING OF WOMEN

In short, law school is tough for everybody. But it's so much tougher for women. The reasons are numerous and originate from the fact that the very law being taught has been written by and for affluent males, a truism most women will be confronting for the first time in law school. As they pore over case after case, this phallocentric core at the heart of Anglo-American law will emerge in any number of ways. The cases studied in the case method rarely have women as actors, except as victims. These old cases that serve as precedent embody the sorry attitudes about women from the period in which they were decided and do not even remotely express the realities of women's lives today, the realities of the women in the classroom. Yet women in class are not often allowed to vent their perspective on either the old judgments or whether a given woman's actions in the cases at hand were "reasonable" or not.

Then too, the fixed hierarchy of the classroom, with the professor standing and speaking from the position of a sort of demigod in the amphitheater style of most classrooms, duplicates precisely the type of male/female power relationships—if the teacher is male—that the female law student is likely to be desperately resisting in her personal life. If she isn't, she probably wouldn't be in law school. The style of instruction, with a professor grilling a student to come at the logic behind a decision, was designed expressly to exclude the social, historical and political tenor of the times. Yet in reality these influences are at the center of every single courtroom decision. The students know this, of course, but are asked to ignore this basic truth and dissect decisions as if they were constructed in a vacuum. And for whatever reasons, men generally are more comfortable operating in this abstract fashion, while women generally find this disagreeable.

When this "male" law is taught, in a style that males find comfortable, by a male who acts like the undisputed ruler of the students' universe, the superiority of men is accepted as the norm. Can this be challenged at every turn? Only at the woman's peril. The best response? Silence.

Casebooks implement the male-superior position in society in several ways, beginning with the simple fact that most of the cases written up have only men as actors. How could it be otherwise? Married women, for instance, really had no rights apart from their husband's until the mid–twentieth century and so aren't likely to show up in a substantial number of the cases. Since women were denied access to the bench until modern times, women judges whose opinions are included are rare indeed.

One more factor must be considered: the type of student who goes to law school. Studies have shown that a sizable percentage of women go to law school because they are interested in social justice, men for status and money. "Women are attracted by the perception that law shapes social relationships and if you understand it, you can build, say, a better health care system, or a criminal justice system, or bring more equity to family law," observes Sylvia Ann Law, professor at New York University and former president of the Society of American Law Teachers. "While no one would disagree that these are things that the law should be concerned about, they are not highly valued in law school." Men, on the other hand, she says, are attracted to law for "power and money," as well as "a belief that deconstructive reasoning, logic, and clear thinking will solve complex human problems."

Quite a number of these rational, analytical types also seem to be the ambitious, macho types who tend to mow down anybody in their way or with whom they disagree. By their very nature they are adversarial, and the combat of law suits them perfectly. In the classroom their aggressiveness comes out in put-downs and insults against those not in their sphere or the women whom they may unconsciously resent for the added competition they represent. Even if the majority of male students aren't the loud, pushy types many of us associate with "lawyers," there are enough of them to dominate many a classroom, just as one loud, rambunctious child can throw a children's birthday party into chaos. Put these young men together with left-leaning women interested in changing the world, and it's like mixing oil and water and charging it with a current.

Because the law school does not exist apart from society—even though it often tries to pretend otherwise—it reflects all that is sexist in the wider world. Not enough male professors take it upon themselves to see that the macho males don't control the classroom climate; far too many go along with the sexist jokes and the put-downs of the feminist viewpoint—some even go so far as to make them themselves. Says Professor Elizabeth Schneider of Brooklyn Law School, "Women are given the feeling that if they speak out of their own experiences or their own ideas, or express ideas that are not fully developed, they will be dismissed. The comments men make in class, either consciously or unconsciously, are given more weight by male professors than what women say. Women's concerns and issues are not being raised, and often, when they are, they are trivialized."

As a consequence, women's participation in most law school classes borders on the abysmal. They don't ask questions, they don't volunteer answers, they don't seek out professors as often outside of class. Schneider reports that some of her third-year students in a women in the law course—which during different semesters she teaches at Brooklyn and at Harvard—say that it is the first course in which they have spoken. Taunya Lovell Banks, professor at Maryland University School of Law, and sociologist Jean Blocker, professor at the University of Tulsa, collected data from nearly two thousand male and female students at fourteen law schools throughout the country between 1987 and 1989. "At every single school," says Banks, "students—of both sexes—perceive the classroom to be more hostile to women than men." In an earlier study, reported in the *Journal of Legal Education,* Banks noted that twice the number of women as that of men reported *never* volunteering or volunteering significantly less than the men did. Older women seem to be somewhat less intimidated, and women over thirty, while more aware of the hostile environment of the typical law school classroom, volunteered more in their first year, but their level of participation dropped with each year they spent in law school. By the third year 25 percent of the women—as opposed to 17 percent of the men—said they *never* volunteer in class.

Banks is not the only one to document such discrepancies in classroom participation. Studies at Stanford, the University of California at Berkeley (known as Boalt Hall), the University of Pennsylvania, the University of Chicago, Brooklyn Law School, New York University and Yale came to the same conclusions. A random sampling of 973 male and female students at all nine law schools in Ohio in 1993 came up with numbers that mirror—in some cases exactly duplicate—Banks's findings. At the University of Pennsylvania, Professor Lani Guinier, who almost had a job in President Clinton's Justice Department, social psychologist Michelle Fine, and others reported in the school's law review in 1994 that even the women who did well academically were profoundly alienated by their law school experience.

Monica McFadden, who began law school in her late thirties after having worked for feminist causes for a number of years, explained how the disaffection occurs. McFadden was at first exhilarated when she entered the University of Chicago because, she said, three women were on the faculty and the women's caucus was one of the strongest organizations on campus. Here was a setting where she felt she belonged. But in no time at all she noticed that the women hung back while the men were called on. "You begin by being concerned with what the impact of a law will be on people—but that is not what you are supposed to think about," she said. "In property class, the imbalance of power was clear, but the only question the professor wanted to look at was 'How should we apply these old rules?' even though the rules are automatically going to hurt the powerless person, and invariably that is the female. Yet you are not supposed to consider that, for that is not being analytical. Those ideas are simply nice platitudes. You soon learned you were in law school to learn not what is the best course of action, but what the rule is."

Although the other studies are more recent, the methodology of the decade-old Yale study "The Legal Education of Twenty Women" makes it particularly compelling. A group of female first-year law students came together not only to address their silence and alienation in the classroom, but also to see how they could feel less left out. Two were women of color; most were middle-class, high-achieving women from prestigious undergraduate schools ranging in age from twenty-one to thirty-three.

To document what they felt was their "silencing" in the classroom, they recorded as it was happening how often men and women answered or asked questions in their classes over the course of the three years they were in school. They accounted for the percentages of men and women taking the classes, since they were not equal. To make sure that a few talky students didn't distort the figures, a continuous dialogue between the professor and student counted for only one. Their finding? Men spoke almost *twice as often as women*. In one class the women made up 44 percent of the students, but they accounted for less than 14 percent of student participation: in other words, in a classroom of forty-six men and thirty-six women, men did more than 86 percent of the talking. Although that class, in political and civil rights, was the worst, only in four out of the nineteen classes surveyed did women speak with a frequency approaching parity with the men.

The Yale data is from 1984 to 1987, but to judge from women's comments at Yale in 1993, progress is moving with the speed of a snail. Student Fall Ferguson explains what can happen in a typical classroom discussion when a woman speaks up. In an evidence class, rape was used in a hypothetical, and the discussion centered on whether the victim's prior sexual history could/should be admitted and whether or not it was comparable to a prior criminal record of the defendant. "I raised my hand and said, 'You can't compare a man having committed robbery to a woman's having had voluntary sex with someone—it just doesn't compute,'" Ferguson recalls. "The professor pretty much ignored what I said. Then another woman raised her hand and made what I thought was a sophisticated feminist analysis of the same hypothetical, and the professor said 'This is irrelevant' in so many words as if the feminist herself and the feminist viewpoint were irrelevant. Then I walked out of this class and a fellow student said to me, 'You know, this class would be a lot better if women didn't go off on these *hysterical* tangents.' My point is, the professor gives her this long bullshit rationale why her opinion was irrelevant, the student just comes out and says that we are hysterical. It's just a different way of saying the same thing." When they generate reactions like that, women think twice before raising their hands.

Even at Brooklyn Law School, where *women do as well as or better than men* academically, researchers in 1995 found that the women students there still said they volunteered significantly less than men and were not as comfortable as the men when they did. "The women reported significantly higher rates of anxiety, depression, sleeping difficulties, crying," notes Professor Marsha Garrison, lead investigator of the study. Despite the fact that Brooklyn Law, with a high percentage of women faculty (37 percent of tenure and tenure-track faculty, 45 percent of the full faculty), seems to present a much more benign environment for women than most schools, almost a quarter of the women students reported they experienced inappropriate treatment based on gender, a rate more than double that of their male peers.

Repeatedly students from close to thirty schools* told me the same old story, and it is quite a depressing tale. Although no one is reminding the women that they are taking the seats of capable men, as the dean did at Harvard until the late 1960s, women are still demeaned, their views belittled, and their concerns ignored. One would have expected more progress, given that the world has undergone a seismic change since the 1960s as far as women are concerned,

* *Students interviewed attended the state university law schools of Alabama, Arizona in Tucson, California at Berkeley, Idaho, Iowa, Michigan, Nebraska, Pennsylvania, Texas, Texas Tech, Vermont, Virginia and Wayne State (Michigan); also Birmingham, Brooklyn, Chicago, Columbia, De Paul, Emory, Fordham, Georgetown, Harvard, John Marshall, New York University, San Diego, Stanford, Washburn, Yale.*

but that's not what the women reported. Many of the women I interviewed were found through women's organizations on campus and thus were more likely to be aware when women's concerns were trivialized, as well as disturbed by the implicit dismissal of all women. But not all the women students I spoke to came from women's organizations—some were recommended by professors (who tended to suggest their star pupils); some I met at conferences; others were friends of friends; and some just happened to answer the telephone when I called a school's law review office, where the individual was just as likely to be sensitive to women's issues as not. Students varied in age from those out of college the year before to women in their forties. The schools ranged from the top tier to the bottom. Several schools were visited in person; some students were interviewed at various conventions and convocations; some were interviewed by telephone. But even at a school where a student said she "had no problems with the professors," at the University of San Diego, she went on to say that the active Women's Law Caucus was dubbed the "Women's Lesbian Club" by some male students. To sabotage the group's programs, pranksters would take down the posters advertising the events and put them in the men's room, something that doesn't happen to other organizations.

One study indicates that female students who go to law school with the same aspirations as men—prestige and money—appear to be not as disturbed by the law school process as the women who come with ideas of social justice and altruism. Another type of woman similarly prepared for the argumentative ambience of law school may be those from working-class backgrounds, young women who had to speak their minds rather than be good girls to surmount the many obstacles they faced in getting to law school in the first place. After that trek they may sense the bias against women, but it presents a less formidable challenge than it does to their more privileged sisters.

But the fact remains that a vast number of women arrive at law school with academic credentials equal to men's, signifying that they have the right stuff, yet the process of becoming a lawyer robs them of their identity, denies them equality, infantilizes them and makes them feel stupid to boot.

"Women suffer from a crisis of confidence in law school," says Jane Larson, professor at Northwestern University School of Law. "It has a great deal to do with the deep message of sex hierarchy in the law itself and law school as an institution." Larson likened the process of becoming a lawyer to getting into a boat that goes over a waterfall and, as students, being expected to stay calm and go along for the ride. "We tell the students they should trust their professors, but that creates a significantly different condition for women and minority students than it does for men because too few of the people whom they are supposed to trust look like them." Because women students' moral and ethical concerns are not reflected in the scholarship or classroom discussion, she adds, "they can conclude that one, their concerns are marginal to the law; two, they themselves are marginal to law school; and three, they 'just don't get it.' " It's a vicious cycle.

At the University of California at Berkeley, Boalt Hall, women feel that much has changed for the better since the 1980s, when women faculty were routinely denied tenure despite their qualifications. Boalt Hall has a woman dean, Herma Hill Kay, editor of one of the first casebooks on sex-based discrimination. Her being dean has given women at Berkeley "a feeling of empowerment," according to Lori Grange, former chair of the student women's association there. But there are still tears aplenty at the annual forum for female students. "In the first few weeks of classes, there is a lot of handholding at Boalt, and the women say nothing is wrong," she says. "But later when we have this forum, several weep and air their feelings of oppression, of listening to demeaning hypotheticals in the classroom, professors avoiding topics, or how they are ignored in contrast with the men. Invariably a couple of women will have kept track of how many times a man talks in class compared with women. They notice right off the bat that men dominate in the classroom."

If a woman dean can't change the system more, what can we expect from other schools? For most women, legal education today is still a constantly denigrating process. Although women enter law school with credentials equal to the men's, by the end of the three years a significant percentage end up depressed, and at some schools the majority fall behind in the grade-point sweepstakes, which puts them at a disadvantage when they attempt to join the job market. In the words of the 1994 Penn report: "By the end of their first year in law school, men are three times more likely than women to be in the top 10 percent of their law school class. . . . These women graduate with less competitive academic credentials, are not represented equally within the Law School's academic and social hierarchies, and are apparently less competitive in securing prestigious and/or desirable jobs after graduation." More astounding than first-year grades is how women end up after three years: the Penn researchers, Guinier and Fine, found that *men graduate in the top 10 percent of the class three times as often as women* and that men were more likely to make law review and be elected editor.

The Law School Admission Council also found that women's first-year grades suffered in comparison with men's. Though women entering law school on the average have a higher grade-point average than men, women score one point lower on their Law School Admission Test (LSAT). But by the end of the first year something has gone amiss. Although the grade-point average difference was slight, the author of the study, Linda Wightman, concluded: "[M]any female law students are not performing academically as well as they could be or should be in the current legal education environment." While the magnitude of the differences often is small in statistical terms, she notes that they bear on class rank, self-esteem and career opportunities. The study looked at data from 29,000 law school applicants to 152 schools and queried 7,000 students who began their second year in the fall of 1992. However, a third survey of academic performance, this one from Columbia School of Law, found that women in the top quarter of the class did significantly better than their LSAT scores would predict. But women began lagging behind when the top half of the class was considered, though at Columbia not by much. And among class valedictorians at Columbia, nine out of the last twelve (1985–95) were women. However, the survey, done by Associate Dean James Milligan in 1995, did not look at all women students, including those in the bottom half of the class, nor did it determine their disposition toward their legal education, and it cannot really be compared with the Penn survey. As noted, women at Brooklyn Law School do not fall behind men academically. (A large-scale study of women's performance and response to legal education at more than forty schools is currently under way at the University of Los Angeles; results were not available at press time.)

WOMEN'S COMMENTS DISMISSED

So what is happening in the classrooms of our law schools? Why are women systematically marginalized, even though their numbers are great? It happens for lots of reasons, and it starts with their lack of participation in classroom discussion, considered the nuts and bolts of legal education, even though grades come almost entirely from anonymously graded test scores.

In the worst scenario, women are not called on—even when they volunteer. "In Property, the women took a count—eight men to one woman were called one day," recalls a student at Stanford. "Yet the professor is young and fancies himself a liberal." Students at numerous schools described the same problem with one or more of their professors. In one classroom at the University of

Chicago the count of males called on reached sixteen before a woman was called on. By the way, Chicago Law suffers from no lack of women students; they make up more than 40 percent of the student body.

Even when women do speak, they are not taken seriously. "When women use personal examples, some of the professors will say, 'Uh-huh, uh-huh,' and just go on to the next person," says Ariadne Montare at Columbia University School of Law. "The men will use examples from their jobs or their life before law school, and it is given more credence than when women do the same thing. Women always have to tread carefully or they will be ignored." The students at the Columbia focus group I conducted in 1993 were far less disparaging of their school than, say, were women students at Yale, Harvard or the University of Virginia, but as a group they talked about how women are not taken as seriously as the men and the lack of female faculty as role models and career advisers.

"The [male] professors cut us off, interrupt us," remarks a student at New York University. "When a woman makes a comment, the professor often doesn't say anything in response, and it is as if she didn't say it, as if she deserves no respect, and they just go on to the next student. It's what the law professors don't do that sends a really powerful message."

At Harvard even a woman with expertise in the subject under discussion was ignored. Her labor law professor had a group of men he considered "the experts," she says, and although she had belonged to a labor union before law school, she was dismissed when she gave a statistic that she knew to be accurate. "The professor said, 'Oh, you think that's so, let's check it with the expert,' and he called on one of the men," says Anamari Oakes. "The young man discounted my answer completely, the professor repeated the young man's answer and then looked at me. 'And so?'" When your ideas are constantly trivialized, even women with healthy egos and thick skins can be dragged down. And silenced.

Race plays a part in the equation, for women of color fare even worse than white women, dropping to the bottom of classroom hierarchy. In Banks and Blocker's large-scale study, the group who reported they were least likely to speak in class were minority women. A full 65 percent of them stated they never or rarely volunteered in class. (Of the 1,930 students surveyed, 14 percent identified themselves as minorities.) White women reported slightly less silence, with 62 percent saying they hardly ever—or never—volunteered. When minority women do gather the courage to say something, more than a third (34 percent) (and a quarter of the minority men, 25 percent) report that their remarks are dismissed as uninformed and unimportant, a higher figure than for any of the other groups surveyed. Kim Robinson, an African American student at Harvard, explains why: "Some of the classes terrify me because God forbid if you are wrong. I would like to be able to ask a question—like, say, I don't know, I am an empty vessel and I am paying you to fill me with knowledge. Because I am trying to engage in an interactive exercise so I can learn something. So I can be wrong and we can talk about it and not feel my self-worth is on the table . . . but that's not possible, so I don't talk." African American women said they felt additional pressure because they feel they are speaking for all African American women, and if they aren't brilliant, all will be stereotyped as stupid women who are there only to fill a quota.

An African American at Vermont Law School, where she was indeed a rarity in the early 1990s, said that she tried to point out in one class that a zoning case that dated from the 1980s actually had the effect of setting up a discriminatory precedent. "The professor acted as if I were off the point, but when I asked him about it later in his office, he said that he didn't have time to get into race issues, even though he could see that what I was saying was essentially correct." Vermont is highly regarded in environmental law, which includes property rights, but, she went on to say, the racist aspects of any laws are typically overlooked as unimportant. However, the worst was yet to come: Another professor told her flat out in his office one day that "women shouldn't be lawyers in the first place, and especially African American women shouldn't be lawyers." Despite the insult, she graduated with honors. Obviously the professor was unaware that the first woman to argue before a Supreme Court justice was a black woman, Luce Terry Prince. Ironically this occurred in Vermont.

What's equally ironic is that many professors actively encourage minority students to take part in class discussion. It probably makes them feel better. That doesn't change the fact that they ignore or belittle the comments of those students. When the professor is a woman, by the way, a significant percentage of both white women and minorities indicated to Banks and Blocker that their opinions and comments were more likely to be taken seriously. But although women teachers now constitute nearly 30 percent of the law school faculties, at many schools they are not given plum teaching assignments, they are clustered in the lower ranks of the faculty hierarchy, and in general they lack the influence and prestige of the male potentates on the faculty.

This may be one reason male students, even though they constitute less than

60 percent of the student body, so completely dominate the classroom atmosphere. Listen to women law students, and it sounds as though law school classrooms are where the gender wars are played out.

Lisa Ilka, a student at the University of Arizona College of Law, recalls that in a class on estates and trusts, the case under discussion was one in which a woman left all of her money to the National Women's Party in the 1940s, but distant cousins challenged her will. They charged that she was suffering from an "insane delusion" even though there was no evidence of that. Nonetheless, the will was overturned. "When someone raised the issue that 'a reasonable woman' standard would have found differently, there was obvious snickering in class—it's by no means the majority of the men, but a small group of four or five," she said. "They will sometimes actually turn around in their seats and look at each other and grin." The female teacher was unaware of the men or unwilling to challenge them.

Milbrey Raney of the University of Texas at Austin recalls the time she asked a question about gay couples in a civil procedures class. "I said, 'Did spousal privileges apply?' and there was this dead silence for a minute and then people started murmuring and talking among themselves. I was engaged at the time, so the reaction I got was ridiculous. But there was a lesbian in the class, and if I were her, I never would have wanted to speak up." A student at New York University concurs that ridicule from the men silences many women. "You don't hear women who are involved in feminist issues speak in class because of the reaction they get. You can hear the whispers—'Oh, it's just PC,' 'It's not relevant,' et cetera."

Even when the professor is a woman, male attitudes often prevail. "In Contracts, we were discussing surrogate mothers," recalls Lisa Kunitz of Wayne State University in Detroit. "One woman mentioned how women entering into such contracts are economically disadvantaged and how this came into play. A group of men laughed—and that was with one of the best professors we had in terms of women's issues. She tried to make the point that she agreed with the woman, but she didn't tell the men to shut up. The woman never raised her hand again."

"A lot of the professors feel pressure from the students to disregard women's issues themselves . . . because whenever a comment about women's rights is made, there is such a charged atmosphere in the class," says a student from Washburn University School of Law in Topeka. "The professors have gotten used to playing the game and found that it is just easier this way."

Another factor that silences women, particularly feminist women, is that their experiences and outlook are frequently at odds with the law as it is being taught. It's as if the professor is talking the same language, but in a different dialect. "With one professor I became resigned that my viewpoint was going to differ with his and there was no point to continually bring up my point of disagreement," says Deborah Stachel, a graduate of Penn who assisted on the survey of women law students there.

"In some classes we read about old cases that were dismissive to women or women who were married and had no independent rights, but we weren't allowed to bring it up in class," says Stachel. "We were just supposed to ignore it—'Oh, it's just old-fashioned and let's move on and talk about something that is really important.' There wasn't any understanding that maybe women needed to vent a bit before moving on." It is as if the professor were to talk about the legal reasoning behind the Dred Scott decision, which validated slavery, and maintained that the fact that African Americans suffered from this decision was totally irrelevant.

Monica McFadden recalls a similar experience at the University of Chicago. "We would be asked after reading a case, 'What is your intuition on this?' and the women were finding that our intuitions were inevitably wrong, and we would be sitting there thinking, This is not how this should come out," she says. "But we would be pooh-poohed for thinking about it differently. You can imagine the frustration of the female student.

"We had one case where the husband got an MBA while his wife, a flight attendant, supported him," she says. "When they got divorced, the question was, 'Was the MBA marital property?' The case came out that while she was entitled to support, the degree was his. I thought, But what about a house? A woman maybe hasn't done anything to earn the money for the house, yet it is marital property. Maybe we need to change how we think about property, but we were actively discouraged from thinking about anything differently. . . . I would speak up in situations like this, but I was told I wasn't being 'intellectually rigorous.' You have to spit back to the professor what he expects to hear."

However, McFadden decided not to go along. "I realized I could learn the law their way, or I could spend three years learning the law and working it into what I believe, and I would get lower grades. You don't have time to do it both ways. A feminist law professor told me to do it their way and work it out later. But I am forty-two years old, I know what I want to do [be a plaintiff's lawyer], and I didn't have time or the patience to just go along." She accepted the fact that her grades—even though she was on her way to graduating with honors when we spoke in 1992—might not be as high as they would be if she toed the line.

"ASSHOLE BINGO"

Some of the silencing of women in law school can be attributed to the puerile atmosphere that prevails in some classrooms, where a reverse spin is put on the dominant machismo. In these classrooms a certain amount of hazing is applied to all students who contribute frequently, regardless of gender or point of view. Too high a profile in the classroom is seen as a ploy to impress the professor. Students who do speak up frequently, female and male, get known as "gunners," or "turkeys," or "assholes." At some schools, Penn and Yale to name a few, the peer pressure to be silent has developed into a fine art. Students engage in what they call "asshole bingo" or "turkey bingo." The names of students who contribute often to classroom discussion are substituted for numbers on a bingo grid, and an "asshole" gets a check mark whenever he or she speaks. You can usually hear an audible buzz in the room when someone has "won."

"Peer hazing by younger males in the classroom is quite effective at silencing women, particularly those who are at all feminist," says Michelle Fine, a professor at the Graduate Center of the City University of New York and coauthor of the Penn study. "Who gets the floor and who doesn't is very race and gender based, and excludes thoughts from being aired. So these boys are jerks—but where is the institution that says this kind of stuff—the insults, the asshole bingo—doesn't go on? The institutions announce that 'we are open to women,' but they are not changing to accommodate them." Social scientists had predicted that numbers alone would transform institutions, but as far as law schools are concerned, the theory appears not to apply.

It isn't just in the school years that becoming known as a woman who has something to say can hurt you. Being tagged a "gunner" or "asshole" or, what's worse, a "man-hating lesbian" can come back to haunt you later. "Women still rely on men as mentors and people to recommend them, and the people who are perceived as troublemakers do not get into the better firms," observes Professor Banks. Everyone is aware that one of the guys might be just the person who can put in a good, or bad, word about you, say, seven years down the road when you would like to join a practice where he's a senior associate or partner. So you keep your mouth shut, and questions you might like to ask go unasked, subtleties of the law remain unexamined, innovative thinking is squelched. Student Lisa Ilka said that not only was law school alienating, it was vastly different from her experience at Smith College, where, she said, there "was an excitement about learning" sorely missing in law school.

Being someone with a feminist perspective is likely to tag you as a "man-hating lesbian" or a "feminazi dyke." Men are allowed to keep their sexuality apart from classroom participation; they can be "turkeys" or "assholes" or "nerds," but their sexuality doesn't come into it. Women are often reduced merely to their sexual function—a "man-hating lesbian," for example. In this simpleton's worldview, smart, vocal women threaten the male role in the social structure. Turn 'em into feminazi dykes and these women can be dismissed.

Women of color may be stereotyped as someone whose only contribution involves race issues. "One student brought up minority issues in the first year, and it became the accepted belief that she would only talk about African American issues," says Columbia student Montare. "But only about a third of her class participation was related to that. She is very bright, and she is capable of arguing issues on a legal ground that have nothing to do with race. Yet people don't seem to remember that."

"Sexual stereotypes abound here," says Celia Lee of the University of Michigan. "If you are assertive, people label you a 'bitch' and assume you are difficult to deal with. As an Asian American, I have a double stereotype: people assume I should be submissive. . . . Sometimes when a woman brings up a point of law where the law is obviously wrong regarding women, you will hear comments in the class expressing impatience with her—'There goes that woman going PC again.' They roll their eyes, they groan, they turn around and stare at the person. I am pretty reticent in class. I rarely volunteer."

It would seem that in these supposedly politically correct days, overt sexual and/or derogatory references to women in the classroom—both from male students and professors—would be relegated to the past. Not so. A Stanford woman recalls an obnoxious student in a contracts class: "He would ask questions like 'What's the statute of limitations on rape?' The professor would joke it off. This one guy would sit with about four guys, and they would make these sexist and gory remarks. The professor did nothing to stop it."

Erin Goldstein, a student at Arizona College of Law, remembers a class period ruined by the professor's casual remark. "This professor had written the textbook on civil procedures we were using, and we all thought, *Whoa*—he's it! To first-years he was like a god. He's a jovial good ol' boy. He liked to use vivid images, and one day he just began a story with, 'In the good old days when women were slaves . . .' Because I was a known feminist, and had spoken up in other classes, thirty heads turned around to look at me. I was twenty-two years old and the youngest person in the class. I didn't learn a thing that hour. I didn't hear a thing he said. Steam was coming out of my ears."

Lisa Kunitz had a similar experience at Wayne State University in criminal law. "We never discussed rape, never discussed child abuse. We had one domestic violence case, and it was belittled and downplayed. The professor said if he only hit her, it probably wouldn't have been a case. I went through the roof and started quoting statistics from the FBI and the state of Michigan, but he pretty much blew me off. I never raised my hand again and didn't go to class much after that."

"In classes you can hear muttering about someone being a slut in a paternity suit . . . who is out to take everything. It's not real blatant, but you can hear it if you listen," says a Washburn student. "I sense a real disregard for the women we discuss in hypotheticals."

What are all these women saying? That at law schools all over the country, sexist comments are allowed under informal house rules. If they weren't—if they invited the same revulsion that racial remarks about blacks, Latinos, Jews and so on engender—the put-downs and insults would be squelched. The students learn it is permissible to be a creep on gender but one should be at least civil on race.

It just goes on and on. Students at one school Professor Banks surveyed wrote that the professor complained that one could not get a good maid or secretary anymore because all the women were in law school; others said that professors referred to them as "bitches." One professor drew a big circle around the title of the subject matter for the day's lesson that he had written on the board. "Pretend this is a large breast." Presumably the students were to suck on it to ingest the day's lesson. A male student commented that a professor put him down by saying that his "ideas are garbage because they are women's stuff."

This kind of woman bashing goes on outside the classroom, too. At some schools (University of Idaho and Emory University to name a few) an overtly misogynist fake law examination, in which an act of prostitution is described in terms of the rental of a piece of property, has been circulated in recent years. The property in question is described as "a garden spot surrounded by a profuse growth of shrubbery," and that's one of the least gross symbolisms in the "exam." At Idaho, Molly O'Leary says that the predominant reaction among the men was: *What's the matter, can't you take a joke?* "There were an awful lot of male students who were upset that others were upset," she says, since it was done annually and considered an institutionalized prank. "So much of this goes on and you just become deadened to it after a while," O'Leary says. When this happened in 1992 the dean declined to call a student body meeting, but at her urging, he spoke to the first-year class. The rebuke was mild, to say the least, she says, as the strongest word he used was *shame*. "His efforts were the equivalent of doing nothing," she concludes.

Sometimes the political becomes ever more personal. At Yale in the spring of 1994 a female student received a postcard showing two females dressed for sex touching each other. The message read: "IS IT TRUE? MAYBE A FACE-LIFT & TWO IMPLANTS WOULD HELP?—THE 'MALE' LAW SCHOOL COMMUNITY." The postcard was posted on the Wall, a student bulletin board, and Yale women expressed not only their outrage, but also the opinion that this was just another example of the woman bashing that goes on at the school regularly. "The woman who has a nontraditional career, who is assertive, who espouses feminist beliefs, is called a 'dyke,' " one student wrote in her commentary on the Wall. A man stated that the card was an isolated event and added: "Some people are just scum." But while his remark is encouraging, the general feeling of the women was summed up by another woman who wrote: "How many incidents does it take before it's not 'isolated'? As a first-year, I've been surprised at the number of hostile events. There are many more than I expected." At Yale, a number of women said, the typical reaction of the law school administration is to blame outsiders—*not* the male students.

Variations of such foul behavior occur all over the country. Some professors engage in it themselves. Some professors have no more idea of how to treat women as colleagues and students than the average plumber. They grew up with the idea of women as people who served them in some way, mothers who made them supper or "girls" who typed their papers or brought them coffee, not people with whom they have to compete intellectually and financially, and many of these men haven't changed with the times. The attitude is apparent in the way the senior faculty treats the women, and the students pick up on it. Things came to a head at Yale in 1995, when flyers listing the alluring attributes of five women in the first-year class were distributed in male students' mailboxes. Feelings ran high, and the Wall once again was full of angry and scurrilous remarks. Dean Anthony T. Kronman was persuaded—some said far too slowly—to look into the war between the sexes. He appointed a student-faculty committee to investigate.

A particularly poisoned atmosphere for women flourishes at Yale, the reasons for which may be found in its years of discrimination against women faculty, to be discussed in a later chapter. If women faculty don't have any real power and aren't respected by their peers, then women students don't have to be respected or taken seriously by fellow students. Then, too, it may be that the kind of high-achieving male student who gets into the hallowed circle of Yale (the entire law school, Ph.D.'s included, has just over six hundred students) may feel that his glorified status allows him to trash women at will. In the world of law school students, Yale (and Harvard) students are kings of the universe.

Certainly one cannot lay the blame for what goes on at some schools as the fault of all male law teachers. Several women told of male faculty at Yale and elsewhere who were helpful to all, women and men, in and out of the classroom, and treated the women with the same respect they did the men.

Sometimes students held widely divergent views of the same school. For instance, a Hispanic student at John Marshall said she was miserable, while a woman of European descent, albeit one who admits to being highly competitive and "one of the guys," says that she found no discrimination there at all. She had no trouble speaking up in class. However, she held a trump card that may have prepared her for the combative style of the typical law school classroom: as a teenager she had played tennis on the professional circuit. Or maybe she and the Latino woman just didn't have the same professors. Or maybe they did. And just maybe their experiences were different because their skin is a different shade.

Critical race scholar Kimberle Williams Crenshaw argues that because minority students' experiences and beliefs clash not only with those of the teachers, but also with those of most students, law school is especially disorienting. Asked to relate to rules and arguments and not evaluate them in light of the worldview they reflect—a white, middle-class worldview—minority students find that they must disassociate themselves and somehow assume an intellectual stance divorced from their existence. Crenshaw, a professor at UCLA, contrasts the options minority students face when slavery comes up: "[C]onsider a discussion in Property where the class is instructed to identify and apply a rule involving a lessee's responsibility for damage suffered by the lessor's property during the term of the lease," she writes in the *National Black Law Journal*. "The professor has asked the class to discuss the application of the rule in a suit for damages by the owner of a deceased slave against who was responsible for supervising the slave when he was killed. The students are asked to resolve whether the slave should be treated as mere chattel, in which case the slave owner will recover, or whether the slave should be treated as a human agency, in which case the lessee's responsibility will probably be mitigated."

Unless the instructor opens the door for students to question the very legitimacy of the proposition, an African American student faces a difficult choice. To participate "correctly," Crenshaw notes, she must disassociate herself from her identity as a descendant of the slave and ignore the illegitimacy of the whole doctrine under consideration. Alternatively she can point out how this objectification of her ancestors—and its discussion in abstract terms—perpetuates the devaluation of African American perspectives. If she chooses that route, she will thus be challenging the premise that the law is without perspective and bias and how holding to that absurd theory immunizes the law from serious criticism. But then "she would risk being regarded as an emotional—perhaps even a hysterical—Black person railing against the law in an obviously biased, unlawyerlike manner." Of course, to those of us who aren't lawyers, her argument would be sane, appropriate, and the only ethical one to make.

Crenshaw adds that while such a dialogue about slavery might be rare (although some minority students said the treatment of slavery in law school was extremely objectionable), other race issues generate similar dilemmas. It might be a discussion of the reasonableness of a white officer's suspicion about black people in white neighborhoods, or the detention of a car of Latinos by Immigration officers or when race concerns are passed over as not worthy of classroom time.

Women's experiences and women's mind-set are likewise devalued, and they are likewise asked to disassociate from their own gestalt when discussing crimes such as rape, providing the basis for much of the profound alienation, exasperation, and finally, depression they experience in law school. While there are those who manage to ride through relatively unscathed emotionally, for most the cost of discarding passions, politics, emotions and identities to an intellectual abstraction is extracted in well-being, mental health, and grades.

"If you survey men and women about their experiences in law school, it tends to sound as though they are going to very different schools," says Professor Fine. "The institution of law school is not gender-neutral in spirit in spite of the impression that they are." Fine, Guinier, and sociologist Jane Balin were the lead researchers on the Penn survey that documented what happened to women in law school in their large-scale study suitably called "Becoming Gentlemen: Women's Experiences at One Ivy League Law School." They surveyed nearly 1,500 Penn students, male and female, from 1987 to 1991. "Women in their first year of law school—with entry-level credentials that were equal to the men's*—had a healthy and critical attitude toward what they saw as the overt maleness of legal education," notes Fine, "but as time went on they became deeply alienated from the institution and the law itself." Women reported significantly higher rates of eating disorders, sleeping difficulties, crying and symptoms of depression or anxiety. And as we have seen, it's not only Penn where women are beaten down. Jesselyn Brown, a high-achieving Yale student who had formerly figure-skated competitively, says that although the atmosphere at the rink was pressured, it paled in comparison with law school: "I have never met so many women with eating disorders as I have here."

* Women's undergraduate grade-point averages in the Penn study were slightly higher than the men's; women's (LSAT) averages were slightly lower (less than a point), a finding concurring with statistics from the Law School Admission Council, which reports a one-point difference between men and women on the LSAT, except for women with engineering degrees, who score nearly one point higher than male engineering majors.

SEXUAL HARASSMENT

Wolves
in the Schoolhouse

In my first year, a professor started telling me he loved me, left notes in my mailbox, tried to put his arm around me when I went to see him. I was twenty-two, he was a married man with several children, a pillar of his church. In a class on gender discrimination the following year, another professor was saying how he didn't think something like this could happen in the law school. I raised my hand and said, "It happened to me."

—STUDENT AT TEXAS TECH UNIVERSITY SCHOOL OF LAW IN LUBBOCK

MANY OF THE EXAMPLES of classroom conduct described here, if repeated often enough, would fall well within what the courts have found to be sexual harassment in the workplace. Justice Sandra Day O'Connor wrote in the 1993 landmark decision of *Harris* v. *Forklift Systems* that it wasn't necessary to have a mental breakdown to legally prove sexual harassment: "A discriminatorily abusive work environment, even one that does not seriously affect employees' psychological well-being, can and often will detract from employees' job performance, discourage employees from remaining on the job or keep them from advancing in their careers." Theresa Harris had charged that a pattern of lewd and sexually demeaning comments by the company's president forced her to quit her job at Forklift Systems. O'Connor stated that the definition of sexual harassment "by its nature cannot be a mathematically precise test." Rather, the courts should look at "all the circumstances" to determine whether an environment is a hostile one. In a concurring brief, Justice Ginsburg went even further in describing what constitutes sexual harassment. She added that the test should be "whether members of one sex are exposed to disadvantageous terms or conditions of employment to which members of the other sex are not exposed."

This doesn't mean that a few lewd jokes constitute the legal definition of sexual harassment. But a pattern of raunchy asides, the constant use of hypothetical cases with sexual overtones, frequent jokes with sexual references, tolerance of vaguely obscene or sexually charged comments from students, or words like "bitch" and "slut" heard whispered in the background do add up to a pervasive atmosphere that makes the classroom a hostile place for women. It puts women at a disadvantage that men can barely comprehend.

While you are not going to find pinups on classroom walls, you do find professors like the one at the Birmingham School of Law who drew a bell curve on the blackboard and then commented on how it looked like a titty. This same professor drew a crude sketch of a woman's breasts on one woman's exam—the highest grade in the class—and let it be seen by other students at a pizza parlor. A student who saw the drawing told the woman in question about it a half hour before she had to take another exam. The woman, incidentally, has large breasts she tries to downplay. "I needed to think about the UCC [Uniform Commercial Code], but all I could think about was revenge," she says. "It ruined my grade-point level." Although she had made B's in the two other classes she had taken from the same professor giving the exam that day, this time her grade was a D. But there's more. The same breast-drawing professor also made suggestive comments in class about African American women's breasts. And he continually embarrassed one white woman because her name was a word that referred to physical intimacy. "The woman was shy and quiet," says the woman quoted above. "But every time role was called the professor harassed her—he would make some comment about her name, he harped and harped on it. Her face would turn red every time." The woman complained to the administration, and to the school's credit, the professor was not invited back to teach.

He is, one hopes, a dying breed. More commonly harassment takes a less obvious tack, such as when a professor brings up sexual references unnecessarily. It still happens at Boalt Hall, where one professor delights in using sexual hypotheticals in his torts class and has done so for years. "One hypothetical is about a man mistaking a woman in an airport and grabbing and kissing her, the other is about a drunk woman coming home but going to the wrong house and climbing into bed with someone she thought was her husband and having sex with him," says Lori Grange. "Then he turns to a woman in the class and says, 'Imagine you are this woman. . . .' If you can imagine hypothetical after hypothetical being framed in these terms, it becomes offensive and demeaning."

Many women at Harvard find famous appeals attorney Alan Dershowitz's class in criminal law offensive because he spends so much time on rape. The day I happened to sit in on his class it came up. Was it because in 1993 he was involved in convicted rapist Mike Tyson's appeal? It doesn't seem so. "Rape is a small part of crim law, but he brings it to the forefront all the time," said a student who had him two years earlier. "The way the discussion would progress was quite insensitive. A great deal of the course was spent with Alan Dershowitz's concern about how many women cry rape when it is not rape. He focuses on the few men who are wrongly accused." Is Dershowitz guilty of sexual harassment? Probably not within the legal definition. But one could legitimately argue that behavior like this does indeed undermine women's ability to learn, as opposed to men's, which might well bring it within the legal guidelines of harassment. More to the point, we are talking about law school here, not Forklift Systems or a short-order cook pinching a waitress's bottom. Isn't it reasonable to expect institutions of higher learning—to which female students are paying customers—to hold to higher standards?

What do we have so far? Women are ignored, and then, when called on, their comments are belittled; their analysis and way of thinking about legal issues that are deeply gendered is frequently dismissed as extraneous or "not rigorous"; put-downs and slurs are common in some classrooms; women are told they are too emotional and that they are not supposed to care which side of an argument they are on, when they do care deeply. Add to the brew a barrage of sexual jokes, innuendos and comments about women—and the occasional professor who badgers women for kisses, dates and so on—and you end up with a pervasive mood that can only be described as hostile. The feeling is vague, yet it fills the room. For women, it feels definitive. And nobody seems to be paying attention. Certainly the faculties at most law schools aren't, nor are administrators. Many law schools seem to be utterly indifferent to what is happening to their women students.

Naturally it is not reasonable to expect that every professor who makes a pass or dates a student is immediately ferreted out. I kept hearing references to teachers or deans (at some of the best schools) who had married their students, sometimes more than one. When you have adult men and women together, some of them are always going to form sexual relationships, and trying to police that is as mindless and bureaucratic as a company dictating that their employees cannot/will not/must not date each other. Some always will. Companies frequently insist that if a superior and underling do become romantically involved, one of them is transferred so a reporting relationship does not exist. At law school, however, no such protections exist, nor is such a rule really feasible. No one can transfer midsemester to another section. Consequently law schools have an obligation to strenuously discourage such attachments as a matter of course because they are uniquely fraught with possibilities for abuse.

In the stressful and fiercely competitive environment of law school, where the professors have so much power over their students, submitting to a professor's requests offers the promise of rich rewards while refusing inherently carries the fear of retaliation. What are we talking about? The difference of one-tenth of one point in a grade-point average can alter job prospects, can alter your class standing at graduation. If the student officially complains, the whistle-blower image can be disastrous on a new career. Taken together, these constraints are a powerful incentive to go along or, at least, not say anything if the professor makes a pass. Everyone knows this—the student, the professor, the faculty, the administration. It would seem to be the obvious role of the administration to create an atmosphere where women students don't feel they have to constantly fend off middle-aged men. But that's not always the case. Sometimes even blatant sexual harassment is shuffled out of sight.

That was the situation for a number of years at De Paul University College of Law, where one prominent member of the faculty was the offender. He had a national reputation in his specialty. For a time he had been the acting dean. In the 1980s and into the 1990s this man, now deceased, would ask female students to his office to talk about their careers. It's an offer most law students jump at, for finding a powerful mentor with lots of connections can open doors like nothing else. It can mean the difference between getting a clerkship after graduation, which is a kind of graduate law school, or getting that all-important first job with a good law firm. So this professor had no trouble getting students to come up and see him. But career matters would segue to hobbies—most specifically his photography. "Would you like to see my pictures?" he would ask, pointing to the stack of prints in the corner. Who would say no? The photographs would start out with landscapes, move to figures, and Surprise! end up with nudes. Female nudes. Next question: "Would you like to pose for me?"

Although his "hobby" was the talk among women students, and was thought to be on the faculty grapevine as well, the school administration chose to do nothing. The wandering professor/photographer/philanderer was one of them, after all. He was also married and in his sixties, and his hobby was treated as a campus joke. Older women students at the school had no trouble putting him off, and he was not known to retaliate. However, in the early 1990s following the Clarence Thomas/Anita Hill hearings, the mood in the country shifted, and what had been tolerated before was no longer. In 1992 former students and members of the school's growing and vocal female faculty took action. Armed with affidavits from students, women faculty took their complaint to the dean of the law school. The man was forced to retire at the end of the semester. At the time, the story was hushed up and De Paul—and the man—spared considerable embarrassment as well as the loss of reputation, not to mention female applicants.

Law schools will go to great lengths to protect their own faculties, especially the most prominent members, in an effort to not diminish their school's reputation. A telling example is how earnestly Emory University School of Law in Atlanta looked the other way a few years back when the alleged harasser was the school's superstar, Abraham P. Ordover.

A 1961 graduate of Yale Law School, a widely admired litigator turned teacher, the holder of the prestigious L.Q.C. Lamar Chair at Emory, fiftyish, slim and athletic, married and the father of two sons, Abe Ordover was enjoying the fruits of a successful career in Atlanta's legal community. He gave a special sheen to Emory, burnishing its reputation as one of the best schools in the country for aspiring litigators. In his ten years as a litigator in Manhattan with the firm of Cahill, Gordon & Reindel, he was involved in several splashy cases. He was part of the team that represented Trans World Airlines against eccentric billionaire Howard Hughes; he took on the notorious Roy Cohn and won; he represented NBC in a celebrated lawsuit. He was recruited by Emory in 1981 and was put in charge of the National Institute for Trial Advocacy (NITA) program. Prominent judges, lawyers and law professors came to Emory for NITA conferences. He produced dozens of films on trial techniques at Emory. Students agreed he could be an exceptional teacher. At the time, Emory was on its way to national recognition, and Ordover was a major player in that goal. But he had a fatal flaw: he was overly fond of pretty women.

The following account of Ordover's behavior and Emory's official response is based on a U.S. Department of Education investigative report obtained under the Freedom of Information Act and a report of an internal investigation at Emory that was published in its entirety in Atlanta's legal newspaper, the *Fulton County Daily Record*. The Education Department's report is vague about the timing of events, and nearly all the names and dates have been blacked out. It is clear from the report, however, that complaints about Ordover and his conduct toward women went back to the early eighties. A woman who was denied a job teaching at Emory told a friend of hers, who did teach there, that she had been denied the job because "she was dating students at the law school where she had been teaching." When she asked, "What about Ordover?" she was told by the then dean "that Ordover's was a different situation." The dean also told her that "the goal of the administration was to keep such things out of the newspaper and that nothing would be done about Ordover unless a formal complaint was filed." And in 1984–85, when David Epstein was interviewing for the job of dean, Ordover's reputation as a womanizer was discussed, another sign that his reputation extended beyond the confines of Emory. Epstein was assured that the talk about Ordover was "based on misinterpretations and innocent conduct." A former student had, in fact, written the school to report an incident of sexual harassment but was told that no action could be taken without more proof. The letter was put aside, and faculty members let Epstein know that it was important to keep Ordover at the school. Around this time, Ordover was given his endowed chair. Sometime during Epstein's tenure as dean, a female faculty member told him that Ordover had made "unwelcome, sexual physical contact" but felt it "would be disastrous to her career" if she filed a formal complaint. Again, the matter was dropped. At some point in the late 1980s Epstein did talk to Ordover about rumors circulating about him at the school. He said he was greeted with angry glares. Epstein left the law school in 1989.

What was it, precisely, that Ordover was doing?

According to the Education Department report, Ordover was known as someone who came on to lots of good-looking, tall, "leggy" female students, particularly the first-years, the youngest and most vulnerable of the law students. As head of NITA he hired lots of them, as well as personal research assistants, to help with his various projects. They were nicknamed "Abe's Babes." Women said that when they refused offers of working for him—being a professor's research assistant is a plum job typically sought after by students—Ordover pressured them to take the job. He left notes in female students' mailboxes, stopped them in the hall, interrupted their conversations, called them at home.

Rumors that he was successful in some of his pursuits circulated, such as, "Who is he sleeping with this semester?" One rumor was that the husband of one female student got into a heated argument with him. Skits in the law school follies satirized "Ordover and his behavior toward women students." Second- and third-year students warned first-years to "watch out for [Ordover] because he is a 'ladies' man' known to 'hit on' attractive women students."

Conventional wisdom at the school had it that pretty women could do well in his classes if they wore short skirts and sat in the front row. He called on his favorite females in class excessively, to the point where students kept track of how many times he called on them or mentioned their names. If any of his chosen "girls" crossed him, he retaliated against them "by criticizing them or making snide remarks about them in class." If this isn't quid pro quo harassment, what is?

Several women stated he asked them "to jog, to dinner, to the theater, and to athletic contests and [did] not invite males." (The report noted, by the way, that he "did give two tickets to a male on one occasion.") He "virtually demand[ed] that female students he like[d] meet him in his office to review exams even if they ha[d] done well" . . . and once there, he "lean[ed] up against them with his body or stroke[d] their arms or shoulder while reviewing the exam."

One woman who went to see him said she took her roommate so she wouldn't have to be alone with him. "Ordover sat between her and her roommate with one hand on each of their knees." Another student said that Ordover sat next to her in the library and rubbed his knees against hers. At one point he sat so close to her that when he turned his shoulder "his whole body was on her body." He then asked her what she was reading.

When one woman tried to leave his office "the professor grabbed her hands, pulled her toward him and kissed her on the lips, and told her how pretty she was." He tried the same with another woman, but because she "turned away in an attempt to divert the kiss" Ordover "kissed her on the side of her mouth."

During one exam period, he "spent a long time looking over the shoulder of an attractive female while she was writing her exam. He had his arm around her while he stood there." One woman left his office hyperventilating and scared. Another woman said he intimated to her that she might join him in Colorado where he was going to lecture, and two women said he asked them to join him in the Cayman Islands.

One woman told me his favoritism toward her was so obvious that everybody began to assume she was having an affair with him, an impression she says he encouraged, much to her chagrin, since she was not and was actively trying to discourage him. "He would look over his glasses, point to me, call my name and tell me to see him after class," she told me. "When I went up to him, he would ignore the students waiting to ask him questions and ask when we could go jogging." Women students said they avoided him between classes by hiding in the bathroom, lied to him when he asked if they had a summer job so he wouldn't offer to help and went the other way when they saw him coming.

Over the years a few faculty members had expressed their concerns about Ordover to the administration, and several students as well had complained about him to various members of the faculty and administration. But no one had ever come forth and said that Ordover offered an explicit quid pro quo, sex for grades, or been willing to file a formal complaint. They would, after all, be out of law school in a couple of years and could put this behind them.

In either late 1989 or early 1990 a sexual harassment survey was distributed as a first step to developing a policy specifically for the law school, even though the university already had one. The one in place outlawed "verbal or physical conduct of a sexual nature . . . when such conduct has the purpose or effect of unreasonably interfering with . . . a student's academic performance or creating an intimidating, hostile or offensive . . . environment." Former Dean Epstein stated that "he was probably thinking about Ordover" when he and the dean of student affairs, Susan Sockwell, went ahead with the survey. But it made the rounds at approximately the same time a faculty contretemps over a tenured faculty member's promotion blew up, in part because he had supposedly "attempted to solicit sexual harassment complaints against Ordover from some female students." The professor hired an attorney to deny the charges. Feeling on the faculty was high, with some supporting Ordover because they felt he was being attacked unfairly, while others felt his actions were a serious problem for the school. The sexual harassment survey only made the situation worse, because Ordover's supporters—and they held sway at the school—saw it as a witch-hunt to get Ordover. It was distributed around the same time as a university-wide survey, and the response was low. However, two students who did not fill it out came forward with specific complaints about Ordover. Yet "because of the small sample size and the uproar and misconception about the survey," the plan to go ahead with developing a sexual harassment policy for the law school was abandoned. Net result of survey: Nothing.

A new dean arrived in 1989, Howard O. Hunter. Students continued to complain about Ordover to Susan Sockwell, but none would file a formal complaint. They said the advice they got from Sockwell was to be aware that Ordover was powerful and they shouldn't do anything to ruffle his feathers—it might only make the situation worse. In other words, "put up and shut up." Women said Sockwell told them that they had to figure out how to handle the situation themselves but did, at least, urge them not to go out to lunch or dinner with Ordover. A few told investigators that she suggested they get help from the university's counseling center; one woman said Sockwell offered to lend her a book called *The Lecherous Professor*. She apparently told some there was not enough evidence to file a formal complaint. Sockwell herself stated that she "would not feel motivated to do anything unless a student said that sexual advances were made." She said that she "is personally more bothered by quid pro quo sexual harassment" than the "hostile environment" the students said they encountered. Too bad she couldn't award them points on their GPAs (grade-point averages) for success in spite of the school's phallocentric policy.

Sockwell's hands appear to have been tied, however, because she says that Dean Hunter told her when she went to him with the students' charges: "Don't bring me innuendo. If you have any hard facts, that's a different story. I don't want to deal in gossip." Apparently investigating to see if the "gossip" had truth behind it was beyond Hunter's or Sockwell's capacities.

Finally, in January of 1991, the university's vice president for Equal Opportunity Programs, Robert Ethridge, held a sexual harassment seminar at the law school. Ordover evidently attempted to intimidate the students who attended. As one student explained, "Ordover walked by the glass walls of the room and then stood there and stared at [the students attending]." He came back at least once, and afterward some of the students said they were "scared to go to [his] class."

But the seminar might have been the prod the women needed, for just over a month later thirteen students filed complaints with the university. Ethridge conducted an investigation, interviewing a total of fourteen current and former students, which resulted in a memorandum sent to Dean Hunter outlining the allegations about Ordover. Ethridge recommended that "serious consideration should be given to permanently severing his employment relationship with the university." That was too much to ask.

Dean Hunter appointed a three-person committee to investigate. Two of the people (one man, one woman) were on the law school faculty, which naturally had a vested interest in clearing the name of their most renowned professor. They held hearings—some said hastily—over a few days early in March, just before spring break. Ordover was questioned about his behavior, and he said that while he might be a "touchy-feely" kind of guy, none of his actions—not the requests for dinner together, the invitations to take trips with him, the kisses, the touching, the knee rubbings, the jogging dates, the personal conversations—none of this was intended to be sexual in nature. Not in the least. The worst he was guilty of, he said, was "bad manners" for interrupting conversations women students were having with male students and turning his back to the men.

Why did he hire so many women for the NITA program? they asked. He told the committee that "most of the work is scut work" and was difficult and detailed and women had *done this type of thing before.* He also stated that because "female students have been in sororities, they have experience *planning details.*" And he didn't remember ever stroking one female's hair and telling her she was pretty, as she had told the committee. He said he was "furious" over what was going on and that he was the one who was "victimized."

The committee must have agreed with his assessment, for they found that much of the students' discomfort was due to *misperceptions* of Ordover's actions. Rumor and gossip at the school had contributed to their mistaken impression, the committee stated, and "did have the effect for some students of creating an intimidating, hostile, or offensive educational environment." But because Ordover didn't *mean* his actions to be taken as sexually suggestive, and the administration hadn't warned him before that he was out of line (Dean Epstein's conversation with him was apparently not a "warning"), the committee determined that nothing he had done constituted sexual harassment. Being stroked on the head and kissed in his office was not "intentional sexual harassment" because it did not recur after the student told him to stop. Other touches students reported? "Not sexual in nature." And again: "No evidence of intentional sexual harassment." The committee also found that he went jogging primarily with female students "because of the unavailability of male runners." The committee's recommendation?

"[N]o disciplinary action."

The dean, however, did give Ordover specific guidelines on how he was to behave and suggested he seek counseling "to develop a better understanding of the ways in which your behavior is perceived by others." He was instructed not to kiss students, stroke their hair or touch them in any manner except to shake hands. He was told "not to sit on the same side of the desk" when conferring with students in his office. He was told not to invite students to lunch or dinner, to go jogging or to arts or sports events. Not that this behavior constituted sexual harassment, of course. Presumably the idea behind these instructions was simply to avoid more "misperceptions."

Before spring break was over, before the students returned to school, in a press release on March 15, 1991, Dean Hunter announced the committee's findings, stating that "it had not been proven that Professor Ordover engaged in sexual harassment." He would be back teaching on March 18.

Dean Hunter went to Ordover's classes the first day after spring break and announced the committee's findings and his decision. One of the complainants, Suzy Kriauciunas, asked, "So when he kissed me against my will, that didn't violate the school's sexual harassment policy?" The dean said nothing. Students applauded. She repeated the question again at a schoolwide meeting. Students cheered again. A male student got up and asked two members of the investigatory committee if they could demonstrate a "nonsexual" kiss. They declined.

The next day students boycotted classes. They marched two hundred to three hundred strong to the dean's office, demanding that Ordover not teach for the rest of the semester and be banned from instructing first-year students. Ordover took a leave of absence for the rest of the semester, citing the "mob atmosphere generated by a small number of nihilistic students." Not that he was to blame for anything, no sir.

Within days six more students—some of them former students who read about the ruckus in the *Atlanta Journal-Constitution*—came forward and filed complaints with the university. That was enough. Two weeks after he had been found not guilty, Ordover resigned. Rumors circulated in the Atlanta media that he was paid a sum in the vicinity of a million dollars not to sue the university. Dean Hunter, in a letter to the editor of *Atlanta* magazine, stated only that Ordover "did not receive $1 million from Emory University." Ordover refused to confirm or deny any settlement, stating that he and Dean Hunter had signed a binding agreement not to discuss it.

In June of 1991 a male student, Jeffrey Straus, who had become the public spokesman for the thirteen women who initially brought the charges against Ordover, filed a complaint with the Office for Civil Rights (OCR) of the Department of Education. In December, after finishing its investigation of the Ordover affair, the OCR sent Dean Hunter a twenty-three-page, single-spaced document spelling out what had been done wrong and what the school needed to do to correct the situation. Dean Hunter was ordered to inform the complainants that the OCR found "an environment of sexual harassment existed last year at the law school" and that "extensive training of University faculty and staff will be required." Four-hour seminars on sexual harassment were held for all faculty and staff over the next several months.

Suzy Kriauciunas says that Ordover's pursuit of her ruined her entire law school experience. "Half of my first-year class was talking about me, and I felt very isolated," she recalls. "I never felt normal the whole three years I was there. I couldn't walk on the faculty floor because a lot of the professors were mean to me. I never felt comfortable going for help." Not surprisingly, she did

not do as well in law school as she knows she could have. Other than in Ordover's class when he singled her out for attention, she says she was called on
exactly twice the entire three years she was at Emory. But there is some justice.
She does practice in her chosen area, immigration law, today in Atlanta. Ordover is involved in dispute settlement there. The dean of students, Susan Sockwell, is now the associate dean of Duke University School of Law. Dean Hunter
remains at Emory.

The Ordover incident caused deep division at Emory. Some of the faculty,
the younger faculty particularly, men and women, felt early on that Ordover
ought to go. But they were the junior faculty without clout. Only one woman
faculty member had tenure at the time. Coming out strong against an influential
professor with powerful friends was, if not political suicide, at least risky, without much to be gained and with a great deal to be lost. A career sidetracked now
might never regain momentum. The other woman faculty member years earlier
hadn't wanted to say anything about Ordover's grabbing her lest it jeopardize
her career.

On the other side were the high-ranking poo-bahs. Many of them were bitter
that the *discomfort* of a few women students would tarnish the name of their
institution and in the process, them too, as well as cost them the school's
superstar.

All this was occurring at a time when Emory was going from a regional
school to one with a national name. To protect that reputation, and their own,
the faculty elders attempted to keep the lid on the Ordover affair, slap his wrist
a bit, sweep it under the carpet in the faculty lounge, and get back to business—
even if it was the wrong thing to do. And they could always fall back on the fact
that since they had decided it wasn't quid pro quo harassment, maybe it *wasn't*
really harassment after all. They could always, you know, think like a lawyer.
Unless there was *proof*—a tape of a conversation, a video, perhaps—they could
always say to themselves that the women were making it up or, at the very least,
wildly exaggerating. Why not? It's what superiors at work and police and judges
and juries in the legal system have done historically when women accuse men
of sexually abusing them. Why should law professors be any different? And who
were these women anyway? Why should they take their word against that of an
esteemed colleague who denies the charges? "[A] major reason that many
women do not bring sexual harassment complaints is that they know this,"
wrote Catharine MacKinnon in *Feminism Unmodified*. "They cannot bear to have
their personal account of sexual abuse reduced to a fantasy they invented, used

to define them and to pleasure the finders of fact and the public." So rather than believe the women, the powers-that-be at Emory chose to sacrifice the women's education and peace of mind to save the school's reputation.

"I never felt comfortable going for help," Suzy Kriauciunas said.

Only combustible force got Emory to act. First the women had to have the courage to take a stand and formally complain, knowing that some would say they were troublemakers. The complainants were supposed to be anonymous, but their names got around school. "The professors were mean to me," Suzy Kriauciunas said.

Then, when the accusations of thirteen women weren't enough, the students had to march. Jeffrey Straus had to be willing to be reviled by the dean who, he says, called him "unlawyerly." Considering what "lawyerly" would mean in this case, the slur was a testimony to Straus's sense of justice. Look how low thinking like a lawyer had brought Emory. Dean Hunter later told the press he didn't remember making that statement to Straus. No matter, all that wasn't enough to make the school act decently. More women had to come forward. The Atlanta media had to make it a running story. Finally, finally, Dean Hunter and Emory University School of Law were forced to do the right thing.

But most law schools don't have such a defining center around which a case of sexual harassment can be made. Instead the harassment is much vaguer. It's the odd professor quietly hitting on a student, it's the offhand remarks denigrating women, it's the sly sexual aside by a student that the professor does nothing about, it's tolerating an atmosphere where students feel free to call feminist women "man-hating lesbians" or "feminazis."

And at many a law school, that's business as usual.

Besides, in a few years the women complaining about how they've been treated will be gone. Next year a new crop of students arrives.

A TALE OF
CASEBOOK CHAUVINISM

Women Get
No Respect

Now we are expected to be as wise as men who have had generations of all the help there is, and we scarcely anything.—LOUISA MAY ALCOTT

BEYOND PROFESSORS who overlook women or dismiss their comments, students who denigrate women's points of view, teaching methods designed to wall out new ideas, professors who harass their female students—what else could possibly contribute to the hostility women face in law school?

The very books they read. Fresh students may be arriving every year, yes, but in most cases the casebooks they are reading are as outdated as pantaloons. Although many casebooks have been revised recently, some with particular attention to gender and race issues, in most a basic antifemale bias remains ossified within the text. Just as the addition of women's bathrooms have not made law schools gender-neutral, so the addition of a few new cases and the exclusion of a few others, and some minor rewording to remove the most egregiously sexist passages, have not significantly reduced the disregard of women's rights and dignity that suffuses the law books used in most classrooms.

It's not just women who are given short shrift by casebooks; it's anyone outside of the white, male, and affluent group of men who wrote the decisions that became our common law. "Generally, you don't find casebooks that use women in the hypotheticals except as spouses or victims—the cases are all very male centered," remarked a student at Brooklyn Law School. As Judith Resnik, professor of law at the University of Southern California, puts it: "Generations of law students read and reread the same Supreme Court cases, and while some of the old cases are replaced by discussions of recent problems and changes in doctrine, the outlines and topics remain undisturbed. While 'supplemental' materials are sometimes added, little is subtracted from the basic story . . . as a generally upbeat tale that depends on not mentioning many aspects of the United States' legal system—the centrality of slavery, the conquest of the Indian tribes and the current a-constitutional relationship between the United States government and the tribes, the oppression of racial and ethnic groups and of women, and the effects of poverty on regimes of property-based rights, *inter alia*."

Casebooks, full of these old decisions and the "upbeat tale" of our legal system, are the basic books used in law schools. They consist of summaries of appellate decisions, chosen by the editors, to illustrate various legal doctrines and sections written by the editors, to illuminate the reasoning that led to the decision. Hypothetical situations that alter the facts of the case follow the court cases to stimulate further discussion and further clarify the legal reasoning under review.

The problem is that the casebooks tend to rely on old cases that predate the modern women's movement and do not reflect women's lives today. Because the law that the old cases reflect is so historically biased, the sexism is built in. The books are purposely devoid of any historical perspective that would explain how the mores of the time allowed the discrimination evident in many judgments. Dealt with in isolation, apart from their historical context, the old cases acquire the status of gospel, and the sexism is passed down intact. The books are not much better on current law. "In the books we used, there was no recognition that the law was still treating the sexes differently," says Monica McFadden, a 1992 Chicago graduate. "We would be asked after reading a case, 'What is your intuition about it?' and our intuitions were inevitably different from the men's and the professor's. We were 'wrong.' We would be sitting back thinking that is not the way that this should come out. Law students are told the words 'fairness' and 'justice' have no place in the law."

"Mainstream casebooks act as if feminist scholars and feminist critiques of the law don't exist," says Northwestern law professor Jane Larson. "What is included in a bound casebook is able to control to a large degree the politics of the classroom." This blind belief in the inviolability of casebooks and textbooks also puts teachers who wish to expand their students' horizons at a distinct disadvantage. "Students believe that what is in the casebook is 'real' law and what the teacher hands out to supplement the material reflects personal, probably political, points of view and is therefore not 'real' law," she says. As we shall see later, this skepticism is largely directed toward women and minority teachers who supplement their course reading.

Larson says she has received student evaluations of her teaching in which she has been criticized for having her students read too many feminist authors, thereby forcing her personal views upon the students rather than teaching "real" law. But when Larson went back over the course syllabus that provoked the criticism, she found that she had assigned only two women writers that semester out of twenty-five.

Gratuitous negative comments about women are by and large cleansed from the casebooks and accompanying textbooks students read today, so the sexism can be quite subtle and its effect all the more invidious because it is hard to pin down. If you don't know what is making you crazy, that can make you all the crazier. When the late feminist scholar Mary Joe Frug analyzed one of the most widely used casebooks in first-year contracts courses today, *Cases and Comment on Contracts,* edited by John P. Dawson, William Burnett Harvey (both deceased), and Stanley D. Henderson (hereafter referred to as *Dawson*), she concluded that while the book purports to be gender-neutral—and she found almost no examples of overt sexism—its underlying dismissive attitude toward women nonetheless charges it with outright sexism. Frug's seminal article "Re-reading Contracts: A Feminist Analysis of a Contracts Casebook" came out in 1985 in the *American University Law Review.* "Re-reading Contracts" awoke a generation of feminist students and feminist teachers, female as well as male, to the real depth of casebook sexism, which before had been bruited about but largely unsubstantiated. Other articles assailing other legal casebooks and texts would follow, but Frug's article aroused the most virulent reaction from conservative academics, largely because the book she chose to attack was one of the most popular contracts casebooks in use. Women students I interviewed frequently mentioned Frug's article without my bringing it or her up. Some professors—including at least one male Harvard professor—who teach contracts assign Frug's article as part of the regular course reading material and then discuss it—even as they use *Dawson.*

What did Frug find?

One, that men vastly outnumber women as characters in the cases cited in *Dawson.* Only 39 of the 183 major cases in the book had women as players at all. Men monopolize more than three-quarters of the cases. They also show up in most of the cases involving women. "Reading the old cases makes it so

obvious that the law is a men's club, that the law is male," observes John
Marshall student Sonia Sanchez. "Women have only a minor role to play in it."

Not only do the women get short shrift in number, they don't fare too well
as characters. They aren't given much of a range outside of old stereotypical
roles. Most of women's legal problems in *Dawson* arise from some dispute in a
family relationship, where the woman is only a wife, mother-in-law, sister-in-
law, or niece. Outside of family, most of the roles they fulfill are conventional
ones: home buyer or seller, nurse, fashion designer, charitable benefactor, welfare recipient, entertainer. While men are in cases as family members, as well
as home buyers and sellers, they also have a number of occupations—doctor,
contractor, farmer and so on. Frug commented that although one could claim
the stereotypical portrayal of women represents real life, editors do not seem
to choose cases on that basis. Casebook editors in general go for the quirky and
unusual cases that make for fascinating reading. But whether the characters in
Dawson are reflective of the real world or not, Frug pointed out that their overall
effect is to confirm the assumption that "women's opportunities are drastically
more limited than men's" and that "because gender has been a factor linked to
career choices and success in the past, it may inhibit their options in the future."
The women sitting in the classroom deny that premise by their very existence,
but the overall impact of few female characters in *Dawson* puts a subliminal chill
on their career options, even as they are becoming lawyers.

Frug faulted the choice of cases for other reasons as well. She analyzed
Fitzpatrick v. *Michael,* a case from 1939 in which the judges writing the opinion
seemingly went out of their way to purposely devalue woman's work. The facts
of the case in *Dawson* are somewhat sparse, but what we do know goes like this:
Ms. Fitzpatrick, a practical nurse, agreed in 1936 to give nursing care to an
elderly gentleman, a Mr. Michael, after his wife died and also act as companion,
gardener, driver and housekeeper as long as he lived. In return he would provide room and board at his house, pay a salary of $8 a week, leave her title to
his cars, and allow her use of his home and furnishings for the rest of her life.
He also confirmed Fitzpatrick's interest in his estate in three successive wills.
Fitzpatrick nursed him during lengthy periods of illness and drove him to and
from his office, as well as on long trips. Michael apparently told his neighbors
he was completely satisfied with the arrangement.

But all that changed in spring of 1939, when, according to Fitzpatrick, distant relatives "poisoned his mind" and he left his house and did not return. Two
days later Michael tried to force her out of the house by having the water,

electricity, heat and telephone turned off, and when that proved ineffective, he had her arrested for trespassing, not allowing her even to remove her own belongings. Fitzpatrick went to court, seeking to retain her modest weekly salary until he died, as well as the other interests in his estate. Her petition was denied.

The principle in contracts law this case is meant to illustrate is a long-standing one. The courts have always held that a contract for personal service, where one party provides continuous, face-to-face, hands-on service of one kind or another to the other party, cannot be enforced against either party's will. This makes perfect sense. No one would want to be forced to keep on a nanny for her child, say, if the relationship between the child and the nanny, or the parent and the nanny, turned sour for whatever reason.

It is not so much the decision itself that Frug objected to, however, as the legal reasoning employed by the judges to reach the decision. Contracts of this kind can be enforced, generally, only when the skills involved in the services rendered are "rare and unusual." Let's turn the situation around and suppose that Fitzpatrick was a skilled shiatsu massage therapist, the only one within one hundred miles, and Michael needed shiatsu and had contracted for Fitzpatrick's services, and she left to work for somebody else at a higher salary. Could Michael then force her to return to work for him? Under the provisions of contract law, the answer might be yes. But the court found that Fitzpatrick's services were not of this nature at all. They "required," said the court, "no extraordinary or unusual skill, experience, or capacity. . . . [T]hey involved no more than doing such as a housewife often does as part of the ordinary routine of life."

The message implicit in this decision is obvious. Woman's work has no value. The *relationship* skills involved in personal service, in hands-on nursing care, in living with and driving around a possibly cranky and certainly suspicious old man, are worthless, of no account, routine. Does it in fact take skill to perform this kind of service for someone over a period of years? Frug's argument is that it takes extraordinary skill of a quite rare kind—the skills, say, of a psychologist. But these are skills traditionally associated with women. Therefore the court can devalue them with hardly a second thought.

To make matters worse, *Dawson* immediately follows this case with a case where one party to an employee contract does have a "rare and unusual" skill and the courts did enforce the contract. The skill involved? Those of a professional football player. Here the court decided that a player of apparently no particular distinction (other than being of professional level) does indeed have "exceptional and unique" ability and can be temporarily enjoined from playing for other teams. Few skills are more "male," not to mention macho, than those required for professional football. "By combining *Fitzpatrick* with *Dallas Cowboys*," wrote Frug, "the editors present without apparent embarrassment two opinions involving the 'ordinary routine[s] of [American] life' in which judges assert that while nursing, housekeeping, and companionship are not unique services, playing football . . . ah, well, that's another matter." Yes: playing football, that boys' game, is a serious business. Women's work is trivial and has no value. Any housewife can do it. All housewives are interchangeable anyway.

It is bad enough that the few women in the book have narrowly defined roles. Frug noted that they are also described in stereotypically unflattering ways. One of the few women with a successful career, fashion designer Lady Duff-Gordon, plays fast and loose with her licensing contracts. Subliminal message here: woman as conniver. An entertainer sues over the results of her nose job: vain and self-absorbed. "Over time, you sense that every time the authors use a 'she' it was when 'she' did something incredibly stupid, or did something awful to a client, or was a victim," remarks student Sonia Sanchez. No one is implying in the least that only men should be the villains in the casebooks, but since women's numbers are so limited in them, portraying them as having unsavory "women's" traits further diminishes them. "[B]y selecting cases in which women are given stereotypically 'feminine' personality traits, Dawson, Harvey, and Henderson offer readers a casebook that furthers gendered ideas that women are not as significant as men and that women are limited to 'female' personalities," Frug wrote.

The language of the casebooks, like the language of the law school classroom, is almost exclusively male. As tradition dictates, the male pronoun is used throughout, even in the problems the editors have created for the casebook in which they have given the parties names such as "s" and "b." The sole exception Frug found is a case in which the editors refer to a shopper interested in purchasing an alligator handbag—read "mindless consumer"—where the party is a "she." In instances where judges used the "he" for "she" for rules that applied to females, and for law review excerpts where the masculine gender is the only one referred to, *Dawson* leaves the language untouched. Historically accurate, yes; biased, unquestionably. *Dawson* also includes passages from the legal writings of eminent judges who have shaped our laws, along with their pictures. Of course, women are absent in this distinguished group, given women's limited opportunities in the law in the past. But by including the pictures of the learned men, contrasted with the invisibility of women as judges, or as authors of law review articles cited, or as strong, ethical characters in the cases, *Dawson* informs the readers that women are not important in the law: not yesterday, not today, not tomorrow.

In addition to the problems with the content of *Dawson,* Frug noted that the overall style of the casebook—authoritarian, neutral, analytical, abstract—encourages students to be cool and distant, devoted to legal principles but detached from emotions. Does this seem the normal way to teach and experience law to everyone? Or is it the predominately male way? And do attitudes and traits associated with females seem substandard? "Readers do not receive positive reinforcement to nourish their emotional sensibilities or to empathize with clients and their problems as part of legal problem solving," she wrote. "Insofar as the activities that the casebook neglects to nurture are commonly understood as feminine, the casebook subtly warns readers, as future lawyers, to repress the feminine characteristics within themselves." Women students found this the most frustrating and depressing aspect of their legal education, as Guinier and Fine documented at Penn and as I heard repeatedly from students.

The so-called feminine characteristics that appear to hinder women in law school include the inability to divorce oneself from the ethical, murky, *human* issues of the law, to act as if there is no real right or wrong, as if all decisions are neutral and equal. And women just don't get it. As Catharine MacKinnon writes, "[P]art of a lawyer's role includes the ability not to care which side of the argument you are on, and women are regularly faulted for failing at that." Men continually fault women for being too "emotional." "Ethical" might be a more accurate term to apply to the women law students who cannot or will not detach themselves from the underlying morality of a dispute.

The cool style of the casebooks, divorced as they are from historical context, divorced from reality, does not accurately portray the context in which cases are decided anyway. Judges and juries are not automatons without emotion. Decisions are not made in historic and cultural vacuums. Cases are not decided according to a mathematical formula. There's the human quotient. And that's when reasoning gets murky and complicated. That's how life is. But that's not how the casebooks present it.

Each criticism that Frug and others found with casebooks, taken by itself, can be dismissed in various ways. Is it so terrible to have a case about a nurse—whose services are not considered rare and unusual—immediately preceding that of a football player whose services are deemed exceptional? Chalk it up to coincidence. Chalk it up to the point of law under discussion. Chalk it up to merely finding two cases that will hold the reader's attention. Does it matter that the pronouns are almost always male? That's the way English works—"he" suffices for both male and female. Isn't it nitpicking to object because the six legal gurus pictured throughout *Dawson* are all male? They *were* men, were they not? One cannot rewrite history to suit feminist ideology. *Dawson* only reflects life. Even today women are more likely to be in traditional roles. This is society as we know it. To portray women otherwise would be false and misleading.

But it isn't any of these by itself that is disturbing: each one can be argued away so that each, by itself, seems petty. Taken together, however, one example after another—Frug's analysis of *Dawson* runs for forty-three pages—presented as the canon in *law,* they become overwhelming and ultimately defining, like the weight of thousands of pebbles crushing a martyr to death. Add to this a classroom in which women are not given the opportunity to vent their anger at being constantly shown to be the inferior, subordinate sex. That's history. That's wasting valuable class time. That's not learning to think "like a lawyer." The entire gestalt, casebook and classroom, reinforces the sense that women aren't important in our legal system. That law is about men.

The casebook editors and strict Socratic teachers argue that discussions of how the law has changed over the years, or how it hasn't, to reflect societal attitudes toward these issues rightfully belong solely in courses on gender and race. Let those study it who are interested in it. Northwestern's Jane Larson says that when she added marital property to her properties course, a student complained that his time was being wasted—marital property belonged only in a course on family law. "Some students believe that they should not have to learn family property questions, that it is more feminist propaganda," she observes. "What they are really saying is, 'My world is the real world, and your world is marginal.'" Odd, considering that family property is one area of law that is likely to personally affect most of the students, male as well as female.

With few exceptions, contract and property casebooks traditionally omit family disputes and concentrate solely on commercial arrangements, the arena where men have traditionally dominated. The rationale here is that the contractual expectations are generally unwritten, looser, more fluid and, once more, *emotions,* that dreadful bugaboo, are involved. But here again the casebooks only reflect the law itself, which also puts family promises—contracts, if you will—into a separate category. Since men have historically held the social and economic power in the family, this is naturally manifested in the casebooks.

Men will accept strict rules and regulations governing their business dealings with other men, but where their wives are concerned, they do not want to be similarly bound.

When family law is included, the authors' comments reflect deeply ingrained biases. Professor Marjorie Maguire Shultz of Boalt Hall recalls as a student reading the one case in her contract law casebook that dealt with marital partners—*Miller* v. *Miller,* in which the promise of a husband to pay his wife for domestic service was unenforceable in the courts. Shultz was angered by the ruling, which was that "a wife should not be paid because she already owed domestic service to her husband." Shultz argues that in severing family promises from the general rules of contract doctrine, the law, in effect, allows the burden of "lawlessness" in family life to fall typically greater on women than on men. How so? Because men normally have more economic power than women and are thus able to enforce their priorities in intimate relationships. And just what is "lawlessness"? That area of behavior not governed by law.

The casebook Shultz read as a student, *Basic Contract Law,* edited by Fuller and Eisenberg, has been revised somewhat, but the current edition, the fifth, still assumes the decision in *Miller* was correct. The authors ask: "Are there any types of legal bargain (other than the type considered in *Miller* v. *Miller*) which are unsuitable for judicial enforcement?" The question implies that families, the realm where women traditionally have a pivotal role, are beyond the law in most instances. The judges' decision implies that the work women contribute to families is simply a moral obligation. Normal laws do not apply. The Law implied the same about the romantic institution of slavery during its existence. Darkies worked the cotton fields by day and sang melodious hymns by night, and their personal relationship with their masters, and with each other, was not governed by law.

The comparison is not extreme. One story that makes the rounds in academia involves a well-known black legal scholar who was a visiting professor at a prestigious California school. When he taught constitutional law, he analyzed the Fourteenth Amendment—the one that freed the slaves—in some detail. The dean of the school took it upon himself to offer outside classes to those students, concentrating on those amendments that he felt were more important. Yet law professors make the argument that it isn't so important what cases or points of law you teach, it's teaching students to think like a lawyer that counts. The dean's action would seem to belie this claim. No matter how you deconstruct it, what is important in the Constitution is a subjective view. Is it freedom of speech or the right to bear arms or the right to equal protection of the law for all citizens?

It is just as subjective to decide to include legal history and leave out the cultural history that explains, or attempts to, crucial issues of race and gender. *Dawson,* for instance, has lengthy comments on various aspects of legal history. Why not women's rights, women's place? Why not a page or two devoted to contracts involving ownership of human beings, as in slaves? Slavery is a seminal part of our culture that shaped our history—and certainly our legal system. Why not something more on reproductive rights, other than the single case involving a woman who attempted to sue an abortion clinic, which a revised *Dawson* includes? Reproductive rights—and contracts, because it always comes down to that—is one of the hottest issues emerging in law today. Should it be shunted off only to courses on family law? And are reproductive issues, in fact, merely women's issues? It is as if men do not contribute to the begetting of children. Family law is an elective course. No one really knows how many men take it, but probably less than half.

Unless the teacher, every step of the way, reminds her audience what's going on in the real world outside of the old cases they are reading, reminds them of the sexist or racist overlay in many of the cases, reminds them what is missing in the books, students are learning that since the law hasn't changed all that much, regardless of the culture, maybe any sexist attitudes they are germinating are really quite permissible.

It is worth mentioning that Frug's article appeared in 1985, and a new edition of *Dawson* was issued in 1993. In the case of *Fitzpatrick* v. *Michael,* the words "doing such things as a housewife often does" have been deleted and replaced with "things customarily done." A photograph of Shirley MacLaine, which showed her in a full-body shot in a sexy dress, has been replaced with a head shot. Other changes have been made in the book, but not in response to Frug; the changes were just a general updating, according to an introductory note by editor Stanley D. Henderson. In an interview, he said that critics of Frug's thesis call it "trash."

CRIMINAL LAW BOOKS

Reading the old cases in a cultural vacuum means that vast chunks of our history of oppression of peoples other than those in power are omitted. Law students are supposed to learn that history doesn't matter, when of course it matters very much, and it has everything to do with why our legal system dispenses unequal justice. And if a seemingly gender-neutral casebook for a seemingly gender-neutral subject such as contracts can be shown to be antiwoman, what about a more obviously loaded subject such as criminal law? When Nancy S. Erickson and Nadine Taub reviewed seven criminal law casebooks in wide use in the late eighties, they found that issues of particular concern to women were not integrated into the texts and that "sex bias continues to be uncritically reflected in the treatment of some subjects."

In the books Erickson and Taub analyzed, they found that the controversial issue of self-defense by battered spouses—cases in which a battered wife, say, kills her husband because she thinks he's going to kill her—was covered in only *one* casebook. Spousal assault—wife battering, in most cases—was also covered only in one casebook. Marital rape, while covered in five of the seven casebooks, typically rated less than half a page, except for one that gave it five pages. Sex discriminatory rules and doctrines were rarely criticized. "Rules that initially appeared to be neutral but, after analysis, seemed to be based on male experiences, perceptions, and values (such as the doctrine of self-defense) were rarely closely analyzed to expose possible sex bias," they wrote in the *Rutgers Law Review* in 1990. "Cases were sometimes edited to remove sexist passages, but this editing (without explanation through notes) left the reader with the false impression that the decision was reached on the basis of nonbiased reasoning. When the doctrinal law ignored the realities of women's lives (postpartum depression or spousal abuse), the casebooks did nothing to remedy this defect." Once again the reader was left in the dark about how law intersects with life. Although some of the editions that Erickson and Taub reviewed have been superseded by later versions, in general casebooks by the same authors typically do not change substantially in attitude—or text—from edition to edition, as we have seen.

One commonly used casebook today is the fourth edition of *Criminal Law* edited by Philip E. Johnson. Students I interviewed found it particularly offensive. *Johnson* contains several cases, for instance, in which sexual jealousy on the part of the man figured into the court's decision. One case, *People* v. *Berry,* involves a man, Berry, who killed his wife, Rachel, and was convicted of first-degree murder. The story of this marriage is a little odd: Rachel, a twenty-year-old girl from Israel, married Berry, forty-six, a cook in California. Three days later she left for Israel and returned approximately seven weeks later. She confessed that she had fallen in love with another man in Israel, Yako, and wanted a divorce. Yako would be coming to this country. Berry and Rachel lived together for a stormy thirteen days. Berry testified that during that time Rachel had taunted him with her love for Yako, kept demanding a divorce, and that they had sex at least once, which she had "demanded." During that time Berry also choked Rachel at least once to unconsciousness, before he strangled her to death a few days later. A psychiatrist, Dr. Blinder, testified that based on Berry's testimony of Rachel's actions, she was suicidal, and this "suicidal impulse led her to involve herself ever more deeply in a dangerous situation with defendant," according to court documents quoted in *Johnson*. "She did this by sexually arousing him and taunting him into jealous rages in an unconscious desire to provoke him into killing her and thus consummating her desire for suicide." Rachel, we learn, "finally achieved her unconscious desire and was strangled."

The jury ignored the psychiatrist's suicide theory, based as it was only on Berry's testimony of how Rachel acted, and convicted him of first-degree murder. However, the appellate court found that the "admissions of infidelity by the defendant's paramour, taunts directed to him and other conduct, 'supports a finding that defendant killed in wild desperation induced by [the woman's] long continued provocatory conduct.'" The appellate court found "this reasoning persuasive." The first-degree murder charge was reduced to voluntary manslaughter.

One could argue that such cases are necessary; that to exclude them because some women are offended would weaken the text to the detriment of all; that if these women don't have the stomach for the gritty, gory details of *real* cases, well, maybe these "little ladies" shouldn't be in the law after all. What do they expect life will be like out there in the real world, once they leave the protective environment of law school?

It might be less sexist than law school. *People* v. *Berry* is a 1976 decision from the California Supreme Court, twenty years old. The culture has undergone a radical shift in attitude since 1976, and it is hard to imagine that the same kind of case and same testimony of a psychiatrist *who never met the dead woman* would be credible today. And it is not just that this one case is insulting to women. Other cases in *Johnson*'s criminal homicide section deal with men murdering their wives because of sexual jealousy; perhaps the topic at hand really is that men kill their wives because they are unfaithful. We never hear of cases where the women kill husbands because of sexual jealousy. So the whole premise of these cases is that while it's not okay to kill if your wife is unfaithful, it is done, and you might get off with manslaughter, which is the same as running someone down with your car. Maybe the judge in Maryland who in 1994 tried the case of a man who murdered his wife when he caught her with someone else, and sentenced that man to eighteen months in a work-release program, read that casebook in law school. It is not any single such case in *Johnson* that is so demeaning, it is the accretion of them that does its damage, informing students and professors that women's place in the law is somewhere far beneath parity.

Some of the cases might have been rescued by a professor who chose to discuss the inherent sexism in them, but all too often—only in isolated cases, I suspect—this is not done because that would be straying from strict legal analysis. A student at Yale said that when women did protest that the psychiatrist's testimony in the Berry case was ridiculous, the professor said, "Let's get back on track," and, "Let's stick to the legal issues at hand," and critical discussion was squelched.

Some women find those cases that portray women as inferior, or that debase women because their lives are not deemed valuable, so disturbing that they don't go to class when they are to be the topic. Although no one denies attending class is helpful, and important, most if not all of a student's grade depends on exams—not class participation. So students cut classes for a number of reasons, often simply because they are boring, or the professor doesn't do a good job teaching, or it's spring outside. For women, there's another reason: they cut classes when they know the discussion is likely to degenerate into an hour-long disparagement of their sex. Because adversarial, flip remarks in classroom discussion are often rewarded, the tone can turn decidedly sinister.

No one should be surprised that women's grades aren't as high as men's. Of course, maybe the problem with exams is that women put context—history, mores, politics—of the cases they are writing about in their answers. And of course, maybe it's that loopy handwriting that gives them away.

RAPE IN THE STACKS

Rape intersects with more aspects of law and culture than any other crime, but editors of law books have absolutely no consensus on how it should be taught. Only some of them cover it as a serious crime in itself. Although five of the seven casebooks Erickson and Taub reviewed covered rape in a separate section, even today some omit it as a topic in itself. Instead rape cases are sprinkled throughout the book to illuminate various related points of law. That's the worst possible way to teach it, according to Erickson, because it gives the impression that the crime itself is not important. "You get no concept of rape as a whole and no concept of its impact on the victim," she says. "You get the impression that it has no coherent theories behind it."

This is all the more surprising, not to say appalling, given the prevalence of rape in our society. According to the best estimates available, 13 percent of adult American women—or one woman out of every eight—have been raped at least once in their lifetimes. Most women know at least one other woman who has been raped. I personally know four; two were reported to the police.

As relationships between women and men change and remake themselves, sexual assault, the legal category into which rape falls, will continue to be a rapidly evolving area in law. The rules keep changing, a fact that demonstrates that "law" is never made in a vacuum, regardless of what law professors tell their students and regardless of the way they teach it. In 1980 only eight states permitted prosecuting a husband for rape. By 1992 only in four states was it *not* possible. Just a few years ago the phrase "acquaintance rape" was not part of the language.

Yet the traditional view of rape—jump-out-of-the-bushes–stranger rape— fails to reflect a realistic view of sexual assault, of when, where and how rapes occur, how victims are harmed, how they react, or why rapists rape, according to Erickson. "[M]uch of the traditional law of rape is based on myths such as 'women ask for it' and 'no woman can really be raped against her will,' " writes Erickson. As a result, she contends, many legal doctrines relating to rape, particularly rules of evidence applied only in rape cases, are premised on a mistrust of the victim's testimony, a mistrust that is not extended to the victims of any other crime.

In some classes, quite possibly in most, the only rape law that is taught is the defense of mens rea, that of the accused's innocence because he didn't know that the attack wasn't consensual, and if he didn't know that, now then, how can he be prosecuted? He didn't even know he was committing a crime. His plunging ahead, pun intended, is a "mistake of fact." These are the sexual attitudes and excuses that are calcified in most casebooks that deal with sexual assault, these are the chauvinistic stances that are indoctrinated even today into would-be lawyers, taught as they are with all the authority of received truth. Of course, some of these women sitting listening to this will be survivors of rape themselves. Given such sexism that women constantly brush up against, what is surprising is that women do as well as they do in law school.

IN CRIMINAL LAW AND PROCEDURE, edited by Ronald N. Boyce and Rollin M. Perkins (hereinafter referred to as Boyce and Perkins), rape is discussed scattershot throughout the book. A number of the cases are indeed quirky ones, seemingly there because of their idiosyncrasies: in one a rogue pretends to be a woman's husband in the dark when she couldn't tell he wasn't. Rather than to elucidate the complex body of decisions and laws that make up rape law in this country, or to make students think about the tough issues in, for instance, acquaintance rape, these cases seem to have been included for their amusement value. An important topic such as the rape shield laws, which mark a historical turning point in rape trials, is noted in Boyce and Perkins in a tiny half-column-width, six-line item, stating merely that just as a victim's prior sexual history cannot be introduced (with exceptions) in court, neither can evidence of the victim's virginity. Interesting—if odd—point, but it certainly doesn't even begin to explain the reason for the laws, and realistically, one is left as much in the dark about rape shield laws as before. The information by itself conveys a tone of "Aha! But at least the woman can't claim she was a virgin!" rather than adding anything germane to the debate. The current edition was issued in 1989, by which time rape shield laws were on their way to becoming universal. Rape shield laws are one of the first examples that acknowledge the legal system's shabby treatment of women in cases of assault against them. While they are likely to be covered in the study of evidence, not every student will take that course. Foundation Press, the book's publisher, reports it is in use at about fifty schools.

Not all criminal law books are so insensitive. The widely used casebook by Sanford Kadish and Stephen Schulhofer devotes a whole chapter to rape, including eleven pages to rape shield laws. Understanding Criminal Law, a textbook by Joshua Dressler, places rape in its historical perspective. Dressler comments that many features of rape law "manifest the attitudes about women and sex held by the male judges and legislators who developed the law." Rape is defined as "at once a crime of violence, of sex, and of power, in which [most often] a male sexually subjugates a female." Thus a woman reading Dressler's book is not likely to feel that women are peripheral to the legal system.

Another trailblazer, this one edited by John Kaplan and Robert Weisberg (also published by Foundation Press), begins its discussion of rape shield laws like this: "Rape has been almost unique among crimes in that, at least until the 1970s, the accuser was treated as an immoral person and her morality was litigated for all to see. The total exposure of the private lives of rape victims has led to the remark that they are raped twice, once by their perpetrator and again in the courtroom." The authors also note that although forty-six states had rape shield laws when their casebook was published in 1991, the many exceptions to them call into question "how much change has occurred in practice." After reading through some of the other casebooks, you want to cheer.

Weisberg, a professor at Stanford, said that when he revised the text (Kaplan is deceased), his aim was to put those cases where there had been substantive changes in the last few years into a historical and political framework, a stunning distinction from *Dawson*'s latest edition. Weisberg culled material from the social sciences and newspaper stories, some of which are included in the book, and then had the revise vetted by women students. "Almost all cases arising under the heat of passion defense in manslaughter cases—a very old traditional doctrine—involved jealous men who discover that their wives have been adulterous and then they kill either their wives or the so-called paramour," he says. "It is amazing to me that the old case books—and many new ones—continue to discuss this doctrine in very abstract terms without noting this unbelievably obvious point—that all these cases are about sexual jealousy and male sexual insecurity. It amazes me that you could spend time on this material without discussing what stares you in the face."

We are not amazed. Views of gender roles and how they have been used to control women are so deeply embedded in the text of most casebooks that these views appear to be the norm. No thought is given to the fact that the "normal" attitude of the textbooks' white male writers and editors is as deeply gendered as any feminist scholarship. Their points of view have been around so long, and we are all so used to phallic drift, the tendency to reflect only the male point of view, that the male attitude becomes the one against which all others are measured. The problem is that the textbooks from which a new generation of lawyers and judges are learning how to run the legal system in this country are considered to be "objective." Overall, feminist critiques have had little effect. New editions of widely used textbooks and casebooks continue to appear, still flaunting sexist ideas about women and the law as if they were not only the norm, but somehow natural, somehow above gender and sexual politics.

Feminist casebooks are beginning to appear, but they are only used in courses specifically dealing with gender issues in the law. Women who have edited law books specifically dealing with women and the law are Mary Joe Frug; Herma Hill Kay; Katharine Bartlett; Mary Becker, Cynthia Grant Bowman and Morrison Torrey; and Beverly Balos and Mary Louise Fellows. The Balos and Fellows book, by the way, is entitled *Law and Violence Against Women*.

All of them place cases in their historical and cultural milieu with readings from the leading experts on the subject. Rape, domestic violence and sex abuse are not given short shrift. Becker, Bowman and Torrey, for instance, include an article by a psychiatrist about how many victims of sexual child abuse turn to promiscuity and drug use, traits that judges and juries in the past determined made these witnesses not credible. However, if promiscuity and drug abuse are shown to be common among victims of child abuse, it supports, rather than defeats, their testimony. Becker, Bowman and Torrey's casebook also includes the kind of supplemental information that other casebooks reserve for teacher's manuals. "We don't play hide the ball—the students have access to all the information that the teachers have," says Professor Torrey. But unless feminist jurisprudence courses are required at all law schools—a great many law schools don't even offer them—this kind of rendering will never be seen by the great majority of tomorrow's lawyers.

For the most part, they are still being spoon-fed unvarnished sexism.

TEACHING RAPE

What Is (Almost) Everyone Afraid Of?

Law is shaped by its practice, and practice by the education of the practitioner.
——NANCY S. ERICKSON AND MARY ANN LAMANNA

IF MANY CASEBOOK EDITORS are bewildered about how to cover rape, law professors appear to be even more in the dark. Yet it is the topic of much discussion around lunch counters and office coffeepots. Turn on the television or radio and you will tune in to the national debate about what is sex and what is rape. In any law school classroom, several students are likely to have some personal connection to rape—some may have been raped themselves, or they may know someone who has. No subject in criminal law more energizes women, and gets men's attention, than rape. Short of murder and mutilation, rape is the most heinous and life-altering crime. Yet law schools, and criminal law teachers, individually and as a group, have largely shirked their responsibility to lead their students over one of the most hotly debated legal issues of the day. Too many professors act as if this great social problem need not concern them or their students. Instead, as a group they remain adamantly committed to the idea that their job is to teach methodology—how to think like a lawyer—rather than content, rather than the nuts and bolts of actual crimes. Many of them are merely lazy, since rape was not taught twenty or thirty years ago when they began teaching and wasn't taught when they went to law school, and they turned out just fine, so they see no reason to bother with it now, especially since it is such a sticky and difficult topic in itself, let alone to teach. It's like volunteering to walk through a field loaded with mines when you can go around it. The laws are complicated and vary considerably from state to state—and keep changing to boot. The gender politics of the day require finesse and sensitivity to the students. Given the numbers on campus rapes today—slightly fewer than one out of six women on campus say they have been coerced to have sex—it's extremely likely that a number of the forty or fifty women sitting in a first-year criminal law course will have been forced to have sex that meets the legal definition of rape.

It's also possible that male students may not have listened hard enough when a woman said no and are defensive about their actions and likely to say things that deflect blame from them. Start with this mix and you have the makings of a highly explosive debate. It's no wonder that many a professor opts not even to teach rape. They contend that its emotional component hinders what first-year courses are all about: teaching students how to *think* like a lawyer, and not the specifics of any one set of laws. Any missteps will certainly be noted at the end of the semester on the students' anonymous evaluations of the teacher. The easiest way out is to sidestep the issue altogether. *You can't cover everything, anyway.*

This attitude is both irresponsible and tragic. Such teachers are intent on making new wrinkles in the brain that add up to an adversarial turn of mind, rather than filling up the wrinkles already there with useful information or, God forbid, an ethical framework to take on the gravest legal issues of the day. If their concern was to teach content about what is happening in the world today, then of course they would have to include rape. "To ignore rape—as many law professors do—is to ignore it as a problem of today," says University of Iowa College of Law student Christine Dykeman. "Teaching it makes people think."

That may be, but listen to these students from around the country. At the University of Texas, for instance, Milbrey Raney said: "In Criminal Law, *no* sexual offenses were covered. There were cases where women were victimized, but the cases themselves were about something else. The points we hit on didn't have to do with rape shield laws or sexual assault, and gender issues weren't touched. The professor was interested in white-collar crime, so that was what we studied. In Evidence, the professor did talk about sexual assault of a child, but only as an issue of hearsay—where a child told a doctor that someone had touched him in a place he didn't like. And that was it."

At Stanford, "a young professor who is an old codger in his thinking," according to one student, brought up rape only to say why he wasn't going to cover it. "He told the class there wasn't enough time to cover rape," she says.

"He said, 'Conspiracy theory is going to be more important. We don't have time to cover rape.'" (Hard to know how he figures this, since one in every eight women is likely to be raped sometime during her life, and nearly half of his students are women.) The woman asked him near the end of the course if they were going to cover rape, and everybody laughed, she says. When she and others pressured him, he reluctantly agreed to give it a cursory overview.

Sometimes rape is taught in an optional session. When that's the case, few men bother to show up. "Almost every woman in our class was at the rape session [held outside of regular class time], but it wasn't brought up in class," remarks Kenly Ames at Columbia. "And if it's not brought up in the class, you don't even think about it because your whole universe is defined by your professor. For some students, the rape section wasn't relevant. It was, 'Well, I don't need to worry about rape, it will never happen to me, it won't be on the exam.'"

Incidentally, rape questions on exams have turned out to be problematic for three reasons: One, women who have been raped say the subject matter can be excruciating to deal with as an intellectual exercise, along with the constraint of time and the added pressure of a course grade hanging on the exam. Two, rape questions are hard to grade, according to one professor who has stopped using them, because rape decisions are hard to dissect on the basis of their legal reasoning alone, and the many variables in convictions and acquittals and reverses by higher courts seem to follow no coherent pattern, depending as they do so much on the personal beliefs of the jurors and judges. "She asked for it because she wore suggestive clothing" is hardly a reasoned opinion, yet it has been the linchpin of many a decision. However, homicide cases can be just as knotty and turn on evidence that is just as convoluted, and law professors have not shunned homicide questions on exams. Three, teachers are skittish about including rape questions, for they may recognize their own unstated ambivalence about what constitutes rape.

The helter-skelter approach with which women at the University of Virginia Law School report they were "taught" rape may be fairly common. One woman said that rape wasn't brought up in her criminal law course at all; another woman said that her teacher went over only statutory rape, sex with someone underage, and while this is a genuine issue, it is removed from the real debate over rape going on today—that is, what constitutes consent. Another woman said rape was talked about in her evidence class; and a fourth woman said that her evidence professor (apparently a different one) did a great job with rape shield laws, as he devoted an entire class to it and put it on the exam. But that teacher seemed to be alone, according to eight UVA women.

One of them pointed out what is fairly common: When rape is discussed at all, the focus is on the intent of the victim, not on that of the defendant. "In any other crime, you don't talk about what the victim intended, you don't talk about how stupid the person was for going to a frat party or wearing a certain kind of clothes," she said. As Professor Banks says, "No one ever questions if a person consents to other types of assault. Nonsexual victims don't have to say 'I didn't consent to be hit with that crowbar.' But with rape victims a simple 'No' isn't enough."

ASSUMING THAT THE STATISTICS are correct, several women in any large section (one out of eight, remember) will have had forced sex, and the memory of that may be just as upsetting as—or even more so than—by rape of a stranger jumping out of the bushes with a knife in his hand. For all of these women, talking about rape is never abstract. Emotional hot buttons are being pressed. Writing as both a scholar and someone who was raped, Susan Estrich of the University of Southern California notes: "You survive rape, but you never leave it behind." Says Deborah Denno, who teaches a rape seminar at Fordham University School of Law, "Even people who are extraordinarily rational in their comments about other crimes become inordinately irrational when talking about rape—their emotions completely take over." To keep the class from boiling over, she says, the professor needs to retain firm control of the discussion. Denno announces at the beginning of the semester that those who may be uncomfortable talking about rape should let her know and she won't call on them.

What happened at the University of Chicago illustrates how heated it can get. A few years ago, when the class disintegrated into a free-for-all, women students asked if they could teach rape. Two criminal law professors agreed. Joanne Hovis, who was a student in one of the classes (and similarly taught the rape section the next year), said that although the women had to overcome skepticism on the part of some male students, "students with nonfeminist views had no trouble speaking," and the discussions were freer than those heard in the student lounge. Different instructors now teach criminal law at Chicago, and the experiment has ended.

At New York University discussions get so out of hand that women leave the class in tears. "My crim law professor only discussed a case [Regina v. Morgan] in England in the section on consent, but in that case you have a woman who was gang-raped after her drunk husband invited his friends to rape her, and then said it was all a big joke," says a student there. "We discussed whether or not the men thought she was consenting, but not the actual crime of rape."

Discussing rape only from the defendant's point of view was the number-one grievance, and according to the students I interviewed, it appears to be the number-one way rape is taught today. This finding coincides with a 1990 study by Nancy Erickson and sociologist Mary Ann Lamanna, who surveyed criminal law teachers in the late 1980s. Of the 238 professors who answered their survey on teaching gender-related material in criminal law courses, the greatest percentage of those who responded—nearly 95 percent—said they covered mistake-of-fact defense in rape—that is, where the accused didn't know that the woman wasn't consenting. Eighty-six percent said they covered the basic elements of rape when they taught it, but in my random survey I must not have come across many of their students, because that number is certainly at odds with what I heard. Erickson and Lamanna's respondents are likely to be predisposed to teaching rape, since the nature of the survey would self-select those interested in gender-related issues, but even among this group the average time they devoted to it is a meager one and a half hours per semester.

WHILE MISTAKE OF FACT, or mens rea, as it is called in law, has a strategic role in rape defense, it can lead to classroom controversy about how a woman was really asking for it anyway because of her dress, where she was, whom she was with, and when it happened or about the lack of injury. It's as if they designed the class not to deal with the real crime, perpetrated largely against women, and how it is tried, but to teach only the best defense. Bringing in rape solely under this heading gives airtime to the debate about ambiguous consent, physical force, or the lack of it and gives guys a chance to talk about, say, "how they didn't know she was saying no," while denying women a chance to talk about rape from their perspective. There couldn't be a more phallocentric way to teach the crime, and this is unquestionably the source of the anger and frustration I discovered. Additionally, if mistake-of-fact discussion is based on the old idiosyncratic cases most of the casebooks favor, more contemporary thinking about acquaintance rape will be limited or remarkably nonexistent, making women feel they are once again being blindsided. Their perspective is dismissed. Unimportant.

One of the most popular criminal law casebooks, edited by Kadish and Schulhofer, includes rape cases (*Regina* v. *Morgan* is one) under the discussion of mens rea, or culpability, but it also has an entire chapter on rape. However, if *Regina v. Morgan* becomes the only vehicle for introducing rape into a criminal law course, the outcome is, quite simply, a distorted and diminished view of the crime. With or without the feminist commentary, analyzing rape only under mens rea gives the illusion of teaching rape, but it is done with smoke and mirrors. If only "I thought she wanted it" is taught, students never get to the victim's perspective. If *intent* is separated from *force,* the crime itself becomes clouded. The hard issues never come up. Students never get to fully discuss what constitutes force in rape, and that is the defining issue today in most cases.

Other troublesome aspects of teaching rape that students described were the fact that professors (admittedly a small number) would sometimes go out of their way to embarrass female students by turning many or most questions about rape to them when they would be largely ignored the rest of the time; or class lectures focusing on the number of women who lie about being raped. "Rape in class becomes a discussion about how women will lie and whether the reasonable woman standard fits into this," said Fall Ferguson about her experience at Yale. The discussion occurred the day Ferguson's class was studying *State* v. *Rusk,* a case that turns on the issue of whether physical force is necessary for a conviction; in this 1981 case a conviction without force was upheld, but much space—and fruit for discussion—is devoted to the minority opinion that it should have been overturned, thereby calling into question the rightness of a rape conviction without physical force. In Ferguson's class, male voices who said it wasn't rape without brute physical force dominated the day, regardless of the fact that a female professor was teaching.

To be fair, teaching rape *is* difficult. Students overreact, emotions run high, personal attacks on other students can take a nasty turn, and the classroom atmosphere becomes heated as it does for no other subject. All points of view need to be aired, yet the session must not turn into a contentious debate that insults and affronts some and silences others. Comments that could be hurtful and extremely painful to some need to be squelched. This is law school, not *Geraldo.* While it may be easier for women teachers to present all sides, as women students will find it more acceptable to hear the man's point of view from another woman or to ask the kinds of questions that come up in real cases, such as "What was she doing there?" male teachers nevertheless need to ask them because these are the kinds of questions that come up in real cases, offensive as they may seem. Even though law school is, after all, a place where free-wheeling, theoretical, contrary—even antagonistic—discussion is prized, this kind of whatever-you-want-to-say dialogue can turn offensive when rape, not taxes, is the topic. And it practically goes without saying that this is a subject where humor, normally a prized law school commodity, never works.

Casebook editor Robert Weisberg, who teaches rape in his criminal law courses at Stanford, says finding the right tone is challenging: "What happens if you don't raise the question of rape is that some students get offended, and want it taught, and other students are made so uncomfortable, they don't want it taught at all," he says. "You don't want to discuss details to the point that they embarrass people, but you have to discuss details to give some reality to the cases."

Fordham's Deborah Denno describes several problems that arise: males may snicker during the entire class period, and female students complain after class about them; females may do the same when the discussion centers on men as victims, and males complain; women may argue that no time at all should be spent on rapes of males—a tactic Denno uses to draw men into the discussion and make them sympathetic to the victim's point of view. "I've even had women tell me when there are cases where the consent is ambiguous, 'Why are we even talking about this at all? Why are you even teaching this when it isn't as important as the number of rapes committed against women?' I have to say that with all that goes on when the topic is rape, it helps to be a woman teaching this subject. It simply is harder for a man."

A male colleague at Fordham, who was petitioned by his students to include rape, brought Denno in to teach it with him. "I can say things about ambiguity, for instance, that male teachers would have a hard time saying without being attacked—women are more likely to go on the attack against male teachers." At the University of Michigan, Professor James Tomkovicz found that female students controlled classroom discussion, silencing a woman who commented that stranger rape is more serious than acquaintance rape. At Fordham and at Michigan you have women taking the offensive and influencing the debate; elsewhere, at Yale and at New York University—in some classrooms—it is the other way around. What happens when rape is taught appears to depend on two factors: how well the teacher handles the class, and whether either group of students—women or men—feels free to direct the discussion.

So FRAUGHT WITH DIFFICULTY is teaching rape that when it is discussed at teachers' conferences, the general consensus among some male instructors is that it is best to avoid the topic completely for fear of being labeled sexist if one does teach it but not to the women's satisfaction. Some male professors say they won't talk about men as victims because that would automatically label them as sexist. Some give the advice that all teachers, male and female, should avoid it completely unless they have tenure and can't be fired. Denno's rape seminar, by the way, has turned out to be so popular that she has had to limit the number of students to twenty-five. Typically, only a few men enroll.

SHOULD WE EXPECT every teacher of criminal law to be able to teach rape well? Yes. Because if not them, then who? Professor Estrich writes in the *Yale Law Journal* that because there is a debate going on in America as to what is reasonable when it comes to sex, the topic demands to be taught. "To silence that debate in the classroom is to remove the classroom from reality, and to make ourselves irrelevant. It may be hard for some students, but ultimately the only way to change things . . . is to confront the issues squarely, not to pretend that they don't exist. Besides, the purpose of education . . . is to prepare our students to participate in the controversies that animate the law, not to provide them with a shelter from reality. . . . [T]he only reason *not* to teach rape," Estrich continues, "is the fear that it is so political, so difficult, and so close to the lives of our students that it can't be turned into just another intellectual exercise. To which I say, what a wonderful challenge for a teacher, and for a student. . . . [P]assion makes classes better, not worse."

PROFESSOR TOMKOVICZ, who had been visiting at Michigan when he included rape in his course syllabus, decided that the risks were worth the rewards when he returned to the University of Iowa College of Law the following year. Christine Dykeman, one of Tomkovicz's former students at Iowa, says, "He prefaced the discussion on rape by saying that you don't know what the person sitting next to you has been through, and he points out that anyone could be a victim, and that we should think about what we were going to say before we said it more than any other time because of the sensitivity of the issue. What surprised me was that more of the aware, open-minded comments came from men in my class. A lot of the women expressed the standard blame-the-victim opinion. But when someone said something like that, he would stop and bring up the other side."

For student Bret Lewison, the dialogue on rape taught him more than the specifics of the crime: "I got a better appreciation of feminist legal thought.

Before, it was something that I could intellectually empathize with, but never from a personal, intuitive sense, and this made me think that maybe, just by the very nature of who we are, we have a different perspective, a really basic difference. It's not easy to gain that perspective through talking about feminist thought in Contracts or Torts. There when the feminist perspective is brought up, the theory is there, but it is abstract." Tomkovicz must be doing something right: he's been one of two nominees for the school's annual teaching award four of the last five years.

RAPE SOMETIMES COMES UP in other courses. At Yale, the class was Evidence, the casebook was *A Modern Approach to Evidence,* edited by Richard O. Lempert and Stephen A. Saltzburg. This hypothetical appears on page 955: "In a rape case, psychiatric testimony that the alleged victim was a nymphomaniac, where the opinion is based on the psychiatrist's observations while sitting in the courtroom during the testimony of the victim." The problem was discussed at length in class, and the point of the exercise was to determine when psychiatric evidence would be admissible.

The whole premise of this hypothetical is absurd: the use of the word "nymphomaniac" plays into an old stereotype about women. The premise here is that this woman had emotional problems, that she had what some would call "loose morals," that she asked for it and then lied about it. Then the students are asked to debate whether all this could be observed by a psychiatrist "while sitting in a courtroom" during her testimony. Perhaps this is the same "expert" who testified in the Berry murder case discussed earlier that the woman Berry killed was suicidal although the psychiatrist never met her. This hypothetical buys into the idea that you can judge a woman by her dress, demeanor and overall appearance, then get an expert to call her a "nymphomaniac," which is a courtroom code word for whore anyway. Students are then asked to argue the legal issues involved as if this were all quite routine and not object that the premise is so obviously dated and biased that even talking about it is ridiculous.

It's ludicrous to believe any casebook editor, or any law school professor, would ask students to debate the legal points if the discussion were about a psychiatrist whose testimony regarding a "satyr" or, say, a man "addicted to sex," the current psychobabble, was based solely on courtroom observations. Neither of the two women in that advanced evidence class the day the "nymphomaniac" was discussed was able to convince the two professors teaching that the hypothetical was too sexist to be taken seriously. "Let's stick to the legal principles here" was the teachers' attitude. In other words, let's teach law as abstract doctrine. Forget reality. Learn to "think like a lawyer."

TEACHING RAPE IS never going to be easy, particularly for male professors, given the current political climate, the emotionally charged nature of the subject, and the incredible diversity of opinion in this country as to what constitutes sex and what constitutes rape. A few students said that some female teachers don't do a good job with it either. But rape is a social issue that is front and center on the legal stage today. The professors know it, the students know it, the rest of us know it. To ignore it, or circumvent it by teaching it as part of another issue, is to lose out on an opportunity to make the law come alive in the classroom. As Susan Estrich writes in the *Yale Law Journal*, "Teaching rape is . . . the best kind of challenge: a subject that is academically and personally alive, where the debate doesn't have to be fashioned just for a class session, forced upon students rolling their eyes and wondering why it matters. . . . [W]e do ourselves, our students, and our enterprise a grave disservice if we allow the forces of conformity on either the left or the right to chill us in doing our jobs, to frighten us from even trying. Our job is to teach what is significant in our fields. In criminal law, rape is significant, and worth our attention."

So far, most law schools and most law professors have yet to get the message.

TENURE TRAVAILS

Law Schools
Are Not Equal
Opportunity Employers

Assistant professors begin their careers as the little darlings of their older colleagues. They end up in tense competition for the prize of tenure, trying to accommodate themselves to standards and expectations that are, typically, too vague to master except by a commitment to please at any cost.

——DUNCAN KENNEDY

IN SOME RESPECTS, law school is a business like any other business. And as in any other business in America, a glass ceiling exists for women who work in it. In law school, however, this inequity directly abuses all who are not male. This is so because the law schools of today are turning out the men and women who will control our justice system tomorrow. If the ingrained sexism of many law schools infuses young minds-in-the-forming with a white-males-on-top message, then that is the sensibility they will carry with them to their law firms, to their cases, to the courts. And as a nation, we will have made little progress toward equal justice for all. Only through the free and equal inclusion of women and minorities on law school faculties can we begin to overcome the gender and race inequities that make our system of justice still unequal.

In the last fifteen years seemingly giant strides forward have been made on many law school faculties in integrating them with women and nonwhite men and women. Tenured law school faculties in 1980–81 were less than 6 percent female; today that figure is close to 30 percent of full-time law school faculty. Approximately 17 percent of full professors and 8 percent of law school deans are women. Women constitute more than 40 percent of associate professors and 52 percent of the assistant professors, according to the Association of American Law Schools (AALS).

But these promising figures hide a depressing reality: Women are still routinely denied jobs, tenure and promotions at a great many schools, and the highest-ranked law schools in the country* are among the worst offenders. The legal profession is almost one-quarter female; law school classes are nearly 45 percent female; yet the majority of the best schools have faculties that are under 20 percent female. For the 1995–96 school year Harvard's permanent academic faculty was 14 percent female; the University of Chicago's is 12 percent. Yale and the University of Virginia are close to 18 percent; both schools' numbers are enhanced by tenured women, two apiece, who are married to men the school wants to keep because of their stature. Yet other women, in some cases with more outstanding credentials, have been rejected in recent years.

At all top-tier schools, Harvard, Yale, the University of Chicago and others, women with indisputably excellent credentials and the esteem of students are being passed over in great enough numbers to indicate something is rotten at the core. Qualified women with credentials that would put some of their male peers to shame are somehow not passing muster with the entrenched and largely conservative, predominately male faculty that rules the roost at the top. New York University is the notable exception, with a faculty that is more than a third female, but even there, numbers alone do not mean that women are part of the power structure. They are not.

Although the numbers of women at some of the elite schools have risen, it is largely only entry-level women (assistant professors) who are being hired. The tactic of hiring these low-level women superficially improves the male/female ratio while effectively retaining male control. Law schools juice up their numbers, filling their ranks with powerless and rightfully fearful junior women who must kowtow to the entrenched powers-that-be on the arduous trek to tenure. Being an outspoken feminist, or too progressive in one's scholarship, unnecessarily sets up roadblocks. Tenure is so important because it connotes acceptance by one's peers at the school and confers a permanent place on the faculty. Tenure makes it nearly impossible to fire someone, but if it is denied, one is expected to leave the school. The next job is certainly at a school of lesser status.

A good—or even adequate—representation of women in legal academia comes only from schools that *U.S. News & World Report*'s annual listing ranks

---

* *The undisputed leaders among law schools are Harvard, Yale and Stanford; other top-ranked schools are University of Chicago, University of California at Berkeley (Boalt Hall), Cornell, Columbia, Duke, Georgetown, University of Michigan, New York University, University of Pennsylvania and the University of Virginia.*

third, fourth or even fifth tier. The leading schools, referred to as "elite" or the more democratic-sounding term, "national," still sorely lack for women on their faculties. The percentages of women faculty at places like Harvard and Yale have only recently risen above 10 percent, and only after some protracted tenure battles or earlier denials of tenure to good women have embarrassed the schools, forcing them to grant tenure to later female supplicants.

As we went to press, the law schools at the Universities of Chicago and Virginia and at Northwestern have not hired a law professor with tenure to teach full-time in a decade, and by denying women these jobs—the way one advances in this profession—the law schools reveal their true colors.

At Chicago, for instance, in the 1995–96 school year, only three women are actually teaching full-time on the permanent academic law school faculty, out of a total of twenty-five faculty who were at the school, not counting the eight emeritus professors, all male, and five or six lecturers, mostly male, who sometimes teach a class. One woman did have a visiting appointment to teach one course during one quarter. Two of the three women are entry-level assistant professors; one is an African American. Only one tenured woman, Professor Mary Becker, was teaching full-time in the law school last year. Chicago is such a harsh environment for women that they leave when the opportunity knocks. In recent years one woman went to the Justice Department; another went to Harvard; another became a judge. Men leave schools, too, but the Chicago numbers are so bad that any tenured woman who departs leaves a black hole in the faculty.

A new dean, Douglas Baird, did bring the nationally renowned philosopher Martha Nussbaum to the law school a few years ago, but she shares a joint appointment with the divinity school and teaches only half-time in the law school and is not a lawyer herself. However needed she was at the school, her appointment is unlikely to threaten the settled chauvinism of the place. Yes, more women are on the teaching staff, but they are the low-status writing teachers and lawyers who staff the legal aid clinic. It will take more than a few women on the academic faculty to change the overwhelmingly white male dominance and conservative bent of the institution, a gloomy glass tower on Chicago's South Side.

A few years ago at a dinner for Chicago alumnae and women students, when a speaker stated that students could now take courses from *twenty-three women,* sporadic hissing broke out among those attending. According to former dean Geoffrey R. Stone, that number was accounted for not only by permanent faculty which then numbered four, including one who was on leave in Washington, D.C., working for the Justice Department at the time, but also by visiting professors, clinical and legal writing instructors, personages of low status and no tenure, lecturers, and teachers from other schools at the University of Chicago who teach a single course at the law school. It certainly would be possible to graduate from law school without taking a single course from anyone other than a white male.

Chicago has a reputation for savaging some of the women who accept a visiting appointment. While they might expect that a year at Chicago would be a plus on their résumés, or that they might even be offered a long-term position, the visit turns out to be a negative because they risk being trashed by the overwhelmingly male faculty when they are up for tenure at their home institutions, or looking for a job elsewhere. Letters of referral are known to contain delicately disparaging comments, which are then expanded upon privately. Consequently some talented women turn down what would normally be a prestigious visiting appointment. Those who have been through the process include several talented women with sterling credentials; some who did get a bid refused. Possibly they were put off by the chilly atmosphere for women at the school.

Professor Marina Angel of Temple University School of Law points out that women faculty have been entering legal education in numbers since the early 1980s, so that old saw about there not being enough qualified women in the pipeline to get tenure at the elite schools is a sham. "Instead of 'There aren't any qualified ones,' they should just come out and say 'We don't think any of them are qualified,'" says Angel.

The sad effect of this near shutout at the top at Chicago and elsewhere is that the same antiwoman attitude trickles down. "If Harvard and Yale don't hire women, then all the Harvard and Yale wannabes feel not only comfortable in not hiring women, but encouraged," says Chicago law alumna Linda Hirshman, a professor at Chicago-Kent College of Law. "If Chicago doesn't hire women, then Northwestern [also in Chicago] doesn't need to either."

Part of the reason for the lack of women with tenure, according to Richard A. White, research associate for the AALS, which collects detailed statistics from its members, is that women drop out before actually coming up for tenure (the faculty votes on whether to extend it) at a greater rate than their male counterparts. Although the numbers for recent years show that more women than men, nearly 53 percent in 1993–94, were hired at the entry level—assistant professor, instructor, lecturer—AALS figures also show they are not gaining tenure at the same rate as men. To begin with, instructors and lecturers are not normally on a tenure track. Assistant professors are, but the ranks of women assistant professors have grown from 1990 through 1994 from just over 46 percent to close to 53 percent, which may only mean that as a group they are not being promoted to associate professor at the same rate as they used to be. This is almost certainly true at the next level as well, associate professor to full. White says that approximately 20 percent of the women who were eligible for tenure resigned before being considered. As Professor Angel puts it, "The system blows out a higher percentage of women than men in the tenure process."

White notes that this dropout rate is especially marked among minority faculty. Although they have a higher success rate of being hired as assistant or associate professors than nonminority candidates—and for the last five years minority women have been doing the best in this regard—women and men of color also *leave law schools at a greater rate than any other group.* Like female students of color, female faculty of color face the double bind of sexism and racism. Until they prove themselves in a really major way, they are burdened with the suspicion of being hired only because they are not white, not male.

Stanford law professor and AALS executive committee member Deborah Rhode notes that a *New Yorker* cartoon perfectly illustrates what is going on at most law schools. The chair of a large meeting looks across the room at the only woman present and announces, "That was an excellent point, Ms. Jones. Now we'll just wait until one of the men makes it." The discrimination, she writes, is myriad: "The same work or the same résumé is rated lower if it is attributed to a woman rather than a man. Male achievements are more likely to be explained by competence and female achievements by luck or affirmative action. Students in both classroom and laboratory studies evaluate women's performance more harshly, particularly those who violate feminine stereotypes of warmth and deference. Male faculty who are abrupt or hard to follow are more likely to be forgiven by students and colleagues. What passes for assertiveness or complex thought patterns among men is interpreted as abrasiveness or confusion among women."

To get along, one has to go along, a lesson apparently indoctrinated in female professors at most elite schools. At Harvard, while some of the women are known to teach lively, meaty classes that do not avoid gender politics, the women themselves are not intimately involved in the politics of the place. "For all their impact, they might as well be men," reports a former visiting professor. While one woman sits on the new hires committee at Harvard, the lateral hires committee—which has a great deal more power and to a large degree controls the future of the school—is all male as I write. New hires can be—and are, as we shall see—turned down for tenure. The lateral hires committee welcomes people with automatic tenure. They can't be fired. They are permanent.

Not only are women less likely to complete the arduous trek to tenure and full professor, even if women make it, they are likely to be kept out of the inner circle. New York University's Sylvia Ann Law, former president of the Society of American Law Teachers and the first person in legal education to win a MacArthur "genius" fellowship, says, "On my own faculty, I am marginalized. There are a handful of guys whom the dean feels he must consult, but I am not one of them." And remember, NYU is the only one of the top schools that has a good representation of women on the faculty. "You walk into a room of men and if they don't know your credentials, they treat you as though you were there to serve coffee," she adds. It's the same story elsewhere.

Women then do not become central to the decision-making policies that determine the nature of the school—that is, curriculum, teaching methods, sexual harassment codes or faculty. Without their input the male faculty unconsciously and routinely ignore or deflect the kinds of meaningful changes that would make law school more congenial to more than 40 percent of their consumers, the women students. "We are still 'outsiders' in legal education," notes Professor Leslie Bender of Syracuse University College of Law. "[O]ur presence has not correlated with an appropriate redistribution of power that enables us to improve conditions for all women in legal education. Until such changes are made, we remain vulnerable to the gender bias within legal education and law."

WHITE MALE BACKLASH

Vulnerable is right. Because some schools have hired more women than men in the last decade, a white male backlash is sweeping many law faculties. Men are threatened because women have taken over many of the teaching slots they feel are rightfully theirs by dint of their sex in a shrinking market. The 1994–95 *Directory of Law Teachers* shows that women now make up more than 46 percent of the associate and assistant professors, and a large percentage of them were hired in the last decade. AALS data show that women and minority job candidates have been more successful at obtaining *entry-level* positions than white men. "Jobs are tight and men with adequate credentials cannot get published," notes Professor Taunya Banks, "so their anger builds."

It doesn't matter what credentials these women coming up now have, the men simply don't want any more of them around. It was one thing to give tenure to a few women, even maybe to a so-called radical feminist, but it is quite another to have a faculty that is a quarter or a third female. Because of this backlash, qualified women are still passed over for tenure, as was the case not long ago at the University of Pittsburgh School of Law, the University of Virginia, Benjamin Cardozo School of Law at Yeshiva University and undoubtedly numerous other schools, or the battle for it can be fierce.

Elsewhere tenured women are being denied promotion up to full professor, even when they plainly deserve it. The faculty at De Paul University College of Law in 1994 initially turned down two highly qualified women for promotion from associate to full professor. One is a recognized expert in international law. The other is an outspoken feminist who was largely responsible for establishing and enforcing the school's sexual harassment policy, which resulted in the quiet retirement of one of the stars of the faculty a few years earlier. Payback evidently came in a no vote for her promotion. Morrison Torrey, coeditor of a feminist casebook and with the full support of the dean, eventually got her promotion; the other, Debra Evenson, resigned.

If enough women get tenure and become full professors, then men will lose control of the school, of the canon, of the whole system, and this is what upsets them. It is not just the older men who are angry; men in their thirties and forties are angry too because now there is competition they hadn't counted on. And it is not that only men are against these women seeking tenure today. Of course women have the absolute right, some might say obligation, not to back each other pro forma simply because they are the same sex, but at some places it seems that the "queen bee" syndrome has prevented younger women from getting ahead. The queen bee syndrome? It is an attitude coming from the one or two women who succeeded in their profession a decade or two ago that says, "I made it when it was really hard, and now I enjoy being one of the few women who did, and I'd like to keep it that way, so not only am I not going to help you, I might even sabotage you." It happens in business. It most certainly happens in law school. The queen bee types are usually women who emulate males in style and scholarship. They are not known feminists. They don't rock the boat or argue for more women or minorities on the faculty.

Professor Bender says that those against hiring more women don't come out and say that is their aim. They say they want an "accomplished scholar," she explains in the *Wisconsin Women's Law Journal*. Although such a preference seems gender neutral, the words are code for scholarship only in those areas where white males tend to write. "[H]ow many of us have sat on faculty hiring committees or in faculty meetings where something is said about all the women who were recently hired, the good job our institution has done in remedying sex discrimination, and how it is no longer necessary to look for more women, or more pointedly, how hiring more women now would be 'reverse discrimination'? Now (finally) the law school can look at qualifications again. . . ." They are a way of getting more white men on the faculty without announcing it, a tactic Bender calls "insidious, yet effective."

THE "BAN" ON WHITE MALES

Because of the number of women now working in academia, some white men have the mistaken impression that law schools' affirmative action policies make it difficult for them to get a good teaching job. "When are we going to lift the ban on hiring white males?" sums up the sentiment uncovered by the Ohio survey of legal education and voiced by a male professor. But that indignation is largely misdirected—even at the entry level. Deborah Merritt and Barbara Reskin, a law professor and a sociologist, found that the thirty highest-ranked schools hired significantly more men (both white and minority) into tenure-track positions than women of any race in the five-year period between 1986 and 1991. But it is not quite so simple: the discrepancy can be accounted for partly by the fact that women come with lesser credentials and limiting preferences; they graduated from a lower-ranked school, they didn't make law review, their clerkships may be less noteworthy, they may have limited the job search geographically, and so on. These are factors that can be accounted for by discrimination well before women are knock, knock, knocking on tenure's door at the top schools. When overall credentials were factored in, as well as the ranking of the 174 schools they looked at, a *slight* preference for white women and men of color was found: when compared with white men of equivalent credentials, they were more likely to be hired by a more prestigious school.

But the effect was slender indeed. "The woman might get an entry-level job at the University of Notre Dame rather than Indiana University," Merritt says, noting that these two schools are so close in prestige that they are sometimes reversed in ratings. So while there may be a small advantage to being a white female looking for an entry-level job in legal education, it has hardly assumed the Goliath-like proportions that led one man, after giving his race as "white male" on the survey, to add: "That's why I don't have a better job."

Merritt and Reskin, however, only looked at entry-level hiring, and even there they found that men with credentials equivalent to women's were hired at higher positions (associate professor versus assistant professor) and that women were relegated to low-status courses and denied the opportunity to teach popular and high-status courses, such as constitutional law, where the opportunities for publishing, public speaking and income are the greatest.

The slim preference for white women noted is fancy dress over dirty linen. It is the lack of lateral hiring of women faculty that makes the real difference. Hiring rules that allow a handful of faculty to blackball candidates make it possible to block virtually any known feminist from a tenured appointment. When full professors change schools, they move from one to another with the tenure at the new school part of the bargain. Although everyone has one vote, powerful people (read "men") are able to control blocks of votes, just as in any election. Without women of clout on the lateral hiring committees, which hand out these invitations, without women able to control blocks of votes, feminist scholars don't get respect—or jobs. And all of us lose.

Linda Hirshman, who won the teaching award at Northwestern when she visited there in 1991, was defeated by four or five votes on a faculty of almost forty. This is in spite of the fact that Hirshman is among the most published law professors in the nation, male or female, ranking in the top forty. In a 1993 survey (done by others at Hirshman's school, the Chicago-Kent College of Law) 33 of the top 150 law faculty who published the most articles were women, roughly the same percentage of female faculty during the period examined. Just over a dozen of them were at top-tier schools; accounting for faculty movement since then, two of the top female publishers are at Harvard, one is at Yale.

But if you looked at the overall picture where the women were, it would seem that many of the most prestigious schools are losing out in the sweepstakes to get to the faculty with the most publishing credentials. Strange, isn't it? Another of the top three women with the most articles to her credit, Wendy Gordon, remains at Boston University. A few years ago she was invited to join Penn's faculty but decided against it, as she and her husband had made their life at Boston. "By the time I got an invitation from an Ivy school," she said, "it was too late." Besides, she added, Boston University has been very good to her. Robin West, the other top publisher, is at Georgetown. Judging law review articles is all so qualitative; undoubtedly men who have voted against asking women such as Gordon (she is one of the many women who have visited at Chicago) and Hirshman to join the faculties of more prestigious schools would say they were not "accomplished scholars." It is worth noting here, however, that the top-ranked man, Richard Delgado, whose specialty is critical race studies, about the intersection of race and law, does not teach at an Ivy League school, either, but instead at the University of Colorado. Writing articles at the cutting edge in law may mean not teaching at the "best" schools.

More women are on law school campuses besides those on the academic faculties, but counting them can be compared to a law firm counting the number of female paralegals to make their numbers sound good. They are clustered in the clinical programs and teaching legal writing courses and have nearly zero input into the direction of the school. When you look at those jobs at law schools, you find that women actually outnumber men by more than two to one today. But by and large, teachers in the legal clinics and writing instructors at most schools are not tenured, although at a few schools that has changed. NYU, for instance, tenures their clinic instructors, undoubtedly related to the higher percentage of women on the academic faculty and their strength in numbers, making it an all-around more hospitable place for women. But regardless, their status is lowly because their work doesn't have intellectual cachet. It's looked upon as a skill that anyone can do. In general, clinical instructors have zero input into shaping the direction of the school, they do not serve on faculty committees, and they are paid less than their academic colleagues and they most certainly do not vote on who gets tenure since they do not have it themselves.

To assume that women who are interested in academic law actually prefer the low-paying and low-prestige work of the lecturer or instructor is to buy the old Sears Roebuck argument that women didn't want to sell high-ticket items such as washing machines and heaters because they didn't want to compete for customers and commissions, but instead preferred selling panty hose and the like. That was the argument Sears Roebuck used to defend itself against a sex discrimination suit in 1973, when it was the largest employer of civilian women. It doesn't wash.

Yet clinical programs, despite their lowly ranking, have appeal for some because they deal with real cases and help people who cannot otherwise afford a lawyer. Instead of teaching, it is really public interest law. Why these women should be low in status is a good question, since it would seem that theory is all well and good, but actually practicing law—ah, that would be something else. A 1993 ABA working paper, "Law Schools and the Construction of Competence," stated, "Law schools teach not how to practice, but esoterica of interest to the professors. Legal education and legal practice occupy different worlds." Writing instructors have even less status than clinical teachers. Yet that same ABA paper found that students rate communication, written and oral, among the most important skills they could learn in law school. These skills "are not particularly legal, but . . . law is a profession of words," the paper's authors noted.

THE RIGHT STUFF

A few words need to be said here about the kinds of credentials elite law schools look for in entry-level candidates aspiring to join their faculties. One is a *law degree from one of the Ivy League schools.* It's difficult to get past the gate without that ticket, so grooming for these positions begins in college, if not before.

Two is *law review,* which is run entirely by second- and third-year students and which nearly every school has. Law reviews, the scholarly journals of the legal profession, consist of articles usually written by law professors, attempting to elucidate some heretofore unanswered questions in a nettlesome area of law; surveys attempting to set a complicated field of law in some kind of order; or criticisms of the law or legal scholarship itself, which is where feminist and race jurisprudence, called critical legal studies, comes in. Students may contribute short notes or book reviews. Most of the articles quoted in this book are from law journals; the articles are often cited in legal opinions, and judges and lawyers rely on them heavily. Although law reviews have faculty advisers, in the main students alone select the articles to be published and may elicit submissions from professors whose points of view and law schools they want to represent in their pages. To work at an Ivy League school, only articles in law journals of other Ivy schools really count.

A third credential top schools look for is *clerking for a judge.* Depending on the judge, clerks may actually write the legal opinions, under her or his guidance, of course, or they may simply find the legal references for opinions and serve more as a sounding board. The more important the judge, the more status the clerkship. Clerking for a federal appeals court judge is better than clerking for a state supreme court judge. Actually clerking for a U.S. Supreme Court justice will hold you in good stead all of your life within the circle of your peers. On law school faculties everyone knows who has clerked for *the* Supreme Court.

Getting these posts are, again, determined by grades, law review and an interview with the judge.

The fourth credential, *working* for a couple of years for a prestigious law firm, or a public interest organization such as the ACLU or Legal Aid, is usually not hard to manage after one has the first two credentials. This requirement may be bypassed for outstanding candidates, but it is rare.

None of these will guarantee that you will be accepted for an entry-level tenure-track position at a prestigious law school; it's just that you don't get into line without them. Once inside the gate, you will have to jump through other hoops before you get tenure, which is basically a lifelong contract with your school so that you can't be fired for producing scholarship or holding opinions not in the prevailing mode. Tenure, for instance, kept left-leaning teachers from being fired during the McCarthy era of the 1950s. And tenure allows feminist women finally to write feminist papers without fear of retaliation.

If Lucinda Finley had accepted that as reality, she might be a tenured professor at Yale Law School today.

OL' BOYS AT OL' BLUE

Lucinda Finley was one of the bright new academics at Yale in the eighties. Her law degree was from Columbia, another of the best schools in the country, where she had graduated near the top of her class; she had been articles editor on law review and picked up a couple of awards there; she had clerked for a federal judge and worked for a prestigious law firm in Washington, D.C. In short, she had all the right stuff.

At Yale she taught core courses such as torts, which deals with injuries and damages, and labor and employment law. In 1983, her first year, another woman who periodically taught at Yale urged her not to write or teach gender issues. " 'Do straight torts or labor law first—wait until you get tenure before you write about women's issues,' she said," Finley recalls. "I dismissed her advice—she was from another generation and I was the young whippersnapper who thought that men's attitudes had changed. I said, 'I'm sure it was like that before, but I don't think it is anymore.' " The woman's warning would come back to haunt her.

Over the next few years Finley's feminism found its voice, and she began pointing out gender-related issues both in her classes and occasionally at faculty committee meetings. And of course they found their way into her scholarship. In four years her articles appeared in four prestigious legal journals, making her one of the more productive young scholars then at Yale. A fifth article was in the works. As part of her normal duties she advised several students on the lengthy analytic papers they wrote in their third year, and because she was one of only a few women on Yale's faculty—while the student body was more than a third female—Finley said she was frequently sought out for this task, as well as to advise women students on their career plans. Her reputation had begun to extend beyond New Haven, and she was often invited to present papers at conferences and to speak at other law schools, both at home and abroad.

The rude awakening came a year before she was actually up for tenure. At Yale, as at most schools, receiving tenure is a two-step process. First the candidate must get the nod from the appointments committee, which is comprised of senior faculty members appointed by the dean, who was then Guido Calabresi. Then the entire tenured faculty must approve by a two-thirds majority. Because of Finley's growing stature in legal academia, it was widely assumed—at least outside of New Haven—that her appointment was no contest.

But Finley would learn otherwise. Calabresi, who is now a federal circuit court judge, and the head of the appointments committee, Anthony T. Kronman, who is now Yale's dean, summoned her to a meeting and told her in no uncertain terms that they would not support her for tenure. Without their imprimatur, few other professors would want to stick their necks out and support her. Deans hold the keys to travel and research budgets, the cooperation of colleagues, and ultimately a professor's standing in the academic community. Calabresi and Kronman told Finley that three of her writings didn't count for various reasons, and the only one that did—a major article assessing the female equality theory and its application to family and workplace issues—they didn't like.

"They said it was not the quantity of my work, they knew how productive I had been, but the problem was my chosen perspective. They said it was not one they were particularly interested in having at Yale," Finley says. "I said, 'You mean the feminist perspective?' They said, 'If that's what you want to call it.' " A few days later at lunch with Kronman, Finley asked what he would write if he were asked about her work when she applied to another school. He replied, she says, that he would say that the genre of her work was not the kind Yale was interested in. "When I pointed out that there were court cases holding that disfavor with women's studies or feminism amounted to sexual discrimination, he said, 'Oh, I guess you have a point there.' "

Calabresi and Kronman's criticism will sound familiar to many a feminist scholar. Professor Gary Francione, who was involved in a tenure fight for a feminist at Penn's law school, says that the words Finley heard were the same as those used against any woman—even when her work is obviously superior—when they just don't want to offer her tenure. "They say the work is not doctrinal, that it is insufficiently rigorous, that it is too theoretical. These words are routinely used to describe feminist jurisprudence, which does not fit into Anglo-American analytic jurisprudence. I can say that because that is what I do."

And Finley's critique? "They said my writing was too doctrinal, too ambitious, too practical, that it didn't bring in enough law and economics* theory," she says. "They said they didn't know the sources I quoted—because they weren't the traditional dead white European males—and they were critical that I used *Newsweek* as a source. That was one footnote out of 244, and it was used as evidence that this issue was now of interest to the public."

It didn't matter that Finley had a fistful of congratulatory letters on her scholarship from others who worked in her area. While most other schools have a tenure candidate's works evaluated by outsiders, that is not the case at Yale. Since the faculty considers itself among the best in the world—are they not at Yale?—they deign not to entertain anybody else's evaluation. Finley was out, and her Yale women were the losers. When she left in 1989 the Association of Women Law Students gave her a plaque that read "She created a space in which we could breathe." For several years after, she was still advising Yale women, by phone and fax, on their papers; the women had been referred to her by male faculty there. By then Finley was a full professor—tenured, naturally—at the State University of New York at Buffalo, where she says the atmosphere is as hospitable to her as it was hostile at Yale. Says Finley, "At Yale I was invisible, and here I am a significant person with a contribution to make." Outside of the classroom she is active in litigation for abortion clinics in Buffalo, where antiabortion Operation Rescue is active; she has testified several times before state and federal legislators on tort reform and women's health issues; and she continues to speak widely on feminist jurisprudence and sexual harassment. But Buffalo lacks the Ivy League stature of Yale.

One of the visiting teachers who came after Finley left was Catharine MacKinnon. If Finley had any lingering doubts about the climate at Yale for strong-minded feminists, they were answered by the ruckus that followed the announcement that Dean Calabresi was considering asking MacKinnon to come

---

* *Law and economics legal theory incorporates cost benefit as a lens through which to examine all legal issues; many consider it a theoretical argument to rationalize the present division of economic power.*

to Yale for a semester or two as a visitor. Coming on the heels of Finley's forced departure, the invitation was seen by some as a ploy to dispel any talk that Calabresi and Yale were hostile to feminists. MacKinnon is considered the most brilliant and controversial of all the academics writing in the area of feminist jurisprudence. Her numerous articles and several books, her outspoken views on pornography and her charismatic personality have made her a celebrity in the wider world outside of academe. Her writings—which grate like gravel against the polished veneer of traditional jurisprudence—and jealousy over her star quality have invoked the ire of more than a few fellows in the academic fraternity. And academia can be a vicious place: reputations depend on the collective opinion of the grapevine, and the collective opinion can often be traced to a very small number of powerful titans in the legal industry. The dean of Yale's law school will always be one.

Understand that MacKinnon was not being asked to come to teach while she was looked over for tenure; this would give her a place to park only for a while, then she would be gone. Typically the dean makes these kinds of offers without taking them to the full faculty for discussion. But this appointment was different, this was too controversial to act on alone, this appointment was taken to the full faculty for discussion and a vote. After it was made public, a well-known ethics scholar who was then teaching at the school harshly criticized her book, *Sexual Harassment of Working Women,* in a memo circulated among the faculty. He stated in the memo that she failed to discuss tort law as a remedy to harassment. When it was pointed out that MacKinnon had devoted an entire chapter of her book specifically to that, he was forced to admit he hadn't *thoroughly* read the book. (He obviously hadn't read the table of contents.) But now he had, he said, and he still didn't think MacKinnon's work was worthy. Besides, a woman whose opinion he did respect didn't like MacKinnon's book either.

Apparently he dismissed as unimportant the fact that MacKinnon had written the brief in the first successful sexual harassment case to be decided by the Supreme Court, *Meritor Savings Bank* v. *Vinson.* In it the court recognized that sexual harassment could be quid pro quo and, what's more, so could a hostile environment constitute sexual harassment. Most law professors would be permanently enshrined at the law school of their choice for having created a new category of legal action; but it didn't buy a ticket for MacKinnon to Yale.

Because of the brouhaha, MacKinnon's offer went to two meetings of the full faculty, each lasting three hours, so hysterical—and that is the right word—

were most of the male faculty over the mere thought her coming to Yale at all. Finley (who was still at the school) learned at these meetings that she was not the only woman who felt alienated from the faculty; the two other women on the faculty did also and all for the same reasons: they weren't members of the ol' boys club that held the real power on the faculty. Women weren't listened to or held in high regard. Eventually MacKinnon came and went (as she had earlier at Chicago, Harvard and Stanford), and there were faculty fights over whether she would get tenure at Yale and Harvard and elsewhere. She didn't. Her nomadic existence finally came to an end in 1990 when she accepted a tenured position at the University of Michigan, one of the first law schools to admit women.

Numerically speaking, the situation at Yale has improved somewhat. In the 1995–96 school year Yale has seven women on a permanent academic faculty of forty. Two are considered feminists, and two are married to men connected to the school (one is a professor, one is a judge on the corporate board that runs the law school) that the faculty wants to keep at the school. None of the seven women are among the small coterie of people with Dean Kronman's ear.

Yale Law School alum Jesselyn Brown, who in 1993–94 was the sole woman in student government at the law school, is not optimistic. She says that the academic atmosphere is so dominated by the conservative white male mind-set that even when issues of particular interest to women—not only rape, but, say, abortion and marital property division—are the topic, the discussion ends up totally slanted toward the conservative-male opinion, *even when women are teaching.* "I had a professor who has pro-choice leanings, but in class she was trying so hard to keep a balanced perspective that she didn't come out strong for it," Brown says. Brown said that she enjoyed "terrific feminist conversations" with women professors outside of class, but added that "in class, the women are afraid to state their politics—yet the men don't censor themselves in any way." Says former student Fall Ferguson, "All the male professors give their points of view as if they were the gospel truth."

A few years ago one of the female professors stopped by the room where the women's law forum meets to suggest that they lobby for a feminist theory seminar. As the professor was leaving she added: "As far as you are concerned, I was never here. . . ." Obviously she didn't want the dean to know that she was agitating the women students to ask for a whole class—for credit!—on feminist theory.

"Yale is an elite school, but for women who have a gender consciousness, it is not a happy place," Finley reflects. "It is not a happy place for anyone who doesn't fit the old boy mold from which the elite institutions have been fashioned—white, male and upper class." The eight women I spoke to agreed unequivocally. The sexism is as rampant as it was during Finley's days. Earlier we heard how offensive classroom discussions of rape could be, for instance, and how mercilessly male students haze feminist women. Perhaps unabashed sexism stems from seeing how faculty women are kept on the sidelines.

Outside the classroom the conservative male voices dominate even more. "At the breakfast conversations, you can always hear a lot of guys say misogynistic things," says Brown. "Every morning it's something else—like, the only reason some women are teachers here is because they are married to one, or Hillary bashing. Feminist women are often called lesbians. When a story about Catharine MacKinnon went up on the Wall, a student bulletin board, a few years ago, someone wrote across it 'SHUT UP BITCH.' "

Moreover, notwithstanding the school's reputation for having a wide selection of minority students, African American Jill Morrison said that racism there is actually quite rampant: "The professors and students talk a good game, but there's a patronizing attitude, which is worse than overt racism because it's like being patted on the head." To defend herself from the inhospitable atmosphere she sensed, Morrison carefully chose her teachers—blacks and women were her preference. "It's not just that you *can do* this, you *have* to," she said, "if you don't want to feel suffocated."

WHITHER THE AMERICAN BAR ASSOCIATION?

Whatever pressure the dozen or so elite national schools feel to diversify comes from the outside world—the students themselves and the social climate—but the resistance historically has been stony. Justice Ginsburg, for instance, tied for first place upon graduating from Columbia in 1959, worked there as a lowly researcher from 1961 to 1963, then taught at Rutgers in Newark for nearly a decade before Columbia discovered this distinguished scholar and offered her a job—but only after the school signed an agreement with the government to hire more women or risk losing federal funds.

Students have certainly tried to rectify the abysmal situation. They have held sit-ins, boycotted classes, staged rallies, and petitioned law school deans. At Harvard two women students tried to sue the school for its lack of diversity (the school has yet to find an African American woman they find acceptable to take a permanent position), but the case was dismissed. Derrick Bell, a respected African American professor, left his tenured post there in protest and went to NYU. Overall, academia is as bad as or worse than industry, because no one is really looking over the shoulder of these vaunted figures who run the schools and telling them they *must* move more women into senior positions. Until last year the government passed the buck to the American Bar Association, which looked the other way.

The ABA accredits law schools, and without its stamp of approval graduates cannot take the bar exam in forty-two states or transfer to do postgraduate work at ABA-approved schools. ABA-approved schools must toe the line in everything from how many books are in the library to the size of the support staff for the faculty to the percentage of students who pass the bar exam. Schools found lacking are subject to disciplinary hearings, which can drag on until they comply with ABA standards. The ABA has done wonders over the years to push schools to diversify the student body. The process would seem to be the perfect vehicle to require schools—even the lofty Harvard—to diversify their faculties. But regardless of what the ABA standards say—and they say faculties must be diverse—the white male stranglehold at the top remains the last great scandal in legal education.

James P. White, who as the organization's consultant on legal education has appointed the small group of deans, professors and law librarians who visit the schools every seven years, has thereby controlled the accreditation process for nearly twenty years. "He appoints people he knows—and he doesn't know many women and minorities—and he runs with his own little boys' network, and it is a disaster," says one outspoken woman who has managed to be appointed to evaluation committees. She says the prevailing attitude is, "We don't have time or expertise to look into allegations of discrimination." Herself excepted, people who would force the issue are not tapped to serve on the teams. The women appointed to the accreditation teams are typically librarians, the traditional "woman's" position in law schools, whose main concern is the library, and practicing women lawyers or bar examiners who really don't understand legal education from the inside and, anyway, are unlikely to rock the boat. Appointments to the teams are status plums, and one doesn't want to seem ungrateful. The site teams are a genteel bunch. They are treated well, too, at the school's expense: They stay at first-rate hotels and dine at great restaurants.

However, White's dominion over the accreditation process was challenged recently. In 1995 the Justice Department was persuaded to file a civil antitrust suit against the ABA, and soon after, the ABA signed a consent decree. One of the points the ABA agreed to was to diversify evaluation committees, appointing more practitioners and judges to the mix of academics and librarians. Others were that the ABA could no longer bar for-profit schools from accreditation or require schools to raise salaries to the median of all accredited schools.

How much the reconfigured ABA evaluation committees will emphasize faculty diversity at the full professor level remains to be seen, since that was not an issue in the settlement. White is under no obligation to appoint people to the committees whose concerns are women's equality. He has every opportunity to keep them off. In the past, even when the site committees came back with a negative report on faculty diversity at elite schools, nothing much happened. The dean might get upset, a concerned rebuttal might be written, but it's all confidential as far as the outside world is concerned; female student-consumers won't be scared off. These reports, after all, are not public, the way *Consumer Reports* lists cars and baby carriages.

In 1992, for instance, four schools were cited for not meeting diversity standards. No action of any sort was taken. A few years back a minority faction on the accreditation team cited Penn for lack of diversity; unlike the minority opinions of the Supreme Court—and the teams and Jim White seemingly have as much absolute power over accreditation as the Court does over the judicial system—their concerns were never made public. Sometimes just getting a negative report energizes the dean to take action. But this is at schools where the dean makes a real effort to achieve diversity, such as the University of Iowa, where women faculty are aggressively recruited. If the dean chooses to ignore it, so does the ABA. "Yet if you don't have the adequate number of chairs in the library, your accreditation gets called into question, but you discriminate against better than half of the human race, and they could care less," says the woman who has served on the evaluation committees. No one can recall an ABA disciplinary hearing held because of a school's lack of faculty diversity.

CHALLENGING THE LAW, CHANGING THE STATUS QUO

In general, the women who get tenure today at the most prestigious schools (and some not so prestigious) are the kind who do not challenge the status quo. With notable exceptions, they don't make feminist waves and they don't make men uncomfortable. Geoff Stone, who went from law school dean to University of Chicago provost, points to the AALS statistics that found that the academics who were called "feminist" by the dean or someone in his or her office who filled out the AALS survey actually got tenure at a higher rate than the traditional instructors. But the sample was so small (thirty-five feminists, one denied, two dropped out) that it is not a reliable indicator. Furthermore the subjectivity involved in classifying some women "feminist" cannot be ignored (are these women all teaching "feminist" courses?), and the status of the schools involved is not known.

Strong, outspoken feminists who want to tear down the old sexist canons of the law, and of law schools, may be the most brilliant and original scholars, but they want to attack the very club they are trying to join. And if you are in charge of the club, and you are comfortable with the way things are, and if the law as is, and the law as taught at your school, suits you just fine, then why let these radical upstarts, *these women,* into your club? It's a Catch-22: If feminists try to maintain their allegiance to feminist principles, they ipso facto challenge the authority of the men who run the club that runs the law school. Those in power would hardly want to give them jobs or have them as lifelong colleagues. Doing that would mean that the way things are would change. The legal canon would crack. So for many feminist women, getting tenure at the elite law schools remains akin to slipping through the proverbial eye of the needle or changing one's stripes to suit the "club."

Why is it so scandalous that the best schools keep women out? Because it is from these schools that so many of the people who run the country come. It is well known that President Bill Clinton and Hillary Rodham met at Yale Law School, recognized as an unofficial prep school of America's power elite. Harvard likes to take note of how many Supreme Court justices have been Harvard Law: sixteen and two-thirds, with Justice Ruth Ginsburg as the two-thirds, since she spent two out of the three years of law school at Harvard. The people who come from the "best" schools hold many, if not most, of the real seats of power in this country. And as Alexis de Tocqueville noted more than a century ago, without a nobility in America, lawyers form the elite. Consequently the kind of law learned at any of these top schools, and the milieu at each of them, is directly related to the kind of law that will hold sway in the future.

If women's influence and feminist ideology is thwarted at the top, the consequences will be felt around America for decades to come. Until women crack the glass ceiling at the elite law schools, real progress in how the Law treats all women will be denied. Tenure—or what's even better, a named chair—at such a school offers greater opportunities to make a difference, in how the law is taught, in what kind of lawyer the next generation will be. Will we raise more individuals who learn only to "think like a lawyer," or will notions of justice, of fairness and equality to all, be instilled in their minds?

Of course, being associated with a great school confers greater pay and prestige to the individual, along with opportunities in the wider world to make a difference. If the ethics columnist for, say, the *National Law Journal* is always an individual from a top-tier school, and if few women are professors at these schools, then the perspective on ethics we are likely to get in the *National Law Journal*—read by an estimated two hundred thousand people in the legal profession—will continue to be that of a white male. When *The Washington Post* or *The New York Times* solicits a legal commentator on some subject for their Op-Ed page, they likewise look to the recognized names from the top schools. Boston University doesn't have the same élan as Harvard or Yale or Penn or Stanford. The same is true of all kinds of publications, all kinds of events seeking eminent speakers and organizations seeking influential members. Professors at the top-tier schools have opportunities to influence opinion makers and leaders that professors at the other schools don't have. Professors at top-tier schools can influence the Law the way others can't. That's how tenure denied to women ultimately translates into justice delayed for all women.

So it is on the faculties of our best law schools that a pitched battle is going on that will, to some degree, determine how many women (and minorities) assume positions of real power in this country in the next generation. If the conservative white men who run the schools can keep out the most effective feminists, then the Law, designed for and by the elite, will not be in jeopardy. And oppression of anybody outside the loop can continue nearly unimpeded. None of this is explicit, of course. But the undercurrent you hear at the elite law schools when you stop to listen is this: How can we keep feminists out of the real circle of power without making it look as though we are doing that?

FEMINIST LEGAL THEORY VS. "NEUTRAL" WHITE MALE LAW

The main excuse that faculties use to deny tenure is that the women's scholarship has been found lacking. Critical Legal Studies, the rubric under which feminist and race scholarship falls, challenge the old order, the very canon of the Law, holding that once it is stripped of its deceptive semantics it is little more than a calcified arrangement of power and oppression that favors the affluent white male over all others. "Fem-crits" argue that the law is encoded with prejudices of race, sex and sexual orientation, and only because the privileged white male has had the power to enforce his experiences and worldview over others is the canon revered as objective, rational, *nongendered,* when in fact it is as gendered as the lacy lingerie carried by Frederick's of Hollywood. But to most white men, or most men, period, it is much more difficult—shall we say impossible for some?—to see the gender fault lines in the Law. It is the way things are and ought to be.

By and large most men can grasp that critical race scholars have something to say: the Dred Scott decision hangs like a large shroud in our history over the image of justice. But with women it is not quite so easy; white men are too close to white women to feel that they have oppressed these women—their wom-en—to anywhere near the degree the African Americans have been oppressed. Certainly in terms of wholesale torture, they are right. But the misogyny has been rampant nonetheless, and the fem-crits who came along and told men they were deeply in the wrong, and their legal forefathers were even worse, vex these men as no other scholarship has. "They find it threatening because it really does challenge the underpinnings of established doctrine, and they are com-fortable with the established doctrine," says Professor Marina Angel of Temple University School of Law. "They say they are not used to scholarship that con-sists of narratives and stories [which characterizes much feminist scholarship], but why should that be when the casebooks are made up with the facts of cases, which are in effect little stories? You use little stories to teach moral lessons—that is exactly what the Bible has been doing for centuries—but many men haven't quite connected that some feminist scholarship does the same thing."

While conservative men can't keep feminist legal writings from being pub-lished—students largely make those decisions, remember—they can find other faults with it and pick at it until, well, anybody can see that the person who wrote that doesn't deserve . . . tenure!

"Usually you're told that it's your scholarship that fails—it's 'unsuccessful,' 'unpersuasive,' 'overly ambitious,' or 'makes no contribution,' " wrote Eleanor Swift after being denied tenure in the first go-round at Berkeley, words that sound depressingly close to what Finley heard. Swift took her case public and announced at a press conference that she had filed a gender discrimination griev-ance with the school, an act that shamed the school into granting tenure to another outstanding woman on the faculty, Marjorie Maguire Shultz, who had been given instead a contract that would have to be renewed periodically. Swift was granted a peer review by five distinguished academics outside of Berkeley who compared her personal file (and her scholarship) with that of the six men who had been given tenure in the preceding years. They unanimously agreed that she deserved tenure, and she got it. Clare Dalton, who won a $260,000 out-of-court settlement* from Harvard after she was denied tenure and sued, says that "the combination of being a woman and being outspoken in these issues, and using both feminism and critical legal theory in my writing worked against me." If these women were truly unworthy, we would not have heard of them again, but most of them are making a mark in the world: Finley has testified several times before congressional committees on tort law reform particularly in the area of women's health concerns; Dalton's work in contracts is considered groundbreaking; Shultz was called to Washington to work on the Clinton health care package; Swift became involved in public interest law; and no one denies that the work of MacKinnon is seminal.

"Nobody in this country has affected the legal relationship between men and women like Catharine MacKinnon," observes Professor Linda Hirshman. "When she is teaching at Harvard or Yale, I will know that the system has righted itself. That she isn't—that she has not been invited to after visiting at both Harvard and Yale—continues to be an indictment of the system." Could it be that the men of Harvard and Yale were envious of her acclaim, her influence, her star quality? Could it be that what she had to say made them uncomfortable and challenged the canon? The answer is undoubtedly *yes* to both questions.

A SIMMERING POT AT PENN

Another particularly egregious case of discrimination was the decision at the University of Pennsylvania Law School to deny tenure to Drucilla Cornell, one of the most important legal philosophers of our time. To an outsider it seemed that she was the ideal candidate for tenure. But since law schools don't hang out a shingle—"Feminist Philosophers Not Wanted"—she didn't know what she was up against when she joined the faculty in 1983. Incidentally, Penn is among the elite schools. It's worth noting here that the pecking order among law schools is taken insanely seriously by legal academics, and the way that each faculty controls its rank is through the quality of the people they invite to be tenured members on the faculty along with them. The status of one's law school is how otherwise undistinguished academics gain prestige, since compared with

---

* *The money was used to fund a law clinic for battered women at Northeastern University in Boston, where Dalton became a tenured professor.*

many of their brethren who actually practice law, they generally don't make as much money. And since law is not, strictly speaking, an intellectual discipline of the same order as other fields, no Ph.D. is required. The intellectual thinking in strict legal scholarship is often less rigorous than it is in more academic disciplines.

By 1988, the year of her tenure vote, Cornell was already recognized as a luminary in legal philosophy. She had published nine scholarly papers and reviews, had coedited a book on the politics of gender and written the introduction, and had six more papers accepted for publication. This was an amazing body of work for someone who had graduated from law school seven years earlier—and several times over what most people have when they are granted tenure. Often two or three published papers suffice, along with demonstrated teaching proficiency. Teaching was not a problem because students had elected her the recipient of Penn's Harvey Levin Memorial Award for Teaching Excellence that very year. Her subjects were labor law and employment discrimination, which she taught along with small sections in legal philosophy. The editor in chief of Penn's law review at the time, Marci Hamilton, said of Cornell: "She is one of the best professors. She is very sensitive to students' needs and interests. She is really loved by a lot of students. If the students voted, she would have gotten tenure many months ago."

Because of her growing reputation, Cornell had been invited to lecture both here and in Europe. Her status in philosophy would seem to be a welcome addition to any faculty, since all faculty members gain stature when they have a genuine star in their midst. At least that's the case if the star happens to be white and male. Although accomplishment after law school can diminish the need for earlier credentials, Cornell had those too: her law degree was from the University of California at Los Angeles, where she was on law review and inducted into the Order of the Coif, an honorary society for law students. Afterward she had clerked for a federal judge. Before law school she had been an organizer for the United Automobile Workers. In short, Cornell seemed easily to have everything that was normally needed to become tenured at Penn.

Tenure votes—even at renowned schools like Penn—can come after three or four years. Cornell was first considered in 1986, but the decision was to delay the vote for two years. Since many of her writings were in philosophical journals, she was told that she had to write something more strictly about the law. She did, and it was published in Penn's law review.

She was also told that she should spend more time socializing with her colleagues. But by this time Cornell's husband was teaching at a university in the New York area. She may not have been on campus full-time, but this was true of other professors as well, for at least one lived in New York, and several had professional commitments (presumably with prestigious law firms) that took them away from the school and Philadelphia. Cornell's prodigious productivity also meant that she didn't have a great deal of free time. "I spent a lot of time writing and teaching, and was young enough to think that was what I was hired to do," she says today, "but I flunked at recess. I didn't walk around the halls making men feel good about themselves." Incidentally, many a female denied tenure has been told that she simply didn't make enough friends of the male faculty. When Clare Dalton was denied tenure at Harvard, she was told that some professors were miffed that she didn't seek them out and chat them up.

Professor Gary Francione of Rutgers University Law School in Newark was a colleague of Cornell's on Penn's faculty at the time. As he tells the story, "People on the faculty started to pontificate about how she wasn't worthy of getting tenure. . . . She was a true feminist, and that made a lot of people uncomfortable." Her standing in the larger world also may have hurt her chances, he says: "She had a support group of people outside the school who were truly well known intellectuals, and the people at Penn took offense that she wasn't sucking around them and playing the little girl game. You see this all the time." But this should not have disqualified her because, he says, "she was an excellent colleague, an excellent teacher, and a scholar whose reputation was widespread." In other words, Cornell aroused the envy of some on the faculty.

After holding up the vote on Cornell, some members of the Internal Promotions Committee (IPC)—under the rules at Penn, two-thirds of whom must support an applicant if the individual is to get tenure—actively solicited letters from people who would be against her, a ploy that backfired. Professor William A. J. Watson, a highly respected scholar and a prolific writer as well (and hardly considered a radical), was asked to be on the IPC after Cornell had been passed over once. "I think the reason was because I had said that I did not understand her work and it was believed that I would be hostile," he says. "Although her work is not about the kind of philosophy that I know about, the people who recommended her were of the highest possible caliber. Jacques Derrida was only one of many who wrote letters for her. He is a philosopher, true, but most of her letters came from people who were lawyers." Watson was referring to the fact that one of the arguments against Cornell was that she was a legal philosopher, not, strictly speaking, a legal theorist. "Drucilla had the strongest academic file in terms of quantity," Watson says, "and the approval rating of highly respected scholars and the whole process . . . seemed biased."

Indeed. Generally, having a specialty outside the law such as economics, history, international affairs and even, yes, philosophy is considered a plus in legal education today. In most cases it should help, not hinder, one's career, especially when one is a recognized authority in that field, as Cornell is. But in her case it was held against her. As Francione says, "If I am teaching interdisciplinary stuff, it is a plus for my career. If she is teaching it, she is not doing law. You can have people doing very similar work, but if it is male, it is looked at one way, if it is female, it is looked at another way. I have no doubt that if I had written Drucilla Cornell's stuff, even though they might find it incomprehensible, they would have said, 'Well, we don't understand it, but everybody who does says it is wonderful. He's made a big splash, so let's give him tenure.' " As for discounting Derrida's enthusiastic recommendation of Cornell because he is not a lawyer, Francione says, "They are right, of course. He just happens to be one of the seminal thinkers of the twentieth century. On their criterion, Aristotle and Plato would have been denied tenure."

By then a nasty smear campaign was under way: rumors were circulating that (1) Cornell had had an affair with a male student; (2) she was also a lesbian; and (3) she and Watson or she and Francione were having an affair, or both. Cornell, Watson and Francione all were having intimate relationships at the time with other people. One would hope that law school faculty, who call upon Socrates for their teaching methods, would be above such tactics. But small minds, it seems, can be found anywhere, even at law schools. Francione finds the hypocrisy behind these rumors absurd.

"There was so much fucking of students going on by male members of the faculty that I thought this talk was ludicrous," says Francione. "Male faculty members routinely acted as if they thought that the student body was a source of dates for them. At the time, Penn had just finished with an incident where a man on the faculty had been screwing one of his students who had a serious eating disorder. The school had her involuntarily committed after she tried to commit suicide—the school did it, they were the movers, not her parents. It was clearly done to keep the incident quiet and protect one of the bright boys on the faculty. There was another faculty member who drank quite a bit and he would send obscene letters to students."

Francione says that when women's groups petitioned the dean (approximately fifty students signed the petition) to do something about the sexual harassment on campus, the dean's response to them was, "Don't make a big thing of it because it could hurt your job prospects. If law firms in New York and Philadelphia heard about this, it could affect your employment, because no law firms like to hear about people making sexual harassment claims." His official response was a letter saying that Penn did not tolerate sexual harassment. Penn, by the way, is known for the number of graduates it sends on to high-paying law firms; something like this could hurt the school's reputation as a trade school for corporate law firms. Francione says he tried to have people from the women's groups come to talk to the faculty about sexual harassment, but the dean vetoed even talking about the matter at a faculty meeting.

The story takes yet another turn. On the morning of the vote, Francione was called in by another faculty member who asked him if her writings could be used to support a totalitarian regime. "I said, 'Excuse me, this strikes me as being a little bit McCarthyistic.' What he was really asking was, Is she a Communist? It was such a sick situation, it is hard to exaggerate it." What is clear is that the cartel against Cornell was using every possible tactic to stack the vote against her. "Drucilla's case taught me that McCarthyism still exists for women academics," says Francione. "One of the most revered members of the Penn faculty is very left wing, but nobody has ever asked me if his work could have been used to support Stalin's regime. And when I said his work was good, no one ever asked me if I was having a homosexual relationship with him."

The day scheduled for the vote, which everyone knew would be close, came when two of Cornell's supporters on the IPC could not be there. Faculty presence is required so that if anyone is not familiar with the candidate's record, he or she will at least be present to hear the discussion before the vote. One had had a long-standing commitment to lecture in Germany, and he made his case for Cornell before he left in a strong memorandum, but his vote would not be counted, nor would the meeting be held when he could be present. Another man, who had served on the committee reviewing her tenure file and had written a positive report, had a wife who delivered her baby that day, and she was in diabetic shock. He was in the hospital rather than at the meeting. Although a few people urged that the vote be retaken when one of these men could be present, the motion was denied.

On March 15, 1988, Cornell was denied tenure by one vote.

Students drafted a petition, and approximately seven hundred students—on a campus of roughly nine hundred—signed. Posters went up around school.

Angry faculty members removed them. Students had buttons made up saying "Cornell, Tenure." The dean, Robert Mundheim, promised to pass on the petition to the provost and the entire law faculty, but according to the law school newspaper, the *Penn Law Forum,* he sent around only a "badly photo-copied reproduction of the cover sheet with a memo that did not indicate how many signatures had been attached."

Student Ann Bartow went on: "There are problems and tensions at every law school, and some of the tensions here at Penn are only tangentially related to Professor Cornell's tenure denial. However, it seems evident that this law school will have a problem attracting legal philosophers in the future should this action go uncorrected. In addition, legal educators who think highly of Profes-sor Cornell's work will now have doubts about the integrity of Penn Law."

Cornell left Penn at the end of the semester for Yeshiva University's Cardozo School of Law in New York City. Some discussion between her and Penn en-sued over the summer, and the possibility of another tenure review came up. But the group against her now came up with another stipulation: they would get yet another batch of letters regarding her worthiness. But this time they came up with a list of people they were sure would trash Cornell's work. Watson, a legal historian who held a named chair at Penn, resigned from the committee in disgust. The IPC asked a faculty member not on the committee to evaluate the list. In unequivocal terms he told both the IPC and Cornell that if he were she, he would reject the list. Cornell resigned.

Watson added that the next person who came up for tenure was a male and "his outside references were extremely lukewarm," yet he got tenure without any problem. Cornell sued the school for sex discrimination but settled in the spring of 1989 for $85,000. She did not sign the gag order the school wanted that would have prevented her from talking about her case. By then she had finished writing *Beyond Accommodation: Ethical Feminism, Deconstruction and the Law,* published by the prestigious academic house of Routledge.

In the spring of 1989 both William A. J. (Alan) Watson and Gary Francione left Penn in protest over denying Cornell tenure. Francione is a professor at Rutgers University Law School. Watson went to a chair at the University of Georgia Law School. Although some of the Penn faculty tried to influence fac-ulty members at Cardozo against Cornell and squelch her chances for tenure there, she became a full professor anyway and, more recently, accepted a joint appointment at Rutgers University, teaching in the law school as well as the

women's studies and political science departments. At Cardozo she was instrumental in turning the school for a while into a major center for legal philosophy
in this country.

What has she brought away from her extraordinary experience? That for
feminists to get ahead in legal education they have had to become coopted by
the very system they set out to attack and change. "Many of us have compro-
mised with the system entirely too much," she says. "To survive you have to
internalize a code that too easily puts you in a position of apologist for a discourse that devalues the feminine."

As is the case elsewhere, women coming after such bruising tenure battles
frequently have a less difficult time. Lani Guinier and Regina Austin, two respected African American legal scholars, have tenure at Penn. Today the academic faculty is more than 20 percent female. However, the school still lacks
a permanent specialist in feminist jurisprudence. The former dean, Robert
Mundheim, left the school to work for a major Wall Street investment firm.

THE GENDER GAP IN THE CLASSROOM

The pervasive attitude that denies women tenure also denies them simple respect in the classroom. Female teachers face a much rougher time in the classroom than do the males. Two-thirds of the students queried for the 1993 Ohio
survey of law schools believe the women teachers encounter hostility from
students, a belief shared by more than half of the female faculty questioned. "I
get the distinct impression that female law professors must prove themselves
capable to students, particularly to male students, whereas male law professors
are given a presumption of competence and must prove themselves *incapable* if
they are to lose that presumption," one faculty member wrote to the task force
doing the survey. Minority instructors face the same skepticism and hostility.

Lillian BeVier, a chaired professor at UVA, recalls what a male colleague said
after observing her teaching as part of the tenure process: "I was struck by his
observations about how strange the class *felt* to him. . . . 'Y'know,' he said, 'it's
really *different*. There's a sort of "prove-it" atmosphere—as though they're waiting in ambush to catch you in a mistake. It must make things uncomfortable for
you!' " From what the women say today, that attitude still prevails.

Says one Stanford student, "I was in a class with a woman professor, and at
midsemester we had a debate [in class] that she was going too fast and making
unreasonable demands. If the professor had been a man, no one would have had
the nerve to suggest that the professor change the syllabus." A student at the

University of Texas in Austin notes that the guys are likely to walk in late for classes taught by women. "The female professors are most likely to be talked back to, or be interrupted, or not have their classes taken seriously," she says. And at the University of Alabama Beth Godfree notes that although she thought the one female professor she had was an excellent teacher, "the guys didn't like her and thought she hated men," a complaint Godfree says was unfounded. The professor may have tried to even things out as far as the women were concerned, and for that she was labeled "man-hating." The woman left the school before Godfree graduated.

Women teachers at Harvard are not exempt from this kind of bullying. Elizabeth Warren says that when she was visiting there in 1992–93, a male student at the beginning of the semester told her that he wasn't going to stand for the Socratic method—*he was paying a lot for his education,* he said, and that's not how he wanted it taught. He wouldn't answer if she called on him unless he raised his hand. She told him that was too bad, but that was how she taught. After a few classes he stopped coming.

When Lucinda Finley at Yale discussed a case written by Justice M. Garibaldi of the New Jersey Supreme Court, she referred to Garibaldi as "she," knowing that the judge's first name was Marie. "You're carrying this 'he' and 'she' stuff too far," a male student complained. "You're turning it into a political rap." Would he have done the same if a man referred to Garibaldi as a female? Probably not. He would have been "informed."

NYU professor Sylvia Ann Law says that whenever she walks into a classroom she still has to establish her authority in a way that male professors don't. "You have to overcome the presumption that you are a mother or a waitperson," she says. "If you don't, the boys in the back of the room will take over the classroom."

"Why does my teaching get labeled political and biased when I discuss issues of particular concern to women, while my male colleagues are perceived as objective or neutral, particularly on gender issues, when they discuss issues of concern to men?" asks Professor Bender. "Why do I have to deal with overt resistance in my classes? Why does my conscious rejection of strict Socratic method get interpreted as a failing, lack of rigor, lack of control or as being 'touchy-feely,' but my male colleagues' alternative methodologies are humane, courageous and challenging? Why is it when male professors supplement their casebooks with articles and cases, they are enriching students' educations, but when I do it, I am trying to indoctrinate students or wasting precious class time by artificially bringing issues of race and gender into the classroom when they are not relevant to substantive law?"

Yet women students are eager to learn from other women. "I've only had one female professor so far," says Karen Rothfleisch in her third year at Georgetown University's Law Center. "It was great to walk into a class and see someone like me teaching." The effect may be in more than feeling. At schools where women excel, observes Professor Hirshman, there is usually a high percentage of women faculty. She compared the female/male breakdown of students to the representation on law review, which is as good an indicator of success in law school as any. By this accounting five of the top seven schools with the best representation of women on law review—Duke, Stanford, New York University, University of Minnesota and Cornell—had more than 20 percent tenure or tenure-track female professors in 1994. These schools, along with the University of Iowa and Columbia, had a greater percentage of female students on law review than the percentage of women in the student body eligible for law review, second- and third-year students.

This is not so surprising, because women faculty are more likely to mentor women students, and women students are more likely to perceive women teachers as approachable, a critical factor in students' perception of their own worth and their role within the institution. One woman at the University of Chicago says that when she needed a faculty recommendation for a clerkship, she didn't even know whom to ask because she did not know any of her professors well. "I went to the one I had the best grade from," she says, "but I don't think he even knew who I was, and I don't know if he ever wrote the letter."

Yes, women need role models, and they need mentors, and they need support for a woman's point of view. As long as the power structure retains its male biases and remains under male control, they aren't going to get it. That's why it is so important that women break through the glass ceiling in legal education. Until they do, women law students are likely to continue to do poorly relative to men. Let us not forget that law school success or failure plays an inordinate part in determining the whole of an individual's career: membership on law reviews, judicial clerkships, jobs with big-name law firms—even law professorships—all are at least partially handed out based on first-year grades. And remember, first year, with its huge classrooms and Socratic style that is the norm almost everywhere, is particularly brutalizing to women. There are always exceptions, women who make law review and even become their editors, the Ginsburgs and O'Connors and Renos, but for the majority of women, the oppressive atmosphere, the outrageous bias, the persistent disrespect shown to the few female professors, continue to take their toll.

"Despite identical entry-level credentials . . . women are *three times less likely* than men to be in the top 10 percent of their law school class," write Guinier and Fine of their examination of the academic performance of nearly one thousand students at Penn. Their data shows that within one year white men rise to the top, white women scatter downward and students of color sink to the bottom of the class, a stratification that continues through the next two years. Although they accounted for Law School Admission Test (LSAT) scores, undergraduate grades and class rank, they found that where women and minorities fell in the grading curve could be predicted by race and gender. Although anonymously graded examinations determine a student's grade to a large degree, when the professor sits down and fills in the grades, that ineffable extra that may indeed pull a C to a B or a B to an A or an A to an A plus is class participation. If the teacher hardly knows who you are, you don't get that extra boost. And if he doesn't call on women much, or if you are intimidated from voicing your perspective by fear of being branded a "feminazi," or if what you have to say is dismissed again and again, you're unlikely to raise your hand. In such a manner does the male-dominated climate of most law school classrooms conspire to prevent women from achieving their best.

It's not because they are dumber, because they don't have what it takes. It's because legal education remains one of the premier male-dominated institutions in the country, just short of the military, and if the majority of the men running the law schools have anything to say about it, it is going to stay that way. The classroom atmosphere is unrelievedly hostile to women, to anyone who doesn't buy into its macho approach to life. The faculties of many schools remain determined to keep women out of positions of power and authority and to scoff at feminist approaches to the law. As a result, women experience law school as alien to their interests and hateful to themselves. It is an ordeal to be gotten through. "What law school does for you is this: It tells you that to become a lawyer means to forget your feelings, forget your community, and most of all, if you are a woman, forget your experience," says Catharine MacKinnon. "Become a maze-bright rat. Women lawyers . . . go dead in the eyes like ghetto children, unlike the men, who come out of law school glowing in the dark."

The elite schools are the worst. Bathed in the glow of their long-standing prominence, their unquestioned authority, they are antagonistic to change of any kind. And to a large degree they control the legal system in this country. They send men and women to the most prestigious law firms and the federal bench and the Supreme Court. We will end this section with a look at Harvard, the "best," the worst.

HARVARD

Beirut
on the Charles

That peculiar pride [Harvard has in itself] represents an incredible, if tacit, stake in the status quo, and also amounts to a quiet message to students that their place in the legal world should always be among the mighty. It produces the kind of advocate who is uncommitted to ultimate personal values and who will represent anyone—ITT, Hitler, Attila the Hun—as long as the case seems important.—SCOTT TUROW

HARVARD IS THE TOP, the cream of the crop, the ne plus ultra of law schools. And as Harvard Law School goes, so goes the rest of them. If America's law schools are generally macho, sexist places, Harvard is all the more so. The reasons for this are not so hard to understand. Many students arrive with a certain inbred smugness. A goodly number will have Ivy League degrees and have been at the top of their college classes—in a way they've already made it. They were chosen because the world has already decided, thanks to their industry and ability, that they are special, the proof of which is that they are at Harvard at all. The professors generally radiate the same smug superiority—they are teaching at *Harvard,* are they not? A fair percentage of Harvard's faculty could be characterized as full-blown egos on parade. They are, well, from *Harvard.* They advise presidents, appear on PBS and Court TV and *Nightline,* argue before the Supreme Court. All this high-flying traffic prompts a certain distance, a cool formality, in their dealings with students. Not surprisingly, a student membership on law review does make it easier to make friends with the professors.

The day I chanced to sit in on classes, Harvard's exalted position was the subject being taught. A professor whose name is a household word to, say, readers of *The New York Times* told his first-year students how much more money than their opponents they would get for working on the same case because their degrees would be *"from Harvard,"* not some "state school." Pity the poor slobs who only manage to go to some "state school," he seemed to be saying. The class listened in rapt silence. The coughing and fidgeting and whispering stilled; this was crucial information—he was talking about their futures, their lucky status, their wallets, and he was talking as if none of them would even consider something like public interest law, say, or anything else that did not put to full economic use the status a Harvard Law degree confers. It was a lesson in snobbism and elitism. Only a fool, he was informing them indirectly, would be opposed to such a system as they had access to.

After all, they are spending three years and roughly $100,000 in quest of a Harvard degree. So everyone at Harvard is heavily invested, literally, in buying into the theory of the law school's preeminence. They want to believe that what its degree confers is a "ticket" to life's finer things, including admission to the corridors of power in America. "It is an education in itself, learning to worship HLS," writes Scott Turow in *One L*. "It must be special, you tell yourself; why else in God's name, am I going through this? . . . Of course all the HLS chauvinism would be silly, as well as offensive, were it not for the fact that over time people at Harvard Law School have made believers of so many others."

In this hothouse of acknowledged achievers, all aspire to emerge as one of the Knights of the Round Table; the Holy Grail is law review and graduating at or near the top of the class. To protect themselves from despair, the collective sentiment becomes a we-are-all-in-this-together attitude, and this fraternal feeling generates both a mock derision and a bewildered respect for the students who do emerge as the stars in classroom discussion. "You hear that you are hired on your first-year grades, and by Christmas you get so concerned that you either get to the brink of a nervous breakdown or you have to decide that you don't care at all," said a second-semester student. They all want to make law review, but only a few will; they want to be on the right end of the grade curve, but only a few can be; they want the respect and friendship of their professors who will write the letters that get them the Supreme Court clerkships or the invitations to join the most prestigious firms, but only a few are chosen.

The competition, then, is intense, and white males who tolerated competition from women and minorities in undergraduate school—because anyone can get a B.A.—now resent these interlopers, for *this* competition will determine their pecking order in the world beyond school. Although minorities at Harvard say they sense a real "prove it" attitude (*prove that you aren't here because of affirmative action*), the male students save their deepest rage and animus for white women—people from the same middle- and upper-class backgrounds, but *women*. How embarrassing to be beaten by a *woman*. If minorities and *women* can get Harvard Law degrees, the value of theirs will diminish. In short, if other schools are competitive and macho, Harvard is even more so.

Thus the gender wars at Harvard (and Yale) are among the worst anywhere. At Harvard they are exacerbated, even encouraged, by the deep division on faculty. Here it is not just gender—that would be too simple, too stupid—but a whole approach to the law that is at issue.

THE SPLIT DATES from the seventies, when the radical idealism spawned in the sixties took root in various American institutions. Harvard gave a home to a group of young, brilliant and charismatic radicals of the time—Duncan Kennedy, Roberto Unger, Morton Horwitz—during this period of flirtation with educational experimentation and the burgeoning deconstructionist theory that attacked social institutions. The basic idea behind Critical Legal Studies, or CLS, as their school became known, is that social and legal codes constitute a "mystification" designed to give the privileged control and influence over the rest of society. In other words, law is designed to insure that the privileged retain their privilege. Harvard initially welcomed these young Turks for the intellectual energy and sizzle they brought to a campus that was notoriously dweeby. It was legal education's brand of radical chic.

In time it would be clear that if the objective of the young Turks was to do battle with our legal institutions along Marxist lines, then they would ultimately have to do battle with the very institution—Harvard—that both housed them and gave them credibility. So Critical Legal Studies turned to internal reform, and the Harvard adherents, now tenured, settled in and began to redo the school: On student selection committees they pushed for students who were known activists; on hiring committees they fought to appoint their disciples.

In the mid-eighties the traditionalists balked and launched a counterattack. Harvard's—and America's—dalliance with radical makeovers of its major in-stitutions was over. The eighties were about making money, not tearing down the institutions that provided it. And the international Marxist ideology that formed much of the foundation of CLS was dying. Soon Harvard Law was "paralyzed by spasms of intellectual violence," as one journalist put it. Both sides dug in their heels when it came to teaching appointments, each wanting to enhance its own ranks and block the other's candidates.

By this time CLS had spawned the "fem-crits" as well as scholars of critical race theory. While the fem-crits moniker has more or less evaporated, feminist legal studies has not, and it flourishes in the law reviews. With the new emphasis on gender and race scholarship, regardless of what it was called, would come a new objective, one that could seemingly be implemented: diversity. And now it wasn't just the strict CLS adherents who argued for it; the diverse population of students did too. The policies that had opened the doors of Harvard to both women and minority students led to a general disgruntlement among them that their kind was so little represented on the faculty.

They had plenty to be disgruntled about. Harvard and Yale, as well as the University of Chicago and Penn, to name a few, were dragging their feet in granting women and minorities positions on the faculty, and while the proportion of women students climbed to 40 percent by the end of the eighties, these institutions kept the percentage of female faculty members in the single digits. The traditionalists at Harvard and elsewhere never said they were against hiring women and/or women of color. What they were against, although they would never admit it publicly, was hiring women and minorities *who didn't think like them.* The trouble was, they couldn't find enough qualified women who did, since the most interesting women around were strong feminists, or feminist/critical race theorists. What to do?

For one, take no more legal renegades onto the faculty—even white males. In 1987 Derek Bok, then Harvard University president, exercised his veto power over the law school faculty's thirty-to-eight recommendation to grant tenure to one of the leaders of the CLS movement, David Trubek, a visiting scholar from the University of Wisconsin. Trubek called Harvard Law "the Beirut of legal education," a moniker that has stuck to this day. Fem-crit Clare Dalton was denied tenure for the second time the next year.

Leading the fight against both of them had been Professor Robert C. Clark, corporate law professor, the Establishment spokesperson, champion of traditionalism, a former seminarian who was an outspoken foe of CLS. He became known on campus for saying that the liberal-leaning Supreme Court was bent on a ritual slaying of the elders. His words were balm to the traditionalists, and Derek Bok was listening. He appointed Clark dean of the law school in 1989, specifically, it was thought, to break the back of the radical/liberal faction there. Clark's appointment would also insure that the fund-raising campaign at Harvard Law about to get under way wouldn't be stymied by a dean "soft" on legal renegades, as the former dean, who had backed both Trubek and Dalton, was thought to be. Not surprisingly, most donors are not individuals who want to tear down the canon and reform the system from which they have so hand-somely benefited.

With Clark at the helm, the swing to the Left would be halted and Harvard Law would continue to be the training ground for corporate law that corporate law—with its deep pockets for its beloved icon—wanted it to be. The fund-raising effort was stepped up, and gifts to the school grew by 64 percent in a year, from $11 million to $17 million. How much of this can be credited to Clark's appointment is unknown, but no one doubts his ability to attract large donations.

But the fight over Dalton's tenure had been rancorous, and it left the school ruptured. Some teachers were so disheartened by her denial that they an-nounced in class they had lost their zeal for Harvard Law. With the rift on the faculty public, students hardly needed further encouragement to align them-selves with either the Left or the Right. Dalton's denial was one issue. The other was: *Is there not one nonwhite woman qualified to teach at Harvard?* In 1990 Derrick Bell, Harvard's first tenured black law professor, had transferred to New York University in disgust after the faculty's refusal to offer tenure to either of two minority women who had completed visiting appointments. At the time, Clark had invoked Harvard's "year away" policy, saying that the school did not hire visiting professors until they returned to their own schools. Clark maintained that Harvard had its standards to uphold. "I think it's clear the law school faculty should make appointments based on the merits of each case, not because of protests," he stated in a *New York Times* interview. "We do have high standards, and we aren't going to compromise them."

CHIPPING AWAY AT HARVARD: MARY JOE FRUG

Two people who had been at the center of the fight for Harvard Law's soul were the Frugs, Mary Joe and Gerald. Both were CLS adherents. He was tenured at Harvard; she taught at nearby New England School of Law, a blue-collar al-ternative to Harvard that had once been an all-women law school. From there Mary Joe had been chipping away at Harvard. Her analysis of how a contracts casebook subjugates women, discussed earlier, was aimed at a book widely used at Harvard. At least two of the three authors had taught briefly at Harvard. But since Frug was from a lesser school, the crowned heads at Harvard felt they could brush her off. Her critique depended on a subjective reading of the text and was vehemently derided by the opposition in the strongest possible words.

They called it "trash." Her critics ignored the fact that it is impossible to analyze
the sexism (or racism) in a text by number crunching. How do you calculate
psychological damage? How do you do a cost analysis of a put-down? Her paper
was picked up by feminists, including the students, and drove yet a deeper
wedge into the faculty division. To many women at the school and, indeed, to
a generation of feminist legal scholars, Frug became a heroine for her provocative analysis of how the law—as she put it—fucks women. She showed them
that vague feeling they had that something was wrong indeed had a basis in
reality.

And then she was murdered.

Frug was murdered on a warm spring evening when she left her home to buy
some cookies. She was in her late forties at the time. She was knifed to death
in her left breast, with cuts deep into the chest cavity, one slicing her heart and
her inner thighs, fueling the conviction among some—including Boston detec-
tives—that her killing was not a random act of violence but a sexual assault.
There are no real suspects even today. A young white man seen running a block
away at the time a crowd was gathering around her has never been identified.
Frug was dead on arrival at a nearby hospital.

Gerald Frug submitted to the *Harvard Law Review* a draft of an article that
Mary Joe had been working on at the time of her death. He said they had to
publish it as it was or not at all. He would not allow it to be edited. The editors'
reaction was swift: an all-out war over the publication of "A Postmodern Feminist Legal Manifesto (An Unfinished Draft)." In it Frug argued that "legal rules
permit and sometimes mandate the *terrorization* of the female body," because
our culture inadequately protects women against physical abuse. Other rules
permit the "maternalization" of the female body, by rewarding women for
singularly assuming childcare responsibilities after birth, and penalizing conduct, such as sexuality or work outside the home, that conflicts with mothering.
Legal rules also permit "and sometimes mandate the *sexualization* of the female
body," she wrote, through provisions that criminalize individual sexual conduct,
such as prostitution, while at the same time other rules legitimize pornography
and the advertising and entertainment industries that "eroticize the female
body." The essay wanders between the views of Madonna and Catharine
MacKinnon without settling anywhere, but it does confront the basic issue head-
on: that the law "constructs" feminine identity along strict lines that are designed to serve men's aims.

Obviously Frug was controversial. In one section of the article Frug used words normally not found in legal scholarship: "We are raped at work or en route to work because of our sex, because we are cunts," and "women get 'fucked' in the workplace, too, where we do 'women's work' for 'women's wages'. . ." Whether or not she would have left the words in the final version is unknown. The conservatives on the staff argued that it wasn't good scholarship, and besides, it was unfinished, only a draft in need of editing; the other side contended that even fragmentary, Frug's work-in-progress should be published as is. She had been a prominent feminist thinker and besides, her murder in Cambridge made her a symbolic martyr for feminists. When the vote was taken, those on the side of publishing the article, as it was, won. The losers did not bury the hatchet. They would wait, and they would get even.

At the same time Frug's article came out, in March of 1992, Harvard's hiring committee offered four white men tenured positions. Three of the four "pale males," as they came to be known, were visiting at Harvard at the time; now Dean Clark said that the so-called year away policy had been changed. The four men consisted of liberals and conservatives, two apiece, and were a compromise between the two camps; that they were all white males did not deter either the faculty or the dean. It did bother the students. At the time, women made up less than 8 percent of the full-time faculty—*five out of sixty-four*, well below the national average, which was then somewhere between 15 and 20 percent. Students demonstrated and demanded an explanation. A "town meeting" with Dean Clark failed to defuse their anger. Clark called in armed police officers to guard his office.

A few weeks later the law review's annual parody edition, the *Revue* (pronounced "review-ee") included a cruel, sordid satire of Frug's manifesto, supposedly dictated from the grave. A sample of the wit: "Men f∗∗k wom∗n every day," it states. "The male reader may think: 'Mary Doe, you're talking about it as if it's a bad thing.' But I don't mean f∗∗k in the carnal sense. This is f∗∗king scholarship." The parody mocks Frug as a sex-starved child at Coney Island, ogling men in tight Speedos. She was identified as "Mary Doe, Rigor-Mortis Professor of Law." The attack was savage.

The *Revue,* which is always a spoof of the law review, was circulated at the law review's annual banquet, open to former editors, contributing authors from other schools, and all Harvard faculty and their families. Had Gerald Frug chosen to attend, he would have found it set out on his plate when he sat down. The date of the dinner? April 4, 1992.

Exactly one year to the day after his wife was murdered.

The parody lit a match to an already politicized campus. "The parody treats women in general and feminist scholars in particular with a lot of contempt, hatred and bitterness," said graduating student Andrea Brenneke. "The parody is symptomatic of the hostility toward women who are taking over positions of power traditionally held by white males. This was their fraternitylike response to getting back at women who fought to publish Mary Joe's article. Some of the professors have treated it as a sophomoric joke, but the implicit message is that violence against women is just the concoction of paranoid feminists."

A few days later nine students staged a sit-in at Dean Clark's office, protesting the lack of faculty diversity. Dean Clark called for a formal hearing, much like a trial. Expulsion was a possible outcome for the "Griswold 9," named for the building where Clark has his office.

Further fanning the imbroglio was the Harvard Law School Coalition for Civil Rights, which reminded the students what Clark had said previously, in response to an earlier protest over hiring: "This is a university, not a lunch counter in the Deep South."

In quick succession the authors of the satire, Craig Coben and Kenneth Fenyo, two who had passionately protested publishing Frug's piece, issued an apology. Mea culpas also came from other editors, including two women—insensitivity is not sex-specific—responsible for the *Revue*. A reaction from Dean Clark didn't appear for nine days. His hesitation bespoke an implicit "tsk-tsk" tone—*boys will be boys*. His tone? He "deeply regret[ted]" the incident. The article was "disrespectful to the memory of Mary Joe Frug." But he said he could do nothing about the *Revue* because "prior restraint" of freedom of speech was not appropriate in the university context. Convenient that Coben and Fenyo had much the same conservative politics as the dean; and how unlike his swift and punitive maneuver against students whose politics he disavowed.

Women students and a good portion of the faculty did not countenance Clark's tepid response. Nine campus organizations called for his resignation. They cited his selective prosecution of the students who staged the sit-ins to protest the lack of faculty diversity.

The faculty joined the fray in a war of words. Professor Laurence H. Tribe, a leading constitutional scholar, compared the parody to the work of Holocaust revisionists, because the article's message was that "the hatred of women is a hoax perpetrated by feminists," an implication similarly false. "What is the point of teaching?" he asked. "I'm sharpening their knives to stab innocent victims."

Interoffice mail zinged over the next couple of weeks. Memos to suit every political stripe went out. One memo called Harvard Law a "white male preserve." A few faculty members saw the *Revue* incident only as a tasteless mistake. Alan Dershowitz called the parody, while offensive, merely "sophomoric" and "in somewhat poor taste" in a syndicated newspaper column. In case anybody missed it, he circulated the column to the faculty. He charged that the atmosphere at Harvard was akin to a "McCarthyite witch-hunt" and stated that "the overreaction to the spoof is a reflection of the power of women and blacks to define the content of what is politically correct and incorrect on college and law school campuses. . . ." Dershowitz added that there was something wrong at Harvard Law, "but it was not sexism or racism." In his mind the only problem was there was just too damn much political correctness at Harvard and that the First Amendment was being trampled on.

Professor Elizabeth Bartholet replied that such a trivialization of the parody was intent on ignoring how women were treated at the law review, where she maintained the atmosphere was so poisoned, it was possibly actionable under sexual harassment statutes as a "hostile work environment." She told *The New York Times* that the incident, and the official reaction of the dean, "shows something very scary about male anger toward women in this institution." In the *Boston Globe* she was quoted talking about "the level of arrogance and elitism that has developed at the law school."

What happened to *Revue* wits Coben and Fenyo? Harvard took no official disciplinary action; and they went on to prestigious clerkships for two federal judges. Coben went to the U.S. Court of Appeals in Washington, for failed Supreme Court nominee Judge Douglas H. Ginsburg, and Fenyo went to the court of appeals in San Diego for Chief Judge J. Clifford Wallace. Elsewhere the old boys' club reached out to protect another of the male law review editors involved in the parody. When he went to work for a Washington, D.C., firm, a memo went out to the other attorneys that the topic wasn't even to be brought up.

And the beat goes on. Two women who discovered that a man was masturbating three feet away from them while they were studying in a public space at the law school found that the harassment really began when the incident became known. The man, a worker at the school, was eventually prosecuted, but the issue was far from over. The women were made the butt of an article in an April Fools' Day edition of the law school newspaper. "Then came the jokes from fellow students, men were coming up to me and saying, 'Oh, Cindy, has anyone masturbated in front of you recently?'" one of them says. "Or, 'Cindy, how big was his dick?' One man came up to me and said, 'I don't know you very well, but you seem like a sexual person. I heard you were the victim, I hope this incident hasn't affected you sexually. If you ever need to talk about your sexuality, please feel free to call me.' And then he handed me a quarter. It seems to me that Harvard is promoting an atmosphere where stuff like this can happen all the time. This is a very hostile environment for women." Months afterward, she still could not talk about the male students' reaction without becoming distraught and tearful.

This aggressively uncivil treatment of women, replete with sex-related put-downs, is the modus operandi of a seemingly large percentage of the male student population at Harvard. Is it the type of male student who goes into law? Is it the type of male who goes to Harvard Law? Is it the do-or-die competitiveness of Harvard, the attitude that one kills the competition any which way? Is it a backlash reaction now that women, and not just other men, are the competition? All of the above.

Consider what happened to Rebecca Eisenberg. She was known as a strong, outspoken feminist at the law school; as a second-year student on law review, she had fought for the publication of Frug's article and worked on commentary accompanying it. She had not been part of the group of self-selected editors who put out the *Revue* and had vociferously decried its content. That year Eisenberg was also job hunting for a clerkship after graduation and was at a loss to understand why she was having such a hard time finding one. Her credentials were solid. "When I returned from my third trip interviewing judges [at her own expense], a friend of mine let me in on a secret—certain conservative third-year editors were calling the clerks of the judges who interviewed me, 'exposing me as a radical feminist,'" Eisenberg says. "So I announced one day in the editors' lounge that I had given up my search, secretly sent out a final round of applications, flew out west for the fourth time to interview, and came back with an offer."

When a dozen women were asked what they thought of Harvard Law, not one was sanguine. Harvard would look good on their résumés, they said, and they undoubtedly picked up some life lessons from the school of hard knocks where white men dominate, but their comments were succinctly put by one woman who graduated with honors: "I think it's horrible.

"Everywhere you are reminded that this isn't your place, the pictures in the classrooms are of all these dead white men in robes staring down at you," she went on. "There is one room where all the women are, but it's a sad commentary on our place in the law. You realize right away that the opinions represented in the law don't represent your own experiences, and your point of view is that of someone who is ignored by the law. That became clear to me on day one." She was so disheartened by her experience at Harvard Law that she chose not to attend graduation.

At the ceremony that year, by the way, Peter Cicchino, a third-year student who defended the Griswold 9—and called for Dean Clark's resignation in the student newspaper—was selected to give a speech as part of the graduation ceremonies. Despite his earlier comments about "prior restraint," Dean Clark responded by calling high-ranking university officials to express his outrage. Cicchino spoke anyway.

HARVARD LAW, for all its luster, is a cheerless, divisive place for women, to be gotten through and over. Of course, many male students would share the same opinion of Harvard Law, with its heavy workload and rhetorical overkill, but women bear the added burden of being the "other"—in the law, in the classroom—even as they constitute approximately 40 percent of the student body.

Of course, not all professors are sexists. Some let women's voices (and feminist interpretations of the law) be heard in the classroom, and the women are keen on them. And some of the women teachers are known to favor women students—to even things out, one professor has said.

The year following the *Revue* affair Harvard Law was again in turmoil. And once again gender was front and center. Despite the charges of misogyny at the law review, a woman managed to be elected president of the journal shortly before Frug's article appeared, albeit not one who took a stand on women's issues. It was the third time in history a woman had headed Harvard's 106-year-old law review. But Emily Schulman's year was marred by charges from other editors that she was both sexist and racist. She had questioned whether two black women ought to be editing a piece by a black law professor and was said to have discouraged a woman running for managing editor under her. Although Clark's dealing with the *Revue* incident amounted to no more than damage control, this time he acted with a big foot. He hired an attorney to launch a full-scale investigation, and he eventually produced a 109-plus-page report that accused Schulman of "judgmental errors" but nothing else.

Many women students felt that the commotion over Schulman was a belated response to the *Revue* incident—and that an outside investigator wouldn't have been called if Schulman were a man. "It was like the Rosalind Shay character on *L.A. Law*—I never saw Rosalind Shay do anything a man wouldn't do," said one student, "but she was treated as if she were a barracuda." In the end, Schulman was not officially reprimanded, and the editors voted to allow her to keep her job. While Schulman was in the hot seat, she did head law review the year the editors conducted an internal study to see if law review's selection process discriminated against any group of students. They concluded that the process had adversely affected every group except white males.

WHILE A FEW MORE WOMEN have been appointed to Harvard's faculty since the Frug affair, the school still lacks for an African American woman or any woman of color. An antiwoman, especially antifeminist, stance continues to permeate the place. Outspoken feminist law professors elicit stares of wonder from their feminist colleagues when they say they are going to teach there for a year. Are they ready for the place? "Could it be worse than where I am now?" was the response of a woman from another elite school. Harvard, the school that belatedly let women in—not until 1950—welcomes them in theory but shuts them out in practice.

Not surprisingly, working-class women (and men) who come to Harvard as students have a hard time fitting in unless they adopt the style, dress and mannerisms of their peers from the Ivy League schools. One working-class woman told author Robert Granfield how uncomfortable she felt when the professor assumed that all the students had fathers who worked in business as executives and were familiar with family investments. "I remember thinking, Doesn't he think there are any people in the law school who come from a working-class background?" African American students are also especially hazed by their peers. Until proven otherwise, black students say they are presumed to be inferior and there because of affirmative action: "When a black woman speaks in class, it's like 'Oh, my God, she's intelligent,'" one said. The same holds true for attractive blondes, a California blonde told me. "I wanted to scream, 'Look, I am an intelligent person, I have interesting things to say,'" she says.

SOME WOMEN do get through Harvard relatively unscathed. These are the women who do not enter with altruism on their minds, but who go to law school for the same reasons as men, for prestige and money. "[T]hose who entered with primarily careerist goals described an aggressive but fair learning experience," Granfield writes in *Making Elite Lawyers,* his study of how Harvard Law causes students to become more conservative and offers them the path of least resistance into high-paying corporate law. Career-oriented women "generally saw the social justice–oriented women as creating their own problems by refusing to play by the rules," he observes. "Playing by the rules" means not questioning the status quo, both in the classroom and in the law, and remaining silent on feminist and racial issues. "A number of women here have older brothers, fathers, and grandfathers who were allowed into this institution when women were not, when black people were not," says Kim Robinson, an African American student. "Many of these women feel that the system will work for them, they will fit in, if they just work hard. And it just becomes easier not to question anything. You plow straight through, and you don't have to do the kind of soul-searching that some of the others do."

DESPITE HARVARD'S REPUTATION for supplying corporate America with its legal eagles, which it does, the school also turns out a surprising number of students whose desire to do public interest work is not shaken by the Harvard experience. The school has an Office of Public Interest Advising, apparently the only one of its kind in the country. While the numbers go up and down with the times, in recent years approximately 12 percent of the graduating classes go into public interest law or government, either directly or after a year clerking for a judge. This is double the national average. Although statistics by sex were not kept in 1994, one of the staffers, Kathleen Reich, says that women who go into public interest work make up significantly more of that number than their representation in the student body would warrant. It is worth noting that women in significantly greater numbers than men enter law school because of a desire to restructure society or to be of service to the underprivileged. A third of the men enter for such altruistic reasons, while more than a half of the women say they attributed "great" importance to this as a reason for attending law school. The fall-off to corporate law is significant, but the fact remains that Harvard is turning out a high percentage of lawyers who retain their early idealism. The numbers have gone up significantly since the 1980s, perhaps reflecting renewed interest in public issues such as the environment and a reenergized women's movement. It may also reflect the fact that the CLS/liberal faction at Harvard remains strong, and strong faculty members attract disciples.

HARVARD LAW has been relatively quiet in the last few years, but the gender wars continue. When one woman's name come up for a position on a student-faculty committee charged with drafting a sexual harassment policy, some male students tried to block her nomination because she was "a stark raving feminist," according to Catherine Caprusso, a member of the Law School Council who attended the meeting at which the woman's nomination was discussed. "The Monster Truck Coalition—they were a group of guys on Law School Council whose mock aim was to hold a monster truck rally at the law school—said that she couldn't be objective because she was a feminist and would impose her ideological agenda on men and the law school and First Amendment freedoms would no doubt be stifled," she said. "All this seemed to come from comments she had made during the discussion of rape in her criminal law section. What they were saying was, she couldn't serve on the sexual harassment committee because she was a feminist." In the end, she did serve on the committee. It was not until the fall of 1995 that Harvard had a sexual harassment policy. It is twenty pages long. How effective it is is anyone's guess.

While drafting a sexual harassment policy took many months and many meetings, an executive order from Dean Clark's office was the quick response to the objections of some white male students that some organizations on campus excluded them, namely, the Women's Law Association (WLA) and the Black Students Law Association. The organizations were summarily told they had to open their membership to everyone, which of course would defeat their purpose. Attendance at a seminar the WLA held to help women make law review was between a third and a half male, again defeating its purpose. The process of selecting law review editors, as noted earlier, discriminates against all groups except white males. At this point the Women's Law Association is deciding whether to cut its official ties with the law school.

"The irony is that when a few white men complained, the law school reacted immediately without any dialogue with students or discussion in the law school community," notes student Shannon Lis, a member of the WLA board, "whereas others, namely, women and students of color, get locked into endless dialogue. It shows how hypocritical the administration is."

Harvard has given a few more women positions since 1992. In the 1995–96 school year, out of a total of sixty-nine tenured or tenure-track teachers at the school, eleven (or 14 percent) are female. None are African American. Dean Clark (and Alan Dershowitz) actively lobbied against granting tenure to Catharine MacKinnon in 1993. Mary-Louise Ramsdale, a student leader and one of the Griswold 9, said: "They have always said they want the top person in any field, and anyone knows that there is no one better than Catharine MacKinnon in feminist jurisprudence."

Harvard does make a nod toward it; Elizabeth Schneider, professor at Brooklyn Law School, teaches it every other semester at Harvard. If you are writing a paper on feminist jurisprudence, you will only have her in residence as an adviser for one semester, not the two that major papers require.

The school continues to do extremely well financially, however. The fund drive that Dean Clark jump-started with his appointment netted $175 million.

2

Women at the Bar

THE HISTORY OF
WOMEN LAWYERS

The Door
Is Slammed Shut . . .
or Nearly So . . .

Mistress Lockwood, you are a woman.—CHIEF JUDGE CHARLES DRAKE OF THE UNITED STATES COURT OF APPEALS, IN DENYING BELVA A. LOCKWOOD'S PETITION TO ARGUE A CASE BEFORE THE COURT IN 1876.

WE ALL KNOW that in earlier times bright women who wanted to live lives out of the ordinary faced incredible obstacles, but it is hard to imagine just how formidable they were. Women could not even vote. They were disqualified from serving on juries. If married, they could not own property under their own name, meaning they could not even inherit property—it was the husband who would hold legal title. They could not enter into contracts that would hold up in court. If they divorced, they automatically lost custody of their children. "By marriage, husband and wife are one person in law: that is, the very being of the legal existence of the woman is suspended during the marriage," is how old English common law was written down by Blackstone in the 1760s. Susan B. Anthony would amend this to "Husband and wife are one, and that one is the husband." Marriage both secured a woman's place in society and secured a yoke of servitude around her neck.

Given these handicaps, given the inflexible role into which society crushed women, given their status as less than equal citizens, it is no wonder that the history of women _in the law_ is a tale of gears (and undoubtedly tears) grinding exceedingly slow. Women were kept out of law schools until they proved it was absurd to bar them, and then they were kept out of courtrooms with the same vigor. The toll on women's lives was great. Here is a disheartened Sarah Grimké writing in the 1850s:

"Had I received the education I craved and been bred to the profession of the law, I might have been a useful member of society, and instead of myself and my property being taken care of, I might have been a protector of the help-less. . . ."

Two decades later in Rochester, New York, suffragette Anthony would be arrested for voting, tried under a trumped-up charge, and not even allowed to testify in court in her own behalf. Despite all the roadblocks, a few amazing women managed to distinguish themselves in the world. Margaret Brent was one.

Brent had several things going for her. Brent arrived on these shores in 1638 with letters from England, written by her cousin, Lord Baltimore, that gave the right to buy land on favorable terms. Baltimore's brother, and thus her cousin, Calvert, was the governor of St. Mary's Parish. Brent, well-born and educated, soon became a large landowner in the territory that would be known as Maryland, and her skills at negotiation, deal making and litigation made her indispensable to Calvert.

And he sorely needed help. He was visiting back in England during a period of unrest when civil war broke out in St. Mary's. Virginia colonists were in charge of the territory when he returned. Calvert amassed an army, promising to pay his troops with corn and tobacco from both his and Lord Baltimore's land. Calvert's troops were successful, and he was reinstated as governor. Soon after, however, he became mortally ill. On his deathbed he directed Brent to "take all and pay all" but named Thomas Green his successor, undoubtedly because Brent was only a woman. Brent immediately declared herself Calvert's executor, and ten days later the Maryland Assembly ratified that claim, giving her the authority to clean up the legal mess Calvert—and civil war—had left behind. Many said that Brent should have been appointed governor.

Settling the estate turned out to be a major job, as it had been left in disarray. Numerous claims were made against Calvert's holdings, and there were numerous debts to collect as well, a process complicated by the fact that legal documents were destroyed wholesale during the civil strife. Court papers show that Brent tried 124 cases in eight years. She frequently asked for a jury trial, as was her prerogative, even though that meant she incurred court costs of fifteen pounds of tobacco a day per juror. She obviously believed in the fair-mindedness of the working-class colonists, in contrast with the large landowners who formed the nucleus of the Maryland judiciary, such as it was.

But despite Brent's name and influence, she was turned down flat when she asked the Maryland Assembly for a "voyce and a vote." She was summarily dismissed—she was a *woman*. Brent then announced that unless she could vote in their proceedings, she would protest all the acts of the Maryland Assembly. Brent's spirited and solitary stand for women's rights is the first on record in the colonies.

Although rebuffed by the good and true men of the Maryland Assembly, Brent continued as Calvert's executor. A crisis was looming, because the soldiers had not been paid and were threatening mutiny. Governor Green was unable to quell the impending riot, and Brent took charge. First she ordered that her own cattle be slaughtered to feed the men immediately. Then she set about paying them their due. As suspected, Calvert's estate came up short. Brent announced that she would pay them, as promised, out of Lord Baltimore's estate. Back in England, Lord Baltimore was not amused.

By letter from England, Baltimore demanded that the Maryland Assembly rebuke Brent. Now with their own peace and safety at stake, the gentlemen stood behind Brent. They wrote back a strong letter stating that for the safety of the colony, his estate was better "in her hands than in any man's else, in the whole province" and that she had, by her skillful dealing, pacified a mutinous bunch of soldiers, and furthermore, Lord Baltimore owed her his thanks for the colony's public safety and not the bitter invectives he had railed against her. This is the woman that couldn't be allowed a voice or a vote, remember?

Brent had had enough by this time. Bitter over the assembly's refusal to give her a vote, as well as Baltimore's slanders, she left the territory and spent the rest of her life outside of public life, living quietly in Virginia. Margaret Brent— smart and able—is prescient of all those women who are good lawyers but not "partner material." Not "qualified," that is, to vote on how the firm is run or to share in the profits. Or maybe they do make partner but are still denied the "voyce and a vote" that makes a difference.

But history has brought her justice and recognition: every year the American Bar Association's Commission on Women in the Profession gives the Margaret Brent Women Lawyers of Achievement Award at the annual convention of the American Bar Association. Previous winners include Justice Ruth Bader Ginsburg, Anita F. Hill, Professor Lani Guinier, Attorney General Janet Reno and Professor Barbara Jordan, among others. Governor Green is a footnote in history, noted only for his incompetent governing.

But Brent stands alone, an aberration in American history. Men of the times (and much, much later times) saw her as the exception to the rule, blind as they were to the scores of women whose abilities in public life matched, or exceeded, their own. It is a defect that still afflicts some men.

IF GOD HAD WANTED WOMEN TO BE ATTORNEYS . . .

Although some women argued their own cases in colonial courts,* more than two centuries would pass after Brent before the first women attorneys put up their shingle and began practicing law. The very first female lawyers did not appear until the 1860s, and these hardy souls had to endure much derision from a male elite that did not want to share political power with women. Lawyers held office, passed judgments, controlled political power, made *law* for the rest of the population, just as they largely still do today. And these men knew that women weren't fit for such labor—exceptions such as Cleopatra, Queen Elizabeth, Catherine the Great, Catherine de Medici, Margaret Brent and Luce Prince notwithstanding.

The men who kept women from the bar were only representative of their times. Today their reasons for keeping women out of the loop of the law sound comic.

There was precedent: ". . . female attorneys-at-law were unknown in England, and a proposition that a woman should enter the courts of Westminster Hall in that capacity, or as a barrister, would have created hardly less astonishment than one that she should ascend the bench of Bishops, or be elected to a seat in the House of Commons. . . ." There was "the woman on the pedestal" rationalization: "Whether . . . to engage in the hot strifes of the bar, in the presence of the public, and with momentous verdicts the prizes of the struggle, would not tend to destroy the deference and delicacy with which it is the pride of our ruder sex to treat her is a matter certainly worthy of her consideration." There was the "We can't believe you are even asking" argument: "When the Legislature gave to this court the power of granting licenses to practice law, it was with not the slightest expectation that this privilege would be extended equally to men and women. . . ." There was the "How will women change the system?" dilemma: "But the important question is, what effect the presence of

---

* *The first woman to address a justice of the Supreme Court was a black woman, Luce Terry Bijah Prince, who successfully defended her husband's claim to a land grant in Vermont in 1795. At the time, the custom was for Supreme Court justices to travel outside the nation's capital to sit with federal judges in each circuit. Justice Samuel Chase sat in the circuit court when Luce Prince's case came up. Although represented by two white Vermont lawyers, she also addressed the court at some length, and Chase stated that Prince "made a better argument than he had heard from any lawyer at the Vermont bar."*

women as barristers in our courts would have upon the administration of justice. . . ." And there was always the God excuse to fall back upon: "That God designed the sexes to occupy the different spheres of action, and that it belonged to men to make, apply and execute the law, [is] regarded as an almost axiomatic truth. . . ." The Illinois Supreme Court rendered up all these justifications in 1870 to deny Myra Bradwell's admission to that state's bar.

Myra Bradwell had worked in her husband's law office before the Civil War. She founded and edited the *Chicago Legal News,* the most important legal newspaper of the West and Midwest. It covered the legal news of the day, of course, but also ran fervent editorials arguing for the rights of women. Suffrage was one; so was getting women (including herself) admitted to the bar. Before the Illinois Supreme Court called upon the Deity to refuse Bradwell that right, the court had rejected her because she was . . . *married.* The court didn't actually say that but instead referred to "the disability imposed by your condition." Bradwell responded that marriage, to which the judges certainly had been alluding, was "neither a crime nor a disqualification." But there was some logic to the judgment, for remember, in those times a woman had no legal existence apart from her husband. He was her head and her representative in public life. Woman was much too delicate to withstand the rigors of public commerce or to be so involved in the squalor of public life that she might actually sully herself by voting. Boston society ladies organized against the women's vote much the same way Phyllis Schlafly lobbied against the Equal Rights Amendment.

However condescending the pronouncements from the bench were, Bradwell was determined. She took her case to the U.S. Supreme Court, which didn't want to have to decide the issue. They hung on to the case for nearly two years before turning Bradwell down. The opinion stated that while there were privileges that the states could *not* restrict, "the right to admission to practice in the courts of a State is not one of them." In a concurring opinion, Justice Joseph P. Bradley went even further: "Man is, or should be, woman's protector and defender. The natural and proper timidity and delicacy which belongs to the female sex evidently unfits it for many of the occupations of civil life. The constitution of the family organization, which is founded on the divine ordinance, as well as in the nature of things, indicates the domestic sphere as that which properly belongs to the domain and functions of womanhood. The harmony, not to say identity, of interests and views which belong, or should belong, to the family institution is repugnant to the idea of a woman adopting a distinct and independent career from that of her husband. . . . The paramount destiny and mission of women are to fulfil the noble and benign offices of wife and mother. This is the law of the Creator." The Religious Right couldn't have said it better.

But by the time the Court announced its decision, the Illinois State Legislature had made it illegal to bar any person from any occupation, except the military, on the basis of sex. Bradwell and two other prospective female attorneys had lobbied hard for the new law and won. The Supreme Court decision of 1873 then had no effect in Illinois, but it was still able to stall the influx of women into law, since now women would have to fight the battle state by state.

Judges in Wisconsin and Iowa faced it around the same time and came to diametrically opposed decisions. In Iowa a brilliant young woman, Belle Babb Mansfield, applied to the bar in 1869, after being valedictorian of her class at Iowa Wesleyan College and reading the law in her brother's law office. She was allowed to take the bar examination, even though the Iowa code limited membership to "any white male person" who demonstrates that "he possesses the requisite learning." Nonetheless the attorneys who read her examination were so impressed with her responses that they urged the court admit her, "not only because she is the first lady who has applied for this . . . but because in her examination she has given the very best rebuke to the imputation that ladies cannot qualify for the practice of law."

The judge was sympathetic. Calling upon another Iowa statute, which held that "words importing the masculine gender only may be extended to females," Justice Francis Springer agreed that Mansfield should be allowed to practice law. His written opinion went further, noting that even when a provision made specific mention of a sex, as the Iowa one did, it could not be construed as an implied denial of females. On that note, Belle Babb Mansfield, a twenty-three-year-old woman from Mt. Pleasant, officially became the first woman recognized as a lawyer by a state bar association in the United States. Iowa seems to have been a particularly agreeable place for women, because there are earlier reports of women practicing law locally there, and the University of Iowa, as noted earlier, was one of the first schools to admit women to its law department.

Wisconsin was another matter. Lavinia Goodell, who had a successful practice in Janesville, applied to the state supreme court when one of her cases was appealed. But since only members of the state bar were allowed to address the supreme court, and since only men were granted membership in the bar, she was effectively prevented from appearing before Wisconsin's highest court.

Goodell, using the reasoning of the Iowa decision, argued that the admission statute of the state bar did not specifically limit its membership to men, but only referred to "he" and "him," and that these words obviously were meant to refer to women as well as men. Furthermore, Goodell stated, the University of Wisconsin—a state-supported institution, she pointed out—was already admitting women to study law. The lawyer who argued her case let the court know that Goodell had prepared all the briefs. All to no avail.

Chief Justice C. J. Ryan was not impressed. His language, disguised as high praise, rivals that of *Bradwell* v. *Illinois:* "The peculiar qualities of womanhood, its gentle graces, its quick sensibility, its tender susceptibility, its purity, its delicacy, its emotional impulses, its subordination of hard reason to sympathetic feeling, are surely not qualifications for forensic strife. Nature has tempered women as little for the judicial conflicts of the court-room as for the physical conflicts of the battle-field. . . . [Our profession] has essentially and habitually to do with all that is selfish and extortionate, knavish and criminal, coarse and brutal, repulsive and obscene in human life. It would be revolting to all female sense of innocence and sanctity of their sex, shocking to a man's reverence for womanhood and faith in woman, on which hinge all the better affectations and humanities of life, that woman should be permitted to mix professionally in all the nastiness of the world which finds its way into courts of justice. . . ." The date was 1875.

But Ryan's sentiments were not universal. The *Wisconsin State Journal* replied swiftly: "If her purity is in danger, it would be better to reconstruct the court and bar than to exclude women." His antiquated view of women had the opposite of its intended effect—women who had been silent on the matter now lobbied publicly for women's admission to the bar. The following year the Wisconsin State Legislature revised its statute, and Goodell was admitted to the state bar. Not surprisingly, Ryan dissented. There's always one.

The same pattern repeated itself for the next forty years: some states allowed women to practice law, albeit after a battle; others resisted. Not until 1920, when the Nineteenth Amendment, which granted women the right to vote, was passed in Congress did Delaware and Rhode Island finally admit women to the bar—nearly three centuries after Margaret Brent proved that women were, in fact, sometimes more effective in public life than men.

Women's right to practice law in the federal courts was more easily won. After being rebuffed in the U.S. Court of Claims, Belva Lockwood, Esq., the woman who had petitioned President Ulysses S. Grant to issue her law degree from the National University Law School in 1873, steered a law through Congress six years later that opened the federal courts to women. The issue became clouded, however, by an 1894 Supreme Court decision that upheld Virginia's interpretation of its legal code, to wit: While any "person" who was admitted to other state bars, or to that of Washington, D.C., would be admitted in Virginia, "person" meant "male." The Supreme Court, maybe not so surprisingly, agreed. By the way, Belva Lockwood is the one who brought this case to the Supreme Court. The end result was that although she could argue in the Supreme Court—and she did so successfully, winning a $5 million claim against the United States government for the Cherokee nation—she was still denied the right to practice in Virginia. This decision was not legally overturned until 1971, although women had been admitted to state bars, including Virginia, prior to that. Ruth Bader Ginsburg made the winning argument before the Supreme Court.*

THE DOUBLE BIND OF RACE AND GENDER:
BLACK WOMEN ATTORNEYS

If white women had a hard time being able to practice law, their struggles pall in the face of how African American women fared. Although Charlotte E. Ray may have amazed the president of Howard University with her acumen, and been the first woman lawyer in the district, as well as the first black woman lawyer in the United States, she suffered the prejudices of the times. Although several reports attest to her superior intelligence, she could not find enough clients. Ultimately she returned to teaching.

The situation changed little over the next several decades. While the number of women attorneys rose steadily, if slowly, the number of black women attorneys rose ever more slowly. By 1910 census data lists 556 white female attorneys and only 2 black female attorneys, although 10 were listed a decade earlier. Thirty years later the number of white female attorneys would rise to 4,146, yet black female attorneys were still in the double digits, at 39.

Nonetheless, a few of them succeeded. In the 1930s, for instance, Eunice Hunton Carter was ultimately responsible for possibly the biggest organized crime prosecution in the country up to that time. Carter was originally hired by the New York County district attorney to handle low-level criminal cases, and

---

* Ginsburg argued in the landmark case of Reed v. Reed that a man could not automatically be preferred over a woman as an executor of an estate. The Supreme Court ruled that the Equal Protection Clause of the Fourteenth Amendment forbade such a preference.

her job included prosecuting prostitutes. Few of these resulted in convictions, but Carter, who actually listened to the women, noticed that they told almost identical stories—about how they were poor farm girls who had been visiting a friend when they were picked up—and that they were usually represented by the same law firm, and that often hovering in the background was a disbarred lawyer with connections to the Mob. Carter surmised correctly that the prostitutes were part of an organized ring and told her boss, but he paid no attention. Carter then took her suspicions to a new special prosecutor, Thomas E. Dewey, who hired her. Carter's hunch was confirmed: for 50 percent of the take, racketeers provided "protection" and lawyers when the prostitutes were picked up. A major raid of the city's whorehouses in 1936 turned out to be disappointing for the small number actually arrested, but Carter convinced three of the women to cooperate and was able to compile enough evidence of a prostitution ring to go to trial. Thus to the surprise of nearly everyone but Carter and Dewey, "Lucky" Luciano was convicted. Dewey got the job of the man who had ridiculed Carter's suspicions, that of New York County D.A., and from there he launched his successful bid for governor of New York. While Dewey was D.A., Carter was appointed chief of the Special Sessions Bureau, and she supervised more than fourteen thousand cases each year. Not bad for someone who entered Fordham Law School as a "housewife and . . . the mother of a young son." Around the same time that Carter was polishing off Luciano, Mayor Fiorello La Guardia appointed Jane Mathilda Bolin, with a law degree from Yale, to the city's domestic relations court. Appointed in 1939, she was America's first African American woman judge.

But while a few black women were succeeding, they were not able to break into the ranks of the American Bar Association, which kept out blacks until 1943. In 1899 white women formed their own association, the National Association of Women Lawyers, but admitted no black women. White women were admitted to the ABA in 1918. A few years later, in 1925, African American lawyers had formed their own organization, the National Bar Association; a woman, Gertrude Elozora Durden Rush, Iowa's first black woman lawyer, was a co-founder. While the NBA remains a networking organization for African American lawyers, the ABA remains the organizational center of power and influence in legal and political circles. In recent decades prominent black attorneys have helped to bring in other black attorneys, but at ABA annual conventions the faces, male and female, are overwhelmingly white.

THE BATHROOM DILEMMA

The early women pioneers in the law, white or black, encountered discrimination just about everywhere—no matter their grade-point average, no matter who they knew. Even with stellar family connections, women simply couldn't get hired. Nanette Dembitz, who graduated in 1938 from Columbia near the top of her class and was an editor of the law review, was a niece of Supreme Court Justice Louis D. (for Dembitz) Brandeis. But although she had plenty of interviews, she had no job offers. At last a partner at one firm asked if she could type, saying that perhaps he could find a spot for her as a secretary. She never made it to a prestigious firm but made a name for herself instead as a civil liberties lawyer for the ACLU before becoming a much respected family court judge in New York.

Just how poor were the prospects for an African American woman during that time? Very. Constance Baker Motley was in her final year at Columbia in 1945 when she heard that a small midtown firm was looking to hire a recent graduate. "The women in my class had high hopes but few offers," she recalls. "When I appeared for my interview, a balding, middle-aged white male appeared at a door leading to the reception room where I was standing. The receptionist had not even asked me to have a seat. Even after the door to the reception room quickly closed, she still did not invite me to sit down. She knew as well as I that the interview was over." In retrospect it was just as well she was not hired by the firm, for Thurgood Marshall would soon hire her for the NAACP Legal Defense and Education Fund. Alongside Marshall, Motley would go on to become one of the great civil rights lawyers of the century, arguing ten cases before the Supreme Court. She would eventually become a chief judge of the federal district court in New York.

When Cecelia Goetz, who delivered the opening argument for the prosecution at the Nuremberg trials, asked to be among the lawyers prosecuting war criminals in Nuremberg, she needed special authorization. Why? Because, she was told, it was impossible to find accommodations for women lawyers in Germany. That the army had no trouble finding lodgings for the female secretaries who were going didn't seem to register with the authorities. However, she prevailed. Later, when Goetz was job hunting in the early fifties, she was told that when her résumé was in front of the general counsel of a major firm looking to beef up its in-house lawyers with people with government experience, the man said, "Bring him in. What are you waiting for? This is exactly the type of person for whom we're looking." When her sponsor told him that "he" was a "she" the response was: "What are you wasting my time for? You might just as well recommend a Negro."

In 1952 Sandra Day O'Connor, with the credential of *Stanford Law Review* on her résumé, received only one offer from all the major California firms to which she applied; the job was that of legal secretary. O'Connor, of course, in 1981 became the first woman to sit on our Supreme Court.

Cynthia Fuchs Epstein reported in *Women in Law* that a Wall Street firm told one of her interviewees that "they would love to hire me, but they couldn't because what bathroom would I use? Really, they said, you couldn't use the secretaries' bathroom, and you couldn't use the lawyers' bathroom, and they couldn't build another one, so what bathroom would you use?"

Bathrooms or not, the women did not give up. In 1960 the Census Bureau reported a total of 7,140 female lawyers; a decade later there was nearly that many women *law students*. Soon the trickle of women going into law turned into a river. The established bar hardly knew what to do with them. Law in those days was generally looked upon as a genteel profession, particularly in the larger law firms found in every city with more than a dozen traffic lights. In many cases, one—as in man—became a lawyer because one's dad did it, because one had the "right" family connections to build a successful practice just by servicing one's own crowd. These were the "white shoe" firms, called that, I suppose, because of the white bucks partners sported in the summer, perhaps on the way to the golf course with their clients. Social class and religion were as crucial to getting hired as grade-point average—perhaps even more crucial—or being on law review or winning the moot court competition. By and large, corporate law firms were white, male and largely Protestant. There were separate law firms for Jews and, to some degree, Catholics. People who went to lesser schools or who came from working-class backgrounds went to less prestigious law firms and worked for less prestigious and wealthy clients. But however these men might be discriminated against, they all had more points in their favor than did blacks and women. In getting hired, they were at the absolute bottom of the pecking order.

When Ruth Bader Ginsburg's dean at Harvard Law in 1960 suggested to Justice Felix Frankfurter that he hire her to be one of his law clerks since she was one of his star students, Frankfurter replied that he just wasn't ready to hire a woman.

Roxanne Barton Conlin, former president of the Association of Trial Lawyers of America, recalls how her law school would not even set up interviews for her in 1966 because she was pregnant and previously had not sent her to some interviews because she was female. Around the same time, the first woman to run for vice president for a major party, Geraldine Ferraro, who graduated with honors from Fordham Law School, went through four interviews with Dewey Ballantine, only to be told on the fifth go-round that "we're not hiring any women this year."

BUT TIME MOVES ON and progress comes in spite of obstacles. The women's movement was a major factor in the changes that would sweep this country in the seventies and eighties. The numbers and percentages of women in law school increased dramatically. The job market would open up—wide in some places, just a crack in others. The ERA would fail, but the Civil Rights Act of 1964 would bar discrimination on the basis of sex. Theoretically there were no more barriers for women entering the legal profession.

But theory is not actuality. Although women were hired, the next barrier white males stood behind was that of partnership, where the golden egg of prestige and money was safely sheltered from intruders. And because they were "partnerships" of good men, honest and true, some thought that they were above the law. They couldn't be forced to take a partner they didn't want, now could they, even if they had solved the bathroom dilemma?

Elizabeth Hishon changed all that. She took on the venerable Atlanta firm of King & Spalding after she was "passed over" for partnership, as being rejected is euphemistically known, and was asked to leave. The year was 1979, and Hishon sued under Title VII of the Civil Rights Act, which applied to firms with more than fifteen employees. The next year Federal District Judge Newell Edenfield threw out the suit, saying that "to coerce a mismatched or unwanted partnership too closely resembles . . . the enforcement of shotgun weddings." He agreed with the partners' contention that their right to reject anybody for partnership was protected by the constitutional right of free association. The Supreme Court was not similarly awed by King & Spalding's argument. Chief Justice Warren Burger, writing for a unanimous court, held that if the opportunity to become a partner is a "benefit" of employment, it is covered by Title VII, and "partnership consideration must be without regard to sex." Burger thus laid the way open for Hishon to bring her case to trial. Five years had passed by the time the Supreme Court ruling came down, and by then Hishon was a partner at another firm.

King & Spalding may have been encouraged to settle by the unfavorable story that appeared in *The Wall Street Journal* six months earlier. In it, writer James B. Stewart reported on the summer picnic at which a group of King & Spalding lawyers decided it would be fun to stage a wet T-shirt contest for the female summer associates. Slightly cooler heads prevailed, and the event was turned into a bathing suit competition; the winner was a Harvard student; the prize was the offer of a permanent job. Lawyers told writer Stewart the event was an example of the "rollicking good times that characterize the firm's social events and contribute to an unusually high esprit de corps among the firm's lawyers." But female associates said they were humiliated and felt they couldn't complain because they were vying for permanent positions at the firm. Other women lawyers who had worked at King & Spalding cited other examples of comments demeaning to women, and the all-around impression that the *WSJ* article reported was that the place was rife with chauvinism. The "wet T-shirt" incident (that didn't actually occur) became the talk of Atlanta's legal and social circles for months afterward, as the partners of King & Spalding operate in Atlanta's rarefied circles that included, at the time, the exclusive white-male-only eating and golf clubs in the area.

Today Hishon, who still practices in Atlanta, will say only that she is glad that she sued and that it was important to open that door to women. "The large firms hadn't faced the issue of sex discrimination at the partner level," she says. "This opened their eyes." After Hishon came other charges of discrimination at other firms around the country, but these were settled quietly out of court until the nineties.

Yet, as in every other profession, the women kept coming. Percentages of female law school graduates have evened off in the mid-40 percentile in the last few years but show no signs of being turned back. But what happens to these women? The percentage of women in private practice hasn't kept pace with the numbers who have graduated from law school. Why? Are they having the careers they dreamed of? Or are they leaving in disgust and despair? Are women changing the profession? Or is the profession changing them? What is their impact on the courts? These are the questions of the nineties.

GETTING STARTED

Many Are Called . . .

I had seen six different lawyers during the day, and the interviews had gone well. A senior partner was the last, and he basically told me that I would get an offer. That night I had dinner with two male associates who joked around a lot. One joke was about a woman who uses a vibrator—I felt they were checking me out to see if I would laugh. I just felt weird. After that, it got uncomfortable. I didn't get an offer. Later I heard from someone at the firm that these guys are well liked and the older guys see them as the model of what they would like to be.—**YOUNG LAWYER** RECALLING AN INTERVIEW IN SAN FRANCISCO

"I HAD A YOUNG GIRL, she filed an application for employment with me. I looked, and she was a law clerk with a federal judge, she was magna cum laude, law review, and all these things. She came in and had an interview. It was a perfect interview. I had everything. All her little files were in the right place, she asked the right questions. Thank you very much. She was very impressive. A young man comes in, I look at his file, it has nothing—not anything stellar or outstanding. He had graduated from law school. That's about all he had. And I sat, and I concentrated on which one to offer the job to for three days . . . so I hired the girl. And then it dawned on me. I should have hired her. It shouldn't have even taken me two minutes. I just had an internal visceral reaction that a lawyer—a man lawyer—is going to be better than a female lawyer."

The biases women face when they go out job hunting with a fresh sheepskin from law school are much more subtle than they were a few decades ago. Women are not likely to be told that women are not hired as lawyers or that the firm "had their woman." Lawyers are not likely to be fired when they are pregnant. Although the dark ages are over, female lawyers still confront a different universe from male lawyers. The man who told the above on himself is not some old boy at one of the nation's corporate law firms where sexism is as palpable as the flower arrangement on the receptionist's desk. He is an assistant state attorney in charge of hiring for Florida. He works in that sector—govern-

148

ment—where one might reasonably expect women to be treated more fairly than they are in law firms. But still the obviously superior candidate for the job *almost* didn't get hired. Because she was female.

For the brand-new lawyer, several options exist: She can go into private practice, whether solo in some small town or for an international firm of several hundred lawyers; she can go into government work of some sort, at the federal, state or local level in one of a thousand different agencies, or become a prosecuting or state's attorney; she can go to work as a lawyer in the legal department of a corporation; she can go into public interest law, either as a legal aid lawyer or for an organization that helps, say, battered women or immigrants; or she can go into academia. Fresh law graduates also have yet another option, to clerk for a year or two for judges, where they research and frequently write drafts of the judge's opinions. Clerking is basically considered another year of training, valuable to all and necessary for future academics.

So how do the sexes break down in their choice of employment? According to the National Association of Law Placement (NALP), the clearinghouse for such data in Washington, D.C., the class of 1993, six months after graduation, was situated this way:

	MEN	WOMEN
Private Practice:	60.6%	53.2%
Government	12.1	13.7
Clerkships	11.4	15.8
Business	10.5	9.3
Public Interest	1.4	3.3
Academic	.7	1.3
Unknown	3.2	3.4

The disparities between men and women at first glance appear to be slight. Women are somewhat less likely to end up in private practice than men are. Earlier data show that when the overall figures for men entering private practice rise, as they did in 1988 (62.5 percent), they also rise for women (57.4). One might assume that although there is a gap, there is every reason to believe that women are closing in on men—at least at the entry level. Other NALP figures also reveal only small differences. Six months after graduation women are more likely to be unemployed (18.1 percent) than men are (15.5), and more women (5.2 percent) than men (4.2) are likely to be working part-time.

But let us look at these figures more closely. NALP was able to gather data

on more than thirty-seven thousand individuals, 93 percent of the graduating
class of 1993 of ABA-approved schools. In a population that large, the 7.4
percent differential between men and women going into private practice—
where the real nucleus of the law profession is—becomes more telling. And
when you go back a decade earlier, to 1983, you discover that not only has there
been no movement forward, there actually has been a slight *backward* slide, since
the differential between men and women going into private practice was 6.5
percent that year. Even when you compare figures only for white males and
females—the two groups most likely to enter private practice—the disparity
between the two groups is greater in 1993 than it was in 1983 by a few percentage points. The gap is certainly not closing.

The statistics become even more telling when we break them down by color
as well as sex. Then much greater disparities appear, revealing most probably
where the greatest prejudices still lie. For instance, nearly 62 percent of white
men in 1993 went into private practice upon graduation, while only 45 percent
of minority* females did. The combination of being both an attorney of color
and a woman is a double negative. The interview at the University of Chicago that
Linda Golden Chatman had with an attorney working for the world's largest law
firm, Baker & McKenzie, in the late 1980s may not be typical, but it indicates
the level of abuse black women must endure. Golden looks as though she might
be a model and is a stylish dresser as well; and at thirty-two she was a few years
older than most law students. She is African American as well. Since her name
then was Golden, the partner conducting the interview, Harry O'Kane, began
by asking whether she had a Jewish connection. He remarked on how fashion-
ably she was dressed. He asked how she got into the University of Chicago, then
went on to share his belief that the university "loves to admit 'foreigners' to the
exclusion of 'qualified' Americans." He asked for her high school, college and
law school grades. But that was just the warm-up. "I had put down 'golf' on my
résumé as a pastime, and he wanted to know where I could have learned to play
golf," she says. "He asked whether 'we' had our own country clubs—like the
Jews—and then went on to say that he wouldn't want to belong to one [a Jewish
one], but then he added, 'They have their own.' In the end, he concluded that
the reason blacks don't have country clubs is that there aren't many golf courses
in the ghetto."

O'Kane wasn't done yet. While discussing the practice of law, he asked,

* *Throughout the book, "minority," "multicultural," and "people of color" refer to individuals who
identify their heritage as African, Hispanic, Asian/Pacific Islanders, and Native American.*

"What would you say if somebody called you a 'black bitch' in court?" Chatman mumbled something about how she wouldn't respond because the person was obviously ignorant, and anyway, how could you respond in a professional setting to such a sexist and racist slur?

How to respond to O'Kane's comments became clearer over the next few days. Chatman says that at the interview itself she was too stunned to object. But she soon learned that another black woman had been subjected to O'Kane's inquisition a few years earlier—he'd refused to shake her hand and asked her what kind of contraceptive she intended to use. Hearing that, Chatman went public with what happened to her. She wrote to Baker & McKenzie and copied the dean of the law school, as well as a few student organizations. Baker & McKenzie swiftly apologized with hand-delivered letters, the firm was barred from on-campus recruiting at the University of Chicago the following year, 1989–90, and O'Kane retired. Chatman believes that race is the initial barrier to be gotten through any time a black woman attorney is introduced. "The first thing people see is your race," she says. "Then they see you are a woman. Then they try to find out how comfortable they are with you—this has to do with appearance, your attitude, what law school you went to. And once you get through all that, being female plays a larger role than being black."

THE 7 PERCENT DIFFERENCE

But setting aside the obvious biases of corporate America, let's look at the overall 7 percent differential between men and women going into private practice. It could be that some women self-select themselves out of the running for a job in private practice. They may know that most big law firms invite many freshly minted graduates into their ranks, but few will be chosen to be partner, and even fewer will be women. "The major concern for women considering private practice is what the climate of the firm is for women," says Roberta Kaskel, assistant dean for career services at the University of Maryland Law School. "They know that the decision they make at graduation about a job may affect any decision they might make five or ten years from now about having a family. The male students only want help comparing firms on the nature of the work and the salary potential."

It is possible that women are not choosing private practice as often as men because more of them are interested in some notion of social justice, a goal unlikely to be realized in a law firm. But several studies attempting to determine whether this is true have come up with contradictory findings. The most recent evidence is that men and women currently in the profession rank service to others equally as a motive for their choice of a career. A corollary to this is the finding that just as many women as men entered law school for career reasons, such as money, job security and advancement, an attitude that this shift reflects women's evolving mind-sets, as well as society's changing expectations of them. The idea that preferred careers for women were some form of social work (nursing, teaching, dispensing justice for the downtrodden) appears to have been replaced with an awareness that more women can and must be their own breadwinners and that some women are just as interested in high-status and high-paying jobs as men.

Yet there still appears to be a difference—a difference that becomes more obvious over time: women appear to have a harder time selling themselves—Hire me! Hire my law firm!—and feel uncomfortable doing it. A frequently heard explanation from women about their choice to go to government or public interest rather than private practice was that not only were they interested in making some sort of contribution to the common good, but also that they realized that they were unlikely to be rainmakers and thus didn't have a chance to rise to the top. If one takes a job in government of some type, one need not advertise for clients or brag about your abilities: clients come to you.

Furthermore, the tenor of the times has something to do with the kind of women who become lawyers. A Minnesota recruiter noted that the type of woman he saw in the seventies—"almost a suffragette, very activist sort of person"—had been replaced with a "more mainstream type of candidate." Kathleen Brady, director of career planning at Fordham Law, says that the job choices made by the students she advises appear to be based not on gender or race, but strictly on grade-point average: students with the highest grades—male and female, white or minority—want to get into the big firms where the money and the prestige is the greatest. "What I hear is students saying, 'I've got a 3.4 GPA, where do I have a good shot?' " she says. But as we have seen, for whatever reason, men as a group are likely to have higher GPAs in law school, and it thus follows that men as a group will have more job offers from law firms.

If that is the case, the obvious conclusion is that private practice is selecting women at a lower rate than they are men. A 1990 survey by the Indiana State Bar Association, which found no significant differences between the motivations of women and those of men in choosing law as a profession, or their reasons for choosing their current employment, notes that we should "question more closely why women are more highly represented in certain types of law practice. . . ." Law firms are not under the kinds of pressures large corporations are to have a diversified workforce. The Equal Employment Opportunity Commission almost never questions their numbers.

The only law firm in the country that underwent a "glass ceiling audit" by the Department of Labor was the New York firm of White & Case, with 550 lawyers, which was targeted because of a contract with a federal agency. White & Case was spared a "finding of discrimination" but was slapped with fourteen "major" violations, mainly for failing to adhere to a written affirmative action plan that would determine if women and minorities were leaving disproportionately before making partner. That's one problem.

Another is that although clients may suggest that they want their legal teams to be diversified, as are their own staffs, this often turns out to be no more than a perfunctory request. Firms sometimes bring a minority to initial client meetings to put their diversified foot forward, but the token individual may be there for show only and not given substantive work on the account.

A second notable difference in the NALP figures is the higher incidence of women who choose to clerk for a judge after graduation. Nearly a third more women than men choose this route, and even more minority women do so. In fact, this is the one category in which minority women are represented in higher numbers than the national average. A clerkship, which typically lasts only a year, accomplishes three things: it adds another premium to a résumé, since the position is high prestige and high visibility and women more than men may still feel the need to add more credentials; it puts off for another year the decision about the kind of law to practice for the long haul.

What is interesting about the higher percentage of women, and women of color, who clerk after graduation is that these positions are highly competitive and the pool of women judges is small, 12 percent on the federal bench, 9 percent on the state court bench. So women graduates cannot count upon any sort of gender allegiance in helping them win these jobs in any number. In spite of this, women, black and white, do extremely well in securing clerkships. Since 1983 minority women outpaced the national average of students taking clerkships in all years but three. But we don't know if men who might have been highly competitive for these jobs chose not to pursue clerkships because higher-paying jobs at firms were awaiting them and not the women, particularly not minority women. One African American woman who was second in her class at the University of Tennessee Law School, for instance, reported in 1993 that she was unable to find a job in east Tennessee.

WHY DO WOMEN GRAVITATE TO PUBLIC INTEREST/GOVERNMENT?

The third significant differential the NALP statistics reveal is that although the overall numbers are small (less than 3 percent of all graduates), more than twice as many women as men choose jobs in the public interest sector. Bar association studies that query people later on in their careers find a much greater disparity. For example, the Indiana survey found more than four times as many women (3.7 percent) than men (.8 percent) in these jobs. However, the overall low numbers in public interest, which normally includes legal aid to the poor, make this data difficult to interpret.

Worth noting is the comparatively high percentage of women of color who go into public interest law. In the legal pecking order this is where pay and prestige are low. Since 1983, the first year the NALP began separating out minorities from their data, women of color have doubled or tripled the national average of law graduates who go into public interest law. When compared with white men, in 1993 women of color were *five times* more likely to go into public interest law than white men. Although government is a separate category, the people who choose it often do so for reasons that are similar to those given by lawyers who go into public interest. It gives them a chance to do public service—and there may not be jobs elsewhere. Ellen Carpenter, a white attorney now in private practice in Boston, went to work for the Department of Labor in Washington, D.C., after graduation from Notre Dame's law school because, she says, she "had a sense that public service was where I wanted to be."

But black attorney Celia Jackson didn't feel as if she had a choice: "I didn't bother to interview with the firms who came to school [the University of Wisconsin] because I saw what a lot of my friends went through—it is a form of rejection, and I avoided that path."

No one is saying that men don't have to have good credentials to land at a top firm, but their social skills are given more weight and they are given more personal latitude than women. Women and especially women of color are expected to be, well, *perfect*. Whatever that is. If Harvard, for instance, can't find a single black woman adequate to teach there, then of course law firms can't be expected to find good African American women lawyers either. As one white thirtysomething lawyer who works as an editor for a legal publication put it: "Men aren't perceived as having screwed up even when they do. Women don't succeed even when they have all the right credentials."

While one can say that the standards for hiring are themselves neutral, that becomes a smoke screen once one considers that law school favors white males generally and that minority women are the most negatively affected by the experience of law school. Law firms exacerbate the inequity, ignoring signs of competence that might be different from those of white male students. Celia Jackson had proved herself during a summer in the Milwaukee District Attorney's Office and was offered a job there in the fall of her third year of law school. As she became involved in bar committees, she heard war stories of life in law firms: "You would have to listen to ethnic and racist jokes, and because you were an African American, you were held to lower standards. . . . So few African Americans were getting in the door, and many of those who did, didn't stay. There was a sense of always feeling out of place and having to alter who they were. You know if you go into the public sector, you don't have to go through all that."

It was fifteen years ago when Jackson began practicing law, and she sees little evidence that racial discrimination has changed much, if at all. Now a solo practitioner in Milwaukee, she says that a competent black male law student who works for her wants to join a law firm upon graduation. He has interviewed with approximately twenty-five firms in several midwestern cities without success.

If he follows Jackson's career path and takes a job in government, he will be joined by nearly a quarter of all African Americans after graduation, according to NALP figures. But here again the disparity between white men and minorities of either sex is striking: nearly twice as many minorities (20 percent) went into government in 1993 as did white males (11.4 percent). The figure for minority females who go into government is slightly higher than the average of both sexes, but government is no refuge from racism. The interview process itself can be degrading. When an African American woman was applying for a job in a prosecutor's office in New Jersey a few years ago, she says, her interviewers "expressed surprise that I had no juvenile record, that my neighbors spoke well of me, and that my drug test came up clean." This occurred in 1993, not in the distant past.

Given the numbers, are we to suppose that minority women are unusually motivated by a desire to help people similarly disadvantaged? Or are these the only jobs minority women can get? Are these choices made purely on personal preference? Not likely. Unquestionably they are the end result of racial and sexual prejudices. Even pointing to GPAs as a measure of ability—which is what the law firms base much of their hiring decisions on—does not exonerate a system that favors the white males throughout their schooling and fails to nurture those individuals not white, not male. What are we to say to the minority woman from Tennessee who graduated second in her class but cannot find a job? When statements are made that women are not having a hard time at the entry level, we need to look beyond the gross figures. It's white women who are not having as hard a time finding a job in private practice, and even there the women are not making the headway that might be expected with the passing of time and as barriers fall in other occupations such as, say, journalism and business.

Today the pay differential between going to work for the government and a big-city law firm can mean a difference of approximately $50,000, maybe more. For a student graduating with educational loans of up to $150,000 (for both undergraduate and graduate schools), the impulse to go for the money, white or black, male or female, all other things being equal, is likely to be grounded in practicality.

THE PERKS OF SLAVE LABOR: HIGH STATUS, HIGH SALARY

Although there are many different types of lawyers and many different kinds of law, private practice is where the real action is. In the pecking order of the profession, lawyers at so-called Wall Street firms, called that not because they are on Wall Street but because they do the deals that involve huge sums of money, are at the top of the heap. These are megafirms of several hundred lawyers or smaller specialty boutique firms with big-money clients and lawyers who have established themselves as top guns. These corporate law firms have Fortune 500 corporations for clients: Philip Morris and Exxon and General Motors. These clients are used to paying big legal bills and want the best they can buy. They also want the work done *now,* and since in-house legal staffs have grown over the last few decades to handle most of a company's routine needs, outside legal counsel may be brought in only in crisis situations. Consequently the work is intense.

Ironically, the influx of women into the field coincided with the competitiveness that marked the Decade of Greed, the eighties, and law firms were not immune to this phenomenon. In the 1970s and 1980s the biggest law firms grew at a phenomenal rate, providing jobs for the ever-increasing number of freshly minted lawyers, more and more of them women. The twenty largest law firms in the country grew fourfold, from an average of over a hundred to more than five hundred lawyers. The big firms opened branch offices around the world. The old system of law firm organization meant that new lawyers were hired as "associates," who could generally hope to become partners in seven or eight years. And more partners created a demand for more and more associates at the bottom to replace the new partners who had just moved up. For a while the demand for legal workers to do the deals kept up with the burgeoning supply of lawyers the law schools were turning out—women as well as men—more than forty thousand a year since 1980. But the partners of law firms at this point realized that they could make a lot more money themselves if they had more associates doing work that could be billed at a high rate, more associates than they ever meant to make partners.

With an ever-widening array of more lawyers offering greater specialization, corporate clients became less loyal, and competition for new business became more intense, as did the desire for profits. The amount of money paid to the lawyers who did the deals—mergers and acquisitions—was staggering for the amount of work done, since the lawyers got a percentage of the deal, plus a bonus, as money changed hands between the principals. Partnerships of men who once saw their profession as a calling and were satisfied with a reasonably good standard of living and a three-year-old Buick were now demanding more, a lot more. And the best way to increase profitability was to push their new hires to work more hours. Into this came the women.

RECRUITING NEW LAWYERS for large and medium-size firms is done on campus. Law students often take summer jobs with law firms, and so the interview process begins as early as the beginning of the second year. If a firm is interested in a student for a permanent job, she or he is given a callback, an invitation to visit the firm in the city and meet with several partners and associates where the job is under consideration.

The women I spoke to said that most interviewers did not ask illegal questions directly. They are not likely to blatantly ask in the initial interview if the person seeking a job is going to get married and have kids, and when. But such constraints are gotten around most often at meals, when everyone is relaxed and the wine is flowing, by talking about how "hardworking" everyone is at the firm and how many hours everyone puts in, and then waiting for the individual's reaction. "The buzz phrase is, 'Do you want to go home at five o'clock?' " said one young lawyer who had worked for two firms in Washington, D.C. "The real question is, 'Do you have a family or other responsibilities, and won't want to work from eight to eight every day?' " The hiring partners want to be assured that a new associate isn't going to balk at sixty- or seventy-hour workweeks, and of course volunteering, "I'm used to working on Saturdays," would be a plus. Or they might talk about their own family life and wait for you to talk about yourself.

A 1990 survey by the Young Lawyers Division of the ABA reported that more than a third of the women interviewed are asked their marital status or plans and nearly a quarter whether they plan to have children or how their spouse feels about their careers. While the survey included women who had begun working before 1983, the data for the group who began working after that—in other words, after the major influx of women into the law—show that the questions were not substantially different. This means that no matter whether the questions are improper and illegal, and they are, women are still being asked them. Men too are asked about their personal lives—but only 6 percent of them reported questions about plans to have a family, and less than 20 percent were asked whether they were married. And although everyone should know by now that questions of religion are out of order, women said they are still asked during the callbacks.

Becky Miller was a divorced woman with three children not yet teenagers when she began interviewing in Lubbock, Texas. She found it difficult even to get to the second round. She said she had trouble even getting the medium-size firms to give her the time of day. "I go for an interview and the reaction is, 'You have three kids, how can you possibly perform?' They are not supposed to ask the question, but they do anyway, sometimes within twenty minutes of the first interview. And it's not an issue at that point. Can't they see that I figured out some way to go to law school full-time and make law review, and I will do the same at a job? My personal situation gets in the way of discussing other things." After she remarried, she says, some of the hesitation let up. "Now it's at least as though I am an acceptable human being. But the attitude that grades and law review are all-important when it comes to getting a job only works for a certain type of student, and I am not that type of student."

EVEN THE KIND of women most firms have the *least* trouble hiring—white, high-achieving women unfettered with children—can run into some not so subtle prejudices. One woman, for instance, found that being "too attractive" ruined her chances at the Boston firm of Mintz, Levin, Cohn, Ferris, Glovsky & Popeo. Her credentials were impeccable. She was in her second year at Yale, her grades were good, she was on the school's law journal. She was twenty-three. When the number of callbacks she got was disappointing, she decided to find out why.

She phoned those interviewers she thought she had a rapport with. Now Mintz, Levin is thought to be a good place for women, having "an enlightened group of male lawyers," according to one source, as well as progressive family policies. What she heard stunned her.

"He told me if he were hiring on enthusiasm that day, I would have gotten a callback. I got the feeling that they were looking for older, more mature types. That was okay. I'm very bubbly. But he said, 'You're a very attractive young woman, and when I notice myself noticing, I like to err on the side of *not* calling back.' Then, as we were ending the conversation, he asked me to meet him for lunch the next time I was in Boston." The woman apparently wasn't too good-looking for Cravath, Swain & Moore, where she did work that summer. Incidentally, she chose to clerk upon graduation.

If the Yale woman found that her looks were a problem, another new lawyer with good grades and law review on her résumé found that being seen as "strong" knocked her out of the running at a firm in San Francisco:

"I was recruited by an associate who knew me, and went through the second round of interviews. I had a rejection letter almost immediately," she says. "I called them up and asked why, and the man said I came off as 'too young and bubbly,' not the kind of person they would 'want to introduce to their clients.' A month or two later, the guy who recruited me called and was furious I didn't get an offer. He said he was told the reason they didn't hire me was because I 'came off too strong.' " One wonders how many men weren't hired because they came off "too strong."

With that in mind, the woman took a different tack at the next interview, presenting herself as doggedly serious and quiet. This time she was told when she didn't get a callback that she lacked "confidence." Her boyfriend, with credentials not quite as impressive as hers, went to work for a prominent firm (Wilmer, Cutler & Pickering) in Washington, D.C. She clerked for a judge for a second year.

Yet a woman who was openly gay, and listed on her résumé that she was a member of the Gay & Lesbian Caucus at Boalt Hall, had no trouble finding a job—once she eliminated the New York firms. She had good grades and was fluent in several languages, always a plus for the big international firms. She got no callbacks from New York City firms but found a place for herself at Morrison & Foerster in San Francisco, where she was happily working when I interviewed her.

Since there are no comparable statistics from other fields, it is impossible to judge whether women today applying for entry-level jobs at law firms face more discrimination than other women do. Many law firms hire lots of bright, young women at the entry level and don't expect them ever to rise far in the firm and be a major part of it. White women without family responsibilities fit in best at law firms, but even that group hasn't made any headway at the entry level in well over a decade. Minority women, to no one's surprise, have the hardest time of all getting situated. But the demand for relatively cheap labor, and that's what associates provide to the law firm for the first few years, has lessened much of the old discrimination against women at the entry level. But the situation has not improved since 1983.

And what happens when women get in the law firms is another story altogether.

PRIVATE PRACTICE

Invited in
but Locked Out

We fool ourselves into thinking that by virtue of there being more of us today we will be fairly treated. We come from society, and society doesn't treat women fairly, and that is imported into the law school environment and from there into the profession. We have to fight back. Don't let the bastards get you down.

—ROXANNE BARTON CONLIN, FORMER PRESIDENT OF THE ASSOCIATION OF TRIAL LAW-YERS OF AMERICA

FROM THE OUTSIDE, working at a large law firm seems like a good way to spend a life: it's a place where people (generally) make big salaries, work in (gener-ally) cushy offices and do work that (generally) doesn't dirty their hands. Even in this era of lawyer bashing, lawyers enjoy a certain amount of prestige com-pared to, say, a bricklayer or a beautician. The lady's a lawyer? She works for a big law firm in that office tower downtown? That means she's smart and talented and tough. She wears great clothes and clicks around in Ferragamos. She knows how to play with the big boys and she makes big bucks. She has advantages that aren't available to most of us.

But then why do lawyers seem to be perhaps the most dissatisfied group of professionals around? A 1994 survey of close to 2,700 California lawyers found that if they had to do it over again, nearly half would not become lawyers. A 1990 ABA report similarly found widespread discontent among lawyers: 41 percent of women in private practice said they were dissatisfied with their jobs; 28 percent of the men surveyed said they too were unhappy with their work.

And it wasn't just the junior associates, with drudge work piled on them and few perks beyond their salaries, who expressed deep discontent. All groups— from partners to solo practitioners—reported significantly more discontent in 1990 than they did when the ABA surveyed them six years earlier. The reason? "[I]ncreases in hours worked and the resulting decrease in personal time have become major problems, the status and acceptance of women in general has not improved in the intervening six years, the legal profession has in recent years become a less pleasant place to work, and, as a result of all of these changes, dissatisfaction has increased."

If it's bad for everybody, it's the worst for women. Women continue to be foreclosed out of the power-broker positions at law firms, they are not on management committees in representative numbers, and their earnings are consistently lower than men's, according to a 1996 report from the ABA Commission on Women in the Profession. These findings coincide with Cynthia Fuchs Epstein's 1995 report on eight large New York City firms, a study commissioned by the Association of the Bar of New York. "Although there is a general crisis of morale among all young lawyers, women do seem to be leaving large firms disproportionately more than men, meaning that the profile of the 'Wall Street lawyer' at the very top partnership levels looks nothing like the distribution of lawyers at the bottom of the pyramid," she writes in the *Fordham Law Review.*

She found that of the individuals who were hired by the firms she surveyed after 1981, 17 percent of the men became partners, against only 5 percent of the women. Only 2.4 percent of the partners are people of color, nearly one-fifth of the 250 largest firms have no partners of color, and almost a quarter have only one. No figures are given for the number of women of color who are partners, but it appears to be minuscule. According to Joel Henning, head of the Chicago office of Hildebrandt, Inc., a management consulting firm, fewer than a quarter of the women (23 percent) who remain at law firms long enough to be asked to become a partner are actually invited to do so, while nearly 60 percent of the men are. Since so many leave, the 23 percent actually represents a very small number of the women who started at law firms—probably the 5 percent Epstein found. Consequently the partnership of the nation's largest law firms by and large continues to be a white male preserve. According to the most recent estimates, approximately 13 to 14 percent of the partners of the nation's largest law firms are women. Yes, the number of female partners is increasing—at a meager 1 percent a year.

More than 70 percent of women in fourteen major law firms surveyed since 1990 stated that gender determined how one was treated at their firms, and 60 percent said that qualified men were given more opportunities than equally qualified women, according to Freada Klein, a Boston-based consultant to companies and law firms on sexual discrimination and harassment. A fifth-year associate who had given notice at a two-hundred-lawyer New York firm when we spoke said that since she joined the firm in the early nineties, the atmosphere had become increasingly political. Morale was down, the pressure up. Law as a profession has become law as a business: at many large firms partners' remuneration has superseded other concerns, such as serving the clients' real needs and the care and educational feeding of young lawyers coming up the pipeline, the pipeline that for the first time has a lot of women in it.

THE DISCONTENT IS PROFOUND. Whatever the sex, it is not difficult to fathom why private practice is full of disgruntled workers. All too often any satisfaction to be gotten from lawyering itself must come from secondary gains—that is, money and *not the work itself.* Many women and men go into law because they thought it would be an intellectually challenging way to spend a life. That it may be, but the first few years at a big firm can be boring and dreary; years can go by before a young lawyer is allowed to take a deposition or argue a motion. Paradoxically, because of the competition, the longer one stays at a firm, the more one is expected to spend time courting clients and bringing in new business rather than doing the actual work. Many a senior attorney is turned into a salesman whose main occupation is pitching the firm's merits rather than doing law. "Eat what you kill" is a phrase lawyers use among themselves, referring to the fact that in the jungle out there, you have to bag your own business— nobody else is going to do it for you. Firms have become impersonal, hierarchical and rife with political rivalries. At the big law firms, the ones that pay the most and have the most prestige, the work for new associates can be tedious, with dozens of lawyers compartmentalized into little niches. For women, combine that with sex discrimination and its traveling companion, sexual harassment, and you've got a recipe for ennui.

Meanwhile the senior partners are patting themselves on the back for having hired women—40 to 50 percent of the recruits at some large firms are women today—and made a few of them partners. But they have mixed feelings because they have this sense that the women and minorities don't really measure up. In partnership terms, they are often judged generically: "We had one and she didn't work out" is a common attitude. Besides, the rest of the story goes, so many of the women leave just as they are becoming really useful to the firm and able to handle sophisticated matters with little supervision. What these men don't realize is that the women have sized up the situation and made a hasty exit: "I knew there would be discrimination at the partner level, but I didn't expect

it as soon as I got here," says a disaffected twenty-eight-year-old associate at
Stroock & Stroock & Lavan, a firm that promotes itself as good for women. For
many a lawyer, the realities of life in the wall-to-wall mahogany suites of the big
firms are a far cry from the glamorous settings of the popular imagination fueled
by high-profile TV-covered trials and programs such as *L.A. Law.* Yes, the money
and prestige are generous, but many—and many more women than men—find
that they are not worth the price.

Large law firms work for the largest, richest corporations, and both operate
pretty much the same way. Legions of workers, supervised by managers, grind
out standard legal advice much the same way General Motors turns out Chevys.
The object is to make sure the big, high-paying corporate clients stay big and
profitable, whatever the social cost. The firms are a brutal antidote to idealism.
The little guy who's been pushed around is the adversary, not the client. Not
too many law students, I wager, imagine that they will spend their days working
on some small aspect of General Motors' defense against the Department of
Transportation, which wants, say, a truck with a side-mounted gas tank recalled
for safety reasons. Or defending Exxon against the state (and seals) of Alaska.
Or working all night to complete the paperwork on a stock offering or a merger.
Or spending years on a technical question of commercial law involving two
megacorporations that involves millions of dollars but the cost to any one individual (outside of the value of the stock held by stockholders) in human terms
is negligible.

"Corporate law is only about the redistribution of wealth," says a large-firm
émigré in Chicago.* "My image of it is a group of little white men pushing piles
of money around with little brooms from one side of the room to another
without any particular concern about what it means. Ultimately I felt that I
wasn't doing anything productive, say, such as making a shoe." She is now an
assistant state's attorney.

Large law firms are where the professors at Harvard and the Universities of
Pennsylvania and Chicago suppose their acolytes will wind up. A great many of
them do. It's where the big money is.

But the women don't stay. *Half will leave law within five years.* In analyzing the
personnel surveys of the more than two hundred law firms the Hildebrandt

---

* *Most of the seventy-plus attorneys interviewed for this section asked for anonymity when discussing
past or current employers. They said that speaking on the record would damage their professional
relationships with past employers, some of which referred business to them. Unless noted, all lawyers
quoted are women.*

consulting firm has worked with in the last dozen years, the 50 percent figure has been fairly consistent, says executive Joel Henning. "A few women go to other law firms, but when we do exit interviews we find that they are dropping out," he says. Forced out is more like it. Forced out by the macho atmosphere, the killing hours and, for some, by the kind of work the large law firms do.

Some of the movement from the big firms appears to be built in; that is, the intention to leave one's first job is sometimes expressed as early as law school. A 1989 Minnesota study of the career paths of approximately 250 male and 250 female attorneys found that only a third of the respondents expected to stay at their first job. Among those lawyers who began practicing between 1978 and 1989, there was no difference between the women and men in the number of jobs they held. But when asked why they left their first jobs, differences between the genders became evident: 90 percent of the men said that it was for a better opportunity elsewhere; only 77 percent of the women agreed. Close to a quarter of the women (23 percent) left for reasons other than career development, with 12 percent of the women leaving their first jobs for personal and family reasons. Close to two-thirds of the women (62 percent) reported that "dissatisfaction" was the trigger causing them to leave their first jobs; only 42 percent of the men indicated the same. Men were more likely to state that they left their first jobs for reasons such as "advancement and salary considerations"; women are more likely to leave because of "discrimination" and "other" reasons. The Stroock associate quoted earlier was looking for a job when we spoke. She had been at Stroock two years.

Little has changed since the Minnesota study. Although there are more women in law firms, real acceptance remains elusive. "The situation has actually gotten worse in the last seven or eight years, because now law firms know they must have some women partners," says Esther Rothstein, the first woman to be president of the Chicago Bar Association two decades ago. "Yet since they have one or two women they feel they do not have to do anything more, so the door is shut against other women. Women have really regressed." She is not the only pessimist.

PROGRESS GLACIAL FOR WOMEN, MINORITIES

In a 1993 survey of nearly eight hundred male and female attorneys at large law firms in fourteen major cities, nearly 60 percent of the women said that the glass ceiling has either remained intact or become even more impenetrable during the three previous years. Of the 43 percent of the respondents who felt that opportunities for female lawyers had improved, most said it was because of their sheer numbers, *not because of enlightened management.*

And it appears that given the enormous changes law firms have been through in the last decade, many firms are no more accommodating, or even less so, to women who have young children. At the same time, the women themselves have become less amenable to meeting the demands of a typical law firm. Unlike the pioneers of the sixties and seventies, who put children on the back burner or accepted round-the-clock surrogate care, today's young women don't want to hand over most child rearing to others. The impact of this on women's careers at law firms is nothing short of monumental. When's the best time to have children and combine it with success at a large, intense law firm? The answer may still be: *Never.*

In fact, women lawyers postpone or put off having children in great numbers. The 1990 ABA survey found that not only are far fewer women lawyers married or living with somebody than men (64 percent versus 80 percent), more women than men were also putting off having children, at least for the time being. According to the 1989 California Bar study, 42 percent said they were postponing children, and 27 percent said they were not going to have them at all.

To have children is one reason many women leave law firms. If Henning is right—that 50 percent of women at major law firms leave law within five years—then something is seriously rotten in the system. Other professions, such as medicine or journalism, certainly have their disillusioned constituents, but they do not opt out in such a wholesale fashion. Corporate law is where the real action of the profession is: it's where the money and power are concentrated. Outside of a small number of high-profile plaintiff's attorneys and criminal defense lawyers, a group that can be counted on one's hands and toes, corporate law is where the most powerful lawyers in the country ply their trade. It's the kind of high-status, high-paying practice that John Grisham wrote about in *The Firm.* Once you're a part of it (assuming you're not involved in criminal activity as his characters were), why wouldn't most people want to remain there?

Yet when I mentioned the 50 percent dropout figure to women at law firms, or to those who have left law firms, many say the number seems too low. "I'm surprised that it's not higher, the way women leave around here," remarks a secretary with Pope, Cahill & Chicago. "All my friends at Bingham, Dana have left," says a Boston lawyer now in a small specialty practice. "One is home with the kids, one is at another firm, the first woman partner is on the bench, another went to another firm, where she does research and writing but doesn't go to court, another is an in-house counsel. The women who are there—it's miserable to hear them talk." An associate in the New York office of Paul, Weiss, Rifkind, Wharton & Garrison says that although the number of women partners at her firm is discouraging (in 1993 they constituted 7 percent of the partners), "there have been no women to pass over for partner at the time they would be considered—they left before they got to that point." In Minneapolis one woman said of Dorsey & Whitney: "In my class [the other people who began practicing law the same year], there were eight men and seven women. None of the women are still there, and of the ten who followed the next year, none of them are there either. The individual stories are real different, but partly it's because while I was there the firm developed a fairly macho attitude. You had to be tough, loud and abrasive, and work more hours than anybody else. There was some perception by the people making decisions at the firm that we women were not as effective as lawyers, and we got that sort of feedback."

Sheila Nielsen, a Chicago-based career consultant for attorneys, disagrees that the women are leaving the law altogether in anything like the 50 percent figure. She believes that many women are merely finding ways to practice that are more agreeable than corporate law. "They work part-time or full-time at a corporation [called "in-house" counsel], they do independent contracting for law firms, they develop a private part-time practice, they take work funneled from a large law firm," she says. And some women do drop out temporarily to raise a family but go back on some basis when the children are in school, numbers that would not show up in Henning's exit interviews. But wherever they go, the evidence is that the level of discontent is very high, and an astonishing number of women flee from large law firms.

WHAT'S SO BAD about the firms that women walk out in such great numbers? Is it only women who are dissatisfied with law firm life? A laundry list of what's wrong with law—and law firms in particular—reads like this:

The hours can be murderous. In today's tight economic climate, the pressure seldom, if ever, lets up—even when you get to be a partner. And the pressure is not just to be a good lawyer; given the glut of lawyers on the market, competent workers are a dime a dozen. Those who make partner are those who do excellent work, *plus* generate new business. Given the competition, collegiality and civility even among the attorneys at one's own firm are at a minimum, political intrigue at a maximum. The orientation of the typical law firm is overwhelmingly male, making the women feel unwanted and shut out—and they often are. Women are not as readily given the respect that goes to their male peers—if they ever get it. Forceful women lawyers are labeled bitches, conciliators are wimps. All the while the firm's partners feel they have done a good thing because they have hired women and maybe a few minorities. Women and minorities are less likely than white men to find a mentor, or a network of friends, who will show them the ropes. At the senior level women's compensation falls behind men's. The work environment is cold and impersonal, a factor that appears to count more for women than men, and the work itself often humdrum. A disenchanted lawyer in Augusta, Maine, reflects, "I went to law school because I thought being a lawyer would be intellectually challenging and that I would be able to do good things for people. But those times when I feel good about my work because I have done something good for people have been few and far between."

A little-talked-about aspect of law firm life is that many of the women who do make the grade are perfectionists who watch their diets, their wardrobes, and their work output with the scrutiny of a Sherlock Holmes looking for clues of their imperfections. "At my firm, many of the lawyers who made partner had eating disorders or were hooked on tranquilizers," says a Chicago attorney who left law to become a freelance writer. "They think a fat person is someone who wears a size ten or twelve. They might not actually be anorexic, but they have the 'anorexic' personality type—they have to be best at everything."

THE TRANSFORMATION OF THE LAW FIRM

Today's corporate law firm has been though a sea change from the time when they were genteel places of work for men from the upper classes, which they were, more or less, right up until a generation ago. Firms were usually on long-term retainers with clients and handled all of the legal business of any one client, much the way family doctors took care of patients before the age of medical specialization. That's no longer true. From the sixties onward, in-house legal departments were beefed up and began taking over the routine legal matters that had once been relegated to law firms. Outside counsel was now hired only for the more intense work of litigation, deal making, bankruptcy, and so on, and it was the job of corporate counsel to seek out the best firm for the job. Consequently the old client/law firm loyalties came to an end, and it was necessary for law firms to actively seek business on a regular basis.

This happened at the same time that the number of lawyers and law firms were growing . . . and growing . . . and growing. Between 1960 and 1980 law school enrollment increased three times and bar admissions four times, and the lawyer to population ratio halved, an increase linked directly to the entrance of women into the profession. Between 1960 and 1985 the average size of New York's biggest law firms grew by almost 375 percent, from an average of 45 lawyers to 214; outside of New York the growth was even more phenomenal, from an average of 50 to 261 lawyers. With size came specialization, partly to manage the increased numbers and partly to tout a law firm's expertise to the now choosy in-house counsels, the ones selecting which firms to retain. Litigation, corporate, bankruptcy, tax, real estate, labor, banking, trusts and estates and intellectual property are some of the various areas of specialization. Lawyers who litigate, for instance, don't do taxes.

The firms outgrew their old office space and moved into the gleaming new towers that went up during the Reagan years. The interior decoration at many firms got ever more luxe; so, in fact, did some of the catered lunches the lawyers ordered in. It was the eighties. Much money was spent to impress clients, attract the best law students, and smooth the wrinkled brows (and egos) of the overworked lawyers.

Perhaps not so amazingly, the expansion of the legal profession coincided with an increase in corporate litigation. The surge began in the 1970s and shows no signs of slowing down today. Litigation has a tendency to go on for years—after the judgment there is always the appeal, and the next appeal. Governmental regulations and the hierarchical structure of both government and the law firm also insured that lots of costly legal steps would be taken before a case was brought to a close. All this busywork translates into billable hours upon billable hours, an incentive in itself *not* to settle out of court and bring the work to an end. But eventually the appeals run out and a client's matter does come to an end. Since corporations do not have a steady diet of such jobs to hand out, another client is needed to fill the void. As a result, lawyers have to generate a steady supply of new legal matters to keep the machinery grinding. Marketing became an integral part of a lawyer's job. Just like companies that sell widgets or oatmeal, many firms now actually employ marketing managers—a job that was unheard of two decades ago.

To make matters worse, the growing oversupply of lawyers insured that the competition for business would be fierce. "If you have a cage that is built to house fifty rabbits and there are five hundred in the cage, there is a turf war going on," observes Martha Fay Africa, a law firm headhunter and em-

ployment counselor based in San Francisco. "Society cannot accommodate
the thirty-thousand-some new lawyers coming into the profession each year
in meaningful ways." The ones who "succeed" are the ones who are able to
seize a piece of the turf for themselves. It can sometimes be a less than
pretty business.

As the firms grew, so did the ratio of partner to associate. Each partner
now was supported by more associates than before. Where before the ratio
had been nearer one to one (one associate per partner), it is now closer to
two to one (two associates per partner) and at some places even higher.
Ultimately this would mean that fewer associates would be made partner or
assume shareholder status.* At some firms the chance of making it is no
more than 10 percent. Because of these odds, the old up-or-out system is
crumbling, replaced by a trend to keeping lawyers on after they have
been passed over for partnership. They may be called nonequity partners,
special counsel, staff attorneys and the like. These lawyers, somewhere between full equity partner and associate, have less influence in the firm's management than the senior partners and do not draw from the firm's profits but
receive a fixed salary. Again, and again ironically, this new layer of lawyers
coincided with the full-scale entry of women into the profession. Just as they
got there, the stakes (for more hours, for rainmaking) were raised or
changed, and law firms devised a place to park these lawyers, many of them
women.

In a 1996 *National Law Journal* survey of 82 of the largest law firms in the
country, only 54 percent of the women partners—and minority partners of
both sexes—have equity, in contrast to 74 percent of the men. The survey did
not include a breakdown of minority women partners.

FROM LAW FIRM TO SWEATSHOP

As competition for jobs, for clients, became more and more brutal, so did
the politics of the firm. The civilized atmosphere of an earlier time gave way
to a cutthroat culture where the attitude was, Take no prisoners. Lawyers
now tended to see outcomes in black and white, and were not typically
practiced in appeasement or inclined to worry about the effect of their actions on the people they figuratively slayed in the courts. Lawyers today talk
about leaving only "scorched earth" in their path, of playing "hardball." Mar-

* *Most law firms are structured as partnerships; associates are employees of the partners. However,
some are private corporations (PCs), and the principals are shareholders, not partners.*

vin Karp, former president of the Cleveland Bar Association, says that the courtroom ethic increasingly has become more fractious: "Litigation is war, the lawyer is a gladiator, and the object is to wipe out the other side." Consequently many firms during this time, including many of the biggest and most prominent, became notorious for the harsh treatment of those on the way up or out.

A case in point: Associates in their fifth, sixth, and seventh years—that is, a few years before partnership decisions have to be made—are the most profitable employees to have around. They can work with little supervision and handle complex matters, yet they are not drawing heavily on the firm's profits. Law firms now are increasingly known to beg such associates to stay, then turn them down a year or two later for partnership, and sometimes tell them they are simply out of a job without so much as a by-your-leave. Even partners are now abruptly voted out and asked to leave. It is not for nothing that lawyers as a group have an image problem.

"As we got larger, everything got less personal—and the way people are handled simply became atrocious," recalls a lawyer whose $100,000 salary was halved when she left corporate law to become a deputy district attorney. At a cocktail reception held at a fancy hotel—no expense was spared that night, she recalls—announcements were made about new office space, new computers, and new offices opening in Hong Kong and New Delhi. Yet the event, to kick off the annual recruiting season, was rampant with rumors that layoffs were imminent. And at the end of the upbeat presentation the rumor was confirmed: 10 percent of the associates were being fired. "It was like being kicked in the teeth at a party," she says.

The way not to be pink-slipped as an associate is to make your mark as a conspicuous profit center—in other words, a lawyer who can be counted on to put in long hours, which translates into billable hours and profit. Because many of the firm's expenses are fixed—salaries, equipment, phones, rent, supplies— the only way to increase income is to increase the numbers of hours billed. In the seventies and the early eighties billing between 1,350 to 1,500 hours was the rule, not the exception, hours that today are considered part-time, especially in cities like New York, Boston, Chicago and Los Angeles. Now most firms expect you to bill at least 1,800. Recent surveys report that almost half of private practitioners bill over 2,000 hours annually, a figure that a few decades ago would have been suspect.

While billing an extra 300 hours a year doesn't sound like much, it makes the difference between a well-rounded life and one that is not. Says a veteran of three large law firms: "The effect on your life goes up exponentially after 1,500 hours." That wasn't lost on the heirs of an associate at New York's Cleary, Gottlieb, Steen & Hamilton who killed himself in 1990: they sued the firm,* claiming that he had been worked to death with excessive assignments and unrealistic deadlines. At Paul, Weiss, the associates who stand out are those who bill out around 2,500 hours a year. That's 48 hours a week, 52 weeks of the year; and it doesn't include the other 10–15 hours a week or so you're at the office doing nonbillable work, nor does it account for any days off. Cravath is said to have champagne parties for associates who bill *over a hundred hours in one week.* That amounts to 14½ hours a day, 7 days a week. The more hours worked, the more hours billed, the more money the firm makes. In this atmosphere quality of life is a nonissue. What life? Everyone, from fresh associate to senior partner, is under tremendous pressure to produce.

"Law is becoming an increasingly difficult way to live a life," comments an associate at a small firm in Maine, who seemingly would be far from the maddening pressures of large-firm, big-city law. "It doesn't have to do with juggling kids and a career, it has to do with the nature of the legal profession—it's more competitive and cutthroat. That doesn't have anything to do with gender. It has to do with the number of lawyers."

Many people go into law to make a contribution to justice, and instead they find the emphasis is on the relentless billing of hours and the marketing of their services. They end up feeling they are neither making a contribution to society nor even allowed to be a good technical lawyer because the emphasis is constantly on the bottom line.

"There was a time when a young lawyer would come in and work like crazy for not too much money, but this would pay off and he would become a partner and the pressure would be off and the income would be good and there would be a certain amount of prestige that went with that," reflects consultant Henning. "Now you make a lot of money right in the beginning, but the pressure never really ceases—it may be even more when you are a partner—and you do not have much esteem in the community."

As the firm was transformed into a grueling taskmaster, enter the women of the eighties. These lawyers were not like the lady lawyers of the earlier generation, women who remained single or childless, women who put aside per-

* *The suit was dismissed. It was believed to be the first case involving the long hours and great stress that many large-firm associates endure, according to* The National Law Journal.

sonal concerns to succeed. This wave of women wanted to have careers, of course. And children too.

Susan D., a thirtyish lawyer in Boston, represents the new generation and has lived through the cataclysmic changes of law firms. After law school she went to work for a midsize firm (fifty to one hundred lawyers) that seemed to her more humane than what she called "the morass" of Davis, Polk & Wardwell in Washington, D.C., where she had spent a summer. "Not only did the firm [Hutchins, Wheeler & Ditmar] have access to interesting cases, people were allowed to have lives outside of the firm."

But all that changed overnight when the Wall Street firm of Cravath, Swaine & Moore, the firm that pioneered the associate-to-partner track shortly after the turn of the century, upped its first-year salaries to $65,000 at a time when the highest-paid new associates were getting $53,000. The year was 1987. Other firms in big cities, including Boston, felt it was necessary to follow suit, and although they did not go as high as Cravath, salaries at large and medium-size corporate law firms took a giant step forward. "I was supposed to start at $40,000, but within a week, they told us we would be getting $50,000," she says. "Immediately they expected more from us in terms of hours. That got worse and worse over time." Like a lot of other firms, Hutchins, Wheeler moved to new office space.

"I remember touring the new offices before we moved in with an associate who was a few years ahead of me. Everything was mahogany and marble. She said, 'Whose hide is this going to come out of? Ours, of course. We are going to have to pay for this.' She meant that while we had been working until ten P.M., now it was going to be midnight. And she was right.

"I was having trouble maintaining a semblance of a life outside the office, as I was working nights and weekends. That's built in to some degree in litigation [her area]. Getting ready to go to trial, I would work until ten P.M. on Friday, get in between eight and nine on Saturday and bring my food so I wouldn't have to leave the premises, and then stay until ten or eleven P.M. on Saturday and do the same thing on Sunday. Sometimes I would get three or four hours of sleep. I had no control over my life. I didn't have a family to go home to, but I wanted to have one—and I wasn't going to meet him at the office. You are never *not* going to be single if you are there twenty-four hours a day." Ultimately she quit, took a sizable pay cut, and went in-house for a university.

The testimony of other women point to the same conclusion: the hours are intolerable. Cathy Isaacson, now a solo practitioner, recalls that her hours at a

New York firm were typically ten A.M. to nine P.M. and most weekends. "At one point I realized that I had not used real silverware for about two weeks—I had been eating only take-out food at the office," she says. "That was the rule, not the exception."

"When I was billing 2,500 hours sometimes I wouldn't come home until five in the morning two nights in a row," ruefully recalls a woman who was laid off when Proskauer Rose Goetz & Mendelsohn retrenched in 1991.

"They kept bumping the hours up. First it was 1,500 to 1,600, then they went to 1,700 and a couple of years later to 1,850," remembers a former employee of Oppenheimer, Wolff & Donnelly in Minneapolis. "Those were the minimums. You had to work more to be a partner. You felt guilty if you ever left before six thirty P.M. and didn't work at least one weekend day. You would look at the partners, and see that they didn't seem that happy either." She went in-house.

Law firms had become the legal equivalent of sweatshops, the only difference being that law offices have climate control and the Occupational Safety Health Administration is nowhere in sight. "The system is designed as a macho test—the men love telling each other how long they stayed up, how many hours they put in over the weekend," comments Gina Anderson, a former corporate lawyer who is now an in-house counsel for a publishing house in New York. "It makes them feel accomplished."

Brooksley Born, the attorney who headed Washington, D.C.'s commission on gender bias in the courts, reflects that while subverting your needs to those of the client is inherent to some degree in any service profession, "the life situation of the male attorney who has no other real responsibilities has exacerbated and expanded what is really necessary for the client's welfare." She recalls hearing when she became a lawyer in the sixties, "The law is a demanding mistress," a reference she says only a man would identify with. Consequently that's how men organized the practice of law in large firms.

The 1989 stock market quake and subsequent depression made a bad situation worse at the big firms. When the economy went sour, deals dried up, and lots of those bodies that law firms added in the eighties were now deadweight. Firms that had never laid off people before for lack of work were now firing people in the double digits. The layoffs, interestingly, affected white males more than minorities and women. During that period of adjustment, between 1989 and 1991, the overall percentage of women at law firms actually rose 4 percent and minorities to 14 percent, at least at those firms that provided gender and ethnic breakdowns in a 1992 *National Law Journal* survey. In any case, the work that the laid-off attorneys had been doing was merely redistributed, and everyone was working at least as hard as before. There were still those fancy new offices to pay for. Some firms, however, couldn't make the adjustment and folded.

MONEY MONEY MONEY

With making money as the A-1 priority, billable hours became an end in itself. Bringing both sides in a dispute to a reasonable settlement would keep clients out of court and—*you got it*—reduce the number of billable hours. Under this system, it doesn't matter what the outcome is—win or lose, the client pays. It is like paying a plumber before he fixes the leak and paying him regardless of whether he did or not. Since work on a legal matter may involve only a few minutes' work at a time, say, a phone call or two—lawyers break their days down into six- or ten-minute segments, accounted for on time sheets. "Litigation is enormously expensive in terms of money and time, and there wasn't enough emphasis on working out a reasonable resolution at my firm," says a litigation firm refugee in Los Angeles. "They pushed litigation simply for the sake of litigation." With lots of lawyers and paralegals on staff to provide work for, the number of people who work on an account goes up. Chicago journalist and attorney Stephanie Goldberg recalls that once when she was a paralegal she was told to go with an in-house client's attorney to find a document at the warehouse—and, with a wink from the partner, was told that she and the in-house counsel shouldn't get lost on the way. The presumption was that they would go off and have a good time—all the while the clock would be ticking for billable hours of her time.*

The outcome of an audit of one of the nation's major law firms provides a good illustration of the inflated billing that goes on at bloated law firms. The unnamed firm had been retained by a large international client on a lawsuit claiming $100 million in damages. "But after three years of expensive litigation, the case was close to an unfavorable result," wrote Paul Lerner, senior counsel at the U.S. division of Asea Brown Boveri, Inc. As soon as the time records were requested, the law firm immediately credited ABB with $43,634.50, the result of "duplication of attorney time," which sounds like a nice way of saying "double billing." The law firm said it had discovered this overcharge through "re-

---

* *Goldberg got the best of the situation. "You're two big strapping lads," she retorted. "I'm sure you two can find the document without my help." She says the partner didn't speak to her for weeks.*

formatting" its bills. But that was only the beginning. The audit found that $1.5 million in billing (out of $3.5 million, or more than a third) was questionable, and this ultimately led to ABB's not paying hundreds of thousands of dollars. What ran up the bill? Egregious overstaffing and senior-level people doing junior-level work, billed, of course, at the senior lawyers' rate.

Most stunning was the number of people who worked on the case: "At least sixty-three attorneys, paralegals and other timekeepers worked on the case when most of the work could have been handled by one partner and one senior associate, instead of three partners and four senior associates; two principal junior associates, instead of thirteen; one nonprincipal associate, instead of twenty-nine, and one paralegal, instead of eleven," wrote Lerner. One of the firms ABB now uses is Brown & Bryant, an all-woman firm in Chicago of five lawyers and one paralegal, which specializes in environmental matters.

With dozens of people working on a single piece of legal business, it is not difficult to see how extra hours get tacked onto the bill. Billable hours spawn inefficiency. Spending time on a client's matter is profitable to the law firm, whether the hours are profitable to the client or not. Barbara Billauer, who left a partnership with a large New York firm to start her own legal boutique, comments, "With less business and a higher overhead and managers who are not well trained to manage, you end up with a desperate situation. There is incredible pressure to make the payroll, and if you have no idea of how to cut or what to cut, there is pressure to double bill, to overbill." What is one to make of James Spiotto, a Chicago attorney whose 1993 financial records indicate that he billed 6,022 hours, a figure that the FBI is investigating? Incidentally, 6,022 translates into 16.5 hours a day every day of the year. His spokesman says he actually billed 1,000 fewer hours; that turns into nearly 14 hours a day. No matter how many hours Spiotto billed, the pressure to increase profits means there is less time (or no time) at the end of the day for the old give-and-take between a senior attorney and an associate, when friendships and real learning can take place in an unstructured atmosphere. Before, those hours were not billed to a client; now, "training" generally needs to be accounted for and billed. Clients end up paying for the education the young lawyers get at the firms.

However, clients are getting choosier, especially as they tighten their corporate belts and see just how crowded the legal field is. Billable hours, long the sacred cow of the law firm, is vaporizing because it led to such humongous bills, even when the outcome represented a loss to the client. Billing at anywhere from, say, $90 an hour for an associate in Dallas to $500 an hour for a partner in New York, can add up pretty quickly. Lawyers are viewed as making too much money anyway. Many clients are now insisting on alternative fee arrangements, such as a flat-fee billing and volume pricing, and law firms are going along. With the competition for business, they have no choice. Other large clients simply have demanded discounted hourly rates. Sunoco Atlantic, for example, notified thirty of its law firms that it was slashing outside hourly rates 20 percent, take it or leave it. Alcoa fired 150 of its law firms and consolidated its work with a single firm employing a flat-fee billing method or volume pricing, an arrangement that harkens back to the old law method of having a single firm on a retainer. Fixed fees sometimes have a performance-based bonus, which rewards quick, optimal results and efficiency. It can reward lawyers for working out speedier settlements rather than litigating, which in commercial cases is not so often done on a contingency-fee basis. This of course shifts a firm's emphasis on results, rather than hours, a trend that can work only for those lawyers, those men and women, who don't want to devote nearly every waking hour to legal business. Settlements have less prestige than winning in the courtroom, but they may be less costly to all sides. But these alternative-fee arrangements may not ease the unreasonable and, some would say, intolerable time requirements of lawyers at large firms for many years.

WOMEN AND LAW FIRMS OF THE NINETIES

Unquestionably, then, the atmosphere in today's large firms, and some medium and small ones too, is more than simply unpleasant; working conditions for everyone are awful. But men—married men at least—are able to work the long hours and still have some semblance of a life. "Although they work the long hours, they have wives who take care of the rest of their lives—a family, a social life, clean laundry," points out Carol Kanarek, who left private practice to become an outplacement counselor and law firm recruiter in New York.

The structure and conditions of the large law firm were designed by and for men who have stay-at-home wives. In effect, with such a couple you have two people working on one career. These wives make sure the man's shirts are back from the laundry, they help their husbands pack for business trips, they may have a meal waiting in the microwave when they get home at ten P.M. Sure, nobody except masochists like working twelve- and fourteen-hour days, but it's one thing if you are coming home to supper and somebody is waiting for you, and it's another if you are coming home to a dark apartment. "The more senior partners are likely to be men born before 1950, and they aren't likely to have married a woman lawyer or anyone vested in her career," observes Martha Fay Africa, former co-chair of the ABA's Glass Ceiling Task Force. "Their wives are the equivalent of traditional military wives who run the home until the warrior-lawyer returns home to repack his suitcase." If women lawyers had the same advantage, their spouses would be keeping them stocked with panty hose and fresh silk blouses.

But they don't, and that's only the beginning. Add children to the mix and you ratchet up the tension considerably. As far as the men are concerned, the firm has been clicking along lickety-split as is, thank you very much, so the prevailing attitude is that women have to make themselves fit the firm, not the other way around—no matter their numbers. And if these lawyer-mothers assume more responsibility for raising children than their husbands, as is nearly always the case, that's their choice. They don't have to be partners, do they? Women of this older generation are just as likely to share those feelings as not. The few women who passed through the eye of the needle in the sixties and seventies and became partners were nearly all clones of the men, except for their sex. "You have to dress like a man, write like a man, talk like a man, do everything as male as possible," says a lawyer in Los Angeles. In Miami I heard: "The women who fit in here have to be tougher than the boys. The woman who fits in the best at my firm wears a tie." The speaker is not a disgruntled associate; she is a partner herself at one of Florida's major firms.

But even if the women of an earlier generation are understanding of the younger women, overall it is questionable how much they can actually do for them. While they have been responsible for whatever family-friendly policies are in place, most women, however senior, do not have a lot of influence with their colleagues. "In many firms, the women partners are tokens," comments Martha Sosman, who practiced law in Boston and now sits on the bench. "They are partners in name only but have no clout. A lot of women were made partners a few years ago for window dressing." You don't frequently find women on the finance and compensation committees or the partnership committee, which recommends to the full partnership who should be tapped. Instead you find women as low-status recruiting coordinators, a euphemism for personnel, a job that requires setting up interviews and the like, or in charge of the legal writing program.

It is true that in *The National Law Journal*'s 1994 ranking of the one hundred most powerful lawyers in the country, a dozen women are included. But not a single woman makes the list because of her success in private practice. The breakdown: three, academia/legal theory; four, government; and five, public interest, which coincidentally is normally the lowest-paying branch of the law. It may be the most personally rewarding, but that is another story. Dozens of men, meanwhile, are on the list because of their success in private practice. Although the ABA has been accused of an anti-woman bias for years, women have risen to prominence in it, both at the local and national levels, with the clout that confers carrying over to their overall prominence. Indeed, Roberta Cooper Ramo stepped down as president in August of 1996. When *Chicago* magazine wrote about "power lawyers" in the Windy City a few years ago, one of the eighteen individuals pictured was Laurel Bellows, the second female president of the Chicago Bar Association in 1991–92 and currently chair of the Women's Commission of the ABA. She is in a small but influential firm that bears her name, rather than in a large law firm, as most of the male lawyers are. The other woman photographed, Mary Jacobs Skinner, appears to have been included by virtue of her having married well—and that is how she is identified in the accompanying copy. A third woman attorney named was former federal judge Susan Getzendanner, widely acknowledged as a member of the Chicago clout club. She is known not to mince words. As she put it when she left the bench several years ago, "I'm at Skadden Arps now. We pride ourselves on being assholes. It's part of the firm culture." Chicago is also home to Debora De Hoyos, who was thirty-eight and the mother of two young girls in 1991 when she was named the managing partner of Mayer, Brown & Platt, an international firm with offices in several cities. She herself says her actual power is probably limited by her relative youth among the senior partners.

Powerful women partners do surface elsewhere, of course. Barbara Robinson, mother of two, a partner at Debevoise & Plimpton, became the first woman president of the New York City Bar Association, but again, her clout comes from the presidency, not the partnership. However, Robinson blazed the trail for part-time work at Debevoise, doing it back in the sixties. Brooksley Born at Washington, D.C.'s Arnold & Porter, which has been involved in some of the most important cases of our time, was on the short list for attorney general. In San Francisco Linda Shostak at Morrison & Foerster was the first woman chair of the partnership review committee and also was appointed to MoFo's points committee, which decides partners' compensation, both powerful committees where few women are typically found. In Cleveland Mary Ann Jorgenson heads the corporate practice department worldwide at Squire, Sanders & Dempsey and served a term on the management committee; Michelle Vaillancourt, a shareholder at Winthrop & Weinstine in St. Paul, is also active in the local bar and is widely respected in the Twin Cities. Until Nancy Atlas became a federal district court judge in 1995, she was a rainmaker for Houston's Sheinfeld, Maley & Kay and a major player in Texas Democratic politics.

But being able to name a handful of powerful women does not present a true picture. "Young lawyers look around and see that some women are doing quite well in private practice, but it is not quite as good as it looks," observes Judge Sosman. "What happens to mediocre people? When you see mediocre women have the same career opportunities as mediocre men, then you have equality."

Furthermore the crack in the glass ceiling is usually big enough to let only one woman through. "Firms give one woman power, and appropriate compensation, and the partners can feel comfortable about themselves," observes Chicago attorney Johnine J. Brown. "They can say, 'See, we allowed one woman to reach the heights.' Maybe it's because she is more malleable, more politically savvy than the others. I'm not saying these aren't superintelligent women, but they realize that only one woman is going to head a major department, or be on the management committee or compensation committee—and if it's you, why would you help other women? If she does, she is unseating herself. At most law firms, the guys can be competing for a dozen or so powerful slots, but there's only one place for a woman with power."

Because men are still running the firms, what goes on in them is still very male and very macho. The more macho the firm, the less likely men are able to deal with women as equals or competitors. Yes, a few women might survive all the verbal slings and arrows that go with the job at these firms, but more will ask whether it is worth the internal Sturm und Drang and leave. "I had a female boss who was good at what she did," says a woman no longer with the New York office of Keck, Mahin & Cate. "The men who worked for her would say things like 'She needs to get laid' or 'She's got PMS today.' You heard a lot about PMS. If a woman was aggressive, she was a bitch. If she were nice, she was too weak to be a good lawyer. You couldn't win either way."

Male-dominated firms are exceedingly hierarchical. Careful note is made of compensation, naturally, but also of size and location of offices, parking space allotment, years in practice, you name it. Many women find these rankings comical but ultimately irritating. A female lawyer in Texas was told—when she was named partner—that putting her name on the stationery would hurt the feelings of a male associate, and would she mind her name being left off? Pecking order, however, does clarify who has power and who doesn't. For instance, it is true that partners all have one vote, but some partners' votes are more equal than others. People high in the hierarchy control blocks of votes, because people vote with them to curry their favor or, at least, not antagonize them.

"As a junior partner, your compensation is dictated by the largesse of the other partners, and if you were interested in getting ahead, you didn't do anything to annoy the senior partners," notes Marty S., a solo practitioner in Great Barrington, Massachusetts. She was one of five women among the sixty-some partners at a 150-lawyer firm in New York that has since dissolved. Marty S. recalls constantly being made to feel like an outsider at the monthly partners' meeting: "Somebody almost always said something that made me feel uncomfortable—usually it was a joke about the size of a man's penis or the ability to get it up. I'm not a prude, but I felt the jokes were told partly to make the women uncomfortable, to show us what a macho bunch of guys they were, and to show us that they were in charge. You couldn't ever say anything, because that would put you in the position of being someone who wasn't in the club, so to speak."

Marty S. says her pay was equal to that of her male peers because it would have looked too blatant otherwise. But wide disparity occurred at higher levels. Partners' compensation within a firm varies widely, depending on an individual's perceived worth to the firm. "One woman was the equal, if not superior, of her male counterpart in litigation," she recalls. "I had worked with both of them. It would infuriate me that she was paid less than him—his bonus was gigantic! She agreed, but there was nothing she could do."

As for herself, she flatly states: "The more senior I became, the more I began to feel that opportunities that were available to my male counterparts were not available to me. And I felt it most when I became a partner." Marty S.'s observation is common among women partners. In fact, the ABA Young Lawyers Survey in 1990 discovered that more women *partners* expressed dissatisfaction with their jobs (42 percent) than associates (36.5 percent). Consultant Freada Klein's survey of women at law firms found that two-thirds said they were not satisfied with opportunities for advancement; only slightly more than 30 percent of the men said the same of themselves. Seventy percent of the women said they had experienced some form of gender bias in the past two years; less than 10 percent of the men said they had also. Clearly partnership is not the end of the problems women face at law firms. For example, once you are a senior associate or partner, you have work to hand out to more junior people. Most law firms allow associates some leeway in choosing for whom they work. A former part-

ner at Keck, Mahin & Cate says that male associates shy away from working for
women because they (correctly) perceive them as lacking real power. Of
course, the men's reluctance or outright refusal to work for women exacerbates
the situation.

Johnine Brown was sabotaged several times as she built an environmental law
practice. At one firm where she was a partner, she had built the environmental
department from the $50,000 in billings she brought with her when she came
into a $500,000-a-year-business in three years. As head of the department, she
was supervising two other full-time attorneys and three part-time attorneys.
Without consulting her, the senior partners decided to bring in a man over her.
"Then the guy came to me and said I was to make no more speeches, write no
more articles, and give up my memberships in professional organizations, and
furthermore, I was to hand over my client files, and the only client contact
thereafter would be through him. The managing partner was there to confirm
the decision." Naturally, by taking away her visibility in the field, her potential
as a rainmaker—and someone with clout—would vaporize. Within weeks she
left, taking her clients with her. But the experience was brutalizing.

And it felt like a repeat of something that had happened earlier. Having gone
to law school as a second career, Brown was a few years older than most of the
sixth-year associates she worked with at another firm. She was handling sophisticated environmental matters. This time the partners informed her that she
wasn't qualified to do the work—even though she had brought in business with
the client's assumption that she would be doing the work. "I have never seen
this happen to a guy," she says. "There were a number of men who were good
to me, but I just did not get the kind of support that a guy would have." Soon
after, she left the firm, once again taking the clients with her.

At yet another firm, when she was visibly gaining power, a male attorney she
had hired was involved in a move to reorganize her department; it was simply
absorbed into a new department, which included other commercial matters.
The firm named a superannuated partner who simply needed a job until retirement to head the new department. He had specialized in none of the areas
he would now supervise. Another time she could not get the budget she needed
to boost the department she was heading. The opposition Brown encountered
in the Midwest, supposedly nicer than the rough-and-tumble East Coast, demonstrates just how deeply embedded chauvinism is in the fabric of the practice
of law. Brown ultimately fled the large firms, taking her clients with her once
again, and went into a partnership with another woman, Brown & Bryant.

If these incidents happen to white women, how are African American women treated? It depends on the firm. Laveeda Morgan Battle, the only African American partner at Gorham & Waldrep in Birmingham, says that "everybody's heart is in the right place" and that the firm has been "remarkably good" to her. When she was recruited in 1989, she says there were no other blacks and whites practicing together in Alabama. Ironically, she says that most of the prejudice and bad treatment she encounters come from white women at other firms who seem determined to show their male partners just how tough they are.

Yet in Chicago an African American woman says the discrimination is ever-present: "The white men at the firm enjoy prerogatives as their seeming birthright." She made partner on schedule, the same year the senior partner in her department was retiring. "He divided up his clients—one half to one white male partner, the other half to another white male partner, and none to the third partner—me. I had worked for some of those clients too." Other minority women say they are "trotted out for clients [for show], but then not asked to do the business." And all seem to have encountered the insult "I don't think of you as a person of color [or black, African American, Hispanic, whatever]" dished out as a compliment. How dismal the situation is was revealed in a *National Law Journal* survey released this spring: The percentage of nonwhite partners at 250 of the nation's largest firms increased only .4 of 1 percent in the last five years. Nearly half of all minority partners are nonequity partners.

A STRONG MENTOR IS A MUST

One of the most common problems of women and people of color at law firms is that they frequently do not get the nurturing one needs to succeed. You must have honest feedback, you must be included now and then when senior people go to lunch, you need to meet clients, you must not be stuck in, say, low-status document research for a year. "The men get the assignment with the powerful partners or the plum cases that bring notoriety and exposure," comments a disaffected associate at Paul, Weiss. "There are no powerful women in my department who might want to help other women." Do the men help? Yes and no. "I have found that the men don't mentor other men either, although they may be a little more comfortable with them and so they are friendlier."

That friendship and the "comfort factor" may be the key. When Elizabeth Hishon sued Atlanta's King & Spalding in 1979 for sex discrimination, it was acknowledged by the firm that she was passed over for partnership more because of style than content, underscoring the significance of friendships within a firm. Even the firm's partners agreed she was a hard worker and intelligent and had received compliments on her work from clients. But partners said she didn't fit in with the outgoing types there who know how to have a good time. To a reporter, they pointed out that she didn't go to basketball games with her co-workers, she didn't go to lunch with other King & Spalding lawyers—partly because they insisted on picking up her check—and was rarely seen at the exclusive, white-male-members-only Piedmont Driving Club with the head of her department. He was the club's chairman. Intangible criteria like these are the essence of sex and race discrimination, and these are the hardest to break down.

It is over lunches and drinks and sports events after work that much of the bonding goes on between senior partners and junior associates, and the importance of these unstructured hours cannot be emphasized enough. Women face all kinds of obstacles here. Some men still feel uneasy asking a woman to join them at lunch. Will people think that he's lusting for her? Who picks up the check? Will she think he's making a pass when he's not? "Men are now more self-conscious about helping a young woman attorney because they are afraid of sending the wrong signals, where they wouldn't have before," observes Barbara Robinson. "Before there may have been some concern about appearances, but now there's the specter of sexual harassment, and that is more threatening."

Often the men aren't intentionally setting out to exclude the women . . . it just happens. Robinson recalls that in 1964 when she left her summer associate job at Davis, Polk & Wardwell, no one bothered to say good-bye or offer her a permanent job after she graduated from Yale. This was after she had been left out of the summer associates outing—a day of sports, drinks and dirty jokes— and, to everyone's relief, had declined to go along on an annual pub crawl. While it wasn't the usual practice, she signed up for a repeat interview with Davis, Polk when they recruited at Yale that fall because she had not heard from them. Then she was told, 'Oh, you shouldn't have had to do this, we should have made you an offer.' " When she declined they were shocked, she says, and later heard from one of the partners that they rationalized her lack of interest by the fact that she was engaged. "I was too young to say, 'No, you idiot, I just think I wouldn't be a very happy person in your very, very male camp.' " It's the same old story today. The men still don't get it. At law firms they are constantly scratching their proverbial heads and wondering why they lose so many women.

But women also play a part sometimes. They may fail to understand just how essential close social bonds are in business. If a woman has a husband (who probably isn't getting the dinner) and/or children, she is less likely to take the time or even acknowledge the importance of these informal networks. While these bonds might more naturally form between older and younger women, there are not enough senior women to go around, and anyway, the senior and younger women may face attitudinal gaps—over how much must be sacrificed to get ahead—that most men won't. Most male attorneys, for example, are not going to request parenting leave when they have a child, even if it is written into the firm's policy, just as the firm's senior men did not.

Interestingly, on some surveys from the late eighties and early nineties, more women than men reported they had a "mentor," but it may be that women and men look at their friendships with senior attorneys differently. Men are more likely to have whole networks of acquaintances in and out of the firm who nurture their careers. Yet being under the wing of a senior attorney—and most of them are still men—may be the single most important factor to a young lawyer's success, unless your uncle is the CEO of a major corporation and will steer a lot of business to your firm. How does it work? A Cleveland attorney explains: "He listened, strategized, helped me figure out what cases were hot and how I got them, how to steer clear of this person, how to get to work for another person. He sometimes read my memos before I turned them in, told me how to look up research when I was stuck, helped me write the opening line in a letter when I hadn't written anything like it before." She and the man's wife were able to become friendly, but that is not a luxury most women will enjoy.

Like it or not, attractive women fare better in the mentoring sweepstakes than plain Janes. The first two female candidates for attorney general, for instance, Zoë Baird and Kimba Wood, are both glamorous. Both were competent in their own right, but both lacked the law enforcement background of Janet Reno, a big-boned, plain-looking woman. Yet when Reno got the job, she seemed like the third choice, even though she was unquestionably the best candidate from the get-go. Incidentally, all—Reno included—had strong male mentors close to the Clinton administration.

In the partnership sweepstakes, it's absolutely crucial to have at least one mentor, in your department, possibly the chairman. Without someone to watch over you, even rave reviews and high hours may not be enough. "Everybody loved me, they all wanted me to work on their cases, but nobody championed me," says one woman, "so I didn't make partner. I didn't really have someone I could call a mentor." Mentors also protect you when times are tough. Carol

Kanarek, a New York law firm recruiter, has been in on meetings when the partners decide whom to cut when a firm is downsizing. "They don't sit around and say, 'Let's fire this person and that person,' " she says. "What happens is that the ones who aren't politically protected fall between the cracks. The first people to go will be the part-timers, not because they aren't economically viable, but because they don't have anybody to protect them. Then somebody will say, 'Well, don't fire . . . so-and-so.' It's not that anybody is out to get anybody, but certain people are protected, and ones that aren't are let go."

Or they leave on their own. One black attorney in Chicago watched another, once the star of the summer associates, flounder without inside supporters. The woman I spoke to couldn't do it because the younger woman wasn't in her department. "She actually found the smoking gun in a case when she was a summer associate, and she broke the case," the woman remembers. "But once she was here full-time, she wasn't given the same things to do as the guys were. To develop your skills in litigation [her area], you have to write parts of briefs, do a lot of discovery, take depositions, present witnesses at a trial, make open-ing arguments. There's a checklist of things you need to learn. But if a whole chunk of those skills is missing because nobody ever let you do them, you can stay in brief writing and research all your life. The way to damage somebody is not give them exposure, and that's what happened to her. She left after four years and went to a government agency. She is doing great."

"If you are getting the wrong signals, if you're not encouraged and wel-comed as part of the group, it becomes harder to stick with it," Barbara Rob-inson points out. "So if you are working full-time against pressing demands such as raising a family, you think, Gee, the powers-that-be don't love me the same as they love my young colleague who happens to be a man, they are not as friendly to me, why am I doing this?"

The still tricky terrain between the sexes in business creates yet another obstacle: most men aren't comfortable critiquing women. They are afraid women won't take the criticism calmly, that they will cry. As a result, women don't often get the constructive feedback they need. "Men will say things like 'Well, I wouldn't be too concerned about this' . . . and it sounds unimportant, when it's not," comments Michelle Vaillancourt, a shareholder in Winthrop & Weinstine, a St. Paul firm. "Handling a woman with kid gloves is obviously to her detriment because the woman doesn't get the opportunity to find out what is wrong and what she could do about it.

They may not tell women to their faces that they are not learning their cues properly, but it all comes out in written evaluations. One Michigan woman recalls that women's evaluations at her firm often noted that they were "too much a Pollyanna-cheerleader type" or were "too happy"—comments on style rather than substance that usually don't come up when men are graded. At Dorsey & Whitney, a top Minneapolis firm, women said that they were faulted for "laughing too loudly" or "being too aggressive." It is hard to imagine that a Dorsey & Whitney male attorney would be "too aggressive," since that is the image the firm cultivates. One woman litigator's evaluation stated that she didn't have a broad enough range of experience, since she had worked for several years on a few large cases, even though she had considerable responsibility on the cases. Another woman who had worked on several smaller cases was someone who was "a good small case litigator," but, the evaluators stated, "they didn't know how she would do on large cases." Of course, she had not been assigned any.

One fifth-year associate at another Los Angeles firm had never taken a deposition herself. Coming to the firm after two years elsewhere, she started out on a large case doing the low-status work of reviewing documents—eight hundred thousand documents; and the following year, when another document-heavy case came up, she was assigned to head up the document research because now she had experience in . . . reviewing documents. What did she learn from document research? "Wear lots of hand lotion," she says cynically. Men at her level, she says, got more varied experience. We spoke just before she was leaving for the D.A.'s office at half her $100,000 salary. She was thrilled at the prospect.

Nancy Ezold had the same problem in Philadelphia at Wolf, Block, Schorr & Solis-Cohen. "I was not given the same level and complexity of assignments as the men, nor was I assigned to work with as wide a variety of partners—two things that are critical at any firm for making partner," she explains. "I was given small matters to work on as opposed to class action or antitrust suits, both desirable cases because the clients are considered valuable, the amount of money is more significant, and the cases are complex." When Ezold raised the issue of getting better assignments, she was told she would, but somehow the white-collar-criminal cases she was assigned did not have the same level of prestige as civil cases, which she was not. Ezold, incidentally, let it be known that she believed the paralegal staff would be better paid and better treated (they were not paid for working on weekends but were billed to the clients at up to $100 an hour) if they weren't mostly women. That did not exactly endear her to the senior partners. Ezold didn't go quietly into the night; she sued after she didn't make partner in 1988 and was the first woman to take the case all the way to trial. Other charges of discrimination at law firms rarely make the news, as all but Ezold's to date have been settled quietly out of court.

Ezold's trial caused some commotion in Philadelphia, for evaluations of male associates-turned-partner (with their names) were introduced as evidence. There was the young man who was described as having "a lack of professionalism, both in terms of legal analysis and research." Another was called "slick" and "a bit of a con man." One missed important dates for completing projects, once proposed jurisdiction under the wrong statute, and missed a pertinent U.S. Supreme Court decision that would have been apparent had he done "rudimentary shepherdizing." One partner wrote that his "intellectual laziness will some day embarrass us." There was the associate who simply disappeared without notice and "almost cost the firm a million dollars." And there was the associate whose "outrageous personality" caused the father-in-law of a partner to change firms. "If he is made partner, I will never again submit an evaluation of any associate." He made partner.

Wolf, Block countered by having partners read disparaging comments from Ezold's reviews. One partner wrote he "wouldn't turn over to her matters which involved complex legal theories, creative lawyering in the sense of legal matter, and certainly not things which involved a lot of heavy brief writing." However, the one partner who testified in Ezold's behalf, Greg Magarity, a litigation partner who had worked extensively with Ezold, wrote in an internal memorandum, "Sy would only assign Nancy to noncomplex matters, and then some partners would qualify their evaluations by saying that Nancy does not work on complex matters. Nancy was literally trapped in a Catch-22." And when Sy Kurland (the individual just referred to) left the firm in 1987, he wrote a glowing report, part of which reads: "Nancy is an exceptionally good courtroom lawyer, instills confidence in clients, gets things done, is unafraid, and has all the qualifications for partnership. . . . What I envisioned about her when I hired her was a 'good, stand-up, effective courtroom lawyer' remains true, and I think she has proven her case."

It also came out at the trial that twenty-seven partners recommended that Ezold be given partnership, twenty-one of them "with enthusiasm or favor" and six with "mixed feelings." Only four partners were negative. And it was easy to see why the trial judge ruled that "male associates who received evaluations no better than the plaintiff and sometimes less favorable than the plaintiff were made partners. Gender was a determining factor in the failure of the firm to promote the plaintiff to partnership in 1989." But Ezold's victory was short-lived. Wolf, Block appealed, and the decision was reversed by the ultracon-servative judges in the Third Circuit. A retired Third Circuit judge represented Wolf, Block before his former peers, proving that old boys never really fade away.

. . . LIKE TURNING A BATTLESHIP AROUND

Sometimes, to be sure, the discrimination is blatant and outrageous, even today. A frat house atmosphere that says "Women beware" has a tendency constantly to recharge itself. Even young men who come to the firm with egalitarian at-titudes can be remade by the pervasive atmosphere into new old boys. Business as usual is discrimination, of course. Women who have worked at Little Rock's Ivester, Skinner & Camp rattle off examples of the recent past:

One former law clerk at Ivester knows that she was paid less per hour than males with the same or less experience; when the male clerks got Christmas bonuses, she did not. She was given a parking space across the street, with the secretaries; a male runner who started after her was given a spot in the coveted and covered parking lot (where the attorneys park) attached to the building. Yet she got great reviews and, later, glowing recommendations from the partners. However, she was not offered a job upon graduation, although the partners strung her along for several months. She went to work as an assistant D.A. "In retrospect, it was good they didn't offer me a job, because they treated the women attorneys horribly," she says. "You would think they had never been around women in the legal profession."

One of the female attorneys there confirms what the former paralegal had to say. She told of the time three women attorneys at the firm were working together in a conference room. A male attorney stuck in his head and said: "Well, it takes three women to do the job of one man." Hillary bashing and racist jokes are big there. If one of the women gets into an argument with opposing counsel who also happens to be a woman, it becomes a "cat fight." When one of the women was undergoing chemotherapy and asked for part-time work, the request was denied. "I had to wait a long time before I had client contact, but a male law clerk was taken to meetings right away with the client," she states. "And it's not just that the clients don't want to deal with women attorneys, because more and more of the in-house counsel they deal with are women." In fact, it was from an in-house counsel at a Little Rock bank that I heard about "what may be the most sexist law firm in Arkansas."

While many women said that the younger men whose law school experience included a good percentage of women were less inclined to give women trouble, that was not always the case. "Younger male attorneys are just as likely as the older lawyers to leer, make sexual remarks, push women for dates, and harass them in the office," states a 1992 report from the Texas Bar Young Lawyers Division. Although younger attorneys may come out of law school believing that women peers are equals, the dominant male power structure found in most private law firms signals to them that discrimination against women is acceptable. The report gave a couple of examples: one female associate reported that a male associate, only one year ahead of her, routinely asked her to run to the library to "fetch him a book." Another male associate sent a female associate, assigned to the same case, a copy of a letter with the instruction to make sure his secretary received the letter for filing. The secretary in question sat right outside his office; the female associate's office was on the other side of the floor.

A woman who fled Wilson, Elser, Moskowitz, Edelman & Dicker in New York described an atmosphere that would depress even the thick-skinned: "So much of what happened was so subtle that if you tried to complain, they would think you were crazy," she recalls. "When the firm was handling cases about sexual abuse in the context of professional relationships, there were always these jokes about what the women said happened to them. It was demeaning. But how were you going to complain about that?" She says that male associates were routinely rude to female associates, and it was with the seemingly tacit blessing of the partners. The overall atmosphere for women attorneys was such that the secretaries didn't want to work for women. "The men would bark orders at the secretaries, and that was all right," she adds.

One reason some law firms appear to be run by Neanderthals is that the senior partners, especially senior partners who bring in a lot of business, are immune to criticism. Who's going to tell them they need to change their ways? Certainly not junior partners whose livelihood to some degree depends on their goodwill. Peers are unlikely to do so, either, especially if he is responsible for bringing in a lot of business. "One of the senior rainmakers in the firm was notorious for refusing to have any women working in his department," says a former partner at a New York firm. "Other partners didn't approve, but he was well respected in his field and it wasn't in their interests to go to the mat with him on this. When he finally agreed to take on a few, all of them were either fired or left." Fortunately, she herself had had a strong mentor: although she had never worked with him, she learned that when she came up for partner, he attempted to block it.

Of course, like businesses everywhere, law firms vary in comfort for women just as corporations do. Although many—if not most—seem to be terrible, not all are. But how a woman or minority fares depends on the department head.

One major firm has changed the playing field completely. At Anderson Kill Olick & Oshinsky everyone who joins the firm is an equity shareholder (roughly corresponding to partner in other firms) from the beginning—although a junior lawyer's percentage of the equity is correspondingly low. All salaries are a combination of a guaranteed wage plus a share of the profits, with the percentage coming from profits rising over time to where it becomes the major portion of the wage. At Anderson Kill one never has to wonder if one becomes a partner; one is a partner upon joining the firm. More than a third of the firm's two-hundred-plus attorneys are female. Yet even here, where the opportunities would seem limitless for women—and attorneys are required to bill only 1,900 hours a year—the percentage of senior women at the firm drops off dramatically, and women are not counted among the most powerful members of the firm. Why? Because none are the firm's rainmakers.

Cory Amron, former chair of the ABA Commission on Women in the Profession and a Washington, D.C., attorney, says that in the nearly two decades she has been out of law school progress for women has come at a minuscule pace. "The discrimination is tremendously subtle today. If you were to be a fly on the wall in the workplace, you wouldn't hear those in management say, 'This person is a woman, and I don't want her to get ahead.' A lot of the discrimination comes from people who think they are doing good, but when it comes down to looking at the training people get so they can make partner, or get to the next level of experience, women aren't getting it, and then they are not perceived as having the skills. Or they are passed over for reasons that are never articulated."

The men in charge are often oblivious—sometimes it seems willfully so—to what is going on. When the Los Angeles office of Kirkland & Ellis, known as a swashbuckling group of litigators, hired an outside consultant to learn why the firm was losing so many women, there was an "Oh my gosh" reaction, says partner Vicki Hood. "People say they don't discriminate, but when confronted with a list of their matters, who works on them, and who has responsibility for their various clients, they all turn out to be white males. . . ." Yet, she notes, "it wasn't as if the senior partners were anxious to examine their warts. It was like pulling teeth to get the study into people's hands."

Most, but not all, of the firms written about here are the large firms with fifty lawyers or more. It's easier to find data on them because they are scrutinized by legal publications and sometimes even the government. But overall, many more women work at small firms than large ones. And here the situation for women attorneys is likely to be even worse.

"The problems are much more severe in small firms," says Carol Kanarek, who hears about the trials and tribulations of women attorneys both in her job as a legal headhunter and through the volunteer work she does for law schools and women's bar groups. "The vast majority of law firms operate outside the eyes and ears of anybody. They do not recruit on campus and so do not have to file NALP forms that would show their numbers. They are not covered by the legal press. Most of them are run by men who have no intention of giving a genuine opportunity for advancement to their associates, male or female. People go to them thinking that they are going to have a real lawyer job, when the partners really have something else in mind altogether. Anyone should be wary of firms that are totally run by males and there is a constant turnover of associates. There are many small, wonderful firms, but there are many more that are truly terrible."

BRINGING UP BABY

The Law
and Children

Even when freshly washed and relieved of all obvious confections, children tend to be sticky.——FRAN LEBOWITZ

THE BIGGEST SPEED bump on the road to success for women lawyers is having a family. There are two ways to be a parent, of course. Have children and have another be the full-time primary caretaker, and it's likely one's career will slow down only momentarily. But that's not a lifestyle that suits everyone. If a woman wants to be more involved with her children, it gets harder to stay on course to partnership.

In an atmosphere that emphasizes billable hours so heavily, in a situation where bringing a case to trial is impossible without fourteen- and sixteen-hour days, it is hard to imagine how anyone can find time for children. In fact, many don't. Female lawyers are less likely to have children than the rest of us. The 1989 California study of nearly six hundred female lawyers found that a whopping 62 percent of them were childless. People who bill more than 2,400 hours a year—and over 50 percent of associates do, according to the 1991 ABA study referred to earlier—have little time left to change diapers, attend PTA meetings, pick the kids up at school and help with their homework. Quality time? They're lucky to get any time with their kids.

Marcia Clark, lead prosecutor in the O. J. Simpson trial, stated in court papers that she was working sixteen hours a day. But even that doesn't mean that the single parent has backup child care for every occasion. When the defense wanted to continue questioning a witness who said she was about to leave the country into the evening hours, Clark said she had to be home with her two sons. "I can't stay," she said plaintively. "I can be here tomorrow [Saturday]," she said as she pleaded for understanding and demonstrated her commitment. At the time, Clark was in the middle of a custody battle with her ex-husband, who was attempting to prove that he was a better parent and had more time for the boys than she did.

The classic answer to the child care dilemma has been part-time work. Corporate America has certainly dealt with it effectively. When the Families and Work Institute surveyed a representative sampling of the U.S. workforce, close to three thousand wage and salaried workers, they found that 57 percent of them had access to part-time work, 29 percent chose to work flextime, and 24 percent could do some work at home regularly. Clearly they were not courtroom lawyers.

A 1990 ABA study found that less than 5 percent of lawyers in private practice—excluding solo practitioners—worked reduced schedules. And that figure may be high. Numerous firms that had part-time lawyers in the late eighties laid them off in the cutbacks of the early nineties. Some firms went belly-up. The ones that recovered are still wary about part-time lawyers, an attitude that almost exclusively affects women who want to combine family and career. More than half of the lawyers at large firms believe that being a mother hampers one's career, and nearly as many say that a maternity leave can negatively impact one's career, according to consultant Freada Klein, who has done in-depth attitudinal surveys of attorneys at law firms.

Law firms have not made the same adjustments for their workforce as the rest of corporate America. Paradoxically it is the largest firms that are most likely to offer part-time work, but with rare exceptions it is the largest firms where working part-time is most likely to put you permanently on the "mommy track," with little opportunity to get off—even when you return to full-time hours. The attitude at most law firms is, as one woman put it, "Don't tell me about your kids."

"It's okay to have pictures of children on your desk—the men do too—but you had better not talk about them," she says. "You would never tell anybody you were leaving the office because your kid was sick."

Nor would you ask for part-time work if you had any hopes of being taken seriously as a lawyer. "What happens to people who take part-time?" asks Sheila Nielsen, a Chicago-area career counselor for attorneys. "They come to me and say, 'I've lost my perks, my benefits are reduced, I have no status at the firm,

I'm treated like a second-class citizen, and anyway, *I'm working close to full-time.*' "

Men, needless to add, do not face this dilemma. A 1993 *National Law Journal* survey of fourteen top firms found that 60 percent of the married men queried had a partner who was *not* employed full-time outside the home. They have a partner, in other words, who can take their shirts to the laundry and their kids to the doctor, can run errands, buy food for dinner, and warm it up when they come home late from still another heavily billed day at the office. Not a lot of husbands are performing those services for their lawyer wives. Not a lot of lawyer-fathers are working part-time to help raise the kids. National surveys find that even in organizations that offer parenting leaves to men, less than 2 percent take them, and then only for a brief period. One study that asked how many lawyer-fathers ever worked part-time to care for children found that only 4 of 803 men surveyed did so, and only 3 of them did it for six months or longer.

For a brief moment in the 1970s some optimists believed that the women's movement would make men more responsive to the idea of sharing child care and household responsibilities beyond taking out the garbage. Unquestionably there has been some change. Some female lawyers have worked out arrangements with their employers that allow them to have both a family life and a career. While some fathers do more than their fathers, that almost never includes officially working fewer hours. What you hear at most firms is that Lawyer X, a woman with two kids who would actually like to see them once in a while, "lacks commitment." She has placed family values above billable values. The mommy track is the wrong track to take if you want a successful career; incidentally, it's also the wrong track to take if you are in a custody battle.

With rare exceptions, the top firms are the worst. Why give a lawyer a computer and a desk and an office for thirty-five to forty hours a week when someone else can use that space for sixty or seventy or eighty hours? The sad thing is that the law, unlike most businesses, is peculiarly suited to part-time work. Attorneys almost always work on individual cases part-time, except when they are going to trial or putting together an important deal. Billing sheets are broken down into segments as small as six minutes, reflecting the part-time nature of the work itself. It would be easy—and is in some enlightened firms—to arrange working schedules around the needs of a family. But it seldom happens.

FLEXIBILITY BENEFICIAL FOR MOTHER, THE FIRM

When it does happen the results are usually beneficial for all concerned. A case in point: In 1978, when Dallas attorney Cindy Ohlenforst interviewed at one of the major Texas firms, Hughes & Luce, for a summer job, her résumé made note of her three-month-old baby because she wanted to find a firm where she could work less than full-time right from the beginning. "Of course it helped that I was first in my class at SMU [Southern Methodist University]," she jokes.

As she recollects, Hughes & Luce "had no women at all" back then, but without rules set in stone the partners were amenable to a reduced schedule. In the beginning she went home two days a week around lunchtime. After the birth of a second child, she cut back her hours even further. When her third child was born in 1985, she took three months off, but then came back full-time. On schedule with the rest of her class, Ohlenforst made partner a year later. Hughes & Luce did not penalize her for either her maternity leaves—two within three years—or the short hours she worked for five years.

Ohlenforst did choose a specialty, taxes, that allows for more regular hours than, say, litigation or corporate, which includes mergers and acquisitions, the kind of work that often requires all-nighters. She does litigate tax cases, requiring the superhuman effort that taking any case to trial demands, but mostly she is able to work a more or less humane schedule. Still, as she puts it, combining law with motherhood "requires tremendous energy, planning, flexibility and good luck."

Even a high-pressure New York firm such as Skadden, Arps, Slate, Meagher & Flom can, under certain circumstances, accommodate a reduced schedule. Deborah Tuchman calls the firm's response to her part-time work "unbelievable" and "terrific." In fact, she joined the firm in 1988 specifically to work fewer hours after her twins were born. Because she came in at a relatively senior level and is able to handle complicated matters in securities regulation, she is not assigned the junk that others complain they are given once they work part-time. Like all the women whose part-time positions have worked out, Tuchman notes that you must be flexible enough to come in on days off and attend meetings as needed. Her clients have her home phone number. Yet in 1994 she took a three-month leave. "Maybe when the children are older, I will consider full-time work and think about partnership. But this way, I've been able to keep my career going and have time to be the kind of mother I want to be." She is not in the running for partner, she knows, but she is a trustee of her twins' school.

Skadden has approximately thirty part-timers. A few are men. None of these men are taking the time because they are raising kids. The message of Skadden, Arps is clear. Even in macho firms, arrangements for part-time work can be made to work for both the firm and employee. But it is unlikely that the practice of law itself will change until men see the need to really get to know their children themselves. One notable aspect of Skadden, Arps's flexibility is that in the area where all-nighters proliferate like mushrooms and for which Skadden, Arps is known—mergers and acquisitions—part-time work is available. It's done this way: You work day and night for weeks on a deal, but then take extended time off.

Skadden, Arps has also found a way to make the office of the future—the at-home office—work for one of its full-time partners. When Erica Ward's husband took over a family business in Detroit two years after she was made a partner, it necessitated a move from Washington, D.C., where she was established in the firm's energy division. Ward thought she would have to give up her connection with the firm, but since their clients are all over the world, the head of her department saw no reason why she couldn't get on a plane at Detroit Metropolitan Airport rather than at Dulles to meet with clients at their offices—which much of Ward's work involves anyway. So Skadden, Arps sent in a technical person to her home in the Detroit suburb of Bloomfield Hills and had the place wired to be the ultimate home office. Ward hit the ground at cruising speed in 1989. A few years later her daughter was born.

"I'm a straight corporate lawyer, but I'm sitting here in jeans," says Ward. "I have a secretary who handles the phone, and the people in D.C. can dial me up with four digits—just as if I were in the office there. I have a fax and modem and FedEx arrives every day—of course I miss the gossip and interaction of being in an office, but I couldn't continue the kind of practice I trained for if I couldn't do it this way." Plus she has more time for her daughter—who is cared for by a nanny during the workday—than if she also had to include a commute in her schedule. Ward goes to D.C. for meetings around four times a year. By the way, more than 20 percent of Skadden, Arps's D.C. partners are female, putting it among the firms with the highest percentage of female partners. Sweatshop reputation or not, they must be doing something right.

WARD'S ARRANGEMENT is possibly unique. Many mothers will want to work fewer hours than the norm today, and need to do it at the office. What it takes for part-time schedules to work is flexibility, senior partners who are sympathetic to family needs, and a willingness to accept different styles of lawyering. This all comes together in varying degrees at firms like O'Melveny & Myers in Los Angeles; Morrison & Foerster in San Francisco; Anderson Kill in New York; Brown & Bain in Phoenix; and other smaller firms around the country. Lori C. Seegers at Anderson Kill says, "I have a hard time remembering anyone who left the firm purely for reasons of wanting to be a mother, and that not being consistent with working here." At O'Melveny & Myers, partner Victoria Stratman says, "I have heard of firms where they go down the aisles to see who is still working at seven in the evening, but that's not the case here. I don't know how many hours I bill. The firm looks at the whole contribution in contrast with raw numbers. Everybody expects you to pull your own weight, but nobody is hovering over you to see what time you come and go." California-based Morrison & Foerster have policies that include sick-child days (no need to make up excuses), a twelve-week maternity leave for lawyers, and an indeterminate phasing-back-in period. MoFo Moms and Pops is a noontime teleconferencing group that talks about parenting issues with its own on-line newsletter. Because of its family-friendly policies, a quarter of MoFo's partners are women, and at least a quarter of them are mothers.

How sensible. How rare. These stories are not typical. Much more common are stories in which women try to find ways to have a family life, are abused by their law firms, and leave. And the cost of losing them is enormous. A study by Aetna Life & Casualty of American business concluded that the cost of recruiting and training to fill a vacancy—plus lost productivity from the job turnover—equals 93 percent of the first-year salary. The cost is almost certainly greater at law firms, where initial salaries are high and the training process is prolonged. A Fortune 500 company was able to reduce the number of women who quit after having a child to 2 percent, from 25 percent, after instituting a child care and support system to reduce stress among employees. Most law firms, with their typically macho attitudes, seem more committed to creating stress. At New York's Proskauer Rose Goetz & Mendelsohn (which is known for its *employment* department) a take-no-prisoners attitude extends to the partners and associates as well as to the other side in a dispute. Women with kids say working there is brutal.

PUNITIVE PART-TIME

At most firms part-time is a punishing experience. One Chicago attorney who was a hotshot litigator at a major firm says that the reduced work schedule she was offered when she asked to work part-time was ridiculous. "They only wanted to have the program so they could say they had it when recruiting," she says. "I would be getting 60 percent of my salary for 60 percent of the hours— but then they said things like 'Of course, we expect you to have full-time child care when things really heat up around here, because you'll be working full-time and then some.' And that means eighty hours a week. Maybe that's not a problem if you are not the primary earner, but I was. My husband was doing research and making $30,000 a year, and since we would need full-time coverage for the kids anyway, I couldn't see how I could do it and succeed.

"A senior woman partner at the firm did me in. She's married to a surgeon and they have gobs of money and gobs of baby-sitters and she couldn't understand that I couldn't do the same. She said what I wanted wasn't in the 'spirit of litigation.' And of course the men thought that too. Most of them have stay-at-home wives. I was going to be the first [to go part-time], and I didn't want to fail. So I started looking for a job elsewhere." She found one at the Illinois Attorney General's Office. Part-time.

As we have seen before, some senior women throw obstacles in the way of junior women. "The women who have succeeded here," says a lawyer at a New York firm with two children under six, "don't have the typical problems of juggling kids at home. And they aren't very sympathetic to any of us with kids. Their attitude is, 'I blazed the trail for you, so now why are you having kids?' " The law firm of which she speaks is one of the one hundred largest in the country. It could be said of most of them.

Going part-time, even when it seems to be working, can stigmatize you as someone who isn't interested in partnership. One woman found this out the hard way. To other women at her firm, it seemed that she had everything going for her: She fit the firm's image of an aggressive gladiator type. She was known as a "superstar"—the word was actually written into her reviews. Even after she had two children, she was still billing two hundred hours a month. When she said she had to have part-time work or she would leave, the head of her department readily agreed.

But the arrangement never really worked. "When I said I had enough work to keep me busy, I would get another assignment, and in reality I was working nearly as much as before for 80 percent of my salary." Plus she was definitely off the partnership track. After two years of "part-time," she went back to full-time and was assured that she was automatically back on track to partnership. She was now in her tenth year at the firm.

"They said, 'Oh, yes, nothing has changed, it is our intention to have you on partnership track.' " To remind them of their promise, she brought it up again a few months before she was up for partner. Again she was assured that her name was on the short list, that her having gone part-time temporarily wasn't a demerit. Other women at the firm were watching to see what happened. If this woman didn't make it, it would be painfully obvious that none of them would either. Less than 10 percent of the one-hundred-plus partners at this firm are women.

She did not make it. The head of her department came to tell her the news. "He came in and said, 'There were no partners made in real estate this year, and by the way, I am surprised that you were even thinking in those terms. When we brought it up at the meeting, everyone was surprised. The partners thought that your priorities were your family.' I wish I had a tape recorder going because it was the complete reversal of what they had been saying all along." When we spoke a few months after she had been turned down, she was actively looking for a job as an in-house counsel.

"With ten years experience it is hard to move to another firm," she reflects. "I don't want to be somebody's slave for two or three years before I am considered for partnership, and I'm not sure it's worth taking that chance again to be disappointed. What is the point?" She says that a few lawyers who don't make partner at her firm on schedule have stayed on in recent years, but she finds the category of "special counsel" untenable, calling it "a never-never land" with no influence, no tenure. "You are boxed into a category that is never going anywhere."

At her firm, only one woman who has ever taken maternity leave was made partner. "She did it by having a strong mentor who fought like hell for her," she adds. As for the women who are partners at the firm, she notes that they have little power and in some ways are in a worse position than the female associates: "They are always being judged on whether they are sufficient rainmakers—are they doing what they are supposed to do? If they aren't, the other partners squeeze them out by not giving them stuff to work on."

If she can't have kids and become a partner at this firm, is it worth the effort of the women behind her to even try, women who might be competent lawyers but not "superstars"? Probably not. So they leave. "My firm was hemorrhaging women," says an attorney in Boston. "The management line was, 'Oh, so-and-so left for this reason and that reason,' but the numbers proved the place was really bad for women."

Frequently the atmosphere is so anti–working mother that even bringing up part-time doesn't seem like a reasonable option. At some law firms the birth of a child is treated like a death in the family. When Adrienne Deckman was elected the first woman partner in 1987 at her midsize firm in Cleveland, she was routinely billing *twice* as many hours as some of the other partners. One year she worked on Thanksgiving so that other partners could be with family out of state. But her esprit de corps was not returned in kind. Three years later, when she announced that she was pregnant, at thirty-eight, she expected that her colleagues would be delighted for her. "The reaction was, 'Oh my God, you won't be available for such-and-such a case,' " she recalls dryly. "The question of whether I would be gone for four or six weeks was bandied about, but I knew I was entitled to three months—they had formulated the policy in the absence of anyone who was going to use it. And they were shocked when I took it."

The firm installed a computer, fax and modem in her home, which she took as a matter of course, even though she tried to make her colleagues understand she wasn't going to spend a lot of time at the PC. "The defining moment came when my son was eleven days old and the fax machine went off at ten-thirty at night. A partner was sending a closing agreement that he said I had to look at immediately. I had just started to breast-feed, and I was sitting in the chair, on a pillow, since I had had a C-section, nursing at my left breast and catching the pages from the fax with my right hand. I thought that's what I should be doing. I was going to prove that I could do it." Deckman says she would later look upon that night as her first clue that "private practice as it is presently constituted is not hospitable to women."

But it would take a while. Her can-do attitude prevailed after she went back to work. Her husband was a stay-at-home dad at that point and was able to bring their son to the office. "I would close the door and be breast-feeding, and there would come this knock and I would talk to them through the crack. Or they would call me on the intercom. But there was nothing that couldn't have waited. It's just that they were going nuts with what I was doing. That 'all for one and one for all' notion in the firm prevailed as long as I willingly shouldered the extra work when my partners had heart attacks and bypass operations. But that kind of hospitality turned into 'What have you done for me lately?' when it was my turn to take advantage of it."

On reflection Deckman says she feels that her colleagues couldn't square motherhood with the tough lawyer they knew her to be. "Having kids was a way of saying that I was soft and nurturing, and they didn't want that. They wanted me to be the biggest ball buster in the valley, which was my reputation. They weren't prepared to let me be some of the things they wanted for their wives and daughters. I was supposed to be different. I was supposed to be yoked with them in the pursuit of clients and profits." Deckman is probably right: many men still put women in specific categories—saint or sinner, good girl or bad girl, tough litigator or soft touch—and have difficulty when they cross over and are allowed to be fully rounded, complex beings. She now works in-house for a Fortune 500 company and looks back on her law firm days with amazement: "I ask myself how I ever got brainwashed into believing that what we had when I was in private practice was a life."

Sometimes it's impossible to win. Women have hid their pregnancies as long as they could. Women talk of multiple miscarriages—until they leave their stressful jobs. Women with children are "laid off" for reasons other women at the firm can't understand, when they see less competent men stay on. A woman at Oppenheimer, Wolff & Donnelly in Minneapolis clearly remembers being told by a partner that he assumed that law was a "second" career for her, apparently because she was married. "I said, 'Excuse me, I have no children and there are none on the horizon. I am coming in on weekends at eight A.M. and signing out at four P.M. What are you talking about?'" Women at Stroock & Stroock & Lavan in New York say they notice that when a woman is pregnant some partners pile on the work. As one senior associate says, "It's like a test when you get pregnant around here—the attitude seems to be, 'Let's see what she's made of.' It is a way of drawing attention to the fact that you are a woman. Gender is *always* an issue here." The mother-to-be, meantime, is afraid to say anything for fear that she will be perceived as not able to keep her end up. At another firm one woman said that a senior partner from another department asked her how long she had been working part-time—when she had never worked part-time. He'd just assumed she was because she had kids.

Another woman lawyer who was working at home one afternoon says she was asked by another woman lawyer—a partner—who lived in her neighborhood to watch her kids for a few moments while she went to a pay phone to call her office. The woman was supposed to be on the road that day, not at home with her sick kid, but she didn't feel she could tell the truth to her office. She wanted to make the call from a noisy intersection so it would sound as though she were on the car phone, not at home. Paranoia? Maybe in this case paranoia is knowing all the facts.

As *The New York Times* once noted, "The big time belongs to the single, the childless, or the women with a twenty-four-hour nanny."

DIFFERENT EXPECTATIONS

The older generation of female lawyers, the pioneering generation, that broke into law in the sixties and seventies did not, paradoxically, experience these problems in the same way. They were a small, self-selected group of highly motivated, highly intelligent and persevering women who were willing to place career above motherhood—they had to be to break out of the mold of *Kinder, Küch und Kirche* and get into law school in the first place. They considered themselves fortunate to be able to be working in the law at all. Many sacrificed a personal life that included a husband and children. Or they had their children first and became lawyers second, or married late and inherited grown step-children.

In contrast, young women coming out of law schools today accept as a fait accompli what the women's movement fought for and expect that the law firms have remade themselves to accommodate them to a much greater degree than they have. This younger generation of women lawyers, larger by the hundreds of thousands, is more diverse than the preceding one, culturally, intellectually and psychologically. Many are simply not willing to put their ovaries, or their mothering instincts, on hold for the sake of a career. They know they are at least as competent as their male peers, yet they see them move ahead more easily than they do. So these women drop out.

Catherine Hagen, whose two children were nearly adolescents when she began at O'Melveny & Myers in 1978, recalls that her generation was defensive about proving themselves. "We accepted the idea that some jobs were incompatible with being a mother with young children," she says. "Young women today are less willing to roll with the punches. They are more willing to quit right now and keep looking until they find the right position."

If they did have children, these trailblazers more willingly accepted turning over their care to others. Sociologist Cynthia Fuchs Epstein, who has tracked the career of women lawyers for more than twenty-five years, observes that for the younger generation of women the standards of what is acceptable child care have risen: "The middle-class mothers of today feel strongly that they need to be attentive to their children's activities in a way that their own parents may not have been for them. I hear all the time about needing to 'help with the homework,' but we were told to do our homework by ourselves. The different assumptions about motherhood are not helpful to mothers who want to combine parenting with a career. Part of it is backlash, part of it comes out of a steady stream of a psychoanalytic orientation that says that what parents do at a young age is of ultimate importance to the child, and that the parent can't be replaced by a surrogate."

Epstein, author of *Women in Law* and a 1995 survey of law firms in New York City, also notes that some of the senior women have family responsibilities of their own, a fact sometimes overlooked by the younger women. "They are not all alone, and they don't have a wife at home to help out either. It's not that they aren't helpful to the younger generation, but these younger women expect so much from them. And the older generation may not have a lot of power anyway."

MONEY AND SATISFACTION

If it is true that 50 percent of all women hired by law firms leave law within five years, it is nothing short of amazing that the men in charge don't do more to reverse this incredible brain drain. Women who are able to work part-time, or to find some other way to combine their careers with a genuine family life, do not leave in anything like these numbers. Talking to women who have been able to do this, in fact, I was repeatedly struck by how happy all of them were with their lives—even when it has meant that they make much less money or are out of the running for partnership.

Giving up personal career gains, as well as money, for many women lawyers is no hardship. In many, but not all, households where the wife is a lawyer, the man still continues to be the one who makes more money. While the statistics for women attorneys may be different from those for the general population, given the income of attorneys in general, a number of the women interviewed who work less than full-time said they gladly took a saner lifestyle in lieu of higher income—even when they were the primary earner. "I make more money than my husband, but we don't have a mortgage on a second home," said one woman partner who gave it up to work regular hours as in-house counsel, since part-time was not an option at her firm. "How much money do you need?"

"This is about as perfect as it gets," says part-time attorney Deborah Tuchman. "I won't have to look back and say, 'Look what I gave up.' The time when kids grow up is so short over the course of a fifty-year career. This way, I get to have both." A partner at Brown & Bain in Tucson, Diane Madenci, who also works somewhat reduced hours, says, "I'm pretty smug about it. I can't imagine life being a lot better than it is now, and that is due to the receptive attitude of the firm." These women have found a happy balance between career and family. They are not measuring success in the same way as men. Money and prestige, they assure me, are not everything. Their image of the American dream is quite different from their male counterparts'.

Working part-time obviously entails making less money. The usual figure is 60 to 80 percent of a full-time salary, depending on the hours worked. The monetary sacrifice may be considerable. Female lawyers, as a group, make less money than males in the first place; when you factor in sacrifices made for child care, the difference becomes exaggerated. A 1993 study of University of Michigan Law School alumni fifteen years after graduation found that "the earnings given up are, for those who make the trade [child rearing for money], large and long-lasting." The women who worked part-time did so for an average of three years, but the overall effect on their average earning power as compared with that of men was an "earnings penalty" of 17 percent, even when the reduced hours were taken into consideration. "On the average, the women in the Michigan sample earned $86,335 a year; 17 percent of this is close to $15,000!" the authors concluded. It was care of children and not their mere existence that created the gap. Once hours and experience were figured in, there were no significant differences in salary between women with and without children. Although the Michigan sample included only eighty women who went to an elite school, the disparate findings concur with other salary data for lawyers.

An analysis of 1990 census data found that the mean earnings of all women practicing law was $40,000, compared with $73,000 for men. To come up with that figure, UCLA law professor Richard Sander analyzed the data of a nearly random 5 percent sample of all lawyers whose principal occupation was the practice of law, approximately thirty-eight thousand lawyers in all. Most of the gap is accounted for by differences in hours worked, practice setting, and age, he says. Once these and other factors are accounted for, Sander found only a 3 percent gap in the hourly earnings of men and women lawyers between the ages of twenty-five and thirty. For older lawyers the gap is much larger, he notes, but it is difficult with this database to control for differences in work history. "It may be," Sander says, "that older women lawyers suffer from the effects of past discrimination, or while they may start at equal pay levels they have lower chances of promotion, or that

women suffer disproportionately from interruptions in their careers for family responsibilities." Using figures from six years later, *Working Woman* found
that the differential had narrowed slightly: a 1996 salary survey, compiled
from Justice Department and private accounting firm statistics, found that
overall women in law had a median salary of $47,684; men, $64,324. Whatever the specific numbers, women are not catching up very fast.

It is true that law firms have become somewhat more flexible in the last
decade, simply because of the high percentage of women working in them, and
this flexibility undoubtedly allows partners to justify paying women less. But
overall they have not made the kind of internal shift that is needed if they are
ever going to be truly satisfying places for women generally. It has not been as
simple as putting up parking lots when people started driving cars. Perhaps
"family values" at law firms means making the workplace inhospitable to wom-
en—that way they will be "encouraged" to stay home with the children. And
although the drastic belt-tightening of most law firms is over, they have not
similarly relaxed their image of what a committed lawyer is. "Law firms are still
downsizing, and even if the economy is getting better, people are still very
nervous about asking for special treatment," comments career consultant Sheila
Nielsen. Instead they quit the firm and make up a practice that suits them or find
work elsewhere. In other words, they leave.

And the men just don't get it. When I asked Daniel J. Burns, former
director of recruitment at Baker & McKenzie, the largest law firm in the
world, why women left law firms in such large numbers, he said that he
didn't know. "This is a problem that law firms are desperate to solve. We
are constantly rethinking the issue. We are at a loss to know why there is
such a high rate of attrition."

Perhaps they ought to start by self-examination. Baker & McKenzie was the
firm involved in the recruitment scandal at the University of Chicago in 1988.
They fired an associate with AIDS, who sued and may have inspired the film
Philadelphia. In 1994 a secretary who sued for sexual harassment won a
multimillion-dollar award. As I write, the decision is under appeal. In 1995,
after four years of litigation, the first female partner, Ingrid Beall, settled a suit
against the firm for sex and age discrimination; she charged they had taken away
her clients and shrunk her salary by two-thirds. Through 1995 Baker & Mc-
Kenzie has contributed more than $715,000 in grants to students of color at
twenty law schools around the country. While the grants are not to be denigrated, they are a minute dollar amount of the firm's revenues, with its fifty-

four offices in thirty-four countries and more than 1,800 attorneys, and in reality the grants have zero effect on what it means to be a female attorney, or a black attorney, at the firm.

In 1996 slightly more than 7 percent (thirty-eight) of Baker & McKenzie's five-hundred-plus equity partners are women; in Chicago, the largest office of the firm, the figure drops to below 7 percent (five out of seventy-seven). As we go to press, none are African American.

RAINMAKING

The Last Frontier

You have to close the deal—you have to come out and say, "I'd like to have your business."—**LAUREL BELLOWS**, TALKING ABOUT RAINMAKING

WHETHER OR NOT one brings in business is the Great Wall dividing the haves and have-nots of clout and compensation at law firms. Don't do it, and you're likely to lose out in the partnership sweepstakes, no matter how good a backroom lawyer you are. At many firms partnership confers the added expectation that to some degree generating business, or "rainmaking," as it is known in the business, is part of one's job. Fail, and you're likely to be frozen out of the circle of influence, and what's worse, you could even be voted out of partnership. In plain English, that's fired. As we have seen, good lawyers are a dime a dozen.

Says Nancy Atlas, formerly a partner at the Houston firm of Sheinfeld, Maley and Kay: "Rainmaking is the litmus test for partnership or shareholder status, and it is becoming increasingly more important as the profession constricts." Atlas, once a rainmaker and now a judge, says it's not necessary to have generated a great deal of new business when an individual is typically considered for shareholder, since the person will only be thirty or so, but the potential must be evident. "They need to have brought in new clients in small matters, or induced existing clients to give the firm additional work in new areas, or increased the volume of work that these clients do with the firm."

In the current competitive cauldron of the law, with too many lawyers and too little business, patriarchs of law firms no longer can rest on their laureled behinds as they go gentle into retirement. In the past, senior partners traded on their wisdom and judgment, as well as on their earlier years of toil and the business once generated, in return for a lighter workload as they got older. That's no longer true—even at such bastions of gentility as Cadwalader, Wickersham & Taft, whose origins in 1792 make it New York's oldest firm and whose very name proclaims it to be an assemblage of men with the whitest of shoes. Twenty-five partners in their late thirties and forties led an uprising in the fall of 1994 that resulted in 17 senior partners (out of 105) getting the unceremonial boot. It was an unprecedented move, for Cadwalader had no provision in its partnership agreement for firing a partner. Clearly it does now.*

The obvious message to the entire legal community was, Produce or you're out. How one bills long hours is obvious. But exactly how does a lawyer generate business? Is it all word of mouth? How do you get those mouths going? Until a few years ago lawyers didn't blatantly advertise for business. That's changed, and now the airwaves and subway cars are full of ads for personal injury and family lawyers. But that's not the way most legal business is generated, and certainly not juicy commercial accounts. One has to be more subtle. One could, for instance, be wellborn, as undoubtedly were a number of the elders of the aforementioned Cadwalader, Wickersham & Taft. That way you were likely to end up rooming in prep school or be a member of the right eating club at Princeton with scions of other wealthy families, heirs who would one day inherit the family business and need a lawyer, preferably several, all from your firm. Even today major corporate accounts are gathered in just this way. Being born with a silver spoon also bought you the memberships into the right country clubs and the downtown eating clubs all over America where contacts that lead to business are made.

To be sure, things have loosened up. Life is more democratic today. Lawyers looking for business can rub shoulders with the people who have it to give through all sorts of social, cultural, educational and philanthropic organizations now besides the Brook in New York or the Union Club in Philadelphia or the Louisiana Debating and Literary Association in New Orleans. But it remains

---

* To be fair, the young Turks had a point. One of the senior partners on the management committee continued to be credited with originating more than $17 million in work—and his compensation tied to that amount—even though he did almost no work for the clients and billed only thirty-six hours in 1993, according to a Cadwalader financial document. But until the bloodletting, the senior partners running the firm apparently saw no problem with the arrangement; such is the strength of alliances among partners and the weight allotted rainmaking.

true that social contacts of one sort or another are one of the most productive ways for lawyers to make the rain fall.

Another way is simply to call up the decision makers at companies and ask them out for a meal, charm them, and ask them for their business. A third way is to become an expert in your area, write articles and give speeches, and generate business simply because people will want you for your amply demonstrated know-how. A fourth way is to take on high-profile cases, no matter how impossible, and attract attention to yourself with the publicity that the case generates. Even if you lose the case, people will remember your name. It's an old rule: Publicity, even bad publicity, is good.

Young attorneys don't usually have to worry about becoming major rainmakers until they are in their late thirties, when a good many will have been made partners. By then they are expected to have a certain level of prestige and influence in their communities. "After about twelve or fifteen years as a lawyer who does the actual work, you are expected to devote part of your effort to bringing in business," says a (male) rainmaker at a 150-attorney New York firm. "We'd go out of business otherwise. But it's at this point that for some reason women drop out of the picture."

WHAT'S THE PROBLEM?

The difficulties that women as rainmakers face are real. Let's start with whom they know. Being well connected does not often work the same way for women as it does for men. Even if an aspiring attorney is in the same sorority or rooms with the heir of a family whose last name is Maytag or Post or Deere, it's certainly not as likely that she will turn out to be the person who chooses a law firm to handle her family's legal business as it would be if *she* were *he*. Rich sons may go into law, but heiresses typically don't. Rich daughters still tend to marry well and become involved in volunteer charity work. If they do have a career, it's more likely to be in the arts rather than the law.

Even if a woman lawyer does get in the right club, or serve on a board dotted with important corporate contacts, she is more likely to form friendships with the other women there and get together with them for lunch, or tennis, than she is to cultivate the men. The likelihood of her new friend being able to swing legal business her way is slim. In a 1993 Prentice-Hall survey of more than 550 female litigators, nearly 90 percent stated that their business development opportunities were either "severely" (34.6 percent) or "somewhat" (55.3 percent) limited at their firms, and the same percentage of women said the main reason for this was the lack of women in powerful positions at client companies.

Leila Kern, who started a law firm with four other female attorneys in Boston, says that when she wrote to ten women suggested by the dean of a graduate school of management—women the dean felt would be in positions of power and able to steer business to her fledging all-female firm—she found that "to a person they told me they were not in that position—a guy doing the same thing would not have come up with the same response." Kern was almost forty and a psychology professor when she went to law school in the early eighties. As a child she had dreamed of being a lawyer like Perry Mason. She clearly loves what she does. When asked if being a lawyer was all she imagined, she said crisply, "No—it's too hard to get business. The men have preset networks, and all the referrals in law are made on the basis of friendship, not quality." Medicine, she observed, was more of a meritocracy, with doctors referring their patients to physicians with the best reputations, "but that's not how work gets referred in the law."

One way to get to know potential clients has always been through private clubs, a troublesome route for women and people of color, since clubs for centuries have been restricted. Take golf clubs. It has long been acknowledged that lots of friendships that lead to business have been forged on the links or at the nineteenth hole. But while the barriers are coming down at golf clubs, some of them retain the all-male memberships (or only allow wives) or have policies that deny women tee times when it is most convenient to golf—say, on Saturday morning—or they restrict certain eating rooms to men only. The Mill River Country Club on Long Island, until a few years ago when it was embarrassed by an Op-Ed piece in *The New York Times,* took restrictions to the absurd: women were allowed to eat in the main dining room, but they could not sit in chairs that have arms. (Is it because the men need more propping up?) When the Women and the Law Section of the Texas State Bar Association wanted to push for legislation to end sex and race discrimination at private clubs, the state bar board of directors not only voted not to support the proposed bill, but also voted that the women's section may not sponsor it on their own behalf. That was in 1993. The framework of the ABA itself, long considered an upper-class white male bulwark, caught up with the times only recently: in 1994 the board of governors passed a resolution stating that no officer of the organization could belong to a club that restricted membership on the basis of race or gender. In 1993 both the outgoing and incoming presidents belonged to restricted clubs.

Golf clubs are not the issue for everybody, since fewer women than men play golf (is it because historically they have been barred from so many courses?), but a more critical issue is the downtown all-male eating clubs that used to be found in every city. To crack them it took a 1988 Supreme Court decision that held that state and local laws against their restrictive policies could be enforced. If businesswomen are denied entrance at the places where other businesspeople meet and greet one another, it's axiomatic they are going to have to work harder and longer to get to know the people who have business to give them. While some clubs have bylaws that restrict business from being done on premises, when memberships are examined by deposition it frequently comes out that many members' initiation fees and dues are paid for by their employers.

Beyond the robust health of the old boys' network, corporate attitudes in these increasingly conservative times have not been good for women. While sheer numbers have made it impossible (and financially stupid) not to advance the best people, and some of them are women, a lackadaisical attitude—call it downright resistance—toward affirmative action, whether mandated or voluntary, has hurt all minorities. A considerable number of corporations do not even bother to keep demographic statistics on their managers, even though it is required by the Equal Employment Opportunity Commission. One consequence is that the number of women with the power to select their friends' law firms has not kept pace with the number of women attorneys at said law firms. This is in spite of the fact that droves of disillusioned female attorneys who flee law firms wind up at the more hospitable havens of corporate America's legal departments. As it happens, women don't automatically refer business to other women, says Laurel Bellows, chair of the ABA Commission on Women in the Profession and half of an eponymous law firm in Chicago. "Because women are used to seeing men in a certain role, they may think of them first when they need, say, a bankruptcy lawyer, just as the men do," she says. "Women need to be more conscious about referring business to other women. It may take two or three extra phone calls to check the credentials, but isn't it worth the effort?"

WHITHER THE TIME?

One major hurdle women face is time: if they have a family, where do they find the time to practice law, be involved with their families, *and* generate new business? Just when they are in the best possible position to attract new business—a dozen years or so out of law school—they're likely to be having children. The time that they might have to have dinner, play golf, or otherwise socialize with potential clients is precisely the time many choose to spend with their children, especially if they are married to men who don't share child care responsibilities at home. Most don't. While it's true that lawyers marry lawyers, if one of them is going to reduce his or her work schedule, it won't be the man. The added pressure to go out and sell can be overwhelming. A lawyer who is highly regarded in her firm but who does not see herself as a rainmaker says, "I do good work for my clients, and I am interested in their problems and how we can solve them, but do I have the energy at the end of the day to go to dinners asking people I barely know for new business? No. I want to go home to see my kid and try to keep it [her family, her marriage] all running."

While some men experience the same time demands—but not, of course, to the degree that women with children will—much of the business-getting activities are male bonding rituals, such as playing golf, attending football games, dining at a downtown club after a game of racquetball, or even attending so-called high-class "strip" clubs, all activities that tend to exclude women. Men may not even want them around because their presence will change the tenor of the outing. The jokes might be less bawdy, the drinking more restrained. And there is an added caveat: While some women may have the potential to enjoy this kind of entertaining, generally they haven't been acculturated into it. Are they football fans? Do they play golf? Furthermore if you are initiating the contact, how do you ask a man to meet you for drinks, for dinner, and ask him to give your firm his business without feeling a little, well, odd?

The male rainmaker quoted earlier says that at the seminars on attracting new business he gives for colleagues at his firm, he finds that when the women talk about entertaining to seek new business—targeting people, frequently men, whom they don't know well, taking them out for a meal, and asking if they would like to switch law firms—the word the women use is "prostitution." It's not hard to understand why: soliciting business seems like soliciting, period, and women practically from birth are taught not to engage in this kind of behavior. Whether by nature or nurture, most women aren't geared at this point to make jokes and be entertaining and pick up the check . . . and imply "Hire me!" They fear being misunderstood. They fear being rejected. "Individuals who learn how to ask for business directly from people who are almost strangers have to be able to stomach a great deal of rejection, because more times than not, the answer is something along the lines of 'I like you just fine, but I'm happy with the law firm that I have,'" says the male attorney. "Women have a harder time with it.

Is it because men get used to asking women out at an early age and get steeled to rejection?" he asks. "Or get used to being cut from a team because they weren't as good as the next guy?"

When they ask men to social events, women fear that clients will feel they are coming on to them. Says Sonya Hamlin, a legal communications expert based in New York, "Being socially aggressive gets mixed up with sexual images and what a woman's role is supposed to be. While women lawyers have already broken out of the traditional women's role by being a lawyer in the first place, they need to go the rest of the way and learn how to sell themselves and their firm." Hamlin points out that the get-acquainted outings are just that—the client wants to know that he or she and the attorney get along and will enjoy spending time together. Working on a case, for instance, may involve going out of town together, and if there is no rapport, the trip will be unnecessarily dreary. Assuring clients that spending time together will be pleasant is as much a part of legal skills today as being able to write a brief or present a case.

Another issue when entertaining men is the clients' wives. Not only are women uncomfortable initiating social events, the men's wives may not like it either. It's one thing to go to a hockey game or to dinner with another guy; it's another matter when the "guy" turns out to be female. Some women solve the problem by asking the wife too, but that creates other problems—do you have an escort yourself? Will the two guys spend the evening talking sports to each other, while you and the woman look for common ground? If that happens, how will you bond with the potential client?

In the past, fresh young lawyers eased into the role of sales by starting out as a sidekick to a senior attorney—a mentor—who took them along on rain-making expeditions, whether a meal, a round of golf with clients, or formal presentations to a client, known as "beauty contests" by the participants. Women of an earlier generation, when there were few women at law firms, generally had mentors who brought them along (except to restricted golf clubs), and the mentors were nearly always men. But today, given the time constraints on all attorneys, senior partners have little time or inclination to be mentors the same way the earlier generation was. Young lawyers are more isolated than ever and young women lawyers the most isolated of all.

Even if they do the required socializing, women still have a hard time actually being direct and saying the words "I want your business." Men grow up understanding these professional relationships; women say it makes them uneasy, that it's crass asking an acquaintance for business, which is, in effect, selling a service to be performed for money. "I tell women that to get the business they have to ask for it. They have to close the deal," says Bellows. "And a week later they call me back and say, 'You know, it worked.' Asking outright may feel uncomfortable, but women have to do it if they want to succeed. You can't blame the guys for not wanting a woman who is not a rainmaker for a partner."

I COULD NEVER HAVE DONE IT WITHOUT YOU . . .

The last hurdle to being a known rainmaker in the male-dominated law firm has to do with the difference in men's and women's styles. Studies of gender differences suggest that in general women operate in a more collegial, and less harshly competitive, manner than men. Some men, for instance, say that the women in their firms have made them more humane places to work simply because they are less aggressive. Women are quietly succeeding at some firms as the two or three lawyers directly under the managing partner (or as the managing partner) who keep the place running smoothly with a minimum of tension. They are more likely to govern by consensus rather than strict hierarchy. They are less likely to trumpet their achievements. They are likely to use the royal "we" when talking about how a new client was landed.

Claiming credit for business is a political act, and some women shy away from it. "Other women at the firm are always telling me that I should speak up and take credit for what I'm responsible for," says one woman, "but I've got two kids and I don't want to get involved in the politics of the firm right now." To an outsider, it is hard to see how merely taking credit can be all that time consuming; later will be too late, since everyone will see her a certain way. Women are likely to pass credit around for fear of being seen as too ambitious, an attribute that is still perceived as a negative in women. For having the temerity to have a successful career, *The New York Times* called Zoë Baird, for instance, "ambitious," a word not used about men with similar career paths. And women may be just as critical of each other when one steps out of character and demands the credit that is due her. Men, used to being ranked in sports and business, the theory goes, also assess themselves constantly and have no problem drawing attention to their successes and assuming the role of top dog. Michele Corash of Morrison & Foerster says:

"I see my own colleagues—women in this and other firms—who are for sure the reasons certain clients came, but the women give a lot of credit to others to deflect attention from themselves, and the result is a perception that goes, 'She is a good lawyer, yeah, the clients like her, but . . .' Since she isn't getting on the airwaves saying, 'I got this client,' she doesn't get the credit she should.

"You hear the women say how wonderful the other people are, but when you listen to the big rainmaking males, it is pure self-promotion. The style of women that makes them incredibly effective in the smooth operation of organizations also limits them. By not claiming credit for what they do, the powers-that-be don't think the women have much to do with the success of the firm. There is just this phenomenal mythology about women not being rainmakers. But recognition is a matter of perception. The lack of recognition women get has everything to do with the style of women."

How I came to interview Corash is a case in point. I had called up the managing partner of MoFo's Los Angeles office. The firm is known to be one of the best places to work in the country for women, people of color and gays. I asked him to direct me to female rainmakers at his firm. He suggested Corash, a "terrific" woman in the San Francisco office. Her field is environmental law, an area of the law that didn't exist before 1970, the year the clean air bill passed. As a new area of the law, it was wide open to women, and today they are clearly among the stars in it.

But what's most interesting is that he overlooked two rainmakers right in front of his nose, one in his office and the other in nearby Orange County. Their areas, banking and business, are more hotly competitive with men.

"You see plenty of discrimination against the best women," says another partner at Morrison & Foerster. "If you look at the stars at the firm in each level of compensation, you see a few women in each group who jump off the page and should be in the next higher level. They are just not perceived of as rainmakers as successful as the men." A New York attorney echoes her thoughts: "If the younger men were scrutinized with the same microscope as the women—as to who brings in what—they would come up pretty much the same at my firm. There are a number of women who have done very well for themselves and the firm, but they just don't get the same credit as the men."

Who gets credit for new business? Is it the person who lunches and makes a friend of a prospective client? Or is it the quiet but competent attorney who actually does the work and keeps the client happy so that he gives the firm additional work? It's an ongoing debate that can turn vicious. A lawyer said that while a woman at her large New York firm got a call from an acquaintance who was steering a nice chunk of business to her firm, the woman had trouble claiming credit for it. The firm had a reputation for handling this kind of matter, and the man who headed the department where the business was going said that it was *his* reputation, and not her contact, that was decisive. Therefore he should get the credit for bringing in this new client, not she.

Sometimes even when the woman's reputation is the reason the client came to the firm, more powerful men gang up on her and take it away. Earlier we learned what happened to attorney Johnine Brown, not once, but three times before she started her own firm. Male attorneys at her firms simply tried to take her business away from her. Says Margaret L. Moses, an attorney in New Jersey: "I know a number of women associates who have brought in major business, only to have the client whisked away by a partner who wines and dines the client at firm expense. Excluded from the social events, the woman associate may end up not even working on the matter." At some of the megafirms women have trouble getting their business development plans approved because the men in power find reasons they should go after such-and-such clients once they are presented, or they say that the potential clients conflict with business they already have.

Louise LaMothe, former head of the ABA's litigation section and a known rainmaker, found that switching to a smaller firm increased her clout measurably. "If you have a book of portable business that is worth a million, and you are in a firm where the total connections are between twenty and thirty million, you will be a more significant factor than if you are in a firm where there are hundreds of millions of dollars of business," she says. LaMothe herself went from a larger firm to a smaller one, Riordan & McKinzie. "The bigger the firm, the more opportunities there are for conflicts, and if you are the second person in the door, the other one gets what he wants." Yes, it can happen to anyone, but since some partners have trouble seeing women as potential powers in the hierarchy, the women are more likely to get squashed in the stampede of male lawyers looking to increase their client base. Men do not give up power—and the income that goes with it—lightly. "The glass ceiling may have moved up," says a woman at Morrison & Foerster, "but it is still there. Just look at the top compensation group in my firm—there just aren't any women in the group of six. And there should be."

Morrison & Foerster, by the way, which has hundreds of attorneys, has several powerful women. *Working Mother* has rated it as one of the best places to work. At other firms, such as the macho powerhouse Skadden, Arps, careful accounting of who brought in what may do women more good than what appears to be the more casual attitude of MoFo. Skadden, Arps does have a woman in its top compensation group.

Several women partners who left large firms in disgust to strike out on their own—with success—said that the political infighting and jealousies that arose out of their being rainmakers poisoned the atmosphere and was the main reason they left. They usually took their clients with them. One partner who is the head of her department at a large West Coast firm says that whenever she publishes an article or is quoted somewhere, the men in her office—and only the men, she notes—sarcastically ask her for the name of her publicity agent. "Their attitude is, 'Why else would anyone want to write about me?' Certainly not because I'm an expert in my area." Publishing and lecturing in one's field is one way to attract new business that suits women's temperament.

"I would give a lecture, or be quoted, and my picture might be used—the backbiting and jealousy was horrendous," says another woman who successfully used the expert avenue to generate business at Stroock & Stroock & Lavan. "Because my stuff got into print a lot—and my picture often ran—the rumor at the firm was that I was sleeping with the editor of one publication. If I did what I thought I was supposed to be doing to stand out in my field, I was criticized for calling attention to myself. And if I didn't do these things to get business, then I wasn't doing what I was supposed to be doing. Male colleagues would have been lionized for doing what I did. I just got criticized—I was too aggressive—and so I stopped."

"Women can't win because they stand out at the top simply by being women," she says, "so they are under constant scrutiny. The Japanese have a saying that goes 'The nail that stands out gets pounded down,' and that was me. I was miserable for a long time before I left." She is among the growing number of women who fled megafirms to open their own firms. She employs two full-time junior attorneys and two part-time senior attorneys, both of whom also renounced the status of big New York firms to work in a more civil atmosphere. All are women. The part-time attorneys do most of their work out of their own homes and are connected to the office by fax and modem. The woman whose name is on the stationery says she has never been happier as a professional. She says in some ways it is easier to attract clients than when she was at a large firm because they know that she will be supervising or doing the work herself, and remember, she is an acknowledged expert in her field.

WOMEN ARE SUCCEEDING IN SPITE OF THE OBSTACLES

Despite the obstacles, women are succeeding as rainmakers in some cases. When Victoria Stratman came back from a maternity leave as a brand-new partner at O'Melveny & Myers in Los Angeles, she headed straight into an eight-week trial that kept her busy for months. But during that time another big client moved out of California, and when the trial was over she found herself with no work and the phone not ringing. "It was a frightening place to be," she recollects. "No matter how much anyone emphasizes that business generation is part of the game once you are a partner, you do not realize the pressure until you are solely responsible for feeding yourself and others."

Initially Stratman connected with someone at the firm who generated business, but she found that role unsatisfactory and so spent some of her suddenly free time actively figuring out how to generate new business. She got involved in the litigation section of the ABA, volunteering for committees and the like, and pursued successful women rainmakers to find out what they did to succeed. In time she formed a network of friends around the country, some of whom have turned into clients or referred them to her. "You have to treat finding new business like a new litigation matter," she says. "You have to figure out a plan and how to get where you want to go."

Because her area of expertise is labor law, she made it her business to get to know the decision makers in human resources at California corporations, and as often as not these turned out to be women. She eschews golf for "a lot of lunches, horseback riding, going to the track and horse shows, the occasional baseball game." She and one female client went on an overnight trip to Napa Valley, where they tasted a lot of wine and talked about their personal lives. "You find something you have in common and go from there. Why do women have such a hard time? Time constraints. How did I get over it? Desperation. If you always rely on someone else to bring home the bacon, you are always dependent on other people and you never have any clout or flexibility. You will always be the second chair on a case."

While Stratman sometimes does dinners with spouses as a foursome, she finds them problematic if the client is a man—then he and her husband sit around and talk sports while she and the wife talk about the kids. "It's not that I'm bored, it's just that talking about kids is not the point. Dinners with spouses work out fine if the client is a woman. Then the men can talk about the Giants all night, and she and I get to know each other and fit in some business."

But Stratman's entertaining is incidental to the personal relationships she forms with her clients, a trait she shares with many women rainmakers. They talk not about "entertaining," but about maintaining relationships. They talk about their clients as "friends." "We are basically in the same business," said an education lawyer of her clients, who tend to be members of school boards and school principals, "so we're never at a loss with what to talk about."

"I can't go out and play basketball," says one woman at a firm where that's done with clients. "I have a different style. I develop a good relationship and hope that down the road new business will come because they have been so well taken care of." Another woman said that since women were used to "taking care of people," they were more likely to find out what was going on in other areas of a current client's business, and what his other problems were, and help him figure out how to solve them. That nurturing quality of women may turn out to serve them well in retaining clients, but all too often retaining clients does not get the same recognition, or accounting on the financial ledger, that bringing in new ones does. Any competent lawyer can keep a client, the thinking goes. Of course, given the competition today, that's simply not true.

Some women have pursued other routes to rainmaking for their firms. Nancy Atlas became known in Democratic politics in Texas as a big-ticket fund-raiser, a high-profile endeavor usually pursued by men. She raised hundreds of thousands of dollars at one point for former governor Ann Richards and wound up getting appointed to the chair of a Texas higher education coordinating board. "The statewide appointment gave me the opportunity to deal with executives in business and leaders in the education community, as well as many politicians that I would have never met otherwise. And if I ran a meeting well, and got their respect for doing so, perhaps that sowed the seeds for future business." It probably also got her appointed to the federal bench.

Then there is the "expert" route mentioned earlier. You attract business because you are known for a certain kind of legal expertise. Johnine Brown in Chicago, for instance, writes a column on environmental issues for the *Illinois Legal Times* and gives lots of speeches in her area of expertise; her small and, to date, all-female firm, Brown & Bryant, has corporate clients that include John Deere and Sears. Michelle Vaillancourt in St. Paul raised her own profile and that of her firm, Winthrop & Weinstine, through her involvement in both the local bar and the Minnesota Women Lawyers Association and publishing in the field of securities law. Incidentally Vaillancourt admits to playing golf (rarely) and tennis (more often) with clients. Barbara Billauer, who has her own small boutique firm in Lido Beach, Long Island, New York, says that she found asking for business for herself much easier to do than when she was asking for one of the megafirms for which she formerly and unhappily toiled. M. Ellen Carpenter, of the all-female firm of Kern, Hagerty, Roach & Carpenter in Boston, served on a federal bankruptcy panel for Massachusetts for two years to become better known and now sits on the board of directors of a credit union. Carpenter is one of the group of twenty women lawyers in the Boston area who dine together regularly and call themselves the Bankruptcy Babes. They often refer business to one another—an old girls' network, if you will.

Muzette Hill, the only African American partner at Lord, Bissell & Brook in Chicago, found that while men at her firm were simply handed some clients from a retiring partner, she was on her own. So she developed a niche of expertise in one area of corporate insurance, her specialty. A few years ago Hill became aware of a new insurance product, professional liability insurance. She made a point of meeting all the major players in the field, reading whatever she could find, and eventually she was writing and lecturing herself on the topic. Now when the insurance companies are writing new policies in this area, she is someone they call upon. And she has not scorned seeking out other women and men of color. "I target black managers—the network is really small and I am unique," she says. "I speak their language. Nine out of ten times they are not the people who make the decisions about which person to hire, but they can get me to the decision makers. And it is all beginning to pay off."

Finally there's the publicity route to new business. Think of Leslie Abramson, who defended the Menendez brothers. Think of the women defense lawyers who were all over the television screen, commenting on the O. J. Simpson case. Think of Cora Walker, a legendary African American lawyer in Harlem. She won a big case two years after she got her law degree in 1946, and the press she garnered from it sent her on her way. It happened this way. Her father, whom she had not seen in ten years, read in the *Amsterdam News* that his daughter was a lawyer and called upon her after being struck by an automobile driven by the former president of the city bar. As might be expected, the errant driver had good insurance. At a settlement conference, Judge William T. Powers asked Walker, black, young and female, how come she was handling such a big case, since lawyers can practice for years and not get a case this big. "With all due respect, Judge," she replied, "that's none of your business."

This was a bit too uppity for Judge Powers. When the settlement talks fell apart and the case went to trial, he cited her for contempt for keeping him waiting ten minutes while she phoned a witness to ask him to come down to court. She was convicted but later exonerated on appeal. She also won a $40,000 judgment for her father—analogous to more than a quarter of a million today. Walker became a heroine in Harlem. Her firm, Walker & Bailey [Bailey is her son, Lawrence], now has a client list that runs to Conrail and MCI. But all of Walker's business didn't come walking through the door without her going after it. "I read *How to Win Friends and Influence People,* and it said to join everything to meet people, and hand out business cards, and mention every chance you get that you are a lawyer," she says. "And that's how I did it."

LAW FIRM
LUST

Sexual Harassment

The entrance of sexual harassment into the legal sphere has recently become the favorite target for those who wish to point out the so-called oppressive power of feminism.——DRUCILLA CORNELL

ONE WOULD THINK that lawyers would know better. They are the ones called in to clean up the mess, to offer a settlement, to fight the claim in court, after some bozo is charged with sexual harassment. One would think. One would be wrong.

Fully 89 percent of female litigators surveyed by Prentice-Hall in 1993 stated that sexual harassment in the workplace was either "somewhat of a problem" or a "large problem" or a "pervasive problem." More than half—55 percent—of the women said they had been sexually harassed in the course of their jobs in the last five years. Apparently even lawyers have learned little if anything since Anita Hill's testimony in 1991 about her former boss, now Supreme Court Justice Clarence Thomas. (Of course, Thomas wasn't sued and did get the job he was determined to have. It often works the same way in law firms.)

Other findings from the survey of 553 female litigators—who were the only women surveyed for Prentice-Hall's publication, *Inside Litigation*—portray a picture of sexual harassment that is more than a little tawdry. Associates in small firms have the trickiest terrain to navigate, which should come as a surprise to no one. Nearly two-thirds of them report that they have been sexually harassed. *That means that two out of three female associates at small firms will be sexually harassed at the office.*

This does not mean that each of these incidents of sexual harassment is a direct or implied quid pro quo exchange; but unquestionably enough of them are to make sexual harassment a serious problem for female attorneys, especially those in their twenties and thirties. In general it's less of an issue after that because women get more power and are savvier about how to handle loutish Lotharios. At the same time, men are more likely to feel their hormonal juices flowing with nubile younger women and hit on them more. A 1992 *Working Woman* survey found that almost 30 percent of the incidents of sexual harassment occur when the women are eighteen to twenty-four years old, a vastly disproportionate number given the small size of this age group in the workforce.

Sexual harassment is about power and status, yes; but it is also about *sex*. The demanding hours of a high-powered law career throw together lawyers for twelve or fourteen hours a day, all working intensely for the same goal, with no time for a life outside the office. While female associates are almost always over twenty-four, they are most often younger than, and often single and available to, the men they work with and admire, and this combination of factors is a prime setting for lust and love. Men are attracted to youth; women are attracted to power. It's no wonder that passion strikes so frequently among this populace.

Often it is a relationship gone awry that leads a female attorney to call upon an attorney of her own to deal with harassment. Her former amour, who is most likely her senior, probably doesn't want her around anymore. The partners circle the wagon around the more valuable partner—the senior male—and she's left on the outside, looking back at what used to be a nice place to work. Suddenly the kinds of assignments that would advance a career dry up, which is a sure way to force her out, because so much depends on the kinds of cases one works on. But aside from a real romance or a tawdry affair, sexual harassment is often about other stuff—unwanted sex jokes, sexual innuendos, inappropriate comments and touches, repeated often enough—which adds up to an atmosphere that can make a law firm an unpleasant, if not overtly hostile, place to work. One could say a *more* unpleasant, hostile place.

Freada Klein, one of the best-known sexual harassment experts and trainers in the legal field, says that her 1994 surveys of fourteen medium and large law firms found that 43 percent of the women said that they had been the target of unwanted sexual jokes, comments or questions in the last year. We can't read the minds of the respondents to surveys, so it's difficult to know when a casual remark crosses the line and becomes offensive. And there's a difference today:

Young women now, many of them raised by descendants of the women of the 1960s women's movement and further sensitized by the Anita Hill/Clarence Thomas incident, are much less willing to put up with the kinds of dirty jokes and off-color comments that their mothers did. It also may be that the atmosphere at some places is actually more overtly sexual than what was common in earlier generations when office life was somewhat more formal, sex was not a topic of everyday conversation, and one's private life, no matter what one's inclination, stayed in the closet.

On the other hand, there has also been a shift in the past couple of years to what is considered inappropriate. Comments that were laughed off in the free-wheeling seventies, or quietly tolerated, are now considered offensive by some. Furthermore, many of the women who went to work in the sixties and seventies thought that the way to be accepted was to be one of the guys, and they were treated as such. Today's young women aren't asking to be one of the boys. They are women, and they want to be treated as professionals.

The women in Klein's studies said that while the sexual nature of many of the comments that were directed their way was unwanted, they did not say they added up to *sexual harassment* to their minds, even though legally they might. This countermands the contention of some men today (as well as Camille Paglia) who claim that women are overly sensitive and that a single lewd joke labels the teller a harasser. Klein's lawyers stated that only pervasive comments of a sexual nature and unwanted touching, as well as pressure for dates or sex, constituted sexual harassment.

So exactly what does cross the line from saucy to sexual harassment? If it wouldn't be said in front of one's spouse, sister, mother or daughter, it shouldn't be heard at work. "When you first explain that one person's joke might be another's sexual harassment, you get a lot of complaints from the men about how they are not going to be able to joke around at the water cooler . . . well, if you are courteous and cordial, that always carries the day," says Tom Kayser, managing partner of Robins, Kaplan, Miller & Ceresi, a Minneapolis-based law firm that conducts sexual harassment training for companies. "I don't know when a sexual discussion has been necessary to advance the work of the law firm."

Sometimes the off-color comment is simply bad manners—egregiously bad manners. What, for instance, was a summer associate to make of the comment a partner made on her first day at work at one of New York's oldest firms? The firm has a large Jewish population and a reputation for making all kinds of people feel welcome. One of the senior partners in her department came into her office and she got up from behind her desk to shake the man's hand. The woman is an orthodox Jew, which generally precludes her touching any man not her husband. "With the knowledge that I am an observant Jew in his head, he immediately says, 'Oh, you're shaking my hand . . . what else are you doing these days that you weren't before?' " Fortunately the woman had enough *chutzpah* to respond:

"Whom do I call to file a sexual harassment complaint?"

He chuckled and departed. No, it's not enough to make you walk out in a rage or officially complain. But that kind of sexual innuendo—on the first day from one of the most senior and most protected people in her department—sets a tone that ultimately makes the place uncomfortable for women. Is every hello an occasion for a sexual allusion? you have to ask. What next?

The woman's retort was in some ways the perfect response—a joke, but one with a message: Don't do that around me. Yet too few young associates are that savvy, or bold enough, to reply in kind. In truth almost no one complains: a young lawyer's career can be derailed if she does. "I don't think any entry- or mid-level associate thinks her career will be fine if she files a formal complaint against a partner," says Klein. "Even if it is substantiated, she is going to be ostracized. Probably no male partner will ever ask her out for dinner or to go on an overnight trip. Her assignments may dry up, her informal mentoring will be affected, and she gets a reputation as someone who's difficult to work with. At best she will be known as the victim. Some will question if she is oversensitive and whether she did anything to provoke it. The common euphemism for this is, 'She is not a team player.' "

In fact, she becomes a pariah at the firm. People will whisper about her when she leaves the elevator. Her life will be hell, and filing a suit will make it worse. The deposition in these kinds of cases becomes an instrument of torture in which any past indiscretions, no matter how slight, come back to haunt the woman and question her integrity and intent.

While the individual harassed suffers doubly when she complains, senior partners, particularly high-income-producing partners, are extremely protected from any sort of criticism. Who's going to tell a major rainmaker that his behavior is out of line? After all, he supplies a large share of the bacon the others take home every other week. He may be a creep, and the other partners may know it, but since there is no direct chain of reporting and responsibility, the partners have a tendency to turn a blind eye to bad behavior. Shared responsibility such as law firms can have can mean that no one really is in charge, no one is willing to take the heat of telling someone to change his wanton ways. The partners are like wives who suspect that their husbands are cheating on them but don't want to know for sure—until the firm gets hit with a lawsuit and its name gets dragged in the mud. Then there is a lot of groaning and finger-pointing behind closed doors. The kind of ignorance that shields some from reality in their personal lives can spell disaster in the business world, as Baker & McKenzie, the world's largest law firm, found out in 1994.

A jury delivered a stinging indictment of the firm's inaction in face of evidence that at least some partners knew there was a loose cannon in the Palo Alto office. Plaintiff Rena Weeks, who was briefly a secretary there, won a $7.2 million judgment from a jury.*

"Law firms are the ones who counsel their clients how to stay out of trouble, but some have failed to take even the most modest precautions themselves," says plaintiff's employment lawyer Janice Goodman of New York City. However, there is some indication that women at least have taken Rena Weeks's victory to heart: according to statistics compiled by the U.S. Equal Employment Opportunity Commission, 131 gender-based complaints were filed in 1995, 70 percent more than in 1990. The biggest one-year increase, 33 percent, came in 1992, the year after Anita Hill's testimony against Clarence Thomas. And there are anecdotal reports of women taking stronger and quicker action than they did before and succeeding in getting the bums kicked out.

It happened at the second largest law firm, Jones, Day, Reavis & Pogue. By some accounts the scene in the Atlanta office in the early nineties was quite swinging. The Clarence Thomas/Anita Hill writing on the wall must have been too challenging for these attorneys to read. One allegedly left a pornographic message on a female administrator's answering machine. To Jones, Day's credit, the man was fired soon after. Then a female associate filed a complaint against a department head. He was demoted, and as one woman said, "his career is kaput." The woman who complained reportedly received a six-figure settlement, signed a gag order, and quietly left the firm, as is common when there is a settlement. The good news for women is that Dorothy Kirkley, a well-respected Atlanta lawyer, was brought in as the man's successor to head the department the next year.

---

* *The judge reduced the amount to $3.7 million; Baker & McKenzie, as well as the harasser, Martin Greenstein, were appealing the verdict as we went to press. It probably won't be settled until 1997.*

VULNERABLE EMPLOYEES AT HIGHEST RISK

Throughout the Baker & McKenzie trial, a leitmotif stressed by Weeks's attorneys was that Martin Greenstein targeted new, temporary or otherwise vulnerable employees. "New employees don't know the system and are concerned about making a good impression and keeping their jobs," says San Francisco attorney Philip Kay, co-counsel for Weeks. It happens all the time. Consider this scenario that seems straight out of the afternoon soaps:

Two weeks after a twenty-six-year-old woman reported to work at a prestigious East Coast firm, she was sent to Texas. Her companions were two male partners and another female associate. But only she was called by the lead partner (we'll call him X) to meet him in the hotel bar—to discuss the case, she thought—on the Sunday night after they arrived. They never did get around to discussing the case as the hours clicked by. X said they would all do it together in the morning before they met the client at seven A.M. X had other things in mind. After staying in the bar so long that the dining room closed, X suggested they go to his room for a nightcap. He'd had several cognacs by this time. When she said no to that, he then suggested they go for a swim in the hotel's pool. Although reluctant, she didn't know how to turn him down. "I said to myself, This can't be happening. I was trying to find a way to keep from encouraging him but not to piss him off—I had just started at the firm," she says. Even though it was after eleven P.M., she phoned the other associate to come to the pool also, but she refused.

The object of his unwanted attention did meet him at the pool—wearing shorts and a top, as she hadn't brought a bathing suit with her—and jumped in just to get away from him. We can criticize her for being so naive and showing up at poolside, but perhaps her actions are not so surprising. The women who go to law school are often children of privilege and grow up in an environment that protects them from the abrasive life experiences that might equip them to handle such situations with more aplomb. Besides, blaming the victim is not the point here; she was a new employee trying to please her boss, and she was just out of an elite law school. How do you turn him off without deflating his ego and driving her brand-new job into a dead end?

At the pool, X kept turning the conversation to sex. An hour later she escaped without being pawed, got back to her room, and called several of her friends as well as her parents, even though now it was after midnight. She worried that somehow she had encouraged X. "This was the first time an older male was not looking out for my best interests," she says. "My mentors in school and the federal judge I clerked for had been men, and they had all helped me, so I couldn't believe what had just taken place. Particularly in today's political climate." The incident, by the way, occurred in 1994. The Baker & McKenzie trial was under way.

The next morning the group was to meet at six A.M. in X's room to go over the case. She arrived a half hour late to assure that she wouldn't be the first one there. Although she had no other close encounters with X on the trip, he was so obviously solicitous of her that she was sure the others were getting the wrong impression. When X left Texas to go on vacation, she and the others, including the partner, stayed behind to work on the case. "But he kept calling me to find out how it was going, even though I was the most junior person there. I didn't call him back." When everyone returned east, her contact with him was somewhat limited, as he was not her supervising partner. She was just working for him on this case. She hoped to put the incident behind her and chalk up his behavior to too much drink and overactive hormones. She told no one at work. She was too embarrassed.

But two weeks later a travel agent phoned and asked which seat she preferred on her upcoming flight to Texas. She knew nothing of another trip to Texas, and she quickly learned that only X and she would be going. It was summertime, and her supervising partner was on vacation at the beach. She phoned him immediately, saying she didn't want to go to Texas with X *alone*. She would be happy to go when the other associates were going.

To his credit he immediately asked: Was it because she didn't want to go alone with X? Right. He asked if there was anything she wanted to talk about. She said no. She didn't want to get a reputation as a complainer. "The women almost always try to figure out what to do themselves," says Klein. "Many of the firms have sexual harassment policies in place that say all complaints will be investigated, and there is no option for informal resolution."

Her supervising partner immediately called X and canceled her going to Texas. And like it or not, when he got back to the office he set in motion an investigation. The firm's sexual harassment committee at the office descended upon her, and she wrote up a formal complaint. Through the grapevine, she learned that at least four other women still at the firm had been harassed by X, yet none had come forward. "Among the associates he had the reputation of a real pig—but none of the partners seemed to know about it," she says. Echoing sexual harassment surveys that show very few women actually report harassment, she adds: "No one wanted to say anything. Everyone is much more concerned about making partner, keeping their job, and getting a raise."

The incident troubled her deeply. She dreamed that she "met his wife and kids at the firm's picnic and they were on welfare," and of course it was her fault. In the end, it turned out that X was a contract, not an equity, partner, and his contract was simply not renewed. But even though another woman came forward and also filed a complaint against him, the man still does considerable work for the firm. When the woman runs into him, they do not speak.

It might not have been so easy for her—if what happened was easy—if X had been a major rainmaker at the firm, or a big client. Then he's much, much harder to dislodge. Complaints, for instance, about Martin Greenstein surfaced in Chicago well before Greenstein was transferred to Palo Alto in 1988 to set up an office. A specialist in intellectual properties, he brought in between a million and a million and a half in billings annually. Baker & McKenzie, however, did not keep a record of any harassment until rumors circulated that a young associate—the secretaries were blown off—who had been there only a few months was going to sue for sexual harassment. She wasn't, but that was the rumor. In fact, only when there was the rumor of a lawsuit did the firm finally write up her complaint, concluding it was without merit, according to attorney Kay. The woman left Baker & McKenzie to accept a judicial clerkship with the prestigious Ninth Circuit.

Another associate who worked for Greenstein for a year had been heavily recruited from a smaller firm where she had been a shareholder; a year after she complained about working with Greenstein, she was fired. (She later brought suit against Greenstein and Baker & McKenzie herself.) Until Rena Weeks sued, it appears that Baker & McKenzie was willing to look the other way while Greenstein stepped out of line, grabbing breasts and buttocks, tickling toes underneath a library table, asking a woman to join him in hot tubs, snapping bra straps, sending lewd notes, asking a lesbian if she and her friend would like a threesome. There's undoubtedly more, but that's what came out at the trial. These women all left—they were transferred, quit or were fired; Greenstein stayed. He was the rainmaker, remember? But the collective testimony of six women—five staff women and one attorney—brought down Baker & McKenzie and Greenstein, no matter how supercilious the attitude of Baker & McKenzie's attorney toward Rena Weeks. Court TV reveals all.

In the aftermath of the Baker & McKenzie decision, it would seem that firms would have a harder time tolerating aberrant behavior on the part of rainmakers. Even if they provide the golden eggs for the other partners and associates to feast on, they can also be costly, in terms of money and reputation. In the past this sort of behavior was looked upon as merely idiosyncratic, like screaming at the support staff. That may have changed. At some firms. For a time.

But how much the Baker & McKenzie verdict actually altered the landscape for women at some firms is debatable. While the size of the award against Baker & McKenzie would seem likely to put the fear into partners' wallets, attorney Kay says that from what he is still hearing from women coming to him as clients, many lawyers haven't gotten the message. No one is betting the bank that this one verdict will change things much. Consultant Klein says that partners frequently bring up the Baker & McKenzie verdict but adds she also hears things like "I would never put M&M's into a woman's shirt pocket [one of the many things Greenstein did], so I don't have a problem."

Sexual harassment consultants reported an increase of business soon after the trial, but women at several law firms say that the training doesn't go nearly deep enough to change the behavior of the partners who are the greatest offenders. They might attend, but they treat it all as a joke. Arrogant people don't listen well and don't change their stripes easily.

HIGH JINKS AT STROOCK & STROOCK & LAVAN

"When the worst offender at the firm is the senior guy in the department, he sends out the message that this type of behavior is okay," says a senior associate at Stroock & Stroock & Lavan in New York. Associates emulate their superiors, and some of them turn into "new old boys" just as bad as their predecessors. "You hear everything from constant jokes about body parts to asking me if I would jump out of a cake at some guy's birthday party to patting my ass," she says. "Or the comment that 'I give great codicil,' with the clear implication that 'I give great head.'" The cretin in question, yes, a senior partner and a rainmaker, made that comment at a lunch for summer associates—female and male—and kept up the sexual allusions about the woman throughout the meal, undercutting any authority she held by virtue of her position. "I went to the ladies' room and for the first time ever contemplated running out the back door," she recalls. "But I didn't. I made it through lunch. I got into a taxi with two colleagues—both men—and I broke down and started sobbing. They were good guys and thought he was an idiot—he is, in fact, an equal opportunity offender. The guys were understanding, I was mortified, but nobody could say anything because he is their boss."

In the real estate and corporate departments, Stroock & Stroock & Lavan positively sounds like an out-of-control college fraternity party. Women come and go through these departments with some regularity. Some are fired, some quit. One associate (who's no longer there) told of an instance when she was sitting in her office shortly after she began working there and a senior partner, a man well-known in real estate circles, came up from behind her and started kissing her neck and blowing in her ear. "I was completely green—I just got flustered and said, 'Oh, you scared me.' Today, three years later, I would probably scream bloody murder." The man, she says, frequently makes lewd comments, embarrassing everybody. Another partner feels free to run his fingers through the hair of young female associates whenever the urge strikes—or to invite them to sit on his lap during a business discussion. He does this in front of the women's peers—male and female—compounding the disrespect and embarrassment. "I jumped away, but it made me feel stupid," says one woman. "The women talk about it all the time."

How can you, they ask each other, be taken seriously as an attorney when bosses act as if you are there for their pleasure? Women tell of the degrading comments men make about wives and women in general—anyone's upcoming marriage is the source of much bawdy merriment—and how this makes them feel humiliated themselves. "It's clear that they don't take their women seriously," says a senior associate still at the firm. One partner at Stroock, two women told me, asks them to sit on his couch if they are working on a project together. He sits very close, close enough to have their bodies touch, and talks to their chests. An active grapevine among the women associates keeps them informed of his latest prey. Apparently the partners are, ah, unaware of his way of working.

Maybe. He's a rainmaker with one of the corner offices, the ones reserved for the most important partners.

Most of the women partners, they said, weren't helpful at all. "The attitude was that they had suffered through this themselves and you would have to do it also," says a former employee who adds that she couldn't get out fast enough. "Stroock had female partners but none I felt comfortable going to." The senior women, she said, were either extremely masculine or married to male partners. They don't do anything to fix the situation, and obviously if you are a junior associate, you can't go to them to complain about their husbands. Anyway, these women don't have a lot of clout and they certainly don't set the tone at the office.

It must be said here that women also highly praised a few of the men, both their peers and senior partners, as first-class gentlemen and mentors; but the women couldn't help come in contact with the creeps who use every occasion as a background for a running sex gag. In the course of doing interviews, I must have come across close to half a dozen women who once had worked at Stroock. Except for praising a few individual men, not one of the women had a good word about the place. One woman said that a senior associate, who seemed to have a shot at partnership, told her that if she wanted to be a partner herself, she probably had to "start wearing shorter skirts." She left the firm instead.

The frat house atmosphere at Stroock came to a head in the summer of 1993, when a corporate partner led a group that included two summer associates— one of them a woman—to Stringfellows, a swanky strip club, for an evening of entertainment. The partner who picked up the tab put the receipt on his expense account, the story goes. However, gossip at Stroock about the incident prevented his being quietly reimbursed. The women were outraged, and a meeting for female associates was arranged. It quickly turned into a venting session about the overtly sexual atmosphere at Stroock. Surprise—some of the women partners were appalled—*they had no idea.* "One of the women partners turned some of the incidents around, and it became 'blame the victim,' " says one woman associate who was there. " 'Why are you still here?' one partner asked me. But another woman apologized for the behavior some of us have had to put up with."

Sexual harassment training at Stroock followed, but it apparently didn't have much of an effect. "Everyone going through it thought the sessions were a waste of time, and the worst offenders just gave it lip service," says a former associate. "The guy who was the worst never got disciplined, the sexual harassment policy was restated, and there was a route to file complaints, but what we all understood was that you could file a complaint and nothing got done. And that's the story of Stroock."

One woman who talked about "the really terrible partner" at the meetings said he stopped being a lout for a while. Just as she had feared, he retaliated. "He gave me the silent treatment, he wouldn't talk to me, he wouldn't work with me, he couldn't look at me, and he is the assigning partner in my department," she recalls. "But I am as stubborn as a mule, I had other partners here who really were able to somehow help me through this time, but it took months and months until it started to get better."

Incidentally, the partner who took the summer associates to Stringfellows was reportedly reimbursed by the hiring partner. He wrote a personal check to cover the cost, and this was supposedly a reprimand to the partner who led the outing. Hard to figure out how. Sounds more like circling the wagons, and wallet, to protect the instigator.

Often the person designated as the one to take sexual harassment claims to is the recruiting director. Frequently, however, *she* is a former secretary who may have been promoted because she has played along with at least one of the partners, and her job is a reward. Sometimes it's a way of keeping someone around to make one of the partners happy. She often serves as a cheerleader for the partners and the firm, and in addition to having no voice or vote, in how the firm is run, she doesn't see what the problem is all about when a junior associate says that she is being hit on. She is hardly one to tell an errant partner to stop preying on the paralegals or junior associates—besides, he's *only kidding*. Stroock & Stroock & Lavan did not answer a request for information about their sexual harassment training.

THE SITUATION IS EVEN WORSE in small firms, where there are no channels to deal with the issue at all. If the harasser is one of the principals in the firm, or one of the firm's biggest clients, the woman almost always loses. Small firms may have only two or three partners. If the harasser is a major client, or maybe any kind of client, they are not going to tell him to clean up his act or stop bothering a woman associate, or that it's inappropriate to celebrate or schmooze at a strip club. The smaller the firm, the more likely they are going to be dependent on a few clients. "Jane" can stay behind when they go to the strip joint, Jane can put up with obnoxious behavior, but her choices are more limited if she's the target of someone's attention. Unless she capitulates, her only option may be to leave the firm. "Where do you go when the head of the firm wants to sleep with you and doesn't give up?" says one exasperated woman. "You leave. You leave. You have to leave."

"These men use the workforce as a way of getting attention from women," says a former summer associate at Duane, Morris & Heckscher in Philadelphia. "The senior partners think they can do anything they want . . . and they can. They have been doing it for twenty years and see no reason to stop." The summer she was there, for instance, a young associate had an affair with a senior partner, who rewarded the woman with good assignments. He became her mentor.

KATHLEEN FREDERICK VS. REED SMITH

How the casting couch at law firms can function is illustrated in the story of Philadelphia attorney Kathleen A. Frederick. When Frederick stopped sleeping with Richard Glanton, a VIP partner at their firm, Reed Smith Shaw & McClay, she says, her chances of partnership went up in smoke. In the City of Brotherly Love, Reed Smith is a branch of a century-old, large, prestigious, and very, very Republican Pittsburgh-based firm.

Glanton is active in GOP circles, and among his boards and affiliations is the Barnes Foundation, a distinguished private art museum with a stunning Impressionist collection that is owned by Lincoln University, the first school of higher education for blacks in this country. Glanton is president of the Barnes Foundation and general counsel and trustee of Lincoln University. He was deputy counsel to ex-Pennsylvania governor Richard Thornburgh and once worked at the EEOC in Washington, though not at the same time as Clarence Thomas. At Reed Smith he commands a corner office and has a reputation as the firm's biggest rainmaker—the kind of partner that his peers have every reason to protect, should they be so inclined. He was, after all, only in his early forties in the late 1980s and would be a valuable asset to the firm as long as he was there. Certainly anyone looking to get ahead at Reed Smith would want to be on Glanton's good side, particularly if he were one's supervising partner, the one who hands out assignments, the one who can nurture a career or kill it faster than you can squash a ripe peach. Glanton is also an imposing African American. Friends call him charismatic, detractors call him arrogant. Probably both are right.

Frederick, a graduate of Villanova Law School, was a thirtysomething lawyer and a disposable commodity, eminently replaceable at Reed Smith. While at Villanova she was an editor on law review, published two articles, managed a symposium on torts, graduated cum laude, and had a baby. After working for another Philadelphia firm for more than three years, she was hired by Reed Smith at the end of 1987. She is a trim blonde, but race really doesn't play any more a part in this story than it did in the O. J. Simpson trial. Frederick reported mainly to Glanton, and for well over a year he had nothing but praise for her work.

However, after a while he began making sexually explicit comments to her, she says, making clear his desire to have more than a professional relationship with her. Frederick says Glanton told her that as she was at her sexual peak she needed a lover, and that he lay in bed the night before, wondering what she looked like in bed. He gave her a gold pin from Bailey, Banks and Biddle, an expensively tasteful jewelry store in Philadelphia. He gave her tickets to the Bush inaugural and arranged to have her picture taken with George Bush at a $1,000-a-plate dinner, to which he had also given her a ticket. He took her to a lounge near his home, the Swann Lounge at the Four Seasons Hotel, a place his wife later would call "an extension of our home." One night, Frederick recalls, he told her that he might get a job with the Bush administration in Washington and asked if she would join him as an aide. They were having dinner at the Monte Carlo Living Room, a dark, plush Society Hill restaurant furnished in one room with . . . couches. It is the kind of place where people are more likely to make indecent proposals than discuss torts. "I want to take you upstairs and show you what's upstairs," she says he said. They went upstairs to the room with the sofas, where they danced. "I felt that under these circumstances, I should dance with him—he was being very good to me," she says. There's more, but it all sounds so much like so many other come-ons—and harassment.

Frederick's marriage was going through a rocky period during this time, and she and her husband, a violist with the Philadelphia Orchestra, had separated for a few months. She told her psychiatrist about Glanton's advances and how torn she was: she felt it was her career or her moral code, her psychiatrist says. She told Glanton, she says, that she did not want to get involved with a married man. And somewhere in the middle of all this, Frederick attended a lecture on how not to be shy around strangers. More about that later.

In the spring of 1989, Glanton told her that he was going to have her appointed to the recruitment committee at Reed Smith, a post that would make her more visible to other partners in the firm. Around the same time, Glanton evaluated her work as *one plus*—very strong candidate for partner. Interesting. Michael Browne, for whom Frederick also worked, also gave her the same high grade—in contrast with the other partners, whose aggregate score came in much lower. Browne and Glanton are good friends. But before the marks were known, Glanton took Frederick to a piano bar and told her that he had given the evaluators the best review of her that he could. Then, she says, he suggested that they "go somewhere" so that he could give her a full body massage. She declined, she says, but the message was clear. How about a little gratitude?

But Glanton's and Browne's high marks couldn't keep the main office in Pittsburgh from grading Frederick a mediocre three plus overall, which placed her near the bottom of the associates in her class. In a firm that makes approximately half of its associates partners, her ranking realistically meant that she would have to do something spectacular or have friends in high places to make partner. This was her critical fifth-year evaluation, one that gives both partners and associates a strong indication of what will happen when the partnership decision is made in two years. Associates whose chances are dim often start looking for a new job at this juncture. Browne suggested to her that she did poorly in the review because she was "too lively," she says, and that he said, "Comments like that are weighted more heavily for women than men." It's the same old story here again: women lawyers have to follow a straight and narrow path—serious, but not too serious, et cetera—if they are to be accepted. Guys can be, well, guys. All kinds of guys. Even spirited.

According to Frederick, Glanton increased the frequency of his sexual advances to her during the spring and summer, asking her frequently to lunch, to dinner, to drinks. One night he allegedly stopped by her house on the way home from a trial in Harrisburg with a bottle of Italian bubbly, Asti Spumante. "I want you to be my mistress," Frederick recalls him saying to her. " 'If you become my mistress, I can help you, I can take care of you. . . .' He indicated that I needed his help to become partner, and he would take care of me if I became his mistress." Frederick says she was miserably conflicted because "Mr. Glanton had been very, very good to me for a long, long time in terms of promoting my career. He had been a big booster of mine."

Glanton kept up the heat, Frederick says, and she kept resisting, even the time in September of 1989 on the dark road when they were in his Mercedes-Benz and "he hugged me and pressed himself against me and unzipped his pants. I told him again that I valued him as a mentor and friend, but it was not something I felt I could do." That was the last straw—almost—for Richard Glanton. People do not say no to him. At work, she says, he retaliated by saying negative things about her, not giving her new assignments, not returning her phone messages. "I didn't know how to say no to Mr. Glanton," says Frederick. "Every time I said no to Mr. Glanton since September, there were adverse consequences." One day he stood her up for lunch with a prospective client, the Philadelphia Orchestra, which Frederick, with Glanton's help, hoped to land for Reed Smith. She learned that he gave the promised position on the recruitment committee to another woman. He canceled a meeting in which her becoming general counsel to a Philadelphia hospital was to be discussed. Any or all of these things would have markedly boosted her partnership chances. Frederick's worst nightmare was coming true: if she didn't sleep with Glanton, her future at the firm was doomed. Law was a second career for her. She was thirty-seven years old. Her marriage, though shaky, seemed to be improving. While this was going on, Frederick was telling her psychiatrist all about how torn she was by Glanton's requests for sex. Ironically, as Glanton increased the frequency of his demands for sex, her psychiatrist noted that his unwanted attention may have brought her and her husband closer together, even though he knew nothing of the real pressures on her at work.

And then, Frederick caved in. She and Richard Glanton had sex. It happened like this, and it is not the stuff of romance: Sometime in October, when Glanton was "acting more like his old self," according to Frederick, she accepted a ride home from him. "We got off at an exit in Gladwyne off the Schuykill, parked by the river. . . . He indicated he wanted to go there and have sex with me." And, yes, they did it. They had sex in his Mercedes one more time, she contends, and once in her house. Her psychiatrist says that afterward she felt "ashamed, degraded and very depressed. . . . She had decided to go with Richard only to save her career and then felt terrible about it," he says. He considered putting her on antidepressant drugs. She didn't want to, because she didn't like the side effects of the tranquilizer samples he gave her to try. A friend, another woman lawyer, says that Frederick told her, crying and sobbing, one night, of the affair and that Glanton had "threatened that if she told anyone about the sexual relationship, he would destroy her."

But a few weeks later, after three trysts, Frederick says she ended the affair, if it can be called that. That's when the retaliation began in earnest. And Kathleen Frederick made a few phone calls that her psychiatrist says were the result of anger and rage. She called up the husband of a woman Frederick suspected was now sleeping with Glanton, and left three messages at his office that were tape-recorded. "This is confidential—she's cheating on you," the recorded voice said. For some, the phone calls were the last bit of evidence that corroborated her story: only a woman really desperate and mad, only a woman who had been unceremoniously dumped for another, would be so crazy as to make such damning phone calls. Though Glanton was not mentioned in the tape, although Frederick had tried to disguise her voice, an Unnamed Female Associate, as she was called in early press reports before her name was revealed,* brought it to Glanton's office. Glanton then called Frederick in and

---

* There is no point in repeating her name here. The woman is now a partner at Reed Smith and a rising star in Philadelphia legal circles.

told her to stop. The tape was also played for Glanton's friend, Browne, who would later become the firm's managing partner. Mysteriously, the tape was never played for David Auten, then managing partner in the Philadelphia office. Three months would go by before he would hear it—and then Frederick would be fired.

On February 1, Auten told her that she would not make "active partner" and there was no point in her waiting around for two more years only to be unceremoniously fired then. He urged her to leave the firm now. Frederick took two weeks of vacation, and when she returned on Valentine's Day, Auten again told her someone in her situation would certainly want to leave. He then said the firm would pay her through June 30. A few days later, Frederick tried to contact the managing partner of Reed Smith, S. Donald Gerlach, in the Pittsburgh office, to inform him about Glanton's harassment. But she was never able to do so. She left a phone message asking that Gerlach call her about a "highly personal and confidential matter." At three P.M., when he still had not returned her call, she sent him an E-mail, reiterating her earlier request. Through the miracle of electronics, Frederick learned that Gerlach read her message the next morning, but he did not bother to call her. That afternoon Auten, the managing partner back in Philadelphia, repeated his offer to pay her through June and told her it would be best if she did not come back to the office anymore. If she would leave immediately, he said, the firm would provide her with career counseling and a good reference. He would not discuss why the firm had come to this decision.

But by this time Frederick had a lawyer of her own, Alan M. Lerner, and the process that ultimately led to a lawsuit for sexual harassment was set in motion. Once Auten learned she had engaged a lawyer, Reed Smith began to retaliate. She would not be paid until June 30. She would not get a good reference unless she signed a release. In fact, Reed Smith would not even respond to requests from prospective employers for references. They would not let her look at her personnel file. Before the case would get to court, however, Glanton would threaten to sue Alan Lerner's firm, call the suit "extortion" in public, claim in front of a TV camera that Frederick was a "disturbed woman" who had been "under psychiatric care" since starting at Reed Smith, and maintain that she had been fired from her last job and wanted only to extort money from him. In pretrial depositions, he branded Frederick's allegations "an unspeakable, murderous, just disgusting lie."

In and out of court Glanton denied everything—that he had ever done anything in the least improper, that they had ever danced (he said he dances only with his wife), that he didn't know what Asti Spumanti was, as he was a non-drinker, that they'd ever had sex, along the way implying that of course they'd dined at nice restaurants because he ate breakfast, lunch, and dinner only at places that use cloth napkins—and more to the point, all those dinners and lunches were at Frederick's behest: he only went because he was trying to be a nice guy and help an associate who clearly needed it. He gave her an expensive pin—whether it was worth $200 or $400 was a matter of contention at the trial—because he was a caring colleague and not cheap. Other people might give $50 scarves. Not him. "Never, never, never," were words Glanton repeated several times over in his testimony. His wife swore that Frederick made a pest of herself, calling their home and inviting herself over, and that her husband "tends to help people—I encourage that," she said.

Glanton, however, betrayed at least a lack of memory when he claimed that he made no more than four phone calls to Frederick's home. Lerner confronted him with his telephone bills, which showed he'd called her home nineteen times from his car phone after her poor evaluation. It couldn't have been that he was pressuring the woman, now could it? "Never, never, never." Glanton had also stated under oath that the first he'd heard about the whole nasty business was when the lawsuit was filed, and that's when he'd made his defamatory comments to the media about Frederick. Hey—he was caught off guard! But Alan Lerner's story is somewhat different; he stated that between December and January of 1991–92, Reed Smith and Glanton were trying to work out a deal with Frederick to make her shut up. Lerner says that the firm offered Frederick $450,000 plus a letter of reference if she would settle with no claim. The deal fell apart, he says, because the confidentiality clause would have precluded Lerner from using information from his own investigation of the case in the event *he* was sued, which Glanton was threatening.

The attorney for Reed Smith, William J. O'Brien, attempted to make mince-meat of Frederick, attacking her as being incompetent, neurotic, insecure, a woman whose mental and emotional stability crumbled after she received a poor grade in the partnership sweepstakes. He suggested that her psychiatrist had fabricated his notes to Frederick's advantage. She was called a "flake" in court. It was charged that she had been fired from her previous firm, but nothing backed up that claim, and witnesses testified that Frederick had handled their legal work competently. O'Brien bluntly asked her if she had agreed to "exchange sex for work assignments." She said yes. Reed Smith's psychiatrist was a woman, not surprisingly; they make the best counterattackers in sexual harassment cases. Dr. Elissa Benedek testified that she didn't believe Frederick, including her graphic descriptions of the sexual encounters. Also not surprisingly, Frederick's psychiatrist corroborated her contention about the sexual encounters. In court it was another case of "she said, he said." In the end, the picture painted of Frederick would be every sexual harassment litigant's nightmare. The defense was basically the "nuts and sluts" defense: the woman is crazy, and a tart, obviously. And, of course, *nothing happened.* She's lying. Destroy her.

Frederick herself did not win the hearts and minds of many people in the courtroom. She sparred with O'Brien, the Reed Smith attorney, and did not win. He was condescending and demeaning, referring to her as a woman who "can't find fulfillment" and stating that "no competent, dignified woman would put up with" the events she described. Lerner, however, turned that around to point out that O'Brien's statement implied that only incompetent women were sexually harassed. In truth, these are the most vulnerable and they have the least resources if they complain. If you're barely hanging on to your job, you are the least likely person to complain about sexual harassment or feel you are in a position to turn somebody down. Such women are, in fact, the most likely targets of sexual harassment. The lecture Frederick attended on how to overcome shyness became a full-blown course in flirting, down to questions such as "Did you bat your eyes?" When Frederick made a sarcastic retort, O'Brien returned with a "Isn't she *cute?* What a trip." Yet the firm had had no problem with the time Frederick met someone at a train station who later became a client.

What the judge, Robert F. Kelly, didn't allow into court was equally as interesting as what he did. Testimony from sexual harassment expert Freada Klein certainly would have enlightened the jury as to the power structure of law firms and why associates and staff are prey for the all-powerful partners. In some sense the power differential between partner and associate is even greater than it is between law professor and student. Your very livelihood can depend on one or two people, and in the late 1980s jobs for new lawyers were not plentiful.

"I was not permitted to testify about the unique aspects of a partnership structure and the power partners have over all associates and how this makes sexual harassment more difficult to complain about," says Klein. "I was not permitted to talk about that which is most relevant in cases like this—the rates of sexual harassment in law firms, or to compare Reed Smith policy of complaint procedures and investigation with what other law firms are doing. It was a hot and humid day, and I got on and off the stand pretty quickly, and I thought, Why did anybody bother? All of my expertise in the field was ignored. I recollect that I was on the stand for less than an hour." Klein was at least allowed to put in an appearance.

Not so for other past or present female employees of Reed Smith. None were heard from. However, apparently a great many were deposed, given the number of documents that were sealed by court order and not allowed into evidence: 185. *Something* was afoot at Reed Smith. The number was high in spite of the fact that some women went to great lengths to avoid being subpoenaed, including one woman who was allegedly happy to be relocating to another city at the time and thus escaped before being subpoenaed, and those who were deposed only did so kicking and screaming, according to Lisa De Paulo, who wrote an impertinent report of the whole affair for *Philadelphia* magazine. (Obviously, the women who were deposed could see a career killer coming. Talk and you'll never work in this town again.) Maybe some of the women would have been like the woman who called *A.M. Philadelphia* during the trial and said Frederick should have just left when she was sexually harassed, just as *she* had when it happened to *her* at Reed Smith. And of course, some of those 185 documents were alleged to be—oh, you know, telephone records, hotel credit card receipts of Glanton's that bore witness to the frequency with which he booked single-night accommodations in the area, and lots of dinners, and you know how those all add up so quickly. Frederick's lawyers wanted all the documents made public and other women to testify; Reed Smith and Glanton did not.

But there was Reagan appointee Robert F. Kelly presiding. He is hardly what you would call a feminist. He is decidedly pro-defense in civil cases, according to the *Almanac of the Federal Judiciary*. He truly outdid himself this time. Chalk it up to old boyism, chalk it up to a lack of legal smarts, whatever: once he decided that this was a case about Kathleen Frederick and Kathleen Frederick alone, that insured there would be no parade of witnesses testifying about the kind of environment for women that existed at Reed Smith. It would be strictly her word against his, as if the Glanton affair were an isolated incident. After the Philadelphia press argued to have the aforementioned documents unsealed, Judge Kelly did allow some of it out—but they contained lots of blank pages.

"Redacted" is the legal word for leaving out the juicy parts, and redacted these documents were. The deposition of the associate Frederick accused of having an affair with Glanton after she turned him down appeared to be 250 pages long but was redacted down to—are you ready for this?—*three* pages. Nearly three weeks after the trial Judge Kelly released more documents, but again most of the pages available were irrelevant to the nub of the case: was she sexually harassed? It was hard to figure why Judge Kelly was so intent on keeping these documents secret or why he refused to let other women testify, the norm in cases like this. When Rena Weeks went up against Martin Greenstein and the world's largest law firm, Baker & McKenzie, a year later, no matter how weak one thought Rena Weeks's case—she had worked for him for only twenty-five days, was transferred once she complained, and left the firm a month or so later for another job—the six other women who testified they had been sexually harassed by him more than made up for it.

But all that was missing in the case against Glanton and Reed Smith. It was as if this had happened in a vacuum. Candid comments about Kelly from lawyers who have come before him, all there for anyone to look up in the almanac, are less than complimentary: "He may be the bottom of the barrel—neither smart nor judicious." "He's mean. He's just not qualified." "There is very little to talk about when talking about his legal smarts." "He's opinionated and jumps to conclusions from the beginning, and then it's hard to change his mind." "He hates anything that has anything to do with a plaintiff's case—he's very defense oriented."

In this case his distaste for Frederick and her lead attorney, Alan Lerner, was evident to the point of not letting Lerner sit shiva for his mother, who died midway through the trial. The trial was halted for two days while she was buried, but Lerner asked for a day or two more to mourn his mother. The answer was no—even for a day—though Lerner's rabbi and bar leaders petitioned Kelly and other members of the federal judiciary. So the very day after burying his mother, Lerner returned to the courtroom to what was probably his most critical task of the entire trial: cross-examining Glanton. It was painfully evident to everyone in the courtroom that day that Lerner was under par, both physically and strategically. He knew it too and later asked for a mistrial. Motion denied.

In the Third Circuit, where Kelly sits, he is known as a judge whose decisions are frequently reversed. Robert F. Kelly will stay on the bench as long as he likes, for federal judgeships are lifetime appointments. He was, incidentally, nominated for the bench in 1987 by Pennsylvania senator Arlen Specter, who performed so well for the GOP during Anita Hill's inquisition by the Senate Judiciary Committee. In his instructions to the jury, Kelly stated that to decide in Frederick's favor, they had to find on a claim of "quid pro quo harassment" and that the harassment was the sole cause of her being fired. Lerner wanted the wording changed to "significant," but again, Kelly wouldn't agree to that.

In the end, the jury—five women, five men—came back with a verdict O'Brien was able to put a spin on and call a win. Although Glanton was found to have sexually harassed Frederick, the firm was held blameless. They said that Frederick failed to prove her ending the affair was the sole reason she was fired. And Frederick was awarded nothing for her claim of sexual harassment, undoubtedly because she had slept with him. She was, however, awarded $125,000 for defamation of character for the public statements Glanton made about her before the trial.

Now it gets curiouser and curiouser. As expected, Frederick's lawyers appealed the decision, basing the claim on the mountains of alleged evidence that Kelly excluded, including evidence that other Reed Smith partners harassed other female employees. There were also those alleged expense receipts, his alleged involvement with another female attorney, his calling a secretary at home and asking her to dinner, and so on. But before it got to the court, Glanton and Reed Smith settled with Frederick for an undisclosed amount. The settlement included a strict gag order on all the parties, including Frederick's lawyers, and—this is the best part—Judge Kelly set aside the jury verdict and cleared Glanton of all charges. This was almost certainly a part of the settlement agreement. The trial then became nothing but a show trial, even if it was the vehicle for Reed Smith and Glanton to come to a settlement with Frederick. The final details were worked out in late 1994; Judge Kelly set aside the verdict early in 1995, an amazing coincidence—if that's what it was. And should any problems arise—should, for example, Frederick or her lawyers talk—Kelly will intervene and decide what happens next. This means in the end that if Richard Glanton is asked, "Have you ever had any judgment [of sexual harassment] against you?" the man can answer *no*. At least at this point.

Since the trial, Glanton has continued as a partner of Reed Smith and the president of the Barnes Foundation and general counsel of Lincoln University, among other appointments. He's been written up in *Time* magazine and *The National Law Journal* with nary a mention of his previous troubles, as if none of this ever happened. However, his political aspirations may have been dashed. The trial occurred in the middle of a slow news summer in Philadelphia, and the media there were over the story like glue. When he briefly floated his name for the GOP nomination for mayor in Philadelphia a year or so later, it sank like a two-ton boulder. Frederick, after a rocky start, is a solo practitioner in a Philadelphia suburb.

The National Law Journal, recounting the Frederick and Nancy Ezold cases— she was the Philadelphia attorney who sued when she didn't make partner at Wolf, Block, Schorr & Solis-Cohen—which were going on at roughly the same time, wrapped up the two cases in a story headlined CITY OF SISTERLY SHOVE. And Philadelphia, remember, is where Professor Drucilla Cornell got the boot from the University of Pennsylvania Law School a few years earlier. Maybe it's in the water.

BECOMING A PARTNER does not necessarily protect one from harassment. True, partners—older and probably shrewder—face a somewhat different problem. Somewhat. They still can be targets for senior partners. But now clients are more likely to be the harassers. In fact, in the Prentice-Hall survey of female litigators, nearly 31 percent of partners in large law firms reported that clients had sexually harassed them in the last five years. Opposing counsel is another source of harassment, which ranges from disparaging or inappropriate remarks to actual physical or emotional abuse, and here again the percentages of women who said they had been so harassed were over 60 percent. While the numbers may seem high, other surveys in recent years are consistent with these figures. It appears that a great many clients think that when they buy legal services they are also buying the right to proposition the attorneys, and far too few firms are telling the clients that they are out of line.

But happily, sometimes they do and it's the harasser who gets fired as a client. Lorna Scholfield, a partner at Debevoise & Plimpton in New York, tells of the time an obnoxious client really got out of hand at dinner. As she usually does, Scholfield brought along a junior associate—in this case a man—to join her and the client. Throughout the evening the client was generally a boor, making disparaging ethnic remarks. If that wasn't bad enough, in the cab on the way home the client reached over and kissed Scholfield and asked her if she would go to his hotel room and look at pictures of his girlfriend. The client chose the wrong target. Scholfield is a former federal prosecutor. The next day she reported the incident to the head of litigation. At her superior's suggestion Scholfield called the man and told him that it would be better if he took his business elsewhere. The client had been fired.

But that kind of response is not par for the course. More typical is this story: A few years ago a female associate who attended a firm dinner with a client twice had to endure the client announcing from the podium, "Take your hands off of her!" although no one was bothering her. The client—a big money client—whom she had just met, knew this but felt no compunction about making her the brunt of his sexually laced comment in front of sixty or so of her law firm co-workers. Everyone in the room laughed except the men at her table, who shared in her embarrassment. "I complained, but the response was, 'What can we do? He's the *client*.'" Oddly enough, this is at a firm where other women assure me sexual harassment is at a minimum; obviously, clients have different rules. Clients often expect their service providers, such as lawyers, to entertain them however they wish. At Stroock partners have been known to ask male associates to make arrangements to take clients to strip joints for an evening's entertainment. They are not the only firm where this goes on. Lawyers sometimes make "dates" for their out-of-town clients. Out-of-town clients want to . . . have a good time when they are in the big city and wives and children are far away.

WITH THE HEIGHTENED AWARENESS of sexual harassment comes a caveat: some men will shy away from working with women to avoid even the suggestion that something might be amiss. I've heard stories about men not wanting to travel anywhere with female attorneys because of the danger of being falsely accused—and sometimes they are—and of men retreating from mentoring young women because they are afraid of giving the wrong impression. "Men are now more self-conscious about helping a young woman attorney because they are afraid of sending the wrong signals, where they wouldn't have before," says former New York City bar president Barbara Robinson. Consultant Freada Klein agrees: "The biggest change in partners' behavior since the Baker and McKenzie decision has been the reluctance of some to mentor female associates." Innocent men have been scared off, but the roués are still wandering the halls.

Adding to the confusion, many men feel that women coming out of law school today are overly sensitive. Is every remark with a sexual overtone sexual harassment, a cause for complaint? they want to know.

Says Lee Ann Bellon, president of Bellon & Associates, a legal personnel search firm in Atlanta: "In some situations that I hear about I do feel that women have overreacted and that something that was meant as relatively innocent turns into a full-blown disaster. On the other hand, that is the typical defense—'I didn't mean it to be offensive, I didn't mean what I said.' It is a hard issue.

Nobody wants to be physically grabbed or to constantly have sexual references in the workplace. You are not going to stop flirting and dating at the office, but what is flirtation to one is sexual harassment to another. In my own office, there are seven women and three men, and at times things have been said in here by the women that could be misconstrued by the men, and I have to stop and ask myself, What would I think was meant if it were said to me?"

That may be the best test. Sexual harassment sensitivity sessions can do only so much. The same is true of sexual harassment policies. Both will accomplish little if they are not taken seriously. Law firms need to weed out the creeps whose every conversation includes a sexual innuendo and who are always looking for someone new to *shtup*. Plaintiff's attorneys and sexual harassment consultants say that when they go to a firm to begin discussions for a settlement, the partners turn out not to be as blind as they have pretended to be all along. They almost always know who the harasser is before they are told.

The shared responsibility of law firms has meant these men are accountable to no one. This is what makes sexual harassment at law firms so common and so difficult to eradicate. But until lawyers drop the "see no evil, hear no evil" stance about their own businesses, sexual harassment will remain an incredibly big problem for them.

Of course, men and women working together under intense conditions for long hours is a recipe for sexual attraction. Lawyers will have affairs with other lawyers; lawyers do marry lawyers. Outlawing office romances is paternalistic as well as unrealistic. So is making one person leave if they marry. The firm can lose one good worker unnecessarily, and since *she's* more likely to be lower in the pecking order, it's usually the woman sending out résumés. The answer is really not so complicated at all: Common sense and good manners will carry the day.

3

The Law and the Courts

HISTORY OF
WOMEN'S PLACE
IN OUR LEGAL CODE

In the Beginning . . .
There Was Sexism . . .

If you got the sayso you want to keep it, whether you are right or wrong. That's why they have to keep changing the laws—so they don't unbenefit any of these big white men.—RUTH SHAYS

STARTING WITH THE GREEKS it has always been a paradox of Western culture that justice and liberty stand as its defining ideals while relegating slightly more than half the human race to the status of nonpersons. The difficulties women faced getting into law school in the 1800s, and then to gain acceptance as lawyers, were but skirmishes in the context of 2,500 years of institutionalized oppression. The major battle has always been to win full equal status for women before the law. The battle has not yet been won. Ancient traditions of male privilege are built not only into law schools and the hearts and minds of male attorneys everywhere, but into the courts, into the attitudes of judges and the police, and most of all into the law itself.

Indeed, it goes back even further than the Greeks, but let's start with William Blackstone, whose *Commentaries on the Laws of England,* first published in 1765–69, codified English law, which is the backbone of American common law. Blackstone summarized centuries of statutes and court precedents in which women hardly rose above the level of chattel. "By marriage," wrote Blackstone, "the husband and wife are one person in law: that is, the very being of legal existence of the woman is suspended during the marriage, or at least is incorporated and consolidated into that of the husband; under whose wing, protection and *cover,* she performs everything. . . ." Known as *coverture,* this doctrine would later be compared to slavery, in that it effectively stripped married women of any legal rights except the right to be prosecuted for heinous crimes. Rank, to be sure, always has its privileges, and wealthy women were sometimes exempt. But in general married women could not own land, retain their own wages, enter into contracts, or sue anybody.

Whatever a woman owned at the time of marriage became her husband's. He did not have to account to her for any rents or profits. The only thing he couldn't do legally was dispose of her property on his own. If a wife committed certain misdeeds in her husband's presence or with his knowledge, she was not responsible unless it was a major crime because she was considered "as inferior to him, and acting by his compulsion." A woman could not give evidence against her husband in a court of law because it was assumed that they were one person under law.

Some scholars believe that Blackstone exaggerated women's subordination; whether he did or not, the very act of organizing the chaotic body of the law eliminated the numerous loopholes and legal vacuums in which women might retain some rights and enforced women's lowly place in the scheme of things. Women have been trying to undo what Blackstone wrought ever since.

Because North America was colonized more than a century before Blackstone wrote, the *Commentaries* did not have the degree of influence here that they did in the mother country, and women had other advantages here as well. For one thing, they were in short supply, making them more valuable and necessitating better treatment. Simply being an ocean away from the conventions of the Old World made new ideas and more fluid conduct acceptable. The hardships of making a life here demanded that women work side by side with men, and they were indeed granted enough freedom to fill certain occupations, such as innkeeper, butcher, and mortician, though if married, they functioned with the permission of their husbands.

Indentured female servants were another story. The shortage of women meant that some of them were sexually exploited by their masters and their sons, and if they became pregnant by anyone, they faced a grave punishment for bearing a bastard child. In the latter half of the seventeenth century in Maryland, for instance, nearly a fifth of the female servants who came to Charles County were brought before the court because they were pregnant but unmarried. If the man in question could not buy her freedom—and there is good evidence many did—she could not marry him, her child was taken away from her, she was heavily fined, and if she could not pay the fine, she was whipped. Furthermore, she had to work another year or two to repay her master for the time lost; the purported fathers did not have to pay damages. A female servant's lot improved dramatically once she was a free woman, and almost all went on to marry men with prospects, thus joining those free women with more latitude in this world than those in the old.

However, things were not so improved here that women could be cheerful about their status. One of the scandals of the colonial period of American history is the number of women who, having been captured by Native American tribes, chose to remain with them when given the opportunity to return to their homes. In most Native American cultures women had a say in the management of tribal affairs. The whole atmosphere of these tribes was more egalitarian than that of the colonists. And when the colonists rebelled against the yoke of English rule and English law, it was certainly not the rights of women that concerned them.

One could even say that they made light of the rights of women. When Abigail Adams, in a 1776 letter to her husband, John, asked him to advance the cause of women's equality, he treated it as a joke. Wrote Abigail, ". . . by the way, in the new Code of Law which I suppose it will be necessary for you to make I desire you would Remember the Ladies, and be more generous and favourable to them than your ancestors. Do not put such unlimited power into the hands of the Husbands. Remember all Men would be tyrants if they could. If particular care and attention is not paid to the Ladies we are determined to foment a Rebellion, and we will not hold ourselves bound by any Laws in which we have no voice, or Representation." She also asked for "more generous and favourable" treatment so that women would not be at the mercy of their husbands, as they were under common law.

In his reply John dismissed her as one would a child: "As to your extraordinary Code of Laws, I cannot but laugh," he wrote back, ". . . you are so saucy. . . . Depend on it, We know better than to repeal our Masculine systems. Altho they are in full Force, you know they are little more than Theory . . . in Practice you know We are the subjects."

But when John Adams wrote to a friend and colleague—a man—addressing the question of who should be allowed to vote, he came down emphatically on the side of male privilege. Only men of property should have the vote, he argued, stating that if men without property were allowed to vote, then "you ought to admit Women and Children: for generally Speaking, Women and Children have as good Judgment, and as independent Minds as those Men who are wholly destitute of Property. . . ."

Interestingly enough, women of property were allowed to vote in New

Jersey from 1776 to 1807. Since only single and widowed women could actually *own* property, it appears they were the only women allowed to vote. Spinsterhood did have some rewards. But women lost the vote after possible fraud in the balloting over where a new courthouse was to be built—it seems that boys and men had dressed as women in order to vote more than once. Anyway, a new state constitution in 1807 stated that the franchise of "all inhabitants" did not include "married women, aliens and negroes, [for if they had the vote] they would have the right to hold office." Egad. It was necessary to keep these groups disenfranchised, it went on, for the "safety, quiet, good order and dignity of the state. . . ."

From the great protoliberal Thomas Jefferson we get no better: "Even were our state a true democracy there would still be excluded from our deliberations women, who, to prevent deprivations of morals and ambiguity of issues, should not mix promiscuously in gatherings of men." To be sure, these men were merely expressing the sentiment of the times. Nevertheless it is their limitations that denied women "a voice and a vote" in the political life of this country until the Nineteenth Amendment passed in 1920.

By denying franchise to women in the Constitution, white men of property assured that the laws that bound women to an inferior status would be extremely difficult to change. For without a voice in the government that drew up the laws, or the courts that enforced them, or in deciding who the judges were, without women on juries, women legally were completely at the mercy of men. Consequently generations of women weathered laws and rulings from the bench that often were designed solely to keep them in their place and men in theirs, all the while whitewashing their pronouncements as a worthy, practically saintly, certainly preordained from on High, effort to preserve—*nay, to cherish!*—woman's natural delicacy and inclinations. The pedestal had indeed become a cage.

It was not lost on some that woman's status legally and politically was not unlike that of slaves. Dolley Madison, for instance, is reported to have said that the southern wife was "the chief slave of the harem." An 1854 book entitled *Sociology for the South* characterizes woman's lot this way: "Wives and apprentices are slaves; not in theory only, but often in fact." Scarlett O'Hara to the contrary, a more modern history notes that women in the antebellum South "took no part in governmental affairs, were without legal rights over their property or the guardianship of their children, were denied adequate educational facilities, and were excluded from business and the professions." The situation was hardly better in the North.

BLACK WOMEN IN COLONIAL AMERICA

But of course women could not be bought and sold as slaves were, and in fact they were unquestionably better off than slaves—especially female slaves. Nobody was lower in status and power and had fewer legal rights than black women. In addition to the hardships and loss of freedom endured by black men, the black woman was also sexually exploited by her white masters. In other words, she was available for rape. Any children she might have, regardless of the father, were a source of additional slave labor, cheaper than could be had on the open market. The system maintained a comfortable standard of living for the ruling class.

The economic benefit of slave children was obvious enough to be incorporated into Virginia law in 1662, a year after slavery was officially recognized there: "Children got by an Englishman upon a Negro woman shall be bond or free according to the condition of the mother, and if any Christian shall commit fornication with a Negro man or woman, he shall pay double the fines of the former act." Who, one wonders, was going to collect fines from a plantation owner if he impregnated one of his slaves? White women too were exploited under laws that dealt with race. Maryland attempted to enslave any freeborn Englishwoman who married a black man for the lifetime of her husband; in Virginia such couples were banished from the territory.

Historian Paula Giddings writes: "So, by the early eighteenth century an incredible social, legal, and racial structure was put in place. Women were firmly stratified in the roles that Plato envisioned. Blacks were chattel, White men could impregnate a Black woman with impunity, and she alone could give birth to a slave. Blacks constituted a permanent labor force and metaphor that were perpetuated through the Black woman's womb. And all of this was done within the context of the Church, the operating laws of capitalism, and the psychological needs of White males. . . ."

In these early statutes lie the seeds of the laws that have governed sex and rape into our time. Gender, class and race biases have been more or less automatic. The lower the class of the victim, the higher the class of the rapist, the less likely he was to be punished. Rapes of black women by white men were often overlooked, particularly in the South, yet when race and gender were reversed, the black man might expect a lynch mob to show up at his door while the sheriff looked the other way. Even today less attention is normally paid to such an offense than the other way around.

Early English law also contained these types of class distinctions. The rape of a propertied virgin, for instance, was always treated as a serious offense—perhaps even a capital crime—because her worth on the marriage market was thus rendered negligible, affecting not only her fortunes but those of her father. Regardless of the actual relationship between daughter and father, legally he owned her as he might a piano or farm acreage, and the stringent rape laws were as much a crime against *his* property as they were against the woman. That this is so can be inferred from the lesser punishments for the rape of a married woman, a nun or a widow. Since women received their status from the men who "owned" them, so were the punishments determined accordingly. The rape of a nobleman's maid cost twelve shillings, that of a commoner's only five. Whether the pain of a commoner's maid was any less than that of a propertied virgin is not a matter the law took an interest in.

THE FIGHT FOR SUFFRAGE

Because the denial of rights to women and to slaves ran parallel, the fight to gain those rights was originally closely connected. Early suffragists began their political involvement in the abolitionist movement, and only gradually did they begin to speak out for women's rights and the right to vote. Sometimes it takes an outrageous affront to one's consciousness to raise it. The women who attended the 1840 World Anti-Slavery Conference in London were greeted with the news that they would be seated in the balcony behind a curtain and were certainly not expected to speak. Eight years later Elizabeth Cady Stanton and Lucretia Mott convened the historic Seneca Falls Convention, where the radical motion to seek the vote for women passed, but only after strong resistance from Lucretia Mott and others of the old guard who thought it was going too far.

The Civil War put woman suffrage on hold, and after the fighting was over the nation was consumed with how to handle the newly freed black man: did he have the right to vote? Male abolitionists who had previously supported women's rights now told them to hush up—it was the black man's time. So the Fourteenth Amendment, which virtually guaranteed all *males* the vote, became law, and the Fifteenth Amendment, which stated that the right to vote could not be denied on the basis of "race, color, or previous condition of servitude," became law without the inclusion of the word *sex*. Feminists lobbied hard to have the word *male* deleted from the Fourteenth Amendment and the word *sex* included in the Fifteenth, but to no avail.

Black women were divided about the Fifteenth Amendment, some fearful that if black men were given the vote and not black women, their oppression would not be lifted. In a famous speech Sojourner Truth stated: "There is a great stir about colored men getting their rights, but not a word about the colored women; and if colored men get their rights and not colored women theirs, you see the colored men will be masters over the women, and it will be just as bad is it was before." White feminists and black women had an uneasy alliance then as they still do now. All were told to be patient.

Susan B. Anthony's patience ran out in 1872, when she voted, along with fourteen other women, in the presidential election after convincing inexperienced male inspectors that the women were "citizens" of the United States as well as anybody. Anthony, as the instigator of the crime, was tried a year later. Her attorney gave an impassioned three-hour speech outlining why she should not be found guilty under expanded women's rights. The judge instructed the jury to find her guilty. They did.

Anthony had not been permitted to testify in her own defense, but she brazenly spoke up before she was sentenced—even though Judge Ward Hunt tried to silence her three times—railing against the male-dominated legal system and arguing that since all men were her political superiors, she was not being tried by her peers. The argument must have inflamed Judge Hunt, but today her bold commentary stands as an inspiring record of both her acumen and her grit.

She had been tried, she agreed, by established forms of law, "but by forms of law all made by men, interpreted by men, administered by men, in favor of men, and against women; and hence [we have] Your Honor's ordered verdict of guilty, against a United States citizen for the exercise of, 'that citizen's right to vote,' simply because that citizen was a woman and not a man. . . . As then the slaves who got their freedom must take it over, or under, or through the unjust forms of law, precisely so now must women, to get their right to a voice in this Government, take it; and I have taken mine, and mean to take it at every possible opportunity." Anthony was fined $100 plus the costs of prosecuting her.

When Anthony died in 1906, it was still a crime to be female and vote.

REDEFINING MARRIAGE

Without the vote, attempts to recognize the legal existence of married women followed a slow and ragged path. Stanton, who had seven children, and Anthony, who never married, attempted to reformulate the marriage contract as a civil contract between two consenting adults, condemning what Stanton called "marital feudalism." Their efforts were dismissed as the rantings of the radical fringe.

Attempts to break free from the loss of autonomy imposed by marriage were not countenanced lightly. Lillian Harman, the sixteen-year-old daughter of Kansas publisher and free thinker Moses Harman, married her father's coeditor, E. C. Walker, in a ceremony where she pledged, "I make no promises that it may become impossible or immoral for me to fulfill, but retain the right to act always as my conscience and best judgment shall dictate." She would, in other words, continue to be her own person. For his part, Walker vowed: "Lillian is and will continue to be as free to repulse any and all advances of mine as she had been heretofore. In joining with me in this love and labor union, she has not alienated a single natural right." By doing so, Walker spoke out against marital rape, a right that would not be recognized for nearly another hundred years and is still doubtful in some states. At the ceremony Lillian's father, Moses, declared: "I do not 'give away the bride,' as I wish her to be always the owner of her own person. . . ." The year was 1886.

"News of the marriage brought threats of mob violence to Valley Falls [Kansas], and the officials—seeking to soothe the situation—arrested the couple on the morning after their wedding night," according to feminist scholar Wendy McElroy. The charge? Living together as man and wife without being lawfully married. Walker was sentenced to seventy-five days, Lillian Harman to forty-five. When asked if she had anything to say as to why sentence should not be passed, Lillian stated in court: "Nothing except that we have committed no crime. But we are in your power, and you can, of course, do as you please."

The Kansas Supreme Court upheld their conviction. The couple refused to pay court costs and spent six months in jail until the fine was paid.

Although the marriage contract wasn't rewritten, in the nineteenth century the common-law rules denying married women the right to own property of their own were shed in state after state, beginning in 1835 in Arkansas. Ostensibly they liberated women from some of the strictures of the past, giving them the right to retain property they brought to the marriage or acquired afterward by gift or bequest, to enter into contracts, and to retain their separate earnings. Actually the Married Women Property Acts were motivated less by male generosity than to assure the economic well-being of the state and gave women a great deal less than the name implies.

True, they freed widows from their husband's creditors, but this was done largely so they would not be a drain on society. Yes, they allowed married women to sell inherited land held in trust more easily, but this was done because the economic health of the growing nation depended partly on the easy transfer of property. While the laws lifted some of the worst legal disabilities of marriage, they sometimes complicated women's rights, making ownership of property more ambiguous than before. A good many of them presumed woman's inability to deal with the world at large, and none of the laws dealt with the many areas where women and men were treated differently under the law. By 1900 married women property acts were in place in three-quarters of the states, but as historian Joan Hoff notes, they were too little or too late, given the rapid economic growth and social changes that occurred between 1800 and 1900: "This century-long, tortuous demise of coverture took place against a confusing and changing backdrop of a political and economic drama in which women played consistently secondary and reactive roles."

In Kentucky, for instance, as late as 1921, when a Mrs. Williams and her husband tried to sell land that she had inherited in trust for her heirs, they were taken to court because the Williamses could not convey clear title to Mrs. Williams's property. Mrs. Williams, furthermore, could not be party to the suit, because under Kentucky's Married Women Property Act, she was not allowed to transfer title to land she owned. As a married woman, she really didn't own it. Consequently Mr. Williams was the one named in the lawsuit. Although Mrs. Williams had no children who could inherit the land—a condition stipulated in her father's will—and had passed what is normally considered childbearing age—the Kentucky Court of Appeals held that she might have another child who could then inherit the land. It was not until 1942 that Kentucky amended the law.*

Indeed, as late as 1964, in Washington, D.C., the court held in *Hardy* v. *Hardy* that a married woman who had discharged the maid and performed her

---

* *The case was in the* Dawson *contracts casebook discussed earlier. Although deleted from the current edition, it was included up until 1993 without mention of the Married Women Property Act or the incapacity that state law imposed on women. The current edition has no reference to the acts in the index, and I could find no mention of women's historical legal disabilities under headings that seem appropriate, although several other historical perspectives are included.*

duties for twenty-two years, using money saved from her household allowance to buy securities in her own name, did not really own them. After
twenty-two years of marriage, the husband sued for divorce and demanded
the stocks and bonds, worth $25,000 at the time, that she had purchased.
She contended that it had been understood that she should keep what she
saved as long as she continued the necessary operations of the house, but the
court held he was entitled to the whole portfolio. The husband gave her
money for food and entertainment, not for stocks and bonds, the court
stated, adding that "to hold otherwise would be to invite disruptive influences in the home."

Until it was repealed in 1970, one statute upheld in Florida required women
to prove their "character, habits, education and mental capacity" before being
allowed to engage in business. Men were not expected to prove anything. In
1971 a court in New York upheld a provision of the law that gave certain
exemptions only to women, explaining: "Plaintiff is in the wrong forum. Her
lament should be addressed to the Nineteenth Amendment state of womanhood
that prefers cleaning, cooking, rearing of children, television soap operas, bridge
and canasta, the beauty parlor and shopping to becoming embroiled in plaintiff's
problems with landlords."

In that same year, it took a court fight for Arizona to do away with a statute
that revoked a woman's license to operate a motor vehicle if her husband failed
to pay a judgment debt for negligent driving—his driving, understand, not hers.
If that sounds ridiculous, consider that as late as 1974 the Georgia Domestic
Relations Code began: "The husband is the head of the family and the wife is
subject to him. Her legal existence is merged in the husband except insofar as
the law recognizes her separately either for her own protection, for her benefit,
or for the preservation of the public order." Sounds like Blackstone dressed up
in modern language.

Left untouched by these acts were those areas where the law treated
women as inferior in status to their husbands or weak and in need of protection, or afforded them less favorable treatment, or gave men special advantages. Another major problem with laws designed ostensibly to equalize
women's status is the age-old one that plagues us today: Judges of different
temperaments and predilections interpret laws as it suits them. No matter
their design, married women property acts laws did not question man's natural dominance and woman's subjugation in marriage, a concept deemed to

be rooted in the law of God. And who could question that? Certainly the judges and lawmakers did not, not in the eighteenth century, not in the nineteenth century, not even in the twentieth.

Senator Sam Ervin of North Carolina, railing against the proposed Equal Rights Amendment in 1970, sounded as if he had stepped in from another era: "From the time whereof the memory of mankind runneth not to the contrary, custom and law have imposed upon men the primary responsibility for providing a habitation and a livelihood for their wives and children to enable their wives to make the habitations homes, and to furnish nurture, care and training to their children during their early years. . . . For this reason, any country which ignores these differences when it fashions its institutions and makes its law is woefully lacking in rationality." Ervin didn't leave a lot of leeway in a woman's choice of career. The ERA would have done away with the legal restrictions and gender-based laws that make women less than full citizens. Intense lobbying by feminists could not overcome the passion against it. Time for the passage of the ERA ran out on June 30, 1982. It was short of ratification by three states.

However, by this time several Supreme Court decisions had altered the legal landscape. In 1971 sex was not to be a hindrance in administering estates and trusts (*Reed* v. *Reed*). In 1973 women won the right to be granted equal benefits from the government (*Frontiero* v. *Richardson*), and in 1975, from their employers (*Weinberger* v. *Wiesenfeld*). In 1979 women were granted the equal right and responsibility to serve on juries (*Duren* v. *Missouri*). While the right to serve as executors of a will may seem like a small step forward, it was a giant leap. The decision in *Reed* v. *Reed* marked the first time that the Supreme Court declared gender stereotyping inconsistent with the equal protections guaranteed by the Fourteenth Amendment. That's the one from which the first wave of feminists fought to have the word *male* excluded. Stanton and Anthony—with the help of a lawyer named Ruth Bader Ginsburg—succeeded, more or less, more than a century later in intent, if not in fact. Ginsburg, not so incidentally, brought the other landmark cases mentioned above as head of the ACLU's Women's Rights Project. In all, between 1972 and 1980 she litigated a total of twenty cases that succeeded in heightening judicial scrutiny over gender-based distinctions in the law. These decisions marked a major turning point for women. What difference will women at the bar and on the bench make to the law? The question has already been answered.

"MODERATE CORRECTION" OR DOMESTIC VIOLENCE

Other abrogations of women's rights have deep historical roots in the law as well. Today it's called domestic violence or spousal abuse; but wife beating—or just slapping her around a bit—is solidly entrenched in our cultural heritage. Before Blackstone, a fifteenth-century friar noted that there were times when it was, in fact, recommended. As Friar Cherubino wrote in Siena's *Rules of Marriage,* it was preferable for husbands to "punish the [wife's] body and correct the soul than to damage the soul and spare the body." It was not necessary for wives, however, to likewise save their husbands' souls. Feminist scholar Deborah Rhode notes that by the Reformation, wife beating was legally out of favor, but it remained publicly acceptable if kept within "reasonable" bounds. Blackstone called it "moderate correction," and while he stated that the upper classes in the eighteenth century didn't indulge in it, the "lower rank of people, who were always fond of the old common law, still claim and exert their ancient privilege; and the courts of law will still permit a husband to restrain a wife of her liberty, in case of any gross misbehavior."

Although by 1870 there were laws against beating one's spouse in almost every state—in Massachusetts the law predates the Revolution—wife beating or spousal abuse has always been tolerated to some degree. Historically, the most effective control has been vigilante justice, whereby the batterer was beaten up or whipped by neighbors or the wife's family. But the absence of real controls in society, other than those imposed by groups such as the Quakers and Methodists, led to women's support of the temperance movement at the end of the nineteenth century, since drinking frequently accompanies battering. Laws seem to have been useful only when the violence left permanent damage, and by then the wife was disabled. Some courts interpreted the marriage contract to allow a husband to administer "moderate" discipline without threat of prosecution.

Whether or not the "rule of thumb" phrase originated in English common law as a measurement of the thickness of the instrument with which a husband was allowed to beat his wife—not thicker than his thumb—is unknown, but what is known for sure is that in this country judgments were referring to the "rule of thumb" in this manner as late as the middle of the nineteenth century. In *State* v. *Rhodes* (1868), for instance, a North Carolina judge found that the husband "had a right to whip his wife with a switch no larger than his thumb." The appellate court that affirmed the decision noted that the thumb ought not to be the standard of size for the whipping instrument, because "a switch half the size might be so used as to produce death."

In modern times all we need be reminded is that after being arrested for battering his wife, Nicole, after it was abundantly clear that this was not the first time he'd physically abused her, O. J. Simpson's "punishment" consisted of telephone therapy, two years' probation, $970 in fines and penalties, and 120 hours of community service. Hardly the kind of punishment to alter the behavior of someone as wealthy as O.J. Certainly society did not censure him: he continued as a spokesman for Hertz, continued as a second banana in movies, continued as a football commentator for NBC. The Los Angeles District Attorney's Office had wanted Simpson to do jail time—thirty days for spousal abuse—but Judge Ronald Schoenberg saw it differently and Simpson walked out of court that day.

Little more than a decade earlier, in 1983, Torrington, Connecticut, police stood by and did not intervene while Tracy Thurman was beaten senseless by her husband. Thurman's spinal cord was damaged. Today she walks with a limp and has severely limited use of one of her hands. Her successful civil suit against the police led to the passage of the 1986 Family Violence Prevention and Response Act in that state, but one has to ask, how many women must be sacrificed before we take spousal abuse seriously?

WHAT'S IN A NAME?

One of the common-law precedents that remains with us is the woman's taking of the husband's name upon marriage. The effects of this name change may appear to be minor, even negligible, to the women who take their husband's name, but the result is ultimately profound. By altering her name to that of another person, a woman subsumes her legal and social identity into her husband's. The distinct person she formerly had been known as before no longer legally exists. In effect she is saying that *she* does not matter as much as *he,* and henceforth *she* will be known by *his* name. If the name change did not symbolize such a submersion of her legal identity into his, did not symbolize his primacy in their "partnership," now exposed not to be a partnership of equals after all, and the state's acknowledgment of this, then the state would not have acted, as it has in the past, as if retaining a woman's own name after marriage was an affront to the state's well-being.

Furthermore, if the name change were not so symbolic culturally, it would

not be such a bone of contention between tradition-minded men and women
and those who chose to keep their own names. I have encountered both irritation and resistance to my retaining my name from some relatives and acquaintances. Some whom I have known for decades refused to send Christmas
cards that were not addressed to Mr. and Mrs. until I told them it was annoying;
others feel the need to point out that I did not take my husband's name when
introducing me; some older men have never been able to say my name without
making an inane comment about what my last name is or is not; and if I take
on a local issue in my small-town newspaper, the opposition seems to delight
in using "Ms." in their rebuttal as if this were somehow a slur upon my character. My asserting my identity as separate from my husband's offends these
people because it challenges the concept that man's place is at the head of the
line. Women are discomfited because my name challenges their choice to have
taken their husband's. The issue may seem incidental as a point of law, but what
it represents is nothing short of monumental.

And the law has taken it seriously. Not until the 1980s could a woman easily
retain her own name upon marriage throughout the country. Numerous states
wrestled with the issue through several court decisions and laws. In 1971 in
Alabama a woman was refused a driver's license under her maiden name because of the "administrative inconvenience and cost of a change to the State."
However, she could, the court noted, go to probate court and have her name
legally *changed to her maiden name,* though this probably required the express
permission of her husband. This is hard to figure, since if she wasn't changing
her name, what "administrative inconvenience" could they be talking about?
Overlooked, naturally, was how much administrative inconvenience would decrease if *nobody* changed their name when they got married. Less than a decade
ago—in 1988—when Wendy Jean Alldredge wanted to go back to her maiden
name on her driver's license, factotums in the Utah driver's license bureau told
her she would need her former husband's permission. This was after she had
been able to change her name on her taxes, Social Security card and bank checks.

I read somewhere that approximately 14 percent of all women today keep
their names upon marriage. But the legal name game is not really settled. The
issue now is whether children after divorce retain their father's name or whether
their names can be changed to that of the mother if she has custody. In 1995 the
Supreme Court of New Jersey said, yes, the custodial parent could select which-
ever name was in the child's best interest, a gender-neutral solution. The court
stated that although the long-standing tradition of using the father's sur-

name reflected society's attitudes toward women, it was not necessarily in the child's best interests.

THROUGHOUT THE LAW BOOKS, throughout the court opinions, throughout the fines and punishments meted out from the bench, one finds all manner of law where the balance between the sexes is still unequal. Historically, the gender-based laws can be as silly as the Kentucky statute that read, "No female shall appear in a bathing suit on a highway unless she is escorted by at least two officers or armed with a club." And they can be as harsh as the more severe sentences women receive when they commit crimes that are typically thought of as male.

Because the legal landscape in which we live comes out of one that was drawn up by privileged white males, for privileged white males, we are always trying to alter an environment where women are always behind, always secondary, always less than the class that made the rules. Full equality under the law always remains just over the horizon. Men may dispute this, given how far we have come the last few decades, and in some instances men are the recipients of gender bias in the courts. This is typically in cases involving custody, but these are rare, even noteworthy.

COURTROOM DEMEANOR

Lady Lawyers
and "Gentlemen" Judges

Justice does not depend upon legal dialectics so much as upon the atmosphere of the courtroom, and that in the end depends primarily upon the judge.
—JUDGE LEARNED HAND

No MATTER HOW the law is taught—cold, pure reason will rule the day—and no matter how the law is writ—without mention of status or sex—the law is what the judge says it is. And how he or she interprets it depends to a large degree on inherent inclinations as well as on the complex experience that makes up a life. If the individual hasn't a clue about or can't imagine what it means to be female, or poor, or otherwise second class, and makes no attempt to find out, or to bring some compassion to the matter at hand, then the justice administered will reflect the mind-set of traditional law: male and moneyed.

Equal justice for all must start with respect for all the women and men who work in the legal system defending clients—lawyers, that is. If they are treated badly, the same shall be true for the rest of us when we come seeking justice. And how female lawyers are treated by some male opposing counsel and some bailiffs and some judges is abominable. Sex discrimination in the profession does not end at the courthouse steps, for justice is no more blind than a three-card monte dealer. If dirty tricks can be made to work against women before they get to the counsel table at the courthouse, they will most certainly be put to use there. And that is the real heart of the matter about why sex discrimination in the law school and in the profession matters so much: it sets the stage for women's less than equal status in the courts.

A commonly held belief today is that the worst excesses of injustice in the courtroom are behind us, that the older generation has retired or is about to or has changed its ways through judicial training, either in a classroom or from their own attorney-daughters. The worst may be over, yes, but there is plenty of prejudice left to go around. New judges who think of women as less than their equals are appointed to the bench all the time—remember, they are only men, some of them those who gave women so much grief in law school and the profession. Our culture is so bifurcated along gender lines that a man can be a perfectly good citizen of the world in every respect except as to how he treats women. Even if they get judicial education on gender bias, and some resist it, they may not stay on the bench long. The turnover among judges is great. You educate one judge today, tomorrow he's gone. Then too, much depends on the kinds of individuals who are elected or appointed to the judiciary. A conservative governor, for instance, largely appoints conservative judges. In California, where a Republican governor has been in control for several years, women say that the bench has taken a clear turn for the worse as far as gender bias is concerned.

Additionally, a new incivility between opposing counsel that cuts across gender has surfaced, and it goes well beyond the facetious banter that all new lawyers encounter. All young lawyers have to prove themselves to their opponents, but women have to prove more. Maybe it is the increased competition women represent that is the source of this teeth-baring hostility. Maybe women are more sensitive to such cruel razzing because it's not their style. Maybe they are more sensitized because of their experience in law school, where a great many of them learned that as a group and individually they are not granted the presumption of competence that is ascribed to men.

The wisecracks are often gender-specific, whether stated or not. For instance, male counsel might overenunciate "Ms." throughout the proceeding, hoping for sarcasm, a ploy that has lost some of its punch as the address has become more common. Sometimes it is not in what is actually said, but in how it is stated: "They might talk down—do it in their tone of voice—they will make some reference about the law implying that the woman doesn't know it," says attorney Cornelia W. Honchar of the ABA's Center for Professional Responsibility. She adds that because lawyers are always looking for ways to defeat their adversaries, they will use whatever they think will work, and some men will make gender put-downs even though they don't think of themselves as sexists that way and would probably argue that they are not. "It seems that being obnoxious goes with the territory," Honchar remarks.

One Chicago lawyer tells of opposing counsel on a $30 million transaction who was "condescending, arrogant, harassing" and who frequently made chauvinist remarks. As soon as the deal was done he began calling her. She finally agreed to see him so he would stop bothering her. They are now married. She swears that he is one of the least biased people she has ever met. . . . "What this shows is that this [abusiveness] is part of the game," she insists. "You size up opposing counsel for everything they are and develop a strategy that is most productive for your clients." Even if it means engaging in obnoxious, uncivil behavior apparently.

Would she have had dinner with him, one wonders, if he had used racist tactics and she were an African American? Although he's married to an attorney, does he continue to be rude to other women attorneys? Given examples like this, it is debatable whether the overall situation is any better today than it was in the past.

The woman who has her antennae tuned to courtroom demeanor more than anyone else in the country, Lynn Hecht Schafran, director of the National Judicial Education Program to Promote Equality for Women and Men in the Courts, remarks: "When it's lawyer to lawyer, when you are in negotiations, at depositions, the interplay is as vile as ever—if not worse—because of the breakdown of civility between lawyers. And now men see women as an economic threat, so they are more vicious than ever. Whatever might have been left of a patronizing courtliness is gone."

Schafran sees an incongruity between what happens from the bench and how male attorneys treat female opponents. Today, she says, one is less likely to hear offensive language and unwarranted rebukes coming from a judge and directed at women than a decade ago. "The judges learned that you don't call women lawyers 'honey,' that you don't tell sexist jokes in the courtroom," she says. But if the judges don't reprimand offensive lawyers, of course it affects how the hearing goes. "Comments that belittle you and suggest that you are not competent do a lot to impeach your credibility with a jury," says Patricia C. Bobb, a plaintiff's lawyer in Chicago who heads her own firm. "It hurts no matter what side you are on."

Bobb and others agree that once you prove yourself to be tough and smart, the patronizing pretty much stops, at least with lawyers who know your reputation. Mary Alice McLarty of Lubbock remembers starting out a decade ago: "I am little and I am short, and I would get that 'honey' and 'sweetie.' It doesn't happen to young male lawyers." Once she shared counsel's table with a tall and imposing ex-military man during a custody case. He would lean toward her threateningly and stare at her for long periods of time. Other maneuvers included slamming books, throwing around papers and pencils, and whatever other body language he could think of with his large physical presence. But in this case the judge and jury were aware of his sexist tactics. Not only did McLarty win the case, the judge awarded more attorney fees than requested. Maybe it was combat pay.

Be that as it may, not all judges are so sensitive. Consider the response a female attorney got in 1993 in the Supreme Court of New York County when she asked a judge to intervene at a hearing because opposing counsel, a male, was abusive and patronizing. The matter being discussed was only the types of discovery that would be allowed; no jury was present. After the second time the man stated the female attorney was "not entitled to respect," the woman asked the judge to intervene. Instead of doing so, he began some chitchat about his golf game, she says, and then somebody nearby said that the judge's back was hurting. "Then the judge stated that he was now going to tell a chauvinist story," she recalls him saying. "He launched into a story about when he was young and a bellhop and used to carry women's heavy baggage and this is what caused his bad back. . . . 'And you know you women are very poor tippers,' " she says he remarked. "He also said that maybe he acquired his bad back as a result of carrying his wife's heavy suitcases," she says. "The judge then went on to discuss how this meant that he could not follow through on his golf swing. He then proceeded to discuss another attorney's golf game and the fact that he is a 'scratch golfer.' This was in open court with several people present."

When the woman asked that another judge be assigned to the case, she was refused. Eventually the matter was brought to the attention of the New York Judicial Committee on Women in the Courts. The male opposing attorney, who was well connected in the courthouse, told a completely different story about the incident, and according to the letter from the chair of the investigating committee, the Hon. Kathryn McDonald, to the woman attorney, the judge himself stated that he had "no intention to discriminate." The letter continued: "Indeed, he prides himself on his interest in and responsiveness to women's concerns in the courtroom." But imagine the uproar if the judge had said he was "now going to tell a racist story" or added, say, that *Jewish* women had too much baggage.

In Little Rock a relatively young female assistant prosecutor had to take action herself rather than get any help from the bench. Blair Beavers had put up

with the outrageous remarks of a public defender several times. One Monday
he was checking out her knees, and when she asked why, "he said he was
checking for rug burns," she says. When she told him he was not funny, he said
that "he would 'come over there and ram my tongue down your throat and see
what you will say then.' " Another time when they disagreed, he asked loudly
in front of the judge, the police who were present, and other courtroom personnel, if she was having her period. The judge did not reprimand him. Later
that day, with the go-ahead from her superiors, Beavers wrote a scathing letter
to the man's boss, the county public defender, and had it delivered by mes-
senger. Within half an hour the man's boss was on the phone apologizing.

SEXIST COMMENTS GET SLAP ON THE WRIST

The difference in how a New York judicial conduct panel reacts to sexist versus
racist remarks from the bench amply illustrates how differently we respond to
these separate biases. In the 1995 annual report of the New York State Commission on Judicial Conduct, which summarizes that body's work since 1983,
judges are shown to have been removed from the bench for racial and ethnic
comments but not once for sexist insults. One town justice was removed from
the bench for using a single racial epithet, as in "So long, kikie," which he wrote
to a defendant who had stopped payment on a check sent to the court. Another
was removed for using racial epithets when taunting a group of youths in a
tavern parking lot. Yet using comparable offensive language about women results in a mere admonition, the lightest punishment possible, analogous to a slap
on the hand; only in one case did a judge receive a public censure, the next level
of reprimand. In this instance the judge had made light of violence toward
women. Commenting publicly about a pending rape case, he stated that the
victim "ended up enjoying herself." Making repeated comments about the physical attributes of women attorneys appearing before him—and thus belittling
them every time he did it—brought only an admonition to a district court judge.

New York State Supreme Court justice Anthony T. Jordan Jr., for instance,
asked a legal services attorney, Martha Copleman, several questions about her
legal background and the length of time she had been practicing. He addressed
her as "little girl" several times. She objected and asked that she be called
"Counselor." Jordan apologized.

However, when the hearing was concluded, Jordan apparently couldn't contain his wrath over her standing up to him. In a raised voice conveying disdain,
he said: "I tell you what, *little girl,* you lose." Copleman, who left the court-

room close to tears, later filed a formal complaint with the New York State Commission on Judicial Conduct, which has judges, attorneys and laypersons among its nine members.

Jordan contended that "little girl" was analogous to "sweetheart" or "darling" and suggested that these were terms of endearment. But the panel didn't buy that. Six of them held that the judge should be admonished publicly; two said he should be admonished privately. Either way, an admonition is the lightest rebuke the commission orders. A prominent male litigator on the panel dissented with the idea of any punishment at all, calling the incident "trivial" and the lawyer "oversensitive." He wrote that "little girl" was analogous to "young lady," a matter that can reasonably be debated; both, however, have the effect of disparaging a woman's authority. If Judge Jordan had said "little Jew" or called an African American "boy," would the lawyer have made the same excuses for him? This particular incident happened more than a decade ago, but it is telling in that Jordan was not removed from the bench but instead received only an admonition not to do it again.

Overall, five judges were *admonished* between 1983 and 1995 for making denigrating or otherwise insulting comments toward women. None of the judges cited for making derogatory racial and ethnic comments received so light a penalty; they were either censured or removed from the bench. According to the report, to be removed from the bench for exhibiting gender bias, a judge has to have actually sexually harassed a woman or women—and that usually meant having sex with employees or physically assaulting them. It happens. In New York five judges were removed from the bench between 1983 and 1995 for just this reason.

LESSONS FROM THE O. J. SIMPSON TRIAL

For a vivid and recent example of the differences in how America responds to racial and sexist comments, we need only look at the O. J. Simpson trial. Simpson's unctuous lawyer, Johnnie Cochran, certainly did not think it was necessary to restrain himself from calling prosecutor Marcia Clark "hysterical," as he did on two occasions when Clark objected strenuously to defense motions. Another time he dismissed as feeble her reason for not being able to stay later than scheduled: she had to get home to the kids. Clark objected to both comments, but the point is that Cochran felt no internal compunction not to call her "hysterical," and doing so got only a mild rebuke from Judge Lance Ito. If Cochran apologized, I missed it.

By putting her down as "hysterical," he attempted to inform anyone listening that her argument was to be discounted because she really didn't have control of herself and was just blathering "hysterically," a word that has been used to insult women since the Greeks. Certainly there were times during the proceedings when Cochran's vigorous remonstrations to prosecution evidence—say, when a witness said he heard a black man's voice at the crime scene around the time of the murders—were "hysterical," if that's the word one wants to use to characterize energetic argument. Cochran was quick to scream—emotionally, volubly, angrily—that this was racism and should not be a part of the trial. Yet no one called him "hysterical."

"When you describe a woman who is displaying strong emotions, she is going to be described in feminine stereotypes, which are uncomplimentary, such as 'hysterical,' rather than in masculine terms, which are complimentary," observes litigation consultant V. Hale Starr of Phoenix. "Men are 'enraged,' women are 'hysterical.'"

But turn the tables and imagine what would have happened if Clark had used a racial stereotype of equal magnitude to disparage Cochran. Imagine, if you can, what would have happened if she had referred to Cochran as "chuckin' and jivin'" with his multiple theories of why O. J. Simpson couldn't possibly have committed the double homicide—it was really a drug-related hit, and the intended victim was Faye Resnick, O.J. has really bad arthritis and can't use a knife with force, but he was able to practice his golf swing that night before he took a nap, and so on. It just wasn't done. In any case, Cochran's multiple theories sounded like a lot of fancy footwork, but no racial slurs were used against Cochran or his client. Had they been, the outcry in the media and from the public, and most certainly from the bench, would have been heard around the country.

When Simpson lawyer Robert Shapiro made an ethnic crack about criminologist Dennis Fung, his comments were much bigger news than Cochran's "hysterical" put-down. I even recall seeing a couple of sidebars in the press devoted wholly to Shapiro's statements and the following mea culpas. Shapiro apologized profusely soon after, both to the public via the press and to a group of Chinese Americans. What are we to learn from all this? That women are still fair game in the courtroom. Sexist cracks are still publicly approved. "Hysterical" gets an objection only from the woman so branded. "Chuckin' and jivin'" is so unconscionable, it's not even spoken.

Of course, aspersions against Marcia Clark because she is a woman didn't end there. The country's best-known divorce lawyer, Raoul Felder, also felt free to make a wisecrack about Clark. Interviewed in the *New York Post* when the prosecution case wound up, Felder said that Clark "wins the award for shrillness and giggliness." *Giggliness?* I watched the trial intermittently all those long months and never once saw the woman *giggle*. But, you know, kids and women and other assorted lightweights *giggle*. Call her a *giggler* and you diminish her. Men have hearty belly laughs. Even Jimmy Breslin, in a paean to Clark in *Esquire*, couldn't help calling her "shrill," though he then attempted to excuse his use of the stereotype by saying that shrill is "the word everybody uses when any woman argues above a whisper."

"Even though terrible racist things go on, there is tacit public agreement that racism is a bad thing and we should not and do not expect it in the courts of law," says Lynn Hecht Schafran, who's been monitoring courtroom conduct as it relates to the sexes since 1981. "We self-censor ourselves all the time. But if you substitute 'black' or 'Jewish' or 'Irish Catholic' or whatever for 'woman' in most of the comments or jokes that go by with no problem, then you would understand immediately why you should not say them.

"It is assumed in public discourse that you can say derogatory things about women in any venue, that it is okay to comment about a woman's appearance— indeed, that it is always a good thing to do—and you can always make a put-down joke or a little throwaway derogatory line, because the men insist 'we really love the girls,' " she continued. "Until there is a public commitment that this is not good, and that we are not going to do this anymore, it won't stop."

Possibly one reason so many sexist comments pass for innocent banter while racist talk does not is that lawyers have grown up reading a body of civil rights law founded on the idea that bias based on race, religion or national origin is wrong. "Everybody is sensitized to those classifications, but when I was in law school sex was not one of the biologically predetermined factors that we studied," says ABA attorney Cornelia Honchar, who is also an administrative judge herself in Chicago. "We learned that it was against the law to be racist but it was okay to be sexist. Women have always lagged behind in securing their rights." But since 1964, the law has included sex as a classification that is not to be the basis of discrimination. It is just not adequately taught or taken seriously.

LET'S LOOK AT what happens when a woman makes a sexist remark. Marcia Clark, for instance, got off her own riposte in the Simpson show. As the "Do

the gloves fit?" debate dragged on, Clark commented about the size of a glove
that the defense wanted to enter as evidence: "Size small. I guess it is Mr.
[F. Lee] Bailey's," an innuendo referring to his potency. Now Judge Ito got
angry. While he'd ignored the "hysterical" reference, which is certainly as demeaning, he used that comment of Clark's to illustrate what would not be
tolerated in his own seven-point conduct code for the lawyers. Message learned?
It is permissible for Cochran to call Clark "hysterical," but a woman similarly
impugning a man is verboten.

But how much good will excising gender-biased slurs from courtroom dialogue actually do? "I don't discount the importance of raising consciousness
through exposing language that gives continued viability to stereotypes that
disadvantage women," says employment discrimination attorney Judith
Vladeck. "I am, however, cynical about the process. It took two wars in which
there was a need for women in nontraditional jobs, and a civil rights revolution,
and the massive political efforts of feminists and other women to make even a
dent in the thinking that informed the attitudes expressed in the *Bradwell* decision," she states, referring to the infamous Supreme Court decision that denied women the right to practice law. "Those attitudes are still echoed in
decisions today. It is the attitudes we must attack. The words will take care of
themselves."

THE BAD OLD WAYS ARE HERE TODAY

From the Ninth Circuit Gender Bias Task Force comes evidence that very little
in courtroom behavior has changed overall: "Without exception, we found the
same differences in perceptions [regarding gender bias in the courtroom] between men and women under 40 years of age as we found between men and
women age 40 and over. These data provide little basis for believing that the
differences found in the Task Force surveys will diminish naturally with the
passage of time." This conclusion is the result of surveying more than 3,400
lawyers in 1991, including nearly 900 women attorneys. Interestingly enough,
the under-forty female attorneys reported observing more instances of inappropriate behavior than did the over-forty women. What kind of behavior?
Making suggestive comments about female counsel during the proceedings; cutting off female counsel's argument; and commenting on the female attorneys'
appearance during the proceedings. For example, 81 percent of the under-forty
female attorneys said their arguments were cut off by male counsel; 70 percent

of the over-forty female attorneys concurred. The final report was published in 1993.

There is no reason to believe that behavior has changed since then. The courtliness that included a dose of condescension toward women that once characterized courtroom behavior has been largely supplanted with "Rambo" lawyers who practice "scorched earth" tactics leading to a "winner take all" resolution. As law has changed from seemingly a gentleman's profession (although some, including Dickens, would say it never was) to no-holds-barred combat, the profession has responded with civility codes—seemingly to no avail. Obnoxious, abusive conduct is often mistaken for good lawyering. Civility nowadays is seen as a sign of weakness. Women, particularly women of color, particularly young and inexperienced women, are perceived to be easy prey: if insults and suggestive comments will fluster them so that they lose their train of thought, or otherwise distract them, so much the better.

Schafran, who has been educating judges about gender bias for more than fifteen years, comments that some men—whether judges, lawyers, or other court personnel—really don't understand why gender-related gibes are unethical. She recalls a male defense attorney on a panel with her in Florida recounting a case in which he deliberately made a sexist remark to distract his female opponent during cross-examination. He admitted it would never occur to him to use a racial slur to fluster a minority adversary. But there's hope: listening to other panelists and reading the background material for the program convinced him, he said, that what he did to the female prosecutor was equally reprehensible.

As Johnnie Cochran has shown us, it's not that the man is alone. In Prentice-Hall's female litigators survey, nearly 88 percent of the 553 lawyers who responded stated that discrimination from opposing counsel was a problem. Nearly 25 percent said it was a "large" or "pervasive" problem. The figures for judges in this regard were hardly any less, with close to 80 percent of respondents in the Ninth Circuit report saying that gender discrimination by judges continued to be a problem.

Evidence of sex discrimination in the courts has been gathered by more than three dozen states (forty-one to date) that have appointed gender bias task forces since the early eighties. They have conducted hearings and surveyed judges, lawyers and others to document the problem, so no judge can say, Yes, it's a problem in New York, or Kentucky, or Idaho, but not in my backyard.

The task force reports are replete with horror stories about women's treatment as lawyers, litigants and defendants.

The task forces found an appalling situation: commonly used demeaning terms of fake endearment, as in oft repeated "little girl"; outright hostility on the part of the judge to any motions the woman attorney brings; condescending questions; pointing out rules of law to women only to embarrass them, when it is obvious they know the law; obvious favoritism and familiarity with the male attorney, who in fact might have shared a meal with him at one of the new cigar-smoking/fine dining clubs, or high-class strip joints, that are springing up across the country.

The state of Washington, for instance, found that 71 percent of the more than 700 female attorneys who took part in its survey stated that they had observed demeaning remarks directed at women or been the target themselves, and what is worse, 52 percent of them reported that it was judges who said them. Nearly half (47 percent) of the more than 750 male attorneys surveyed said they too had observed other lawyers act condescendingly toward women lawyers, and 27 percent said they had seen judges do it. In Louisiana 36 percent of the female attorneys and 12 percent of the male attorneys surveyed thought that judges attributed more merit to the arguments of men than those of women lawyers.

One Denver-area attorney reported to the state's gender bias task force that two judges were so hostile to women that she has had to consider "whether I am hurting clients if I represent them in front of one of these two judges." In the same survey a male attorney wrote that he has a "fairly obvious advantage" in front of judges who display "a strong bias against female attorneys" by exhibiting "an unwillingness to listen to arguments and objections which I knew had merit." In Colorado over half the women who responded to a state survey, and 20 percent of the men, reported hearing remarks or jokes demeaning to women, use of first names or terms of endearment for female but not male attorneys, and comments about female attorneys' personal appearance as part of the courtroom interaction. Most of the comments came from male attorneys, not judges, and the Colorado report goes on to conclude that "the problem is not so much biased or abusive behavior by judges as it is *judges' failure to control the behavior of male attorneys.*"

Well, yes and no. As we saw earlier, when a New York lawyer asked a judge to intervene, the situation went from bad to worse. Here is a taste of what is happening to women in some courtrooms:

Margie Lehrman was trying a class-action case in a Washington, D.C., district court when the judge asked if anybody had anything new to add. "The case had gone on long enough and the judge didn't want attorneys repeating the arguments unnecessarily, and since the point I wanted to make had already been stated by another attorney, I said nothing," she says. "With that, the judge looked at me and said, 'Who is this pretty little lady sitting at the counsel table? Do you have anything to add to this, *little lady?*' I handled sex discrimination and sexual harassment suits at the time, and I remember thinking, So this is what it is like to be the real victim. I had a new sensitivity to my clients." Perhaps for reasons like the above, Lehrman is now a director of the National College of Advocacy, a division of the Association of Trial Lawyers of America in Washington, D.C.

Tampa attorney Ruth Whetstone Wagner recalls the time not long ago when a judge ruled for her—she had a recent Supreme Court decision on her side— but apologized to her opposing counsel, a male, for doing so. "It was like the guy was his fraternity buddy, and he had to say he was sorry that he had to rule for me. The judge said something like 'Well, she's got you—I've got to rule for her' as if he were sorry he did. There is a lot of old-boy cronyism in the courts." It seems as if the judge were surprised that Wagner could possibly be right. Having to prove yourself all the time depletes energy and undermines your ability. It's like a white person constantly being on the defensive to a roomful of blacks to prove that she is not racist.

In Westfield, New Jersey, Susan Brandt McCrea remembers when a motion she made in a divorce case was turned down by a judge, even though she knew the law was on her side. A few weeks later her father, with whom she was in practice at the time, came before the same judge and presented the same motion, just as McCrea had written it. The judge, understand, knew her father from years of courthouse familiarity. The judge granted the motion. McCrea was in court that day. "The judge said something to the effect of 'Gee, your daughter was here asking for this, but I didn't give it to her . . . I'm not sure why,' " she recalls. She now has a successful partnership with another male attorney in an adjacent county.

And in one northeastern state an attorney who was seven months pregnant asked for a continuance on the grounds that a crucial witness was in military service in another state and could not be subpoenaed. The county courtroom was packed. (The woman asked that the state not be mentioned for fear that the judge will recognize himself, as she still appears before him.) The other side did not object. "The judge started questioning me—'Do you really think you are trying this case?' he said," she recalls. "I asked him what he meant, and he looked at me and said, 'Well, you *are* expecting, aren't you?' My face turned red and I didn't know what to say, so I mumbled something about how I intended to try this case, and he responded by saying, 'Well, I wasn't sure because you are wearing a big dress.'

"I stammered out that if it came to that, someone else in my office would cover for me. I got the continuance that day, but I sure paid dearly for it. I never reported the incident to the panel that oversees judicial conduct. I felt that if I had, it would be difficult for me to function in the state."

BOYS WILL BE BOYS

Much—if not most—of the worst behavior occurs out of earshot of the judge, where many a Rambo-style lawyer feels that anything goes. For example:

"Should you succeed on your motion, we would merely dismiss the case, refile it shortly thereafter, and in the interim send somebody over to perform a clitorectomy on you."

"Tell that little mouse over there to pipe down." "What do you know, little girl?" (That phrase again.) "I don't have to talk to you, little lady." "Be quiet, little girl." "Go away, little girl."

"Male lawyers play by the rules, discover truth and restore order. Female lawyers are outside the law, cloud truth and destroy order."

All three incidents occurred in the last few years. Chicago attorney David Cwik sent the "humorous" clitorectomy threat to opposing counsel Marilee Clausing. Cwik was ultimately reprimanded in 1992. By the way, he insisted that it was all a joke.

Attorney Lawrence Clarke addressed the "mouse" and "little girl" comments to attorney Beth Rex at a deposition in New York. Rex says the name-calling was accompanied by disparaging gestures by Clarke, such as "dismissively flicking his fingers and waving a backhand at me." In 1992 Justice Diane S. Lebedeff fined Clarke $500 and another $500 for attorney's fees.

But Frank Swan, the attorney whose blanket statement about female lawyers clouding the truth was included in a letter to Assistant U.S. District Attorney Elana Artson, got off scot-free. A federal district court judge, Alicemarie Stotler, initially sanctioned Swan for violating a local regulation that prohibits an attorney from acting in any way that interferes with a court's ability to administer justice; with the support of the ACLU, Swan appealed; the Ninth Circuit

Court of Appeals overturned the sanction in 1995, stating that the language in the statute was unconstitutionally vague.* One wonders what the outcome would have been if a racial or ethnic slur had been substituted for "female." But then even someone as boorish as Swan might have censured himself and not sent the letter. I mention this again because without making the comparison, some might not understand what the fuss was about.

But most incidents never get reported. Tricia Tingle, a Native American lawyer in a San Antonio suburb, remembers the time an attorney tried to bully her into submission. "This guy shows up unannounced and demands to be seen," she recalls, still angry over the way he treated her. "I had some other business to take care of, and before I was done he barges into my inner office and leans over the desk and throws a settlement agreement at me. He says, 'YOU HAD BETTER SIGN RIGHT NOW!' I say I'm not signing, so he screams some more and threatens to have me removed from the case. I'm thinking, What have I done, the clients need to be talked to and hear what this means, and he's insisting, 'You sign this right now!' "

But when her co-counsel, a man she shared an office with, walked in, "the guy sits down right away and crosses his legs and his whole tone changes," she says. "He is no longer threatening. He is totally different once Vince was in the room."

"You hear a lot of stuff about PMS," says Virginia McGrane, a medical malpractice lawyer in New York. "If you can carry it off, the best retort is to say, 'And you are acting like an old man with a dangerous spermatic buildup.' " Not all of the "PMS" and "menopausal" comments come from attorneys; the Ninth Circuit report notes that female attorneys described being disparaged that way by judges.

Put-downs with a sexual subtext are, in fact, extremely frequent. One woman wrote to the Ninth Circuit task force that during a deposition a male attorney placed his face near her derriere and asked if she was dieting. He continued to make remarks about her body during the deposition in front of other lawyers and a doctor, completely humiliating her. When she told the magistrate and judge, they refused even to listen to her. Another told of the time the stockbroker client of a male attorney tackled her to the ground in her office, and when she asked the other attorney to take control of the man, he said: " 'I don't want to hear about it.' Both men said, 'You must be frigid.' "

* *The State Bar of California and the state of California subsequently argued at a rehearing that the statute was constitutional; at this writing the Ninth Circuit has not yet issued its final decision.*

As a male attorney wrote to the Ninth Circuit task force: "Disparaging remarks about females tend to be more sexually oriented. The same conduct of a male would draw nonsexual disparagement." In fact, the report notes, 20 percent of the female judges and 6 percent of the male judges say they have heard their colleagues make comments about female attorneys' presumed sexual orientation. You know, if she's tough, smart and strong, she's probably a "lesbian" or a "dyke."

MORE WOMEN ON THE BENCH should—will—be akin to fresh air blowing into moldy courtrooms, but they do not assure a bias-free atmosphere. Los Angeles bankruptcy judge Lisa Hill Fenning, who worked on the gender bias task forces for both California and the Ninth Circuit, says it is sometimes still necessary to give out protection orders to women attorneys who are unable to complete depositions because of the outrageous gender and racial slurs made against them. "One lawyer said to a woman attorney, 'Women should be barefoot and pregnant,' and made some anti-Semitic remarks referring to her," she says. "You would think that a lawyer who knows that the case is before a woman judge wouldn't behave that way, but some of them will stop at nothing. Sometimes opposing attorneys will refer to the female attorney as 'madam' with the clear implication that she is equivalent to someone running a brothel. I admonish them, but it takes a long time for some of them to learn the lesson." Since 1979, when the National Association of Women Judges was formed, the number of women in both the federal and state judiciary has grown from little more than 5 percent to over 10 percent. The casting of women judges on television— where they are seen seemingly as often as men—is way ahead of reality.

Whatever the number of women judges, some male attorneys are far different creatures in their courtrooms than when they are appearing before a man. "Their general lack of respect is reflected in their demeanor throughout the trial," observes LaDoris Hazzard Cordell, a judge in superior court in San Jose. Judge Cordell, who is both a woman and an African American, contends that male lawyers say and do things that would not be tolerated—or even tried—in a courtroom with a male judge. "They are overly combative if they get an unfavorable ruling, they will throw their papers and pencils down in disgust, you can hear them say, 'I will never try a case here again,'" she says. "In their eyes we are not seen as important and serious. It's as if they think we are playing at being a judge, so they will humor us for a bit."

Several incidents stand out in her mind. One male attorney stated at the outset of a divorce trial, "Well, I don't think the court can be fair because both the judge and the opposing counsel are women." Since it is unthinkable to ask a male judge to recuse himself on the grounds of his sex, and males for years have represented both parties in divorces, the trial went ahead in Cordell's court. "I had to work very hard and not let my feeling about the man interfere with what was fair for his client," she says. Also annoying on a more or less regular basis are the frequent references to "girls" when the male speakers mean their secretaries and others, who are presumably grown women. "In one probate case a male attorney kept saying something like 'The girls would like to divide this money up.' I kept hearing 'the girls this, the girls that,' and I finally said, 'Excuse me, how old are these girls?' 'They are in their forties' was the response. So I said, 'They are women, not girls.' " Not so very long ago a male attorney actually called her "honey" at a bench conference. "I said, *'Excuse me.'* He had not a clue of what he had said. Then he says that of course he didn't mean any disrespect. What he meant of course was to trivialize my presence on the bench."

Judge Cordell, who is famous for not taking a lot of guff,* says she has become numb to the insults and sometimes just ignores them. More difficult in a way is stopping the attorneys who put down women plaintiffs and witnesses with their asides and forms of address. "If you affirmatively say, 'We don't tolerate that in my courtroom,' you run the risk of being labeled a pain in the rear. It is easy to have these gender bias rules, but for a woman, especially a woman of color, the effect of implementing them can be devastating on her career." Word goes out, she explains, that she is a bitch and can't be fair. Such malicious talk leads to cases not being assigned to her. The administrative judge who assigns cases is not impervious to comments about judges that he hears around the courthouse. Then too, judges are elected, and while they don't normally run campaigns as vigorous as other elected officials, who gets the nod to be on the party line in the voting booth depends largely on the individual's

---

* In the late seventies, when Cordell was in her twenties, one judge kept calling her "young lady" throughout the entire trial, while the opposing counsel was "Mr." with his surname. Finally Cordell could stand it no longer. When the judge asked if the "young lady" would stipulate to a certain fact, she stood up, looked him in the eye, and said: "Yes, I will stipulate to that, old man." The judge got red in the face and told her that he could hold her in contempt of court. "I said, 'I wasn't the one who raised the issue of age and sex. You did, Your Honor.' " The judge, she says, was really angry then. But he stopped calling her "young lady" and used her name instead. Cordell vaguely remembers losing the case.

reputation among the party loyals. The "boys," old or not, are still usually in charge.

Then there is the frustrating pattern of men just not hearing what women say. "In chambers, it isn't always obvious that the judge or other lawyer is dismissing what the woman has to say, because it's all very subtle," explains Holly Sellers, formerly staff attorney for the gender bias task force in Connecticut. "A woman will make a suggestion about a course of action or a possible resolution, and the discussion will continue as if she hadn't said anything, and then later one of those same suggestions is made by a man and it is acted upon. I've heard that many times."

WOMEN'S CLOTHING A HOT TOPIC

Women's clothes are a big issue in the courts. Some male attorneys and some judges can't seem to stop talking about them. Yvonne Huggins-McLean of Seattle was arguing a motion a few years ago when the judge asked her to do something overnight. Before she could respond, opposing counsel said, "Your Honor, this is the first day of the Nordstrom sale and if Ms. Huggins-McLean is anything like my wife—they send a limousine for my wife—I'm sure she will want to attend," remembers Huggins-McLean. Fortunately the judge told the attorney he was out of line. But his comment was heard by the jury. Was she a lawyer or a fashion plate?

"When women lawyers are evaluated you hear about their personality first, their looks second, and what they are wearing third, before you ever get to 'Are they smart? Are they prepared? Are they dynamic? Are they talented?' " comments Leslie Abramson, the dynamic, prepared and smart Los Angeles attorney who got a hung jury in the first trial of Erik Menendez, who had confessed with his brother, Lyle, to the murder of their parents.

The kind of evaluation that sounds as if it belongs in a beauty contest rather than in a legal setting happens all the time. It is never harmless. "You go to trial and someone says, 'You sure look good today,' or, 'You're the best-looking thing about this trial,' and that demeans your professionalism," notes JoAnn C. Maxey, an attorney in Little Rock. "By constantly focusing on what you're wearing, they make you a woman first, an attorney second. If I were to make the same comments to men, they would be perceived as a real come-on. Clients say the same thing all the time. I had a client tell me how nice looking my legs are, and that is the last thing I want my client looking at."

Superior court judge Faith Enyeart Ireland of Seattle recalls a rape case that resulted in a hung verdict. After the trial the jurors, she says, had a lot to say about the way the female prosecutor dressed. "She wore something with a sailor collar or something with a bow in the front—they did not like it. At a second trial where she dressed conservatively, she got a conviction." Judge Ireland, chair of the Gender and Justice Implementation Committee for Washington, also remembers an antitrust case in which she is sure that the verdict went against the corporation partly because the main witness was an attorney whose stylish outfits resembled those worn by the women of *L.A. Law.* "She was not provocative, she was just too gorgeous, and the jury just didn't believe her. In their minds, she was too attractive to be credible," says Judge Ireland. "I have heard people talk about the way men have dressed in the courtroom, but it does not determine the outcome."

Lorna Scofield, a Debevoise & Plimpton partner in New York, is aware that the last time tough-guy tactics were tried against her was the day she wore a Laura Ashley dress with puffed sleeves. "I was dressed more girlish than I usually do and looked more vulnerable to the opposing counsel," she says. "He said something that indicated he thought I was easy prey, and I just jumped down his throat and that was the end of that."

Litigation consultant Hale Starr observes that when it comes to choosing her outfit for court, a woman attorney labors under a heavy burden. "The more you adopt a masculine look and the more you adopt a totally feminine look and the more you adopt a unisex look, the more you are going to offend someone in the courtroom," she explains. "And since different people have different ideas about what is masculine and what is feminine and what is unisex, it is hard to figure out what to wear."

RACE ADDS ANOTHER FACTOR

African American women attorneys encounter an even greater burden, dealing as they must with the double whammy of sex and race. "Minority women are more likely than any other group of attorneys to be berated by a judge for no apparent reason," notes the Massachusetts gender bias report. "Finally, minority female attorneys are more likely than white women (and both groups are more likely than white or minority men) to be subjected to inappropriate sexual comments or touching by court employees." In one case reported in the Massachusetts survey, a black female attorney said that she was required to give testimony in one case that she was not related to her black client. When another African American female attorney was assaulted by a black male defendant, an officer of the court refused to restrain him.

A black woman attorney in Washington, D.C., says point-blank: "Every time I go before a judge I have to prove myself in a way that a white woman doesn't. You hear all these comments, 'You are such a competent attorney.' When I simply do a decent job, it is viewed as the exception." One doesn't hear outright racial slurs, she says, but there are other ways to show disdain. "The older male lawyers particularly try to intimidate you by being unnecessarily nasty. You hear the condescension in their voices, in the aggressiveness . . . it is as if they expect you to back down. I usually ignore them because there is nothing else to do. You can't go to the judge and say, 'Hey, Judge, I think this person is discriminating against me.' "

Unquestionably, black women lawyers are asked to prove more often than white women that they are indeed attorneys. They are frequently mistaken for court reporters. Yvonne Huggins-McLean recalls that one time her bar membership card wasn't enough with the bailiff; she also had to produce her driver's license because it had her picture on it, which could then be checked against her bar membership card. Another African American attorney told of the white female judge who addressed her client, a white woman in tattered jeans, as "Counsel" while she, the lawyer, had on a suit and carried a briefcase. "You know you don't just get black today, you were black all your life and you learn to get by," she says. "Today, every day in court, they underestimate you." Another remembers ruefully the day she was dressed in a business suit and pearls and was mistaken for a cleaning lady.

In Florida Assistant State District Attorney Marie LaCroix of Miami told the Racial and Ethnic Bias Study Commission that "partially as a result of exclusion from vital male-dominated networks, minority women are put in the worst divisions, get heavier caseloads, and are often not asked by supervising attorneys to jointly try larger cases." Another woman of color, Bertila Soto Fernandez, an assistant state attorney in Miami, reported that she is expected to act as an interpreter for victims and witnesses and expected to take on clerical duties that male co-workers are not, all of which detracts from her ability to do the job she was hired for: be a lawyer.

Rachel Patrick, director of the Commission on Minorities for the ABA, says that at every roundtable discussion the commission has held for women of color someone ends up crying. "I just assumed that the problems I had in law school and in employment were isolated incidents that had happened to me," she says, "but now I know that other women are carrying the same scars."

IS THE GLASS HALF-FULL OR HALF-EMPTY?

We can say that the glass is half-full at this point rather than half-empty, but the amount in the glass is the same. Yes, women in the courtroom have come a long way. Lynn Hecht Schafran and others throughout the country have been teaching judges since the early eighties about gender bias in the courts, a phrase, by the way, that was substituted for sex discrimination because the judges were affronted by the idea that they could be guilty of discrimination. Sociologist Norma Wikler, founding head of the National Judicial Education Program in 1979, remembers that the first time she presented a program—the first ever—on the subject at the National Judicial College in Reno, it was called "Sexism in the Courtroom."

"They let me talk about twenty seconds and they began challenging every single thing I said—really screaming and yelling, and it was just chaotic," she says. "Instead of being at a lectern, I was on the witness stand." Before the now infamous meeting was over, the judges threw spitballs at Wikler. Yes, spitballs.

The climate, of course, has calmed down since then, but some judges still balk when it comes to learning about sexism in the courts, whatever it is called. Schafran says that not long ago when a New York judicial education program entitled "New Issues in Criminal Law" was offered, the judges attending knew that part of it would be on wiretapping because one of the two presenters was a specialist on the topic. The topic the woman judge would be speaking on was unknown; it turned out to be child sexual abuse. "They all sat there looking as though they were sucking on lemons," Schafran says. "They didn't want to be there, they didn't want to hear the issues, they were furious, they felt as if they had been tricked. They felt that this was 'girl's law.'"

So when I hear that we've come a long way in the courts—and I do hear it—and that several states, Florida, New York and Ohio among them, have issued slim booklets of what is not appropriate language, that judges are a whole lot better than they used to be, that the worst of the lot have retired or died, that enough judges have been educated themselves and see that in their courtrooms, at least, overtly sexist comments or addressing a female witness by her first name is a thing of the past, that you don't hear women addressed as "young lady" or "sweetie" or "Ms.," dripping with sarcasm, as often as you used to, or that *some* judges no longer tolerate snide and sarcastic lawyers, the answer is that any time gender stereotypes and insults creep into court is one time too many.

For it may be that the one insult or the casually tossed off "little lady" or "my hysterical opponent" is the comment that unconsciously convinces at least one juror or judge that the female attorney is weak and thus so is her claim or her plaintiff. Besides, if the gender-related put-downs can rattle the woman opponent, maybe she won't do her best work—and the other side will win.

When women lawyers themselves are overtly aggressive in their advocacy—wearing the Rambo badge proudly themselves—a favorite maneuver to undermine them is the age-old one of name-calling: Women are "strident" and "shrill" and "bitchy" and "abrasive" and "hysterical." If their arguments are creative, they are "tricky" and "manipulative." And if they win too often—*you know how men hate that*—or if they are outspoken feminists, they are "dykes." They need to "get laid." Men are merely go-getters or aggressive or creative or assertive.

A federal prosecutor in Maryland recalls how during a long trial she and the defense attorney had a big argument. When it was over the man said to her: "I don't know how your husband lives with you." One Orlando lawyer recalls one of her cases in which both attorneys were female: "Debate got fairly heated, and the circuit judge said there was nothing worse than two women arguing. It gets better, because then the bailiff commented, 'Meow.' " Meow, hysterical, cat fight . . . all of them demean the women's zeal in fighting for her client and reduce a legal argument to nothing other than two females fighting, and that's generally, well, amusing. Somehow different from the straight-shooting way men fight. All of the nasty things said about women lawyers are also ascribed to women judges who are not bowled over by male braggadocio.

The bench may or may not be better as a whole than previously, but judges are all individuals and quite independent of one another. Forward-thinking judges can be replaced with conservatives who aren't even aware that they are biased, and furthermore they don't want to hear about it either. A fair and impartial judge can be across the hall away from another judge who discharges sexually biased decisions like an old Chevy in need of emission controls. But if you are in *his* courtroom, it matters not that *in general* things have gotten a lot better. Your life will be affected by the decisions of an individual judge, not the members of the bench as a whole.

Most women attorneys do learn to let the barbs and gibes bounce off them, and that usually stops men from using them. Sometimes the judge's obvious condescension and/or the opposing counsel's constant derisive comments to his female opponent without intervention by the judge work to the woman's advantage. Juries do figure out what is going on. Assistant U.S. District Attorney Elizabeth Lesser recalls a murder case she was prosecuting in Brooklyn where the defense lawyer and judge seemingly worked in tandem to prevent her from presenting her best case. The judge denied motion after motion of hers while granting the defense practically everything he asked for, even when they were in violation of the law. However, the jury wasn't buying his line of defense and found the defendant guilty after an hour of deliberation. "Then the judge set aside the verdict," remembers Lesser, "saying, 'I don't find these witnesses credible.' It was something he legally couldn't do. Lesser's office appealed, the decision was reversed, and the defendant is serving twenty-five years to life. "Members of the jury spoke to the court officers after they were overruled and said that the judge and the lawyer had ganged up on me and wouldn't let me put my evidence in," she says.

But that story is the exception, not the rule. For as long as gender games are a part of the way the justice works, the scales will be tilted against women, regardless of individual successes.

JUDGES GUILTY OF SEXUAL MISCONDUCT

"Judges have solicited sexual favors from criminal defendants, civil litigants, lawyers (including prosecutors, public defenders and private counsel), law clerks, law students, court employees, job applicants, probation officers, juvenile court wards and jurors," notes Professor Marina Angel of Temple University School of Law. "Some have specifically demanded sex for favorable treatment and have retaliated when their demands were not met. Despite the seriousness of this conduct, however, sanctions imposed against offending judges have been surprisingly light."

A judge found guilty of sexual misconduct—and it is usually quite egregious once it gets to that—typically receives nothing more "than a censure, reprimand, or admonishment," Angel writes in the *University of Miami Law Review*, enumerating fifteen cases of judges who were charged with sexual assault or everyday sexual harassment and what disciplinary action was taken, if any. New York, in fact, may be an exception to the rule, for as noted earlier, judges were removed from the bench for sexual misconduct there—five, in fact, between 1983 and 1995. But even if a judge is removed from the bench, other discipline may consist of only a short suspension as a lawyer. "Tough love" is apparently not a concept the judges use when dealing with their own. Even when minors are involved and the man in the judicial robe could be charged with statutory rape, judges often avoid any further punishment once they resign, as if that were all it took to repair the damage.

For instance, a former Kentucky judge, Robert Dean Hawkins, could have been charged with statutory rape. Instead Hawkins, who was found to have engaged in sex with two underage females under his jurisdiction in the 1980s, was allowed just to resign. And since he had resigned, the Kentucky Judicial Retirement and Removal Commission did no more than censure him publicly, according to Angel, believing that it was the most severe sanction it could impose. A censure by one's state supreme court is public humiliation indeed and remains on the man's record, but it involves no fines, no sentence. Such a man usually goes on to have a lucrative law practice, with no trouble finding clients, since it is known he is on familiar terms with his past colleagues on the bench. This is how the old boys' club works.

Kentucky seems to be particularly lenient to its wayward judges. A few years after Hawkins was slapped on the wrist, the state bar charged Judge Thomas F. Hardesty with making "untoward propositions to females who were before his court as criminal defendants." While the Kentucky Supreme Court found a "strong indication" of quid pro quo offers of leniency in return for sex, Judge Hardesty resigned before the judicial commission investigating him finished its report. The Kentucky bar then began proceedings against him as a lawyer, but the supreme court stated that while a one-year suspension from the practice of law "would have been appropriate," the matter was dismissed on procedural grounds. End of story.

Equal leniency was accorded a judge in the state of Washington. There Mark S. Deming harassed so many women that the supreme court simply categorized the numerous complaints under "district court personnel, probation personnel, prosecuting attorney personnel, and assigned counsel personnel" and listed only "illustrative excerpts" of the judge's misconduct.

"Judge Deming once asked a third-year law student in his chambers to 'take [her] clothes off and bend over.' He told a docket clerk to stand up and then hugged her and unlatched her bra strap: 'He then said something to the effect of "Gee, I haven't lost my touch," and was kind of tickled with himself,' " Angel writes. He told a deputy prosecuting attorney that he felt a "heightened state of excitement" in seeing her on the witness stand; he told another that he "would really like to jump your bones"; he winked at a public defender and then blew her a kiss. When her client asked, "What's going on?" observers in the gallery giggled. When a probation officer he liked to touch refused, he chased her around a desk, finally jumping over the top to assault her. In another instance, when a female law student intern appeared in court to give a message to a prosecutor, he told the judge the interruption would be very quick. Deming's response? "Oh, she's here for a quickie, uh."

Although Deming was removed from office by the state supreme court, which called his behavior "inexcusable," the court in its wisdom went on to call the years of sexual harassment the result of a "lack of social graces, restraint and decorum." Chasing a female probation officer—someone in no position to challenge the judge's authority or retaliate—represents a "lack of social graces"? Publicly ridiculing dozens of women amounts to a "lack of decorum"? Considering that Deming's outrageous behavior went on for years, it's surprising the judges didn't say, Ah, shucks, can't the women take a joke? In the end the only punishment Deming got was the public humiliation of being fired from his job.

Deming was brought to account in the eighties, before Anita Hill's wake-up call, but the judicial system today is far from purged of such gross behavior. Sexual misconduct may occur among only a small percentage of the judges, but if you are the woman it happens to, it doesn't matter that it's only one in a hundred or one in five hundred judges who are out of line. If the man is assaulting you, he's the only one who matters.

Because judges are at the apex of our culture, in both the legal system and society in general, the fear of retaliation protects them as efficiently as an alligator-infested moat. Whom can a woman complain to? Who is judging the judges but their friends and colleagues? Who will, in fact, believe her? Afraid of being thought the provocateur—"Judge So-and-so couldn't do that, I know the man" is a common response—afraid of the backlash from the judge and his colleagues who will rally around him, the woman keeps silent. One Kentucky woman told the gender bias task force there of a judge grabbing her in his chambers. She said the experience was so unbelievable and shocking, she could not talk about it for years. "Moreover," the report states, "she was dismayed as to any recourse; she simply avoided that court after the incident." Maybe the grabber was Hardesty or Hawkins. Maybe not. She didn't say. And as long as she is silenced, the lout can do the same with another, and another, and another; only the women he hits upon know about it, and each is likely to think she is the only one. A woman might be able to handle a sexually wayward remark or a pat on the fanny if it came from a peer, but what does she do to a judge? Slap him? Loudly embarrass him? Give back a stinging retort, a sexual put-down? Not if she is going to be in his court next week, next month, next year.

Without question this kind of behavior directed against women lawyers undercuts their ability to represent their clients. Which is another reason for them to keep silent about it. Here's how a group of women lawyers in Kentucky put it to the gender bias task force: "Although we are willing to share these anecdotes with the task force, none of us are willing to come forward publicly and identify the particular judges, lawyers, firms or governmental agencies for two basic reasons. First we do not care to put ourselves on a line to become a further victim of gender bias by pointing fingers and we cannot afford to jeopardize our clients or our law firms by such public identification.

"Second, all of us have persevered and become relatively successful at the practice of law and we choose to keep our public facade that the following anecdotal experiences are not painful, discouraging or detrimental to us as individuals and practitioners."

Before we leave the Bluegrass State, here's what another woman reported: At a social function given by the bar association, a judge before whom she was scheduled to appear commented on how much "I like to watch women's tits during oral arguments."

Kentucky is not alone in having judges who are captivated by women's breasts. This is from the Iowa gender bias report: "A woman attorney reported a particular judge continually made comments regarding her breasts." This from a New York plaintiff's attorney: "When I started out, one judge used to ask me to lean over the bench, and I am a little busty, so it was obvious what he wanted me to do," she says. "Another judge said how he was going to make me 'judicial by injection.' I felt he wasn't kidding. I was intimidated." From Texas: "One of the most offensive things ever said to me by a judge was the time that a male judge asked me what color my nipples were. . . . [T]he judge said that to me in front of other male attorneys. I was flabbergasted." Also from Texas: "I have had judges stroke my hair and caress my shoulders as we discuss the upcoming docket." And a female legal aid attorney said a judge "surprised her . . . by poking her on either side along her breasts." Only those who are higher up the feeding chain feel free to wantonly touch those who are below them; it is why we humans feel at liberty to stroke our pets whenever the mood strikes us.

While the following incident doesn't particularly involve breasts, it illustrates how silence allows sexual harassment to flourish. In Chicago in the early nineties one woman in her twenties realized that only the young female attorneys at her firm were sent to appear before a certain judge to settle the smaller claims in a large product liability suit. The guys, she said, did not get these dinky cases. The proceedings were held in chambers. "He was notorious in our firm," she says. "He touched the skirt of one of the other attorneys. Once he got me to come over to his side of the desk while he signed a settlement agreement. He called me by my nickname, 'Bunny.' The guy was in a wheelchair, so he was harmless in the eyes of everybody at the firm. The unspoken agreement of women who got sent over to him was that to zealously represent our client, we had to agree to be harassed. To stand up for yourself with some sense of pride would be to compromise the client. You began to feel like cannon fodder after a while—if you had wanted to adjudicate cases that way, you could have become a stripper. The partners knew about this, and to my discredit, I went along with it. In one of my reviews, one partner [involved in the case] commented about my show of good judgment. I knew it referred to this."

In Washington, D.C., a judge who signed the fee vouchers for the court-appointed attorneys made a regular practice of carrying on "flirtations" with the women lawyers—individuals, in other words, who were dependent on him both for case assignments and to get paid. These "flirtations" often involved drinks and dinners and who knows what else, says a woman who was there in the eighties when these shenanigans went on. Despite this carrying on, the big juicy cases were still likely to go to men—unless it was a sex-related case. At least one judge was openly hostile to women lawyers and made a regular practice of assigning all the sex-related cases to them. "He would say in court, 'You want a tough case, here, take this case,'" says the woman. "So you would end up representing the rapist and the batterer. He took delight in making you uncomfortable." She says women had no choice but to take whatever they were assigned because if they didn't, "you would get a reputation for being *too choosy*, and if you didn't take the cases, you wouldn't survive."

In Brooklyn, whose court several women agreed was "real ol' boys' club," one prosecutor found herself at a loss over how to deal with a relatively young judge visiting the jurisdiction about whom she said, "Harvard Law, he had a rocketing career ahead of him." Married? Yes. After a case during which he was particularly harsh on her, he asked her to come to his chambers and kept her there for three-quarters of an hour, quizzing her about her love life. "I didn't know how to leave—I mean, he's the judge—but I felt as though I were in a bar and being hit upon." There was no one—besides a friend who could do nothing—to tell that his questions were inappropriate. She could hardly tell him. Finally she said, "Your Honor, I have to be in court," and got out of there.

Judges' harassment of women lawyers is not the greatest crime of judges, but in a very real sense the act does not differ from your garden-variety workplace harassment. The courthouse is the litigator's workplace, and the judge, even if he does not sign her paychecks, is her ultimate boss. Whether she does well or poorly on a case depends to a large degree on the rulings he makes for or against her. If she loses in front of a particular judge time and time again, she loses credibility as well as clients. If she depends on court-appointed work, she's in no position to challenge a judge, or comment that his rulings are biased, for he's not likely to assign any cases to her after that if she does. If he's pressed her for sex, and she's turned him down, and he's humiliated and spiteful, she has no recourse to a sexual harassment policy—even if the court does happen to have one—or to a human resources department, or to any sort of an informal channel to get the judge to lay off. She has to bring charges to a judicial conduct board and, with that, jeopardize her standing as a member of the courthouse club, for it is not just that one judge who will likely hold a grudge, but all the others who are his friends, as well as the lawyers who want to curry his favor. Even if they know she is right, they are unlikely to say anything publicly. After all, they don't want to get on the bad side of any judge. They want to encourage favorable rulings. And she will be seen as a "troublemaker."

BECAUSE OF THE WIDESPREAD unwillingness of women to complain, no one knows exactly how serious the problem of sexual harassment by judges is. No one is collecting definitive statistics. There is no way to prove, for instance, that sexual harassment by judges is declining, even though the received wisdom is that improper language from the bench is on the wane. We do know that no state is immune. Angel's collection of outrageous incidents by judges is drawn from Arizona, California, Florida, Michigan, Minnesota, New York, North Carolina, Washington, Wisconsin and, of course, Kentucky. In the nationwide Prentice-Hall survey referred to earlier, 31 percent of the litigators surveyed stated that judges had sexually harassed them. The survey was completed only a few years ago, in 1993. We don't know what the women mean, specifically, because sexual harassment includes anything from a sexual reference or dirty joke that makes a woman ill at ease to unwanted touching and pressure for sex, and we don't know how far back the harassment goes, but a harassment rate of 31 percent—nearly a third of the women queried—is high enough to indicate that a great many judges still don't get it.

RAPE IN CHAMBERS

Sometimes a judge goes completely out of control, and his behavior transcends ordinary harassment and becomes not just criminal, but evil. One such judge is David W. Lanier of Dyersburg, Tennessee, population 19,000. In 1992 eight women testified that Lanier, a member of a family dynasty that held sway over western Tennessee for half a century, sexually assaulted them; and a dozen more who did not testify talked to the U.S. District Attorney's Office in Tennessee. Lanier was a sexual predator in a judge's robe: the women told investigators of violence, stalking, obscene phone calls, legal repercussions, loss of employment. Vivian Forsythe Archie, once a local homecoming queen and an honors student, testified that on two occasions Lanier "stood over [her], exposed his penis, and pulled her head down and her jaws open," according to court documents. There's more: "He then forced his penis into her mouth and moved his pelvis back and forth with great force. Archie testified that this hurt her throat and jaw." He did not stop until he ejaculated. To call it "oral sex," as some court papers and news reports have done, is like calling rape "genital sex."

Lanier was threatening to take her eighteen-month-old daughter away from her. At the time Archie was a drug user, a fact she admitted to on the stand. Archie grew up in Dyersburg and was well aware of the power the Lanier family wielded in western Tennessee. Lanier had presided over her divorce in 1989 when he had awarded her custody of her daughter. A year later she was out of work, and she and her daughter were living with her parents. When she heard that a job was available at the courthouse, she went to see Lanier, who told her then that her father had said she was not a good mother—possibly because of her admitted drug use—and he wanted custody of his grandchild. This was when Lanier accosted her for the first time.

A few weeks later Lanier telephoned her home and told her mother he knew of a job for Vivian, but she had to come to his chambers to find out where it was. Vivian Archie knew a job would give her more leverage when Lanier made his decision about her daughter. When she went to see him, Lanier told her the job was that of the secretary to Dr. Lynn Warner, Archie's physician since she was a child. Before she could get away, Lanier once more forced himself on

Archie, again ejaculating in her mouth. She ran crying into the bathroom to clean up. Then she went to the interview.

Lanier wasn't the only scum in town. Dr. Warner would testify that the judge told him Archie "would do 'anything' for a job," a signal, he said, that meant Archie was "willing to perform sexual favors," and "[a]s a result agreed to interview Archie for the job."

Another woman, trying to find a way to make her husband pay child support, said Lanier forced himself on her in his chambers and that she went along because she felt it was the only way the judge would agree to sign any orders to get her ex-husband to pay up. "I'm always prepared," she quoted the judge as saying as he pulled out a sleeping bag.

Some charged that he exposed himself—actually masturbating when he called them into chambers—or repeatedly fondled them. He manhandled breasts and buttocks, he thrust his pelvis while he had an erection into a woman's back, simulating fornication, he retaliated against those who fended him off. One secretary was fired after she rebuffed him; she testified that he told her they would have gotten along fine if she had liked to have "oral sex." Another secretary, a recently divorced woman with two young children, put up with him for two weeks before quitting. She took the job, even though he hugged her inappropriately at the interview, because for a person without a college degree the job of Lanier's secretary was a good one in a town like Dyersburg. She testified that at first he just touched her breasts, but as time went on he became more aggressive, as the court document records, "grabbing and squeezing her breasts, rather than just placing his hands on them. She confronted him . . . but he told her that if she reported his behavior it would hurt her more than it would hurt him. [She] testified that since the Lanier family was so powerful, she thought that no one would hire her if she reported the defendant's behavior."

One woman went to see Lanier concerning her work in a federal program, Drug Free Public Housing, which offered parenting classes for people who lived in public housing and were the parents of children being tried in juvenile court. Since Lanier was the juvenile court judge in two counties, she hoped that he might refer parents to the classes as part of their children's sentencing. They tussled in his chambers—Lanier fondled her breasts and her crotch before she could pull away—and he told her she could have all the clients she wanted if she came back to see him. She did not, and Lanier referred only two individuals to the program. The woman stated that she did not report the incident because the man was a judge, and she did not want too many people to know he had attacked her.

LANIER HAD BEEN THE MAYOR of Dyersburg for fourteen years, from 1965 to 1979. He controlled jobs in city hall and intimidated opponents and voters. In 1982 he was elected to the bench and became the juvenile court judge and the chancery court judge for two counties. In western Tennessee Lanier was the man who presided over probate matters, boundary disputes and divorces, hearing between 80 and 90 percent of them, along with child custody and child support cases. He determined who worked at each of the courts, including secretaries, clerks and juvenile officers. Women whom Lanier harassed were afraid to tell their husbands because they knew it would ruin their chances of advancement and they would be suspected of encouraging him. They also knew that if they said anything, their husbands' jobs might be in jeopardy. Lanier's influence on the lives of the women who lived within his jurisdiction can hardly be exaggerated.

To make matters worse, the family was deeply entrenched in western Tennessee. Lanier's father had been county clerk in the 1930s and once held the county largely under his political control. Lanier's brother, James, who died of cancer in 1991, was at various times a representative to the state legislature and a district attorney. At the time of his death he was under investigation for taking kickbacks from drug traffickers, possible ties to illegal gambling, and placing a spy within the Tennessee Bureau of Investigation. Although the two brothers were political enemies, the women of Dyer and Lake Counties felt that it was useless to go to James to ask him to prosecute his brother for sexual assault or coercion. The word on the street among attorneys in Dyersburg was that if they wanted something from Judge Lanier, they should send their secretaries over to ask for it, the same way the Chicago firm sent young female attorneys to the crippled judge seeking favorable decisions.

In a town where not that many good jobs were available, where one man could decide whether your child stayed with you or was taken from you, what happened when your child appeared in juvenile court, how much child support or alimony you might receive, where there was no one to turn to who would do anything about the judge because no one in Tennessee would prosecute him, it is not hard to understand how these women protected a sleaze like David Lanier with a wall of silence. Those of us who live in big cities, where there are more resources, more judges, more people to help, where one family cannot hold sway over whole groups of people, may be skeptical of his seemingly absolute control, but Lanier himself had no doubts about it:

"Don't worry. I am a judge, and I can do anything I want," a court employee said he muttered to her behind the bench as he placed his hand on her crotch. Court was in session.

Eventually the women found help from the U.S. District Attorney's Office in Memphis, which got wind of Lanier's behavior with women when they were investigating him for other possible charges of corruption. The U.S. District Attorney's Office soon involved the FBI, which at first did not want to deal with the sex charges, believing them to be beyond their purview. But because of the women's distress, and the knowledge that it would be impossible to successfully prosecute Lanier in the state courts, the FBI and the U.S. District Attorney's Office teamed up and went ahead, with the approval of the Justice Department.

Charges against Lanier were brought under a statute dating back to the Reconstruction era (18 U.S. 242), which was designed to protect citizens from police and other public officials who abused their office. Most of the acts occurred under the "color of law," a phrase that means they occurred while Lanier was acting in his official capacity. As a matter of fact, Lanier was wearing his robe when most of the incidents occurred. He was indicted in May of 1992 for three felonies and eight misdemeanors in depriving eight women of their constitutional rights by using his position to sexually assault them. He denied everything—except one act of what he said was "consensual" sex with a woman who had a child support matter before him. He claimed his political enemies were out to destroy him. Trial was set for fall, and he was out on bond. Two days after the indictments were handed down, he was back on the bench.

THAT SUMMER one of the women who had testified against him in the grand jury hearing brought another matter to his court. He was under orders not to contact any of the women—but not to recuse himself from their cases. The woman wanted to transfer custody of her child to her parents so the child could attend another school. She had testified before the grand jury that had indicted Lanier. With the woman's parents present, Lanier heard the case in chambers. According to Stephen C. Parker, one of the attorneys who prosecuted Lanier, he clearly tried to frighten the woman, warning her that if he transferred custody, she would have to come back to him if she ever wanted to change that status.

She then asked to see him in private. Unbeknownst to her, Lanier was taping the conversation. She apologized to him for testifying for the grand jury, saying that she had been forced to do so under threat of committing perjury. She finally broke down and cried, and then one can hear on the tape the rubbing sound when Lanier reached down and touched—*rubbed*—the woman's crotch, according to Parker. She can then be heard tearfully thanking the judge for the order she was asking for. "Instead of wielding a gun over these women," Parker says, "Lanier used the power of his office. What type of man is aroused by someone breaking down and crying?"

The Tennessee Court of the Judiciary began its own investigation of Lanier, and although he was indicted in May 1992, it wasn't until August of that year that the state supreme court reassigned all his cases to another judge and Lanier was effectively removed from the bench. The state legislature instituted impeachment proceedings, but in the meantime Lanier collected his $85,300-a-year salary.

Lanier was free on an unsecured $20,000 bond. In August prosecutors accused him of contacting witnesses to try to intimidate them into changing their testimony. Several of the women said they received obscene phone calls they believed were made by Lanier. Others complained that Lanier stalked them. One woman said she caught Lanier on his hands and knees, peering into the ground-floor window of her basement apartment, and received explicit obscene phone calls with details as telling as the color of her nail polish. She also said that she twice found dead roses in her car, which Lanier had frequently borrowed, and once she came home to find them all over the front porch of her home. He propositioned another of the women. A federal magistrate ruled that Lanier violated conditions of his bond but declined to put him in jail.

Lanier turned down a plea bargain that would have required him to plead guilty to misdemeanors, resign from the bench, and serve eighteen months in jail. The trial was held in late 1992 and mesmerized the county for three weeks. Eight women and four men returned a guilty verdict of two counts of felony and five counts of misdemeanor. Lanier was found not guilty of a couple of the charges, including the one in which the woman did have sex with him in return for a favorable ruling on her child support case. She worked at city hall across the street from the court, and he later left $100 on her desk, which she did not return, factors that apparently affected the jury's decision. Lanier was the first sitting judge ever successfully prosecuted under the federal statute. It began to seem as if equal justice had been served.

·   ·   ·

WHILE AWAITING SENTENCING, Lanier continued his efforts to get the women to recant. According to prosecutors, Lanier asked Dr. Warner to contact Archie in his behalf, and Warner did so. He was also accused of writing to two lawyers, urging them to contact witnesses and ask them to recant. Finally, in February of 1993, a judge revoked his bail and put him behind bars. A few weeks later he was sentenced to the maximum under the federal sentencing guidelines—twenty-five years in prison with no parole. At sentencing Parker called him "a common rapist" and "a convicted sex offender." His $1,600-a-month pension, to which he was still entitled even though incarcerated, would be effectively collected back by the state as a $1,490-a-month fee imposed for the cost of imprisonment.

Before the indictment Lanier and his longtime wife, Joan, were divorced. Nevertheless she, along with their two daughters, stood by him during the trial. Property the ex–Mrs. Lanier would not normally be entitled to by law was transferred to her as a lump-sum alimony payment, thereby impoverishing him and shielding his assets from any civil claims from the women. Strangely enough, the settlement agreement between the Laniers was filed shortly *before* the divorce papers themselves were filed.

"Our only hope of collecting anything is to undo that divorce," says Kathleen Caldwell of Memphis, attorney for three of the women who are suing for damages. "It appears to be totally bogus. Even so, there is not enough money to make up for what he did to these women." Another lawsuit was dismissed because the statute of limitations—one year in Tennessee—had run out. But those of the women he harassed after the trial are still in the courts. Vivian Archie is one of them; she has moved to another state and kicked her drug habit, and she is doing well. Another of the women, Caldwell says, became divorced largely as a result of Lanier's actions and has fled the county.

But the story doesn't end there.

Lanier appealed, naturally. In 1994 three judges of the Sixth Circuit Court of Appeals, which takes in Kentucky, Michigan, Ohio and Tennessee, reaffirmed the conviction in a strongly worded rejection. (Most of the previous quotes are taken from the opinion.) But the following year, in a move that surprised the Justice Department and the FBI, the entire Sixth Circuit Court of Appeals agreed to hear oral arguments on Lanier's case. By doing so, the judges voided the earlier rejection of his appeal. It was a curious turn of events, since this happens so rarely. Even more unusual was that the judge who had written the previous stinging affirmation of the conviction, H. Ted Milburn, was asked to recuse himself. Why? He had known Lanier since law school and they were friends. Although Milburn's "friendship" did not stand in the way of his upholding Lanier's conviction, Milburn went along. In court that day, June 14, 1994, Lanier's court-appointed attorney, Alfred Knight, was greeted warmly and ceremoniously by Chief Judge Gilbert S. Merritt, a fellow Tennessean. Knight was Lanier's former law partner, whom Merritt had appointed to represent a supposedly indigent Lanier. The story just gets curiouser and curiouser.

According to those present, it soon became clear from the judges' gentle rhetorical questioning of Knight and the skepticism—call it hostility—shown toward the government attorney, Tom Chandler, an appeals specialist from Washington, that a major surprise was in store for most of those present. Judge Merritt questioned Chandler as to what constitutional right Lanier had violated.

"The right to bodily integrity," he replied. Chandler said that this right came from the Fourth Amendment, which protects us from unlawful search and seizure, from the "due process" clause in the Fourteenth Amendment, and from precedent. Chandler cited cases from other circuits in the last decade that affirmed one's right to "bodily integrity," but the judges weren't buying. In Darcy O'Brien's compelling book on the case, The Power to Hurt, the author says that one of the four women judges who sit on the court, Cornelia G. Kennedy, suggested that the trial judge made a mistake when he told the jury that to convict, they must find Lanier's acts "shocking to one's conscience." U.S. District Attorney Parker says this was done not to lower the burden of proof, but to raise it. Now it seemed to be turned on its head.

"What if I went down to Riverfront Stadium," asked circuit court judge David A. Nelson, referring to the Cincinnati stadium, "and beat up a ticket scalper just because he sold me lousy seats? Does that make me guilty of a federal crime?"

"Sure, if you were wearing your robe," responded Judge Merritt. "Ha ha!"

The women and their pain and humiliation? It seems to have been all but forgotten in that courtroom. The next day the judges voted nine to six to release him. Lanier was immediately freed from the Alabama prison where he had been jailed. Lanier returned to Dyersburg and moved back in with his ex-wife, according to sources in Dyersburg. "We're optimistic and praying for him and for everyone involved in this," said Joan Lanier at the time. The only thing that can be said is that the scum served more time than the plea bargain he refused, but that is cold comfort to the women involved or to the rest of us.

When the Sixth Circuit majority released their opinion earlier this year

(1996), it omitted any statement of facts—Lanier's despicable deeds were simply missing. No one could be reminded what he had done. Their reasoning was that since the Supreme Court has never explicitly held that the "right to bodily integrity" includes freedom from sexual assault, Lanier therefore couldn't be charged with a crime because he didn't know raping women in chambers while wearing his robe was a violation of federal law. In other rulings the right to "bodily integrity" has included the right not to be beaten up, but rape is somehow different in these judges' minds. "Permitting federal prosecutions of 'conscience shocking' simple and sexual assaults committed by federal, state and local employees or officials," wrote Judge Merritt, "places unparalleled, unprecedented discretion in the hands of federal law enforcement officers, prosecutors and judges." If you take this statement at face value, it implies that the discretion over whether to force a woman to have sex with a judge lies in the hands of that judge solely. The Constitution, in short, doesn't include the right not to be raped by a judge. This means that until the Supreme Court says otherwise, judges who wish to exchange favorable rulings, or jobs, for sex are violating no *federal* law, and the victims have no constitutional protection. To anyone not raised to think like a lawyer—nay, to anyone who believes in justice—it is as plain as the blindfold on the statue representing justice that this group was looking for a loophole for Lanier. It is as Ambrose Bierce noted in his definition of "lawyer": "n., one skilled in circumvention of the law." These judges are quite skilled.

"What they are saying is that the right to bodily integrity is not a right under federal law," says Steve Parker. "Under federal law, you cannot beat someone, but you can rape them." If the state had chosen to prosecute him, of course, he would have been charged with felonies for the sexual assaults. But no one believed he could be convicted if charges were brought in state courts. The Sixth Circuit did have some precedent: in a biting dissenting opinion in a 1994 case, *Doe* v. *Taylor Independent School District,* in which a fifteen-year-old student successfully brought suit against the school district for not stopping a teacher from molesting her, a Fifth Circuit female judge, Edith H. Jones, wrote: "If Doe has a viable constitutional claim, I say, let the Supreme Court say so."

As I write, the Supreme Court has agreed to hear the case brought by the Justice Department, *United States* vs. *Lanier.* The outcome will determine if sexual harassment and assault by a public official deprives someone of their constitutional rights.

•   •   •

FEAR OF EXPOSING the dirty little secrets of the courthouse only perpetuates the evil. The women of Dyersburg knew what Lanier was up to, but most kept silent because of the fear of retaliation. For years women kept silent about Senator Robert Packwood's habit of sticking his tongue into their mouths when they didn't expect it. Until they talked to the press about it, and to the Senate Ethics Committee, Packwood didn't feel it was necessary to cut the drinking and stop the groping, much of which he says he doesn't remember. Likewise, until women tell others—anyone and everyone—about sexual misconduct and harassment by judges, it will continue because it can, because no one is saying *Stop!*

Unquestionably sexual harassment from the bench is the final betrayal. Judges embody ultimate power, and when they abuse it by sexually harassing or abusing those under their jurisdiction—whether lawyers, court employees, or women who come before them as defendants or victims—our legal system is operating at its absolute nadir.

Our legal system does not choose its judges with merit as the sole determining factor. Judges are usually lawyers first, and typically it is their political skill and standing in the old boys' network that propels them to the bench, not probity, not moral rectitude, not an inherent sense of justice. We know that lawyers as a group are among the worst harassers. Some of them become judges. We know, or should know, that what some men—judges and lawyers both— hear as playful banter, women hear as insults. It is not the women who need to change, any more than African Americans should become inured to racist slurs; it is the men who speak them who must change. Until very recently we as a nation have acted as if a man's sexual proclivities were somehow disengaged from the rest of his character, as if how he treated women bore no connection to his moral being, when in fact the two cannot be separated. Some decry this trend, blaming "the media" for a lack of privacy of public figures; it is in fact a refreshing change, for if a man's relationships to women were of no consequence, then the women themselves were also of no consequence. That it matters today means that women as a group matter more.

It is true that the job sometimes makes the individual, but it is also true that power corrupts. And it is the power of the judiciary and women's silence that have allowed judges who harass women to get away with it, sometimes for years, without fear of reprisal. We would like to think that is changing, that what Anita Hill started cannot be put back inside of a box and stored in a dark corner somewhere, that the gender bias reports are doing their work by shining light on how women have been wronged by our courts. But then we are left asking, Why is David Lanier living quietly in Dyersburg? Where is the justice for the women Lanier wronged? In the end, what happens to any individual woman happens to all of us.

DIVORCE

Breaking up
Is Hard to Do

Divorce is the one human tragedy that reduces everything to cash.
——RITA MAE BROWN IN *SUDDEN DEATH*

MANY——IF NOT MOST——women will have their first direct involvement in the legal system if they get a divorce. Although the rate of divorce declined slightly in the late eighties, it is still true that nearly one in two marriages ends in divorce. For some the split will not feel tragic and the division of assets not that traumatic. Some marriages are of short duration (half of all divorcing parties have been married under seven years) and produce no children (four out of ten dissolving marriages), and the community property to be divided is neither great nor largely the result of one individual's contribution. Marital assets available to divide will probably not exceed $30,000.

But for many people divorce will be a horrendous event. One study measuring people's responses to various "life events" found that divorce ranked as more stressful than a jail term or the death of a close member of the family; it was second only to death of a spouse. So emotionally charged is the breakup of a household for most people that for those who can't easily sort out their property and the children by themselves——and resort to warring lawyers——it's almost a sure bet that no matter the outcome, both sides will end up feeling used and abused, outraged at their ex-spouses, and his or her lawyer, one's own attorney and, should the case be one of the approximately one in ten that actually gets to trial, the judge to boot. "Poll the last five thousand divorces and 80 percent of them would say the system was not fair to them," says Gary

Skoloff, coauthor of *When a Professional Divorces* and a matrimonial lawyer in Livingston, New Jersey. "No matter how you cut it, you can come to the conclusion that you were unfairly treated."

So both sides feel victimized. Some fathers contend that generally they are automatically deprived of a right to take a meaningful role in their children's upbringing and are reduced instead to a monthly check. In 1994 in New York a group of men brought suit in federal court, alleging that custody is awarded to mothers as a matter of custom, often ignoring evidence to the contrary. The suit was dismissed, but another is being pursued in the name of all parents—fathers and mothers—who lose custody, arguing that no court in the state has the right to strip a parent of custodial rights without a jury trial. Around the country other father's rights groups have sprung up to oppose what they maintain is a system that punishes them unfairly. In California women brought suit in federal court, claiming that the state courts, after failing to protect them from physically abusive partners, discriminate against them in custody cases because they have attempted to protect their children from the abusive fathers. In Ohio another group of women is charging in federal court that the entire family court system in the state, from juvenile court to trial court to appellate court to the supreme court, systematically discriminates against women and bends the rules to favor men.

One result of men's dissatisfaction is that lawyers are more likely to ask women judges to recuse themselves than they do male judges, particularly in divorce cases. In 1992, when both of the two judges assigned to family court in supposedly liberal St. Paul would have been women, "it was like a nuclear explosion went off," says Kathleen Gearin, whose normal rotation to family court was delayed to prevent this from happening. Judge Gearin would have overlapped with a second female judge for six months. Male lawyers and other judges had a hissy fit, and the administrative judge waited to assign her to family court until the other female judge had moved on. "Yet from 1848 until the mid-1980s, there *never* was a woman in family court at all," Judge Gearin says, still exasperated. "And if there were two judges, they were two men, and nobody said 'That's not right, we can't have that.' I was left speechless. You hear lawyers say again and again, 'My client doesn't want a woman judge,' and they ask you to recuse yourself. I always wonder how much it was the client and how much the lawyers."

No one can really answer that question, but evidence that women more than men are asked to recuse themselves comes from the state of Washington: when the gender bias task force there surveyed judges—men and women—nearly half said that prejudice against women judges had been used to disqualify them because of their gender, close to double those who said this happened to male judges.

Asked how the two sexes reacted to her decisions, Judge Gearin painted a no-win picture: "If you rule in favor of the husband, they say, 'That's because she's a woman, and she is bending over backward to show that she is fair' or 'because women are always harder on women.' And if you rule in favor of the woman, it is because 'she is a woman and they always stick together.' " Because of the emotional toll of serving in family court, because it has the lowest status ("girl's law," it is sometimes derisively called), most judges don't stay in it too long, and consequently many family court judges are ill prepared for the psychic turmoil or emotionally complicated issues they encounter there. And many of them can't see beyond their gender limitations to be just to both sexes.

So where does the truth lie? It is true that sometimes men are the victims of bias, particularly in custody decisions, but the bulk of evidence from the thirty-four state gender bias reports issued as of June 1996 tips the scales the other way. Overwhelmingly the task forces found that the prejudices women face *because they are women* far outweighed any such bias against men. In the measured words of the Nevada Gender Bias Task Force's report, "[T]he problems of women were more widespread and more urgent than the problems of men." Women are often threatened and lied to by lawyers and ex-husbands, of whom they may be afraid; lack of money to pursue their cases forcefully can cause women to leave the bargaining table impoverished; far too many judges look the other way when support and maintenance payments are not made; even a longtime homemaker in her fifties may end up with few assets and a few years of support while she "rehabilitates" herself for the vanishing job market older women face. "The task forces have written beautiful reports and come out with reams of recommendations, but of course the problem often is that those reports get put on the shelf and their recommendations are not realized," declares Lynn Hecht Schafran, head of a judicial education program to promote equality in the courts that was the catalyst for the more than forty-one gender and race bias state task forces that have been convened throughout the country.*

Retired Minnesota Supreme Court justice Rosalie Wahl, chair of the gender bias task force in her state, observes that the sexism and class discrimination

---

* *Washington, D.C., and several of the federal circuits also have gender bias task forces, as does Puerto Rico.*

particularly impacts impoverished women: "We know . . . from our own bitter experience that the judicial system into which these women come, seeking justice as parties in dissolution, custody and maintenance cases, in personal injury sexual harassment and discrimination cases, as complainants in domestic abuse and rape and other sexual assault cases, as defendants in criminal cases . . . discriminates on the same basis and to the same degree as every other of our major societal institutions because of shared beliefs about the inferiority or difference of women . . . and this 'institutional sexism' . . . is made of the same hard rock as institutional racism."

ACCESS TO THE COURTS

This institutional sexism leads to the first obstacle women come up against in the courts: access. If you can't get good legal representation because *he's* closed the bank account, and he's been in charge of the finances in the marriage, and he left with all the records, she's probably going to find it hard to get her fair share when divorcing. "If a woman doesn't have the ability to get attorney fees at the beginning of the divorce, she won't be able to prove what the value of the estate is or form any reasonable proposal that will favor her, and consequently she will walk away with the short end of the stick," says Carole L. Chiamp, past president of the Detroit Bar Association and one of the "10 Divorce Lawyers You'd Want in Your Corner," according to *Detroit Monthly*.

In a middle-class family the financial estate may consist of a pension and other retirement benefits, bank accounts, certificates of deposit, securities, real estate, automobiles and jewelry. The court can divide only those assets about which it knows the value, location and title. The husband knows, but he's not talking; it's up to the wife to prove where everything is. "Awards of counsel fees in most counties in New York—New York County is the exception—are so pitifully small that the attorney cannot afford to do the proper investigation," comments Susan Bender, former president of the New York State Women's Bar Association. It's no different elsewhere.

Chiamp contends that many judges who have been on the bench for a long time lose track of what it costs to develop these cases, and unless the parties are wealthy, lawyers frequently have a hard time getting even reasonable fees. "Consequently you have a number of attorneys not wanting to represent women,"*

---

* *Several of the family law lawyers interviewed said they take cases that pay next to nothing. They may be the exception rather than the rule, but such lawyers do exist.*

she concedes. "When a man walks in my office, he writes a check that day. When a woman walks in, you have to figure out how you are ever going to get paid." And, say many attorneys, often you don't get paid more than a pittance of what the case cost in time and money. It is not unusual for the woman to be forced to "share" an attorney with her husband, with often disastrous results. As the Nevada report attests, "It is common to hear women in this position complain of being threatened by their husbands, their husbands' attorneys or even by their own attorneys: 'Settle or you will lose everything.' " While legal fees may eventually come out of community funds, more often than not the wife must petition the court for allowances, "which if ordered are to be doled out by the husband to the wife. . . . This arrangement, as a general rule, allows the husband to spend freely from community funds for his own legal needs, while the wife must beg, piecemeal, for a few dollars which she must prove is 'needed' to prosecute her action or defense."

In an acrimonious divorce limited funds at the beginning will almost always lead to a resolution at the end that penalizes the wife. "The affluent spouse can go in there and fight very vigorously with a top-notch lawyer, the less affluent doesn't have the kind of money to buy the best legal advice," explains New York Appellate Court justice Betty Weinberg Ellerin. "And if she does have a few dollars put away, should she have to exhaust herself economically to fight in that arena?"

Because of the uncertainty of winning big fees, or sometimes even marginally adequate ones, lawyers pressure their less affluent clients, typically women, to settle quickly—particularly given the looming specter of a child custody fight. "Some lawyers will use the threat of a custody battle as a wedge to pressure the spouse, usually the wife, into taking a lesser property settlement and less alimony," maintains Sari Jaffe, a New Canaan, Connecticut, matrimonial attorney, echoing the sentiments of many. "They may have no intention of actually asking for custody, but they know they can scare the woman by using it." Lawyers' surveys indicate this type of threat is extremely widespread, and other evidence suggests that it is enormously effective. Women will give up a great deal to keep the children.

Simply arguing a case can dry up the nest egg of even a moderately situated middle-class family. Consequently many women agree to settlements with unfavorable terms. According to a study by the New York City Department of Consumer Affairs, a common scenario in which lawyers collude is for the wife's attorney to draw up a proposed settlement she thinks is fair. Her lawyer sends it to his lawyer, and it is almost always rejected, considered just to be the opening salvo. The wife's lawyer then pressures her to agree to a far less favorable proposal simply to get the matter over with. "The negotiation process is aborted largely because the lawyer knows that the wife can't afford to continue paying fees of $200 to $400 an hour, and there are few other marital assets in sight that the lawyer might be able to apply to additional fees," the report notes. If the judge does not enforce temporary maintenance, it may be that the woman never gets any maintenance at all, although she is ill-equipped to carry on while the divorce and final settlement are pending. Additionally, inadequate counsel at the beginning of the process may lead her to accept less-than-adequate temporary maintenance and child support, which many judges merely confirm by the final decree. A "temporary" disadvantage turns into a lifelong one.

Without the speedy awarding of temporary maintenance, or alimony, many women cannot bargain from a position of strength. "Sometimes a judge will sit on a case for months and then come out with a great decision, but by then the less affluent spouse is starved to death," notes Justice Ellerin, former president of the National Association of Women Judges. "Or maybe she settles beforehand and takes a lot less than she might have gotten if she had been able to wait it out." In the mid-eighties Justice Ellerin was administrative judge for the New York City trial courts, a sort of majordomo for the courts. While she was in the job she pushed through a rule requiring judges to rule on temporary maintenance in thirty days or explain to the administrative judge—at the time, it was she—why they had not.

In a case from the early nineties in a New York suburb, a man who wanted out of a twenty-year marriage was ordered to pay weekly maintenance of $700 to a wife who still had two children at home, according to the attorney, who asked for anonymity because the judge is still on the bench. At the time, the man made $150,000 annually as an executive at a securities firm; two decades earlier the wife had dropped out of school to support them while he finished college and did not go back to work until the husband left. She was able to get a job as a $20,000-a-year bank clerk, and the likelihood of her ever making much more than that was slim. But the man did not pay anything, and the judge would not enforce the order, stating that "it" would be taken care of at the trial.

It never was. By the time the case did come to trial two years later, the man had lost his job and couldn't pay anything, certainly not back maintenance. In this case there was no settlement, since the wife contested the divorce because he would give her nothing but the house. She won. A hollow victory. The wife had hoped he would offer a better settlement in order to get the divorce, but instead he simply walked away from the marriage. By this time he was living with another woman. The wife has possession of the marital home but cannot sell it unless he dies. The attorney who handled this was paid a small retainer of less than $2,000 at the beginning of the case. Attorney fees were not awarded, since there was no divorce. For the wife, a "temporary" arrangement has become a permanent disaster.

Although this man did not file for bankruptcy, doing so is a novel tactic of ex-husbands (or not so ex) to avoid making payments to a former spouse or companion, according to Los Angeles bankruptcy judge Lisa Hill Fenning. The U.S. Bankruptcy Code does not permit the debtor-husband to walk away from spousal and child support payments, but simply filing a bankruptcy petition can substantially delay or prevent collecting them, sometimes for years. Judge Fenning chaired the bankruptcy advisory committee for the Ninth Circuit Gender Bias Task Force, which recommended that the code be revised. In 1994 Congress passed the Bankruptcy Reform Act, making it more difficult to use bankruptcy to shield an unwilling ex-spouse from fulfilling his court-ordered family obligations. Under the revised code, child and spousal support obligations are given priority, and many family matters are no longer subject to the same delays in payment that used to come simply by filing for bankruptcy.

ALTHOUGH WOMEN of every income stratum may find themselves financially strapped and unable to pursue their case forcefully, it is poor women, as Justice Wahl asserted, who face the greatest hurdles. These "forgotten women," low income, unskilled, broke, and with primary responsibility for raising children, may have no place to go. If their income is low enough, they will qualify for state and federally funded legal aid, but in these days of budget cuts for such extras as legal representation for the poor, the wait will likely be long and the attorney assigned to the case hideously overworked. To qualify for a matrimonial attorney from the Legal Aid Society in New York City, for example, a family of four must have an income of no more than $18,400. Because of the heavy demand, each month several hundred cases fall through the cracks; people might qualify, but they get discouraged with the waiting time. Each of the five lawyers who work in the Brooklyn/Manhattan office handle up to three hundred cases a year, double what the busiest lawyers in private practice take on.

Of course, if one's income is not low enough to qualify for free counsel, but the individual still can't afford a lawyer, she may opt to represent herself, a perilous path to go down if the divorce is bitter. Nonetheless the Massachusetts gender bias study found that an increasing number of women were representing themselves in divorces. One woman explained why: "Why do I and other mothers attempt to represent ourselves? The answer is simple. We have no funds, and the legal professionals have no services to offer low-income non-AFDC [Aid to Families with Dependent Children] recipients."

Such *pro se* representation, as it is called, is fraught with difficulties even for the college educated: she may not know what to do or how to do it, and she is likely to encounter hostility and disdain from court personnel, who may give her the wrong information, according to the Massachusetts study. Despite this, a third of all divorcing parties use no lawyer at all; the National Center for State Courts found that in sixteen jurisdictions around the country, two attorneys were retained in only 29 percent of divorce filings. However, in a great many of these cases the separating individuals work out the deal relatively quickly without much hassle between themselves. It's the 60 percent of dissolving marriages where there are children that do not lend themselves to easy or quick resolution.

Going to court does not necessarily buy justice. Judges have inordinate discretion in deciding who gets what as well as custody, and judges are only human, subject to the same influences and prejudices as the rest of society. "Maintenance is totally dependent on the lawyers' and the judge's attitudes, and when you try to counsel a client about what will happen if you go to litigation, you don't have a clue," comments Jean Gerval of the University of Minnesota Law School in Minneapolis. She and her students attempted to categorize the awards given over a three-month period in 1991 in Hennepin, the county where the school is located, but they found that the awards were inconsistent and unpredictable. Knowing this, and aware of the cost of contesting, most women simply settle out of court.

NO-FAULT OFTEN MEANS NO RESPONSIBILITY

Just how far a woman's standard of living falls after a divorce is the subject of some debate, but all investigators agree that the descent is swift and sure. In the mid-eighties sociologist Lenore Weitzman reported startlingly disparate numbers for the standard of living between the sexes *post* divorce in Los Angeles County (women down 73 percent, men up 42 percent), but these figures have not been duplicated by others. Generally speaking, the average decline for women's standard of living after divorce is somewhat more than 30 percent, while a man's increases a little more than 10 percent. Standard of living involves a variety of measures to determine the real purchasing power of a household.

The trouble with such averages is that they hide a multitude of circumstances. Some women experience a rise in their standard of living: using Weitzman's own raw data, Richard Petersen of the Social Science Research Council in New York found this occurred 15 percent of the time. Averages also include those women who, say, had jobs as teachers or waitresses or receptionists and married someone who made more money than they did; if they got divorced after a couple of years, and there were no children, and the woman continues to work at her job or goes back to work, her standard of living typically drops back to what it was before. And no one sees this as wrong or unfair.

Nonetheless averages do paint a broad-brush picture of society. The income statistics following divorce tell us, for instance, that wealthier women face disproportionately a greater decline in standard of living than those from other income groups. But for these women, a plunge in lifestyle can mean that they no longer live in a private home with pool and a gardener who comes twice a week, but instead make do in a three-bedroom condominium without a maid. There may be no more lunches at "the club," and without that backdrop their social life may change drastically. Instead of running charity events, they may take a job as a secretary at the local school. The comedown will certainly be trying, but their straits are petty in comparison with the decline women near the poverty line experience. Their loss of income from the husband, with children to raise, is truly catastrophic. Some—even some formerly middle-class women—will end up on welfare.

Furthermore the one-third decline in standard of living that all women face is an average reflecting the diverse experiences of all divorced women: those who stayed in the job market and are most able to provide for themselves and their families after the divorce, those whose per capita income actually rose, and longtime homemakers, whose prospects in the job market are dismal. Poor white women fare the worst, and their incomes continue to decline even five years after divorce. Furthermore divorced women do not recover easily, even five years after the dissolution of their marriage. Some women do, of course. For all groups, remarriage is the surest route to an economic comeback. "The absence of marriage, not the presence of divorce, is the major cause of poverty for women," notes family law expert Marsha Garrison.

THE DISPARITY IN ECONOMIC STATUS between husbands and wives after divorce is evidence that the divorce reform of the 1970s and 1980s was not necessarily a boon to women. As the rate of divorce was spiraling upward in the sixties and seventies, so was the public clamor for a simpler, less humiliating, less punitive way to end a marriage than had been possible up to that point. Prior to 1970 most divorces legally were the fault of one or the other, and divorces were often difficult to get. In some states the courts looked with skepticism on any reason for divorcing other than adultery. "Incompatibility" or "irrevocable differences" did not pass muster everywhere. The need to establish infidelity spawned a whole industry of private investigators who took photos of husbands entering hotels with women not their wives or caught them in flagrante delicto. The wife then filed for divorce, using the set-up photos to document her husband's infidelity.

With "fault" established, judges based alimony on some loose concept of punishment. Typically the man was the transgressor who would have to pay lifetime alimony until his ex-wife remarried; the court might award nothing to the woman if she were the one who, say, had had an affair or two. And under the old laws wives had the bargaining chip of contesting the divorce to secure a better settlement for themselves. That's how it worked in theory, anyway, and certainly sometimes in fact. Only Nevada granted divorces without undue hassle. Wives who had worked out favorable settlements and who could afford a six-week "vacation" at a dude ranch near Reno went there to meet the state's residency requirement. It was good for tourism. Nevada notwithstanding, by the late sixties the old unsavory practices surrounding divorce seemed more and more unreasonable and distasteful. Legislators who write the laws get divorces too. The zeitgeist called for reform.

THE MYTH is that under the old laws when the divorce was the man's fault, the woman made out well. In fact, she didn't. No more than 15 percent of divorced wives since 1920 were awarded alimony, and far fewer men than that actually paid it. In Phyllis Chesler's groundbreaking study of sixty mothers who had been challenged for custody between 1960 and 1981, 90 percent of the fathers paid no alimony; 67 percent of them paid no child support.

Between 1969, when California became the first state to rewrite its laws, and

1985, when South Dakota became the last to add a no-fault provision to its list of grounds for ending a marriage, divorce law in this country was totally reformed. No-fault divorce took the "blame" out of divorce proceedings. Courts could now treat the breakup of a marriage as if it were the dissolution of a business partnership. Under no-fault divorce either party can end the marriage simply by stating that it has broken down, and the other spouse rarely can stop it. No one, then, needs to be "punished." But make no mistake: the laws were not reformed in order to overcome the disparity in income distribution between the sexes after divorce. That was not the issue.

But since these changes were occurring against the backdrop of the women's movement, the laws were rewritten (by mostly male legislators) to seem as if they embodied feminist concerns. Lifetime alimony supposedly represented women's outdated dependence—and men's long sufferance. Feminists contended that the old laws, which did not normally divide property if it was held only in the man's name, failed to take into account the value of a homemaker's contributions to the family, whether or not she worked outside the home. The new laws were supposed not only to make it easier to divorce, but also to adequately compensate the spouse with the lower (or no) income and to treat the woman as more of an equal to the man, not someone who had to depend on a man for her livelihood. While alimony, or maintenance, as it began to be called, was being phased out, state after state adopted guidelines proposing that the marital property, no matter in whose name it was held, be divided equitably, if not equally.*

These reforms represented two significant changes in divorce law. First, a onetime division of marital property could mean a clean break and a fresh start for both parties. Second, equitable or equal distribution of property, which came along with no-fault, presumed that maintenance award would be temporary for "rehabilitative" purposes only, a demeaning term in itself because it implies that women need to be "rehabilitated," as if the condition of being a homemaker were a disability. In sheer economic terms, of course, it is. Rehabilitative, or short-term, maintenance spread like a firestorm. Although there is no national data, in New York we know that under the old system four out of five alimony payments were ordered for a lengthy period, frequently until death or remarriage. A number of state studies indicate that the average award today,

---

* Today seven states require equal division of property or have adopted a presumption of such: California, Idaho, Louisiana, New Mexico, Texas, Washington and Wisconsin. The forty-three others direct "equitable" division.

in those 15 percent of cases where there is any, is for between one and five
years.

"The attitude of many judges is, Why do the women need money from the
men?" says Lynne Gold-Bikin, former chair of the ABA's Family Law Section.
"Awarding permanent or long-term alimony goes against the state guidelines.
Fifteen years ago there was no question that someone in a long-term marriage
would not be able to go out and get a job. That's all changed." Although the
alimony might not have been paid, and its dollar value went down over time
because of inflation, at least the courts were realistic about a fiftyish homemaker's job opportunities and unconsciously awarded her for contributions to the
ex-husband's life that had made a successful career possible. "Now they think,
Well, you gals wanted to be in the job market, here is your chance," Gold-Bikin
adds. In Delaware, she says, a legislator who was getting a divorce pushed
through a statute that precluded alimony at all unless you were married for
twenty years. Naturally he got in under the cutoff.

The underlying assumption in these reforms was that if the wife was not the
economic equal of her partner, she would be as soon as she got her feet on the
ground. Or remarried. And if she wasn't able to get a job that paid as well as
her husband's, that wasn't the law's fault.

But the move to short-term alimony and "equitable distribution" would
prove calamitous for many women. "[M]ale perspective on family life has
skewed decisions in equitable distribution cases," asserted a legislator who spoke
to the New York task force on women in the courts. "The perception of most
men—and the judiciary is mostly male—is that care of the house and children
can be done with one hand tied behind the back. Send the kids out to school,
put them to bed, and the rest of the time have free to play tennis and bridge.
They think any woman—no matter her age or lack of training—can find a nice
little job and a nice little apartment and conduct her later years as she might
have done at age twenty-five."

Some judges routinely consider maintenance a "bridge" until remarriage,
then make judgments about how long the bridge should be, based on the woman's looks. Some divorcing men try to influence the decision. In 1995 in Manhattan, a Mr. Morrison sought to avoid paying his wife's legal fees by affixing
her photograph to every page of the pleading, thereby suggesting that she was
attractive and young enough to find work (or someone to pay the bill for her).
State supreme court justice David B. Saxe was not amused and in his judgment
called the use of the photographs "blatantly sexist." He ordered Mr. Morrison

to pay his estranged wife $10,000 in legal fees plus $300 a week for the next year.

In 1993 New York attorney Susan Bender had a case in which the judge in chambers asked how much maintenance her client, a woman in her forties, wanted. She was a mother of four teenagers who had spent the entire marriage as a homemaker. "Long enough to get rehabilitated," Bender answered. " 'No, no, no,' the judge said," Bender recollects. " 'Your client is a fucking knockout. She is going to get married in two years. I don't want this poor guy to be on the hook.'

"How judicious of you, Judge," an exasperated Bender responded. "Why don't you help me settle this case so we don't have to go to trial?" In the end the woman was awarded ten years of maintenance as well as child support.

This sort of thing happens everywhere. In North Dakota a judge was quoted in the *Bismarck Sunday Tribune,* from his written opinion, that a woman divorcing a man earning $200,000 a year is "a very attractive person and has a pleasant personality, which attributes can also be viewed as earnings assets." Doing what, the judge did not say. In Michigan attorney Carole Chiamp made no bones about the fact that an attractive woman has a harder time getting a fair settlement from some judges—the presumption is she'll be with another guy soon. In California a few years ago a woman contended during a trial that the man she was divorcing had asked her to marry him even though they were living together at the time. The judge found this hard to believe. "Why in heaven's name," he asked, "do you buy the cow when you get the milk free?"*

In Illinois in 1995 a Mr. Toole asked an appeals court for relief from the $800-a-month maintenance he had been ordered to pay to Mrs. Toole—for three years—after a nineteen-year marriage. Two daughters still lived with her. Mrs. Toole and the girls moved in with another man, and there was a "resident, continuing conjugal basis" to the couple's relationship, according to court papers. In the middle of the appeal the woman moved out of the man's house and testified that she was not going to continue to live with him. Too bad, said the court, and stopped the maintenance. One judge, a man, dissented.

The examples are anecdotal, but they do indicate that not that much has changed in terms of the economic outcome of divorce: women are getting the short end. The new no-fault laws may work for a couple who have been married for a few years and have no kids and no sizable assets to divide, and this covers

* *Iverson v. Iverson,* reversed on appeal. 11 Cal. App. 4th 1495; 15 Cal.Rptr2d 70 (1992).

a great many divorces. Add small children to the picture, or consider the long-term wife whose husband leaves her after thirty years for his assistant, and they do not work so well. Implicit in them is the presumption that lost career opportunities can be overcome easily or at will, and besides, women's economic opportunities are equal to men's today. Explains Jean Gerval, director of the Child Advocacy Clinic at the University of Minnesota Law School, this "ignores the significant wage differentials between men and women, the limited job opportunities available for women who have been out of the paid workforce for significant periods of time, and the loss of long-term job benefits for women who have worked intermittently or on a part-time basis to accommodate family goals prior to the dissolution."

In fact, the wage differentials between husbands and wives are significant: 39.4 percent of all married women are not in the labor force; and 30 percent of those who are in the labor force are working part-time. It should come as no surprise, then, that the median contribution of all wives to family income from earnings is just over 36 percent.

WHAT IT REALLY COSTS TO STAY HOME WITH THE KIDS

Rare is the individual who has been working at part-time jobs to suit her family's schedule, rather than forging ahead in a career, who can make up for the lost time when she wants to resume her career full speed; more likely she will be relegated to a low-paying job. All women whose careers slow down, or stop entirely, for any length of time suffer this decline in earning capacity, and women with advanced degrees suffer the most depreciation: a twenty-year-old degree in anything from English to education is not highly, if at all, marketable in the labor force today. Companies are downsizing, new jobs are scarce, automation is replacing many workers. There are fewer jobs for everyone, most especially for the unskilled individual who has been out of the labor market for even a few years. Older workers have the hardest time of all.

"I see women in their sixties who were doctors' wives waiting on tables or selling clothes at Marshall Field's," says Gold-Bikin, whose office is in the Philadelphia suburb of Norristown. "The courts have said they are only allowing rehabilitative alimony, but to what are you going to rehabilitate a woman who has devoted twenty-five years of her life to raising a family? The job market is not going to welcome her with open arms, no matter what." Managing a household does not count under "management" skills on a résumé.

While she is declining in absolute numbers, the displaced homemaker is still very much with us. The Census Bureau counted more than 17.5 million displaced homemakers in our ranks in 1990, and while the largest percentage are sixty-five-plus (more than ten million), not all of them are old. The number of women either not working or looking for work—in other words, those who are not in the labor force—has stabilized at just over 42 percent. Thirty percent of all women with children under eighteen—the prime working years for most—are not in the labor force. If current divorce figures hold, and there is no reason to assume they will dramatically change in the foreseeable future, "family values" or not, what this means is that the displaced homemaker will be with us for quite a long time.

"In rural America and in small towns, women still stay home and raise the kids," observes Gold-Bikin. "Many men believe that it is an insult to their manliness if their wives have jobs. They think, No wife of mine is going to be working and raising kids. Plus, a lot of men pay lip service to the idea of the modern woman, but they personally want someone who will be available to them. They like the idea that their wife doesn't work, that they can call up and say, 'Pack the bags, we're going on a trip.' " Among my own acquaintances, I can count several women in their thirties and forties who left lucrative careers to either follow their husbands to another state for their careers, or who drastically cut back on their own work schedules, or who changed jobs to one less demanding, to raise the children and not go crazy trying to do everything. Certainly their goal—to provide a good home for their family—is a worthy one, but should the marriage fail, their investment in their husbands' careers, and the sacrifice of their own human capital in the labor market, will almost assuredly not be rewarded in real-dollar value. Whether or not they quit their jobs happily, they do it in a culture that alternately encourages them to be good homemakers and mothers when the marriage is intact, then not only devalues those skills in the job market, but drastically penalizes them for the time they have been out of the labor force.

What the reforms did not take into consideration is that typically the most valuable asset of the marriage was not in tangible goods, but in the working spouse's (usually the husband's) earning capacity, whether it was by having a successful career or running a small business. And in most instances the earning capacity was as valuable as it was because the other spouse (usually the wife) had devoted some of her energy to supporting a lifestyle that made it possible for her partner to indulge in the single-minded pursuit of a career. Even if she hadn't engaged in the obvious contribution of having worked and supported *them* while he was in school, or done research for *him,* her contributions came in the form of managing his family and social life, running the errands (as in picking up *his* shirts from the laundry, dealing with the plumber for *their* backed-up drain, buying presents for *his* family), raising *their* children, possibly entertaining *his* business contacts and being available for dinners out with *his* clients and office mates. One need not be a full-time homemaker to participate in such career building; one need only be the parent most often responsible for picking the children up at four-thirty or five-thirty from the day care center and having to think about what's for dinner.

Now two studies demonstrate that this kind of support translates into actual dollars: Men with traditional stay-at-home wives earn more and get higher raises than similarly educated men from two-career families. Sociologist Linda K. Stroh of Loyola University of Chicago found that over five years the men with stay-at-home wives at twenty Fortune 500 companies averaged salary increases that were 11 percent greater than those of similar men with working wives. Ever the cautious academic, Stroh would say only that she could "not rule out the traditional wife-as-a-resource" as the reason for the salary gap.

Not surprisingly, family law and appellate judges don't seem to be aware of the data. In Rhode Island, for example, spousal support awards dropped from 9 percent to 5 percent between 1985 and 1988; in 1985 the median length of alimony was five years or longer, but by 1988, it was down to two and a half years. Yet consider the options of a woman who unquestionably contributed to her husband's ability to work at his career while she managed their home and children:

In her mid-thirties she had been married for fifteen years to a rising executive making $75,000 annually at the time he decided he wanted a divorce. They met while she was working as a waitress, and she quit when their first child was born and had been a full-time homemaker since. The children were twelve and nine.

To divide the assets "equitably," the family home was sold. Without college credentials the only jobs she could get were minimum wage. Consequently she could not afford a decent apartment for herself and the children with the income from whatever job she might get. Landlords refused to consider court-ordered child support payments as proof of her financial stability. When she did find a suitable place to live, the building manager would not rent it to her unless the husband co-signed the lease. He would not, and the judge would not order him to do so. Living with relatives was not an option. Recalling the poverty in which she had grown up, and concerned about how she would raise the children adequately, she reluctantly gave her husband custody. They now live with him.

The trial judge, constrained by a state statute that alimony be for "rehabilitative" purposes "for a short and definite period" (except in cases of ill health or psychiatric disorder), awarded her two and a half years of modest alimony and ordered her husband to pay her tuition for the next three years at the junior college where she had applied to train for a position as a dental assistant. But a waiting list at the college, the least expensive school in the state, makes it likely that it will take four years—not three—for her to complete the training.

"What I found most troubling about this case was the tendency of some judges to pull the number of months or years for rehabilitative alimony out of a hat rather than look realistically at how long it would take a displaced homemaker to get the training she needs to develop marketable skills," notes the attorney who appealed the case, Amy Tabor, "and there is the very real possibility that rehabilitation may be of limited financial success." Tabor chaired the Economic Impact of Divorce for the Rhode Island Advisory Committee on Women in the Courts.

"The problem is exacerbated by the practice of the [Rhode Island] Supreme Court when reviewing divorce cases to give very great deference to the 'discretion' of the trial judge in family law matters," she says. In 1986, for instance, the Rhode Island Supreme Court rejected long-term alimony in a situation in which there was a significant difference between the two parties' assets, both in dollars and in earning ability. Now they have done it again. Tabor's appeal was denied in late 1995.

Because of that deference to judicial discretion, appellate courts in most states, where the percentage of women judges is less than 10 percent, do not overturn many of these cases. Nor do the cases generally reach that level. "To prevail on appeal, a spouse must establish that a trial court abused its discretion—a difficult task indeed when a statute implicitly authorizes a court to rely on personal notions of fairness," notes Professor Cynthia Starnes, a family law expert at the Detroit College of Law. This means that the financial fate of a homemaker depends on the goodwill or prejudices of a particular trial judge.

It is the same everywhere. Up until last year Texas had no alimony provision at all. As a community-property state, the division of marital assets was supposed to take care of everything. Just as married women property acts were written for the benefit of the state, so was the 1995 law. Spousal support was a provision tacked on to a welfare reform bill when legislators realized that penniless former spouses were often forced to go on the dole. Before this enlightenment the bill had languished in the legislature for a decade. As written, the alimony provided for is meager. It outlaws any alimony at all for marriages less than ten years, and potential recipients must prove that they would be unable to support themselves after the property is divided. Maintenance is limited to three years with a cap of $30,000 annually, regardless of the wealthier spouse's income. It is not retroactive and applies only to marriages after September of last year.

WHY EQUAL DISTRIBUTION IS NOT EQUITABLE

The upshot of all this is that the divorce reforms, with "equitable" distribution of assets—which more often than not means "equal"—has the patina of being fair to women when it is not. "Let me say this," Judge Ellerin says in her characteristically blunt way. "We have many judges here who are very fair in what they decide, but there are still an overwhelming number who aren't fair in their distribution of assets. They put themselves in the position of the man, and think, Gee, how would I feel if I had to give this much away when I have my own divorce?" At one judicial education program on gender bias she attended, domestic violence and equitable awards were the two topics the judges discussed. "One old judge said when it came to discussing domestic violence, 'So he slapped her, big deal, what does that mean, a little slap?' However, when it came to the discussion of support, he had a daughter who was newly divorced, and then he was saying, 'Oh, this is not fair.' Who says that your own personal experiences don't enter into your decisions from the bench? As women [judges] we are more likely to empathize with the women who are the victims of unfair treatment."

How about the judge in Georgia who opened one woman's divorce trial by saying: "I don't know my feelings about child support, but alimony is like feeding hay to a dead horse." The wife's attorney withdrew rather than continue to represent her in court. The woman told the Georgia gender bias commission he had to because his zealous representation of her might hurt his future practice before that judge.

Lynn Schafran recalls a judge telling her that in determining the settlement, he calculated that the man would be eating meals out—since no one would be cooking for him. "I said, 'Excuse me, what are you talking about? The man doesn't need to eat his dinner out every night,' " Schafran told the judge. " 'He can cook. The wife isn't eating out every night.' The judge looked at me and said, 'Hmmm . . . I never thought of that.' Judges need to put themselves in the place of the displaced homemaker and ask, 'What would I do if tomorrow my income were suddenly slashed by 85 percent? How would I live?' "

Then there is the judge in Reno, Nevada, who until a few years ago refused to grant women divorces unless they filed the petition under their husband's last name—*he'd show those feminists a thing or two about who was boss.* Jerry Carr Whitehead had many such lapses of judgment, not all relating to gender bias, but because he had friends on the supersecretive state supreme court, including Chief Justice Thomas L. Steffen, who signed several orders favoring Whitehead, it appeared that nothing would be done about him. This was after the judiciary discipline commission and the state's attorney general, Frankie Sue Del Papa, together tried to investigate his alleged wrongdoings. One allegation was that when lawyers tried to get him off their cases he would call the other side and ask which judge they wanted to hear it. As in the case of David Lanier, the wolf in judge's robes in Tennessee, it appeared that at the state level nothing would be done about "Back-door Jerry," as he was unaffectionately known in the Nevada bar. Even the newspaper in Reno, the *Gazette-Journal,* had to be embarrassed into writing about Whitehead by stories leaking out of other sources, notably the *Review-Journal* in Las Vegas, before they began reporting the story fully. Whitehead was the paper's former attorney. (When I called to talk to a reporter, I got one of his friends on the city desk instead. The reporter I wished to speak to was "never" going to be available.) The Justice Department intervened once again and began its own investigation of criminal wrongdoing. On January 1 of this year Whitehead agreed to retire in return for the investigation being dropped. He was not disbarred, as many had called for. He asserted that the mess was all political. The state supreme court hired a retired lawyer at $145 an hour to investigate who leaked the story to the *Review-Journal.* Apparently the Nevada Supreme Court is more concerned about concealing corruption on the bench than correcting it.

While Whitehead was routinely ruling against women in Reno, appellate courts in some states (Massachusetts, Minnesota, Mississippi and New York, to name a few) have begun to recognize that short-term maintenance is sometimes inappropriate, and thus decisions across the country are still a crazy-quilt pattern. Even in New York City, where trial judges have begun awarding long-term support in appropriate cases, the appellate court recently reduced one long-term award in *Hartog* v. *Hartog* to five years and stripped the woman of property and insurance awards.

While federal regulations ordering the states to enact child support guide-lines have standardized such payments based on income, judges continue to have wide latitude in dispensing maintenance. The idea of long-term maintenance has not yet generally drifted down to the trial courts where the decisions are being made. And with most women having limited means to pay lawyers, only a minute portion of these cases ever goes to appeal.

WHO GETS WHAT

Although most states call for "equitable" division, judges have largely inter-preted "equitable" to mean "equal"—that is, dividing the family estate in half. In fact, all the evidence is that *on the average* women are at least getting half of the proverbial pie. But as Professor Marsha Garrison of Brooklyn Law School points out, these averages don't tell us much because among the individual families who make up the numbers. Some wives will get nearly nothing and some will get everything. "Statutes in different states list several factors that are to be the basis of what judges are to consider for equitable distribution—need, length of marriage, the needs of the custodial parent for the home, income, health, contributions to the marriage," she says. "You would think that needier wives—low-income women, or unemployed, those with few resources to fall back on—would get more property, but if you look at judicial decisions in New York, you find, surprisingly, that these women were likely to receive a small fraction of the marital property. This suggests that judges are looking at mon-etary contributions more than need or anything else when they divide the pot."

Professor Garrison also found that when the couple had little to divide, women tended to receive more of the marital property than when there was a lot. It is in wealthy families that wives fare the worst. All that career support—the dinner parties for the right people, the charity work, providing a family, the conspicuous consumption that seems to go with the job, and it is a job—is denigrated and devalued at divorce time. Being a "trophy wife" may not pay that well if one gets fired.

In most marriages, of course, the tangible assets to divide aren't worth much. The average net worth was under $25,000 in 1984; adjusting for inflation, Professor Garrison estimates the amount would be no more than $30,000 to-day. It is not unusual, for instance, for lower- and middle-income families to live from paycheck to paycheck. "Often, a couple's only important asset is equity in a marital residence," writes Professor Starnes. "When the parties lack other assets, this equity can be divided only if the home is sold, and in fact, sale of the home is frequently ordered. A homemaker may thus leave the marriage with limited income potential, few if any assets and no home." Equal distribution of the assets, while it seems like a fair and tidy idea, is in effect not equitable, even though that is how many judges are deciding how to split up the assets.

In Professor Garrison's study of three New York counties (including Manhattan; Westchester, a New York City suburb; and Onondaga, which includes Syracuse and surrounding farm country), the marital homes were sold a quarter of the time at the time of the settlement. "But even if the home is divided equally, it may be heavily mortgaged and you're not talking about the full value of the house," she comments. "It's likely not to mean much in real assets to the wife. Division of the house ignores what it's worth as a home for the kids who don't have to change schools or move to a new neighborhood. The problem with equal distribution is that you get a strong push to sell the house and divide it equally, and that is supposed to settle the score." In the worst case, the estate may be riddled with debts, and even if the homemaker receives all or nearly all of the assets, they are nearly worthless in actual dollars. However, when the estate is debt-ridden, the man usually shoulders that burden.

Where the inequity of equitable distribution is seen most clearly, perhaps, is when a couple own a business. Who gets it? One of Chiamp's clients in Detroit owned a Hallmark card store with her husband; it was the couple's main asset, worth approximately $300,000. Chiamp explains that one obvious inequity in assessing the worth of a business is that it is treated as if it is going to be sold, not as a long-term income generator, income that the wife will share no part in under "equitable" distribution. Chiamp argued that the wife had been an equal partner in the business, having done the books, worked in the store, ordered stock and so forth, and she, instead of the husband, ought to get the store because it would be more difficult for her to get the financing and the necessary support from Hallmark to open a new store than it would be for him. She lost, and the woman attempted to buy another card store in a different area, but true to Chiamp's prediction, she did not get the necessary financial backing from Hallmark.

Despite the capriciousness of judicial awards to women when divorcing, they turn out to be on the whole more favorable to women than what they will get if they settle before going to court. When Professor Garrison compared the court-ordered alimony against overall awards (including those litigated and those not), she found that the courts ordered alimony three times more often.

One reason was that litigated cases were more likely to involve long-term marriages where the wives' financial contributions were generally not great. Apparently judges recognized the wives' contributions to the earning power of their mates, as well as took into consideration the wives' economic chances for the future. Judges also awarded alimony more often to unemployed wives married for ten or more years, 83 percent, as compared with the larger sample of cases investigated, where only 49 percent of the women got alimony. Judges also tended to award a higher dollar amount, representing a more significant share of the family assets, than settlements worked out between the two parties. Property division was much more likely to approximate an equal division of assets. Low-income wives were more likely to be awarded alimony than high-income wives or wives where the division of property was substantial in a dollar amount. "In a nutshell, judges do not appear to be the primary source of the economic disadvantage experienced by divorced wives," notes Garrison. It is, unquestionably, the culture that is at fault.

Nor are lawyers the problem. Lawyers, in fact, were a significant factor in being awarded alimony: 30 percent of the wives were awarded alimony when both parties had lawyers; but no women received alimony when neither party had a lawyer. Even under child support guidelines, Garrison found that the awards were significantly higher when lawyers were involved.

While this seems like good news, what is sobering is how few women (and men) are actually represented by counsel in divorces. Several studies indicate that in less than half of all divorces do both sides have a lawyer. Even in Westchester County, a wealthy suburb of New York City, only in 47 percent of divorces did both parties hire a lawyer. New York is unusual in that court-appointed lawyers are routinely assigned to indigent parties in custody cases.

CHILD SUPPORT: THE ELEPHANT CAUSING THE CRISES IN WELFARE

Unpaid child support is being blamed as the elephant that has caused the stampede of women seeking Aid to Families with Dependent Children (AFDC). There is some truth to the argument. Nationwide, more than $14 billion goes unpaid each year. The total amount of past due child support is in the vicinity of $34 billion to $44 billion, according to educated estimates. Nationally, only a little more than half of the women (53 percent) entitled to child support get the full amount; one-quarter receive nothing; and another quarter get partial payments. Given women's overall disadvantage in the labor market, given that they have major responsibility for the children, it is no wonder that so many families headed by women end up below the poverty line: In 1991 more than 35 percent of all mothers with custody were below the poverty line; only 13 percent of custodial fathers were.

Despite stepped-up efforts, and success, in collection from a decade ago, collection rates are only slowly improving because of the staggering increase in the number of women who are eligible, according to Joan Entmacher of the Women's Legal Defense Fund. Census Bureau figures show that in 1994 nearly one-third of American families with children were headed by a single parent; in 1970 the figure was 13 percent. More than 86 percent of these families are headed by women. A significant percentage of those women were never married to the fathers of their children, and collecting from these men—in many cases, even finding them—is a herculean task. "Today just standing still with the current demographics is something," Entmacher says.

Thanks to computers and stricter enforcement practices, collection has gotten much better in the last decade, and some states actually do a decent job. Although the $9.9 billion collected in 1994 is still less than a third of the amount owed in child support for that year, according to estimates from the Department of Health and Human Services, between 1992 and 1994 collection of child support grew in dollar amount by nearly 40 percent. Nonpayers may have their wages withheld, their driver's licenses seized, and their income tax returns vanish, and rarely, they may be thrown into jail. Come 1997, under pending legislation, the federal government would establish a nationwide system to match child support orders with employer records showing the locations of all people hired. Collecting from men who have wage-earning jobs in states that enforce wage withholding is actually not difficult. As attorney Susan Bender remarks, "If the guy is working at AT&T or IBM, I am in like Flynn."

It is not so simple to collect from the self-employed, someone who moves to another state or country or changes jobs. Bender has been trying for nearly three years to collect from a self-employed chiropractor with a good income, now that the girl's mother, after thirteen years of solely supporting herself and the girl as a freelance writer, is ill and not able to work. The girl's father has never paid anything of the small amount he was ordered to at the time of divorce, when he was not working. He threatened to take the girl out of the country if she tried to collect. Bender, who has taken the case pro bono, expects that in the end, "we are likely not to see any money from this guy—he's transferred money out of his accounts, he's moved to an offshore island."

Public awareness of the problem and shared anger over deadbeat dads has led some judges to be stricter with men who don't pay, but many judges still have refused to force men to lower their standard of spending or order them to pay back support when they are located. In Cleveland Leona Reiner has pursued her ex-husband through the courts—and the army, as he was a career military man—since 1968 when they got divorced in Texas. Child support had stopped after a few months. When she wrote to his commanding officer through the Secretary of the Army—with the help of an Ohio senator—in the late 1960s she got a letter back telling her that her ex-husband was an "excellent officer." Wage withholding was unheard of at the time, and the army was not going to break new ground.

But Reiner, who became an attorney along the way, did not give up. After appearing before what she estimates to be two dozen judges, after accusing most of them of being prejudiced against women, Reiner won a judgment of $126,000 for back support in 1989. She says her husband is wealthy and can well afford to pay. But he fought the decision, and four years later it was re-versed because, the appeals court ruled, the judge who awarded the settlement was *prejudiced against her.* Her ex-husband, now retired with full military ben-efits, resides in Texas. In 1995 the Ohio Supreme Court refused to hear her appeal and, in doing so, stipulated she not be allowed to bring it again in lan-guage so strong that one is hard put to believe she was asking for back child support. Noting that Reiner has filed several affidavits alleging prejudice on the part of the judges the case had come before, the papers state: "Mrs. Reiner . . . continuously abused this system for ten and one-half (10½) years. No court in this country should be subject to such abuse, particularly over such a lengthy period of time." Excuse me, wasn't the woman trying to collect court-ordered child support? Is the judge, Peter Sikora, saying that because she didn't give up she is "abusing" the system? What about Mr. Reiner? It goes on: "This action was primarily instituted by the mother for her benefit and assistance." So that's what Sikora thinks of child support.

Reiner is charging in federal court that the family court system in Ohio from top to bottom discriminates against women, bringing the suit in the name of six women and two children, herself and her now grown son included. "The judges up and down the system just kept passing the buck around, and I'm not the only one this happened to," she says, the weariness evident in her voice. "Whether at the trial court, or the court of appeals, or the supreme court, the judges in Ohio are systematically denying women the benefit of laws that pertain to their cases, and bend the laws to favor men. I'm getting older, but I'm stubborn, and I am not giving up." Her petition was dismissed in the lower court, and she is appealing to the Sixth Circuit.

Not all courts let deadbeat dads slip and slide through the system. In a landmark case that marks a new direction for how courts deal with unpaid child support, New York State Supreme Court justice Phyllis Gangel-Jacob—note that she is a woman—threw a well-off investment adviser into jail after he returned to New York City to face *federal* charges for failing to pay the more than $580,000 in child support he owed. Jeffrey A. Nichols stopped paying support for his three children in 1990 and had eluded the system by moving either out of the country or to a different state every time a local judge ordered him to pay up. Money was transferred to his second wife's account or out of the country. At one point he delayed payment by denying the children were his, necessitating expensive DNA tests to prove they were. Whenever the local sheriff was close on his trail, he moved, once walking away from a home that he had put up as security for his bail. He was finally arrested in Vermont and charged under the 1992 federal Child Support Recovery Act. After seeing his list of expenditures, including an American Express tab of $77,000 and Saks Fifth Avenue credit card charges of $41,000, the judge decided that he would be jailed until he comes up with at least $68,000, the amount owed when Judge Gangel-Jacob presided over his divorce in 1990. In 1995 he served 114 days in jail before agreeing to a payment schedule for $600,000 in back child support. When last heard from, he was applying for welfare in Vermont—a development that also made the news. Judge Gangel-Jacob has been reassigned to nonmatrimonial work, seemingly in response to lawyers complaining that she was too supportive of women.

But Nichols's jailing is so much the exception, it made news around the country. And only because his ex-wife had the means and persistence to track him down was he ever brought to justice. More likely these men never have to pay the piper. Some courts around the country, however, have found the act unconstitutional. Last year the Eastern Pennsylvania District Court did so, saying that the statute went beyond the jurisdiction of the interstate commerce code, under which the recovery act is included. The opinion notes that "child support" does not "substantially affect interstate commerce," rejecting the argument that unpaid child support allows many families to fall into poverty.

"A fight to enforce court-ordered child support can take anywhere from two to four years and will probably cost more than the sum recovered," observes attorney Bender. "In the meantime, women can't get on with their lives, can't hire people to enforce the statutes that do exist. Without adequate resources, these women can't enforce their legal rights." Most give up. Judge Charles McClure told the Florida gender bias commission that when he first became involved in enforcing child support, he saw women who had been to court so many times, they had "the look of a prisoner of war." One exasperated attorney in Texas told the gender bias task force: "Judges seem to be 'bothered' by family law cases and could better spend their time on 'more important cases.' " In Minnesota a judges' survey found that while the judges said they are willing to use the contempt-of-court powers to enforce child support awards, in actuality they do so infrequently. In two years the median number of nonpaying fathers jailed was two for male judges and three for female judges, according to the state's gender bias report. However, one judge noted the jail was a powerful motivator to pay up: "They all seem to find their checkbooks on the way to the holding room."

Some noncustodial parents claim they don't pay support because their ex-spouses hinder or outright deny visitation with their children. Certainly some of these charges—perhaps even a good proportion of them—are true. However, a Vermont attorney noted that he had seen judges forgive men's failure to meet financial obligations to their families, while severely criticizing women for anything resembling interference with visitation. Perhaps the two can't be strictly compared, but once again it's the woman who feels the hot breath of the law on her neck, not the man who isn't paying for his children's upkeep. "The expression 'Justice delayed is justice denied' is nowhere more appropriate than in the area of child support," notes the Nevada task force report. "Although the individual amounts of money involved may in some cases seem trivial to us, they are critical to the child in need of adequate food, clothing and shelter. Those things cannot be made up later in a child's life."

Lack of child support is one reason women's standard of living plummets after divorce. Six out of ten divorces involve children, and in more than eight out of ten cases the children live with the mother, the parent who as a rule has the lower earnings. Another factor is that child support awards do not realistically mirror the cost of raising children without the substantial income of the higher wage earner. It works like this: If a father takes home $1,500 a month, and the mother takes home $500 a month, their combined income for a family of four is $2,000 a month. If they divorce, Mom gets the kids, and child support is set at, say, $450 a month. Dad now has $1,050 a month for himself, and Mom and the two children live on $950.

Since 1989 states have had to have guidelines in place stipulating how much of the income of the noncustodial parent is to be designated for child support, and awards ordered after the guidelines are generally much better than they were before. In New York most noncustodial parents pay between 17 and 35 percent of their gross income, depending on the number of children. Judges no longer have unfettered discretion in setting awards, and they have risen almost universally. In Rhode Island, for instance, child support awards increased almost 56 percent after the introduction of statewide guidelines.

In setting the guidelines, most states focused on how much the noncustodial parent contributed to the children before divorce and try to keep that same percentage after the divorce. But such calculations fail to acknowledge that when the children live with a parent, really all of them share the entire income, not just some small portion. "Even if you artificially show that x amount is spent on the children, and x amount is spent on the wife, and x amount is spent on the man himself, the portion that the father spends on himself includes housing, the car, food and all of that is shared," explains Joan Entmacher of the Women's Legal Defense Fund. "When the parents live independently, all of the rest of the income that used to support the household is not available to the children." Then too, the value of the awards declines with inflation, and while both partners have a right to seek a modification every three years, doing so requires going back to court and, most likely, hiring an attorney to prove the case, a luxury many women cannot afford.

FATHER'S RIGHTS GROUPS that have sprung up around the country in the last decade—no one knows how many activists there are, but they are plenty vocal—claim that support awards and the amount of visitation set by the courts are severely biased against men. In some states, California, Connecticut, Georgia and Washington among them, such groups have been successful in getting the guidelines lowered, and it appears they will gain ground in others. Ironically, it is typically middle-class fathers—ones who can best afford to pay—who are spearheading the drive to reduce payments. Some have remarried and are trying to raise second families on salaries that do not stretch to cover everyone's needs. Male legislators of course can understand their plight.

To be sure, there may be more to it than that. Attorney Amy Tabor, while a stalwart advocate for women's rights, believes that it is inappropriate to blame the enormity of women's poverty and the crises in welfare solely on deadbeat dads. "There is a growing gap between the rich and everyone else," she says. "In a large number of cases, the fathers are being squeezed more and more in their jobs. Either they have lost good jobs or their companies have demanded givebacks in greater contributions to health insurance. Many of these men have suffered a real drop in salary. People at the bottom are just fighting over crumbs."

IS MEDIATION A BETTER WAY?

Because about half of the civil docket in our nation's courts is concerned with family law issues, and because of the high cost of litigating family disputes, an alternative dispute resolution process is gaining ground. *Mediation* calls for divorcing individuals to resolve their differences themselves, and has been seen by some as the salvation of clogged courts, the remedy against unscrupulous lawyers, the best of all possible solutions for both men and women. Mediation may consist of as little as a single session of a few hours' (or shorter) duration, or it may involve numerous two-hour sessions over several weeks. The mediator can be a lawyer, a mental health expert, a law professor or a professional mediator from one of those fields; some states require training, some do not.

Mediation has caught on like wildfire. Since 1973, when Los Angeles County started a pilot program, it has spread in some form to all fifty states. By 1995 thirty-eight states and Washington, D.C., had some court-based mediation for custody and child support disputes alone. In eighteen states the law either requires divorcing parties with minor children to undertake mediation or gives local courts the power to require divorcing couples to try it before litigation.

Enthusiastic proponents of mediation say it is an informal, nonintimidating process that allows the two parties to work out the financial arrangements, custody and visitation without litigation. They point to a resolution rate of between 50 and 70 percent. Several studies indicate that people who use mediation services perceive it as fairer and less pressured and believe it produces more satisfying agreements than the traditional adversarial process. "Mediation works for most people because it offers a level of protection and help that is not readily available otherwise," says Jessica Pearson, director of the Center for Policy Research in Denver. "Otherwise, most people are just winging it themselves without a lawyer, negotiating themselves with a lot less protection and help than they can get in mediation."

Study after study concludes that mediation is more user-friendly than the typical back-and-forth that goes on when two lawyers are doing the negotiating. Even people who don't resolve their differences state they are not displeased with the process; satisfaction rates of various studies fall between 70 and 90 percent, rates that do not vary between mandatory versus voluntary programs. In the Charlottesville Mediation Project, in which 77 percent of those surveyed said they were satisfied with their mediation, even those who failed to reach agreement believed the process was useful and would recommend it to others. Mediation is so popular, in fact, that in Alaska, where all cases involving domestic violence are excluded from mediation by law (which amounted to the relatively high figure of 68 percent in the period studied), many "women objected to being barred from mediation because they did not expect the violence to continue or they believed that mediation would provide a safe context in which to work out their visitation problems," Pearson states.

Given all this, it sounds as if mediation is a panacea for disputing couples. But many feminists, as well as some lawyers of both sexes, believe just as firmly that women are in general at a disadvantage in mediation and tend to give up much more than they would either by negotiating themselves or by having lawyers do it for them. Some note that women prefer to conciliate rather than prolong an acrimonious dispute, so they agree to unfair settlements because it is in their nature to come to an agreement. Carol Gilligan's research on women certainly backs up this theory. Those women whose lives have been largely in the home also tend not to consider the long-term situation, some say, and lack the confidence and self-assurance that comes from having a successful life in the public sphere.

As for the rates of satisfaction, Professor Robert Levy of the University of Minnesota Law School counters that they are misleading because typically the people who say they are satisfied with mediation are those who were amenable to settling their differences in the first place. "Every study indicates that way over 90 percent of all divorces are settled anyway, so to compare contested divorces to mediated divorces is like comparing apples not to tangerines, but to broccoli."

One of the concerns that mediation raises is that "success" is counted when an agreement is reached, period. It does not matter whether it is fair or not, it is the resolution of the issues that matters. "The mediator wants to have a success—which means a resolution—and in achieving that, the mediator is consciously or unconsciously going to adopt the stronger person's wishes and enforce them because that is the quickest way to an agreement," Professor Levy contends. If the husband has been controlling the finances, there is no way to disprove what he says about assets. If he has been a bad parent, there is no one to back up the woman's claim that he never showed up for a parent-teacher conference or helped with the homework or that he hit the child. Fairness is thus sacrificed to the god of efficiency. And if the man—it's almost always the man—has close ties to the judicial system, or a lot of clout in the county, the woman is especially at risk. Consciously or unconsciously, the others involved in the process see the man's point of view. Cronyism is at the heart of some of the worst divorce stories around.

In Florida a prominent man with considerable influence in the legal system was able to bamboozle his divorcing spouse, with her "feminist" lawyer's complicity, and the mediator's encouragement, into a settlement that left her with a sixth of what she would have been entitled to under equal distribution. The couple had been married nearly two decades. The woman had quit her job as an award-winning newspaper reporter when they married. As his social director and hostess, however, the woman also had a visible position in the community.

But behind the affable veneer they presented as a couple, he was a tyrant at home, both with her and with the children. Although the man had not hit her, his cruelty and control came out in other ways. When she decided to leave him, she could not afford to rent an apartment. He would not leave the marital home. Instead, he allowed her and their three teenage children to live in "his" motor home, parked in a friend's driveway. Nearly penniless, she could not afford to go to a campground for the proper water and electric hookups. The sewage facilities were woefully inadequate; there was not enough power to use the stove. All four of them had to use the bathroom in the friend's house and eat all meals there. Before going to trial, she was told, she must "attempt" to come to a settlement through mediation. The week before the mediation, she slept little, smoked a lot, cried daily. The family assets were worth more than a million and a half—a fact that never came out at the single mediation session.

The man offered her the house and, an hour later, a temporary maintenance of $1,000 a month for eighteen months. She did not want the house, since it needed major repairs, and she knew it would be hard to sell for what it was worth at that time. Both the mediator and her lawyer overestimated by more than 100 percent the value of the home in the current market—they said it was worth a half million easy—and told her he was offering a great deal. They also told her a judge would review the settlement to make sure it was fair. Yes, but only if she contested it at trial and the judge overturned it would it be null and void, which they did not tell her.

"When you are living so horribly you are upset, distraught, and you don't have the strength to fight," the woman says. "But I naively believed my lawyer and the legal system would protect me." Less than seven hours after the mediation began, that same day, upset and crying, she signed the agreement. Resolution? Yes. Check one more off for the mediator.

Afterward, she contends, her lawyer later wrote a CYA ("cover your ass") letter, stating that she had told her that the agreement was not a fair settlement, but the deal was done. A new lawyer brought the case to trial a year and a half later, but the mediated settlement stood. The judge, who of course knew the ex-husband, exonerated her original lawyer in his opinion, so she could not sue her for damages. After eighteen months the house was sold for $245,000. The man retained the fifty-foot cabin cruiser, the condo in another state, the motor home, the securities, assets totaling well over a million. The lawyer who tried to undo the mediated agreement had to sue the ex-husband to collect his fees. By then the ex-husband had bought the house next door to the former family home and moved in with a different woman. The ex-wife lives in a condominium with the children on the other side of town. Since it had been years since she had worked as a reporter, no one at the local newspaper would even respond to her letter or calls. Remember, the man was extremely prominent in the town. He had a lot of friends who didn't want to get on his bad side. She has a job as a $15,000-a-year secretary.

While this case is extreme, critics of mediation contend that some variation of this scenario is far too frequent. "Mediators don't want to be therapists, so the notion that they should stand on one person's side is not appealing to them," Professor Levy says. "They are more interested in their own turf, which is getting the parties to come to an agreement." However, Levy adds a proviso: If the mediator is sensitive to power imbalances in the couple's relationship and willing to do something about them, the mediated settlements will have a better track record than that of couples who work things out on their own.

But critics of mediation say that this does not happen often enough to justify a wholesale shift to mediation because too often the woman ends up losing more than if she'd worked out an agreement herself. "Women usually have some control or authority over the children in a traditional family, and they can use that authority in negotiating an agreement by themselves," explains Penelope Bryan, a professor at the University of Denver College of Law. "The negotiation might go like this: 'You want to see the kids on such and such a day, well, I need *x* amount for support and so much to get my feet on the ground.' Put a mediator into the process and the woman is essentially stripped of any power she might have had, because the wife accedes to the 'expert.' And there is no reason to suspect that mental health workers who do mediation are any less biased against women than therapists and psychiatrists have been since Freud."

Both critics and proponents of mediation agree that mediation does not work for women who have been battered by their husbands, since the power imbalance is so unequal and the woman may be terrified even to be in the same building with the ex-spouse. In some cases mediation may not involve face-to-face discussion between the two parties, and the mediator will act as a go-between. But even if there has been no physical battering, there are still stumbling blocks for women entering mediation.

"They tell you not to talk about the past, only the future," explains Trina Grillo, a law professor at the University of San Francisco and a former mediator. "If you have a spouse who has not been a good parent, or has not fulfilled his obligations, you are not allowed to talk about that. You are deprived of the opportunity to talk about what your worries are and you do not get credit for being a good parent. You are told that doesn't matter, but what happened in the past has everything to do with what might happen next week." Consequently, she and other family law experts say, fathers are being awarded joint custody in mediation when they should not be.

"The bias in mediation is that everything should be divided equally, and that includes the children," observes Professor Bryan. "But too often that means that the man who has been totally controlling the woman's life still has the power to do so through the child. She can't make any decisions about the child by herself, including decisions about schooling, doctors and religion, so the stronger parent continues to enforce his will." Too often in divorce one or both parties are more interested in hurting the other party, or saving face, than they are in the children's welfare.

The greatest indictment of mediation comes from a study that looked at what happens several months after. Mediated custody agreements typically fall apart in three to six months, according to Marilyn L. Ray, executive director of the Finger Lakes Law and Social Policy Center in Ithaca, New York. She compared mediated agreements in New York, where mediators show a distinct preference for joint custody, and Georgia, where it is looked upon more skeptically. In New York, when Ray looked at who was actually taking care of the children on a day-to-day basis three to six months after the divorce, mothers were providing a home for significantly more of the children (74 percent) than they actually had legal responsibility for (66 percent). "Yet when a joint custody solution was mediated, there was almost no child support at all," says Ray. "You see right away that these women who are taking care of the children are not getting the support they should be." Mediated agreements when they include custody and child support distinctly disadvantage women and children, she concludes. "It appears that women are trading property and child support to avoid a custody fight," she says. "Before they go in, he says to her, 'Let's call it joint custody, and I won't pay as much support, but I'll let you have the kids anyway. If you don't do that, I'm going to fight for custody.' " It happens frequently. Nearly 85 percent of the lawyers queried in an Ohio survey agreed that "fathers seek custody for leverage in negotiating alimony or child support." Another Ohio survey found that 90 percent of the attorneys believe that fathers seeking custody are interested not in custody per se, but in using it as a bargaining tool.

In the case just discussed, was the grossly inequitable distribution of assets after an eighteen-year marriage, in which the wife was a homemaker and helpmate, the fault of mediation? Almost certainly. Under the "equitable distribution" law in Florida, she probably would have ended up with a greater piece of the pie than the thin slice she got—depending on the judge and the length of her ex-husband's influence. In Phyllis Chesler's study, a number of the men whose wives lost custody were lawyers, thereby greatly enhancing the man's chances for getting the agreement he wanted.

Some judges are fair. Some are realistic about a woman's opportunities after decades of being a homemaker. But why should justice for women still depend so entirely on the luck of the draw? And why, after all the reform, after all the efforts to change the system, are women still making out so poorly in divorce? Whether divorces and settlements and child custody are mediated or not, whether they end up in court or not, whether they are settled by the parties themselves or opposing lawyers, women are still by and large getting less than equitable settlements for the years they put in as chief bottle washer, career helpmate and child care worker.

CUSTODY

Rights and Rage

Childhood is only the beautiful and happy time in contemplation and retrospect: to the child it is full of deep sorrows, the meaning of which is unknown.
——GEORGE ELIOT

TALK TO THOSE divorced dads who despair over their fractured relationships with their children, if they have one at all, and they will tell you that the system is stacked against them, that lawyers and judges conspire to strip men of the ability to be real parents. They insist that moms have all the leverage when it comes to getting the kids. "You have no idea of the sense of despair that sets in when you are repeatedly told by lawyers that you have no chance of winning in court," one father told the Michigan Task Force on Gender Issues in the Courts.

Talk to mothers who lost custody of their children and they insist just the opposite: if they deviate at all from the stereotype of the chaste stay-at-home mom, they are susceptible to punishment by having their children taken from them. Although mothers by and large retain physical custody of the children after the dissolution of a relationship, those who do lose the children will most likely be devastated, since a mother's identity, as well as society's attitude toward her, is contingent upon her raising the children. When custody battles get to court, although that happens only about 5 percent of the time, the fight is always explosive and expensive and shattering. And again, no matter who wins, the other side feels cheated.

It was not always so. When divorce was rare, English common law automatically gave the children to the father. They were, when they were old enough to work the fields, a financial asset. The mother was entitled only to "reverence and respect." The common law presumption in favor of the father "disintegrated with the advent of the Industrial Revolution" in the nineteenth century, as social historians have noted. Fathers left the farm and moved into the factories, compulsory education reduced the availability of children as contributors to the family coffers, and the courts discovered mothers' maternal instincts. By the twentieth century the prevailing winds had shifted so that "children of tender years" were not snatched from their mother's bosom; legally they might be returned to fathers when they were. "Fault"-based divorces further favored mothers in custody disputes—unless of course she was an adulterer or otherwise unfit. By mutual agreement between parents, mothers got custody more than 80 percent of the time by the early twentieth century. That figure rose to around 90 percent in the late 1980s.

Now the pendulum has shifted back a bit. According to Census Bureau figures, in 1992 fathers had physical custody nearly 14 percent of the time. Family law experts note that many more men are asking for, and getting, either sole or joint custody. Between 1980 and 1990 the number of single-father households almost doubled for the second decade in a row; overall, the number of single-parent households headed by men is growing 2.5 times as fast as those headed by women. The reasons?

They are complicated and various. The women's movement sparked a certain amount of role reversal among many married couples, and it is true that some men are taking more responsibility for child rearing than they did in the past and some women are taking more responsibility for making money. Some men have in the last twenty to thirty years become more interested in being real, participating parents to their children—more than just someone who takes them to the circus. Other men have learned that they can take advantage of the hype over this newfound interest in parenting. They become concerned fathers when the divorce is impending, but their real interest is in punishing and controlling the women and children who are slipping away from them.

In addition, men have learned that the threat of fighting for sole custody (and getting joint) is an excellent way to coerce mothers into signing agreements that are financially favorable to men. In two separate surveys in Ohio more than 80 percent of the domestic relations attorneys agreed that fathers seeking custody are primarily motivated in using it as a bargaining tool. In the process they often wind up with joint custody—and less child support than they would otherwise have had to pay—while mothers still have physical custody of the child and the major responsibility of raising him or her.

Of course, not all dads are conniving monsters who want to walk away from their kids when the marriage ends. Seventy-five percent are paying at least some child support, and a great many of them wish to be more than a wallet to their children and assume a role that is more than that of a friendly uncle who takes them to the movies every other weekend. The question of who is getting shafted in custody cases is a vexed one. It is impossible to determine from statistics who is really interested in a child's welfare and who is using custody as a way to hurt the mother.

No matter how it is negotiated or ordered, joint custody typically means that the individual who pays child support pays less. The idea is that since the children spend more time with each parent, the cost of raising the child is more closely equalized and can be given directly to that child. It sounds good on paper, but it doesn't usually work that way. "If the child support is based on custody and the amount of visitation, these agreements break down rather quickly," notes Marilyn Ray, an authority on social policy. "The children end up living in a home without sufficient support, and Mom is struggling to make ends meet. The economic burden is not shared." And Mom and the children become the statistics of women and children in poverty. In several states if a child can stay with the father more than 100 nights a year, the amount of support the father pays drops precipitously. Consequently the woman with the kids 265 days a year gets a lot less than the woman who has the kids 270 days a year. Joint custody can work, but only if both parents can get along well enough not to fight over the children, or in front of the children, and if the parent who has the child less—100 nights or not—contributes substantially to the child's upkeep, such as paying for some bills that are part of the regular cost of raising a child—doctor's bills, insurance, clothing, schooling and so forth. While fathers are more likely to stay involved with their children when they have joint custody, and are more likely to pay support, the grand experiment of joint custody was not quite the remedy that it was hoped it would be. Warring parents are warring parents no matter what. Joint custody often means that the stronger parent can still enforce his will on all major issues concerning the child—education, religion, health. The Nevada gender bias report observed that the awarding of joint custody—for which the state law has a decided preference—is appropriate only when the parents can agree. "In other cases, absentee fathers may exercise family control which is not justified under the circumstance."

Despite its many problems, however, joint custody is often the outcome of choice for many judges. Several gender bias reports conclude that courts are ordering shared parental responsibility in inappropriate cases. The New Jersey task force made note of "the deeply held belief that judges are ordering joint custody in order to avoid making a decision." Mediators like it too, because it sounds fair. When fathers do fight for custody, they have a very good chance of getting joint custody at worst, full custody at best, according to statistics from several states. Although there are no national statistics to give us a picture of the nation as a whole, the gender bias commission in Massachusetts found that when fathers sought custody, they obtained either primary or joint physical custody over 70 percent of the time. The figures are based on a variety of measurements, including an examination of court records in one of the largest counties in the state and a survey sent to family law lawyers who over five years had represented 2,100 fathers involved in custody and paternity disputes in the late eighties. In Middlesex County (suburban Boston) researchers found that in five hundred cases filed between 1978 and 1981 fathers who sought sole custody received it *41 percent of the time* and joint custody in 38 percent. Mothers contesting fathers seeking sole custody were awarded custody *only 15 percent of the time,* a statistic that is consistent with findings in North Carolina. In California, fathers contesting mothers for sole custody prevailed with either sole or joint custody in 41 percent of the cases.

While it remains true that the vast majority of divorces do not reach this stage, it is significant that when custody is contested in court so many women lose. If *Kramer vs. Kramer* were filmed today, the father would probably win custody rather than the other way around. Women who deviate from the stereotypical norms—as the Meryl Streep character did to go off and find herself as well as a career—are routinely losing their children. Women who combine careers with raising a family are facing increasingly hostile judges.

"Case after case since the early eighties shows that in the minds of many judges, a woman working outside the home is not a good mother," comments Lynn Hecht Schafran of the National Judicial Education Program. "A woman is expected to be on the job for her children twenty-four hours a day." A father is held to a different standard. He is seen as a paragon of paternity if he changes a couple of diapers. "A man with a full-time job who provides any assistance in child rearing, however limited, looks like a dedicated father, while a woman with a full-time job who still does primary, but not all, caretaking, looks like 'half' a mother, dissatisfied with the child-rearing role," comments Nancy Polikoff, an expert on custody at American University College of Law.

While there are no statistics on how often career women lose children to career men, it seems to happen with some frequency when the woman in question is more successful than her mate—she must be working too hard at her job to be a good mom. A case that sent chills through the ranks of working mothers in 1994 was that of Sharon Prost. She had been chief counsel for Senator Orrin Hatch, now chairman of the Senate Judiciary Committee, when she lost custody of her two young sons, who were seven and four. By that time they had been living with their mother for nearly two years, since she'd split up with their father, Kenneth Greene, a labor-union administrator. Near the end of the marriage Greene had been out of work for two years after leaving a high-pressure job. During that time the children were cared for either by day care workers, an au pair, or Prost's mother. At the time of the divorce he was working, but for less than half her salary.

Although Prost testified in a five-day trial that she rose at five-thirty A.M. to spend time with the children before school when they were together, that seemed to be less important than who took over from the nanny first in the evening. He usually did, even though the total hours Prost spent with the children weekly added up to more than Greene's. Although the older son's kindergarten teacher described a regular ongoing relationship with Prost, whom she says she saw nearly every day—Prost was someone who provided cookies and cupcakes as the "surrogate room mom"—this was not mentioned in the judge's decision, which instead focused on the two or three times a semester Greene participated in school activities. The judge misconstrued when the Senate is not "in session" to mean only holidays; in fact, it is nearly half the 260 days a year Congress convenes. Prost's working until midnight or one A.M. occasionally, such as during the Clarence Thomas hearings, was held against her, but the day care records showing that she routinely picked up the children by six, as well as affidavits from co-workers about when she left the office, were overlooked. Prost was accused of being "rigid" and "hysterical" (that word again) by a few witnesses, descriptions the judge saw fit to include several times in the opinion, while commending Greene for dealing with his job-related depression in six weeks. The opinion made no mention of testimony from a social worker the couple had seen regarding Greene's "volatile" personality, his anger and his focus on deflating his ex-wife.

A child psychiatrist who had been jointly selected by both Prost and Greene recommended that Prost be awarded custody, as the children had been thriving in her care. Both sides presented contradicting witnesses over who was the better parent, who had done what to whom. The judge noted that Prost's drive to succeed can be seen in her four degrees; however, they were awarded even before the couple was married. Although it was noted that the children were "doing well" under the present arrangement, the judge decided that because Prost "is simply more devoted to and absorbed by her work and her career than anything else in her life, including her health, her children and her family," Greene should have sole custody. Prost has liberal visitation rights. Incidentally, the judge was a woman, Harriett R. Taylor.

"Clearly those activities that the husband does with the children are considered to be 'remarkable,' and if done by the mother, they are considered to be routine," says Prost's attorney, Armin Kuder. "And when the mother does things that the husband or father normally does, she has to explain herself." An appeal was denied. Prost has taken a lesser job with Senator Hatch's office that is more flexible than her old one, and has filed a motion for a rehearing based on changed circumstances. The children are in after-school care although Prost is willing to care for them at that time. Senator Hatch has started a legal defense fund for Prost. She is paying $22,091, close to half of her current take-home pay, in child support. She says that in the first nine months after the order went into effect, the children actually lived with her more than with Greene. For this privilege she signed waivers that she would not seek a reduction in child support or a change in the custody order. When she did, based on her new part-time work schedule, the arrangement ended. Greene attempted to get an order of protection against her, but the motion was thrown out of court as frivolous.

Cut to Michigan. In another highly publicized case, a sixty-nine-year-old judge, Raymond R. Cashen, awarded custody of three-year-old Maranda to her father, Steven Smith, in 1994 because the girl was in day care while her mother, Jennifer Ireland, then eighteen, had begun attending the University of Michigan on a scholarship. On weekends and holidays Jennifer and Maranda would go to her mother's home. Smith was going to junior college, working part-time, and living at his home; his mother—not Smith himself—would be the primary caregiver.

Testimony at the custody trial focused on Ireland's first two years as a mother, when she left much of the care of Maranda to her own mother while she went on with her life. Ireland graduated third in her class; she was a member of the French Club and the National Honor Society. But it was her cheerleading, the number of her boyfriends, and her partying that became the focus of the ten-day trial, until the judge finally called the character assassination to a halt. Smith's parents testified they drove by Ireland's house frequently—once every night, maybe again at six A.M.—to see if her boyfriend's car was there. They went to her church to see if she showed up. They drove by her workplace. They admitted they were keeping track of her every move on a daily basis. They secretly tape-recorded nearly every conversation she had with them. Eventually Ireland filed two stalking complaints against the three Smiths, father, mother and son. There were incidents of physical intimidation also, which involved pulling and pushing, and Smith testified that he knew Ireland was afraid of him. Although he claimed to have a tape recording of one of the incidents to show his innocence, the tape was never produced at trial.

In his decision Judge Cashen called Ireland "sexually indiscriminate," even though the father "wasn't much better." Mothers seeking custody, obviously, have to be more chaste than the men who impregnate them. The stalking and intimidation by Smith and his family were considered to be totally irrelevant. "The mother's academic pursuits, although laudable, are demanding. . ." and necessitate "the leaving of the child for a considerable portion of its life in the care of strangers. There is no way that a single parent, attending an academic program at an institution as prestigious as the University of Michigan, can do justice to their [sic] studies and the raising of an infant child. There are not that many hours in the day." He noted that "under the future plans of the mother, the minor child will be raised and supervised a great time by strangers. Under the future plans of the father, the minor child will be raised and supervised by blood relatives."

In other words, since Ireland is getting a good education, which will allow her to better support herself and her daughter, and she has to have the child in day care while she's in school, we'll take the daughter from her. Under that reasoning an awful lot of mothers are likely to lose custody to ex-husbands whose mothers will provide care. Ireland's case is not an isolated one. In a snarled case in New Jersey, Judge Katharine Sweeney Hayden gave custody to a father—although he was not the biological father—because he was going to be living with his parents and she thought the mother's life was too unsettled. Woe betide any young mother who isn't as stable as Gibraltar.

"The message of the trial court was that women are supposed to give up their jobs, give up their careers, give up their academic pursuits, and be nothing but a stay-at-home parent," comments Julie Field, the attorney who handled Ireland's appeal.* "Jennifer was doing everything right. She didn't go on welfare, she got a scholarship to a great institution—and what's the punishment she receives? She loses her child."

"There is real schizophrenia between courtroom policy and public policy," adds Lynn Schafran. "We are developing social policy that says a woman who stays in the home on welfare is a bad mother who will lose her benefits, so she is forced to go out and get a job and put her children in some kind of day care. But if she is in another financial situation, if she's middle class, she is punished for not being at home full-time. There is no logic operating here."

But there was in the Michigan Court of Appeals. Last year, before a different judge, the Ireland decision was overturned and remanded for a new hearing. In May, Ireland won permanent custody.

But these cases are not isolated incidents. Women's rights lawyers tell of a string of cases: In San Jose last year a mother lost custody because she had allowed her boyfriend to take care of her son part-time while she attended law school. In New York the appellate court awarded custody of an eleven-year-old girl to her unemployed father even though a court-appointed psychologist described him as "abrasive, antagonistic and indifferent to the human race." But while the mother was in an office somewhere making a living, he could be abrasive, antagonistic and indifferent at home, with his daughter. Also in New York, actress Tonya Pinkins of *All My Children* lost custody of her two sons because state supreme court justice Lewis R. Friedman lent considerable weight, he stated, to her "palpably obvious anger throughout the proceeding." Women, then, had better not show their anger in the courtroom.

In Reno, in 1990, now defrocked judge Jerry Carr Whitehead awarded an infant less than a month old to the father, a carpet layer, after the husband alleged in court that the mother had slept with her boyfriend. This supposedly happened within seven days after she had an episiotomy, a surgical cut made during delivery to enable the passage of the baby. The father took the son and moved to California. The mother, Gale Pearson, had custody of the couple's other older son. Two years later Whitehead awarded custody of the older child to the husband because Pearson, then a medical student, had missed a court-ordered evaluation; the letter informing her of it had been sent to her home in

* *Field handled Ireland's appeal for free through the University of Michigan Women and the Law Clinic. It closed at the end of 1995 because of budget cutbacks. More than half of the clinic's $207,000 budget for the 1994–95 school year came from federal funding sources.*

Reno while she was on a surgical rotation in Las Vegas. By the time she received it the date had passed. Ultimately the supreme court ordered a new hearing. Since both parents were now living in California, the hearing was held there. Pearson won custody of both sons.

In Florida last year an appeals court upheld an Orlando judge's decision that a five-year-old boy should live primarily with his father, Donald Severance, who had a history of alcoholism. The mother, Susan Kopec, was said to be a "volatile, intense person more oriented to career achievement than parenting." Kopec said, yes, she worked long hours, sometimes at two jobs, because her first husband didn't pay support for her two older children and that during her marriage to Severance, he drank often and contributed little income. The child's guardian ad litem testified that the boy was doing well living with the mother. But once again, physical custody went to the father. At this writing Kopec was asking for a rehearing.

In one case that was ultimately overturned, *Burchard* v. *Garay,* a California court ruled that a working mother should lose custody to a father who had remarried and whose new wife would stay home to take care of the children. The case is a famous one among matrimonial lawyers and custody experts; even though it was overturned on appeal in 1986, women's rights advocates say that the original judgment is not so unusual.

An executive in Memphis lost her two adolescent boys this way, to a "stay-at-home mom and a new house on a lake," as she put it. The woman at the time was living in a three-bedroom condominium and working for Federal Express, an egalitarian company but one that demands a high level of commitment. She had to hire baby-sitters when she traveled overnight. "What came out at the hearing [for custody and child support] was how much better a life my ex-husband and Betty Crocker could provide—how she made sandwiches for the school, what they thought of her at the church. The really aggravating part was that it was generally acknowledged that the father was going to hand over the care of the boys to her. It was a tremendous blow because it cut to the core of my maternal instinct. Financially it was devastating. Now I was living in a three-bedroom condo I had no need for and I had to pay $500 a month in child support." The underlying assumption is that mothers are fungible—any woman will do, as long as she's a stay-at-home mom.

Sexuality is another area where women are held to a different standard from men. Baltimore attorney Timmerman Daugherty recalled how one of her clients lost custody because she was having a relationship with another man. Although the woman later married the man, the judge would not reverse his original decision. This occurred in spite of state law in Maryland that says a parent's sexual activity is irrelevant—unless it has a detrimental effect on the children. Daugherty says judges pay the law no heed.

"There was no evidence that the children had been harmed, and one of them, a twelve-year-old girl, testified that if she had to live with her father, she would run away," Timmerman said. And, just as in the Ireland case in Michigan, it wasn't the father who was going to raise the kids—it was the grandparents. "That's a typical situation—the father gets the kids and he shoves them off to the grandparents," she added. A woman in Iowa told the gender bias commission there that while it was considered unacceptable if she ever had an extra-marital affair, "the children's father could have as many affairs as he wanted, and he had the privilege of leading whatever lifestyle he chose." The attorneys and judges, she said, "did not feel these relationships reflected on his image as a role model for our children at all." A woman testified to the Texas gender bias commission that while a divorcing woman better not go out with another man, "a new girlfriend is often seen as a plus for a man, someone who will help him care for the children."

Who is better able financially to care for the children is another consideration used unfairly against women. A 1990 Wisconsin study found that fathers are more likely to get custody when their income is high, when the mother's is low, and when the youngest child is not an infant. Typically it is the man who has the greater resources and can carry on a prolonged custody fight, hire a good attack lawyer to do it, and show at the same time that he can provide a more affluent home. One unintended but nevertheless real result of a woman's economic disadvantage in the labor market is the legal separation of her from her children after divorce. Modern, "egalitarian" laws cannot rid our legal system of the yoke of tradition and practices that principally serve affluent men, regardless of how the law reads.

Without question, women are held to different standards in deciding custody—except when it comes to money, and then they should have as much as the men. Men can work and have careers and still win custody, but women are not supposed to; somehow they must make up the difference between what child support pays and what they actually need, but not be so successful at it that they appear to care about their careers in the same way men do. Men can go to school or to their jobs and let their mothers take care of the child; young mothers must sacrifice everything to child care. Men can have affairs and it's a plus because the new girlfriend (or wife) will help with the child; woe betide the woman who steps out. Even when these cases are overturned they create a climate of fear in women's hearts, and they clearly indicate the bias that still permeates American society and its courts.

Sometimes the bias is incredibly egregious, reminiscent of nineteenth-century attitudes toward women. North Carolina may be the worst state in the union in this respect.

A CESSPOOL IN CHAPEL HILL

When the Committee for Justice for Women, a private research and advocacy group, looked at the 55 contested cases in Orange County, North Carolina, from 1983–87 that were actually litigated, they found that men were winning sole custody in two-thirds of the cases and joint custody in most other cases; if you add in the figure for joint custody, men were successful in 84 percent of the contested cases. More than 40 percent of the fathers were proven or alleged spousal abusers, and some had physically or sexually abused the children as well, a statistic which replicates many other studies which show that violent men are disproportionately likely to contest custody. Only in 16 percent of the cases were women getting sole custody. Although the report of the Committee for Justice for Women was publicized in the surrounding three-county area when it was released a few years ago and was the subject of a CNN special, it's still business as usual in family court in Chapel Hill.

What happened to Ashley Williams is a case in point. Ashley McEachren and James Dale Williams* met and married in 1985 in California. They moved to Chapel Hill in 1987. James—fortyish, graying and good-looking—became head of a writing program at the University of North Carolina there. Ashley started and ran a successful secretarial services business. The marriage broke apart in 1994. Austin, their son, was seven. In a deposition at the time, James admitted that he had sex in his office with students, including one Ako Shimada, who was on a payroll he dispensed; that he and Shimado had attended academic conferences together partially paid for by university funds; that he had sex with more than two hundred women—a result, he said, of "being a child of the sixties"; that while married he had answered an ad and fathered another woman's child; that after he ended a four-month affair with another student and when she pressured him for hush money, he gave her the name of a man in

---

* *Because both use the surname Williams, they are referred to by their first names.*

California he knew who regularly paid for sex. She later told James she flew to California, met him and completed the transaction. There's a name for that, and it isn't "teaching."

As the divorce became more acrimonious, Ashley sued Ako Shimada, a Japanese native, under a state code for "criminal conversations" with James, the legal words for breaking up her marriage. Ashley's business declined and she filed for bankruptcy, owing some $7,000 in back salaries.

A few days before the hearing with Shimada, John Greenlee, an assistant attorney general at the state Department of Labor, had Ashley arrested around four P.M. on Saturday, New Year's Eve. It was either jail or $7,000 in cash on the spot. The request was more than a little unusual, since most such legal chicanery grinds to a halt there as everywhere between Christmas and New Year's. The warrant stated that since she had transferred all her assets into cash, she was an immediate flight risk, though there was no evidence to that effect. She had no way to get her hands on any cash until the following Tuesday because Monday was a legal holiday, so she would be in jail and miss her settlement conference with Shimada and her lawyer. On the spot, Ashley hired a tough new criminal lawyer, Terry Harn, a former assistant U.S. district attorney, who was not afraid to bark at John Greenlee and anybody else in his line of fire, including the sheriff, who admitted he was supposed to keep Ashley in jail until Tuesday. Harn charged that the warrant was itself illegal. Although Ashley had already changed into a crisply cut orange prison jumpsuit, Harn got her out in a couple of hours. On Tuesday, Ashley surprised Shimada and her attorney by showing up for the scheduled nine-thirty A.M. appointment. Shimada agreed to pay Ashley $10,000 and apologized for sleeping with her husband in their bedroom.

Ashley's brush with North Carolina's slippery justice system was not over yet. Two days later the custody hearing was scheduled. That morning yet another deputy sheriff showed up outside her house to arrest her on yet another warrant, although he wasn't sure exactly what it was for, since it was back at the station. While Harn arrived and took the boy to school shortly around eight A.M., Ashley slipped out the back door, disguised in a big hat and sunglasses, dashed through the woods behind her house, and got into a waiting cab on another street corner. Much to the surprise of her ex-husband and his attorney, she made the nine A.M. court date, too. She retained custody of Austin. In order to protect the son's privacy, Judge Patricia Love had previously sealed James's 118-page-plus deposition, with all its juicy pecadilloes. In her testimony Ashley described how James once threw her across the room and how he brought her roses afterward. She thought she would never have to worry about custody again. Her ex-husband's promiscuity was now all in the record. An ex-wife also had testified to James's ill treatment of her and his controlling personality. Although James's attorney attempted to have Ashley declared as someone suffering from a "mental breakdown," he dropped that ploy when she showed up in court both able and fully in control and with reputable witnesses who testified to her mental soundness and abilities.

But she didn't count on the way Chapel Hill cronyism winks at philanderers, or the clout of being a tenured UNC professor in what is basically a company town, or North Carolina's history of notorious disregard of justice for women in family court. A few months later Ashley wanted to put Chapel Hill behind her and make a new life in California, where she had family and friends—after all, she had only moved to North Carolina for his career. James then challenged the original custody agreement, charging that her plans were far too unsettled and uncertain for the boy's well-being, that since she was the one moving, he deserved custody. If she left, he would be denied the right to see Austin regularly.

To her astonishment, district court judge Joe Buckner agreed; the promiscuous professor was awarded primary physical custody. The boy, the judge somehow reasoned, would be better off with his dad. Ashley was given limited visitation, which, oddly enough, would be increased if she *moved* away. Buckner later would admit that he had not bothered to read the deposition outlining James Williams's sexual proclivities or previous drug use or his long history of treatment for chronic depression.

Details contained in James's juicy deposition were made public and reported on the front page of the *Chapel Hill Herald* over the spring. Williams sent a memo to his colleagues at UNC, stating that the charges of his sexual shenanigans were all a lie, part of his ex-wife's vendetta against him. Harn asked for a new custody hearing, requesting that Buckner rescue himself. Williams's attorney, Lunsford Long of Chapel Hill, was widely thought to have been heavily involved in Buckner's last election campaign, a fact that Long denied. Buckner, by the way, is also the former partner of the lawyer who represented the student James had referred to the California john. Apparently it's all very clubby in the political and legal circles of Orange County, North Carolina. Buckner refused to step down. "What's good for the university is good for Chapel Hill—that's the feeling—so since Williams was a big shot at the university, he was protected," says Harn.

Three months later, in June, as she was preparing for another custody hearing, Ashley was arrested once again, this time on a warrant charging her with animal abandonment. It seems that she owed a kennel more than $1,000, and the owners would not allow her to pick up her Labrador retriever without paying the bill. Yet when her father from California tried to find out what was owed so he could pay it, the kennel owners would not return his calls or faxes to let him know the exact amount owed. So it kept adding up. Coincidentally, the kennel is in Judge Buckner's hometown. The instruction sheet with the warrant ordered that Ashley, who now lived in Durham County, be held on $2,000 cash bail because, once again, she was in danger of fleeing. At the hearing the female magistrate of Durham County, Jewel Parrish, said she didn't understand why the magistrate of Chatham County, where the kennel is located, would recommend a cash bond for such a case. Ashley was released immediately.

"The idea was to put her in jail on idiot charges and keep her quiet," said Harn. Throughout the months this case dragged on, both Harn and his wife, as well as Ashley, had the oil mysteriously drained from their cars a couple of times. Ashley's car was ruined.

James's deposition was officially unsealed in July. UNC chancellor Paul Hardin at last got around to reprimanding James. A letter of censure would be placed in his file, but he would continue on sabbatical and collect his $65,000 salary, and presumably come back to teaching when this blew over. A third hearing was scheduled; Harn again asked Buckner to recuse himself, and he again refused. After a perfunctory hearing, Buckner said his decision would stand. Austin would live with James, who was by this time living with his fourth wife, Shimada. If UNC was tolerant of James's proclivities, the state legislature was not, where it was threatened that funding to UNC might be cut off as long as James remained on the faculty. Chancellor Hardin retired from UNC. His replacement, Michael Hooker, almost immediately began dismissal proceedings against James. A few days later James was allowed to "resign."

Within weeks he found a new job at Governor's State University in University Park, Illinois, as director of a writing program. Although administrators there smelled some of the stench from Chapel Hill, UNC officials confirmed that James Williams "resigned," and they wrote it off to a messy divorce. So the professor, Ako Shimada and Austin abruptly moved to Illinois after school one Friday. The boy was not told of the move beforehand and was not allowed to say good-bye to anyone. "He was ripped from his home," Harn said. "He was basically told to get in the car and go without getting to talk to his mother or any of his friends." Harn asked to have custody reconsidered. It is worth noting that legally the couple have joint custody.

At yet another hearing, now before another judge, Philip Allen, a child psychiatrist who had more than fifty sessions with Austin testified that the boy, now eight, should be returned to his mother's care, because, he said, in his father's care "he's more tentative, tense, there's a distinct difference when he's with his father as opposed to his mother. . . . He said he was very lonely sometimes when he's with his father. . . . He would be less at risk with his mother." The next day James was found in criminal contempt for secretly moving his son out of state, but the judge, a man who fills in around the state when needed, indicated that he didn't believe he had the authority to change custody at this time. He was not from Orange County, nor did he appear to be fully aware of all the ramifications of the case. "Based on the limited evidence I have heard, you have won my heart," Allen said to Ashley in court, "but I'm afraid you haven't won my legal opinion." What would it take? A federal investigation?

Ashley Williams has moved to Santa Monica. She has a well-paying job as a headhunter in the computer industry. Austin lives with Ako Shimada and James Williams in Park Forest, Illinois. Although James is supposed to pay for Austin's airplane ticket to California for visits, he was not living up to that part of the agreement last fall, according to Ashley.

Apparently it will take an investigation by the Justice Department to clean out the dung heap of North Carolina family courts. "Women are getting hammered down here on a pretty frequent basis," concludes Harn. "The statute reads so that both parents are on an equal footing as to who can be the custodial parent, but what has happened is that it comes down to who can provide the most goodies, and that is usually the father. It comes down to who has the most money." When I asked him how a UNC professor could have so much influence with judges, the sheriff, even with the Department of Labor, he replied, "I wish I knew. But don't forget," he added, "there are a bunch of people around here who like to party with young girls." Maybe James Williams had met all these people before. At parties with young girls.

The state's supreme court, incidentally, decided to forgo establishing a task force to document gender bias; the court assumed it existed and so is "committed to spending appropriate money and energy to address the problem." Don't hold your breath. And if you're female, don't get divorced in Chapel Hill.

BATTERED WOMEN LOSE CUSTODY

Men such as James Williams are not so much interested in the children's welfare as they are in control—control over their former wives, that is. Ashley couldn't move back to her home state with her son; instead James dragged her back into court, and in a surprise move the judge awarded him custody. Yet soon after James had custody of Austin, when it suited him, he fled North Carolina to another part of the country for *his* career. Family law experts contend this phenomenon is none too rare: once the man wins custody because the wife wants to move away, he is then free to move with the children anywhere he wants. "Most married women relocate because they are following their husbands, and then they get left holding the bag if there are kids when the couple breaks up," contends matrimonial attorney Lynne Gold-Bikin. She recalled a case where the man wanted to move to Alaska and so the wife did, and once there, he left her. "When she wanted to move back to the Lower Forty-eight, she couldn't, not if she wanted to keep the children," she says, "so she gets stuck in Alaska."

California attorney Patricia Barry says that among the hundreds of cases she has handled, she found "a direct relationship between abuse of the mother and the need to control and punish her by forcing her to remain in the jurisdiction if she wants to retain custody of the kids—these are not nice men who are litigating this issue." In California at least, it is no longer possible to prevent the parent with custody of the child from moving away. In 1996 the California supreme court ruled that such a move can only be contested if it can be proven it harms the child.

Certainly not all men who insist that their wives not move away are doing it simply to control their wives—certainly some of them genuinely want to see their children often. But without question continuing control over the ex-wife motivates many men who are emotional and/or physical batterers. The outcome in the Williams case sadly is not a single aberration. The children are the forgotten victims in such custody wars. "Before the welfare of the child is looked at, you have to have broken bones or a dead kid," Ashley says. "Whoever has the most money and the most clout wins, and the judges just look the other way where the child's welfare is concerned."

Despite provisions in state laws specifically precluding abusers from getting custody, despite a federal resolution stating that children should not be placed with such parents, judges are routinely ignoring charges of domestic violence in awarding custody. A recent California study of 150 divorces demonstrates rather alarmingly that when a restraining order due to domestic violence was in place, the man was more than twice as likely to challenge the mother for custody. These men were also three times as likely to be in arrears in child support. Yet when social psychologist Geraldine Butts Stahly, author of the study, looked at who was actually winning custody, she found no difference between batterers and nonbatterers. Consequently, she says, "*a woman who has been battered is more likely to lose her children than a woman who hasn't been battered.* The courts are simply not taking the violence into consideration at all, nor are they looking at the father's failure to support the kids." However, in the absence of national statistics, we do not know if this holds for the entire country.

Stahly, an associate professor at California State University, San Bernardino, also found that residents of shelters for battered women were significantly more likely to report threats of kidnapping, custody disputes and violence related to visitation than were those who had not been subject to physical abuse. Phyllis Chesler found that more than half of the fathers in her study who were successful in winning court-ordered custody had been physically abusive.

Joan Zorza, an expert on domestic violence, says that in her dealings with more than two thousand women in the decade she was with Boston Legal Services, "custody fights were very rare unless there was domestic violence." And fathers were winning, she says, at least joint custody, unless the women were zealously represented by someone knowledgeable in domestic violence. Zorza heard of many cases around the courthouse in Boston, where women were being urged not to raise the abuse issue because it was "embarrassing" to the children and the man." The husband's attorney, and officers of the court such as probation officers who did mediation, would say that if the woman brought it up, it would probably have financial repercussions—the man might lose his job. The irony of all this is that these fathers were not paying support anyway. Many of the mothers had been carrying the financial burden of the family through welfare or working, and the fathers had paid no attention to the children during the marriage. "Now suddenly they show up in court asking for joint or sole custody, and amazingly the court took this as a sign that they were wonderful fathers instead of being suspicious."

The cases are a tangled web. Judges have a hard time following who did what to whom. Many judges believe that if a man beats his wife but not his children, his rage toward her should affect neither custody nor visitation, even though there is a mountain of evidence about the destructive effect of witnessing violence between one's parents and how this perpetuates itself in the next generation. The abuse often escalates after a separation or divorce, when the man is losing control, as the O. J. Simpson case exemplified, whether or not he was the murderer.

But judges don't get it. "Judges look bored, it's 'ho-hum,' even when there is corroborating evidence as to the violence. Witnesses can say they saw bruises, you can bring in a police report and a person you told you were beaten up right after it happened, but the man gets up and says, 'Judge, I never did it,' and the judge says, 'Oh, well, I can't make up my mind, and she is hysterical anyway, so I rule in his favor,'" states Los Angeles attorney Barry. She brought suit in federal court, asserting that courts were awarding custody to battering spouses because, as she puts it, "California employs judges, mediators and psychologists who work to the detriment of mothers and children—the whole system is stacked against women and children." In 1995 she had to drop the suit for lack of funds. As a family law practitioner who takes cases that will never pay even a fraction of their worth—and the time that can be involved as the batterer continues to litigate is substantial—she could not afford to continue the suit without outside funding. Battered women usually aren't well financed.

"The woman comes into court believing that the man can't possibly get custody, and she is afraid of him—she is wigged out, she is hysterical—and the man comes in looking as if he stepped out of a bandbox, he is very calm, very charming, and so he gets at least joint legal custody because the judge can talk to this guy and he seems so reasonable," continues Barry. "He's the one who is going to make sure that the other spouse will have visitation, while she's screaming that she doesn't want the kids anywhere near him, so the judge awards custody to the 'friendly parent.'" Several states have specific "friendly parent" provisions in their laws, urging that custody be awarded by the parent who appears more likely to make sure that the children have continued contact with the other parent, a condition that unwittingly works to the detriment of battered women who have finally been able to break away from their abuser. The "friendly parent" provision helps to justify awarding men custody, particularly when judges don't believe the batterer—that presentable doctor, carpenter, or *lawyer* in front of them protesting innocence—could have done those terrible things the woman is accusing him of.

How else could a known wife batterer, Lonnie Dutton, have won custody of his four children? Apparently everybody but the judge in Rush Springs, Oklahoma, knew he was a loathsome bully who for years had terrorized his ex-wife—she said he beat her unconscious with a hose and two-by-fours. His ex-wife, Rose Marie, says the boys once were ordered to throw steel-tipped darts at her and were beaten if the darts didn't pierce her skin. When Rose Marie fled in 1989 she took the two youngest children, who were six and four at the time, to Texas, but Lonnie eventually got all the kids back, winning custody after telling a judge that they had been abused in Texas.

End of story? Not quite. Lonnie told the boys to kill anybody who molested their younger sister, who was ten in 1993. Following those instructions, Herman, then fifteen, picked up a deer rifle and pointed it behind the ear of his sleeping father. He told police Lonnie had "messed with his sister" that morning. Twelve-year-old Druie pulled the trigger. "While the mother was no prize, there was a willingness to turn the children over to the father uncritically by both the authorities in Texas and Oklahoma without examining to see if he was a fit parent," says James Percival, attorney for the boys. "The allegations about the mother were that she was whorish, and all social workers respond more negatively if a mother has gone wrong than if a father has. And we have to remember that she suffered years of horrible, unspeakable abuse that is hard to believe—Lonnie would pour jalapeño pepper juice in her eyes, he beat her viciously—that doesn't excuse her, but God only knows what the rest of us would have done." The boys were tried as juveniles and given probation. They were ultimately placed, together, in foster care and are reportedly doing better than expected.

What happens when children do not want to visit their noncustodial parent? They too might be punished. An Illinois judge, Will County Circuit Judge Ludwig Kuhar, sent one twelve-year-old girl to a children's detention center because she would not visit her father in North Carolina after he sent airplane tickets. The mother, Kathy Marshall, went to court to block the visit. Her daughter Heidi said her father acted "weird" and that he claimed her mother and grandparents were "wicked." She also said he threw a guitar at her. The father, Sheldon Nussbaum, denied the charges. Marshall was found in contempt and ordered to pay $3,000, Heidi went to a detention center for the night; her sister, Rachel, eight, was confined to her mother's home. The Illinois Appeals Court upheld Kuhar's ruling. At press time, the matter was being appealed to the Illinois Supreme Court.

Sending a child to what is, in effect, jail because her parents' divorce has traumatized her is a sign of how badly the courts can, and often do, function when it comes to family law. As Sheldon Nussbaum, the father, himself said to the press, "Trying to unscramble a situation like this in a court of law is like trying to perform open heart surgery with common kitchen utensils." Ask a divorcing parent of either sex whether he was treated fairly, and he or she will say no. Nobody—except maybe batterers and control freaks who win custody—think justice was served in a divorce. And the children get caught in the crossfire.

Nevertheless the law is all we have. The divorce reform of the last three decades has not in fact leveled the playing field for women and men. Women wind up with the children in the vast majority of cases, but they also wind up significantly poorer. Under the threat of losing their children, they are held to different standards of conduct. They are punished for trying to advance their education or their careers. When they are challenged for custody it is all too often a tactic designed not to ensure a father's involvement with his children, but to lower his support payments or save his assets. They lose custody of their children to men known to attack and injure them physically and most certainly to men who abuse them emotionally. Judges regard women with suspicion if they press too energetically for their rights or evince too much anger in the courtroom. They lose property and alimony and sometimes the children to cronyism among judges, members of the bar, and men of prominence or wealth. Judges think a committed father, says custody expert Nancy Polikoff, "is someone who makes lunch. The father who does more than nothing looks like an extraordinarily committed parent."

Are there good fathers? Of course. Can mothers be irresponsible, addicted to drugs or grasping? It goes without saying. It isn't a question of one gender being "better" or "worse" than the other. It's a question of the law—not only how it is writ, but how it is interpreted. The law always turns out to be what the judge says it is. The judge in one courtroom can be fair, the one in the next notoriously unfair. And in custody matters, it does not appear the law is leveling out for women; it seems as if women are losing ground. Sometimes the person who is awarded custody is the one who can put on the better face in court, a tactic that borderline sociopaths and batterers, emotional and physical, are much better at than the abused individual, who is usually the woman. Some judges see through the stage show, some do not. But enough judges—regardless of gender bias training, regardless of supposedly gender-blind laws—discriminate against women in family law disputes in numbers great enough to add up to a national disgrace.

DOMESTIC VIOLENCE

How Many
More Women Must Die?

Our religion, laws, customs, are all founded on the belief that woman was made for man.—ELIZABETH CADY STANTON

THE COLD NUMBERS are chilling: domestic violence or spousal abuse accounts annually for 12 to 15 percent of all murders in this country. When a spouse kills a spouse, wives are the victims in nearly two-thirds of the cases. One study of all one-on-one murders and non-negligent manslaughter cases over a five-year period found that *more than half of the female victims were killed by their male partners.* In 1992 an estimated 1,432 women were murdered by their abusive partners. For all those murdered, millions more are beaten.

Domestic violence experts Catherine Klein and Leslye Orloff, in looking at the statistics on battered women who do not die, summarize the situation this way: "An estimated four million American women are battered each year by their husbands or partners. Approximately 95 percent of all adult domestic violence victims are women. An estimated 50 percent of all American women are battered at some time in their lives. According to one national survey, violence will occur at least once in 28 percent of all marriages. Among intact couples, one of every eight husbands carries out one or more acts of physical aggression against his wife each year. Repeated severe violence occurs in one out of every fourteen marriages. In a survey of American college students 21 to 30 percent reported at least one occurrence of physical assault with a dating partner. Even these figures are likely to be low. Most national estimates are obtained from surveys that have typically excluded the very poor, those who do not speak

English fluently, those whose lives are especially chaotic, military families, and persons who are hospitalized, homeless, institutionalized, or incarcerated. Therefore some have estimated that the number of women battered each year is closer to six million. Domestic violence is the single largest cause of injury to women in the United States—more significant than auto accidents, rapes, and muggings combined."

It's been with us since the beginning of recorded history. As we have seen, old English common law deemed "correcting" the wife perfectly acceptable—nay, perhaps even necessary—and the remnants of this centuries-old sentiment continue to color public perception and how the legal system handles the abuser. Some men are abused by their wives, but the percentage is small. Perhaps 5 percent of physical abuse among mates is perpetrated by women, and some of that is by women attempting to protect themselves from abusive men.

What to do about domestic violence is a knotty issue because the legal system alone cannot eradicate it. In myth, movies and music, our violent culture glorifies the strong he-man who controls his woman. He may "protect" her, he may even "save" her from danger, but as his woman she is subordinate to him. If she gets out of line, if she talks back, if she, God forbid, sleeps with another man, if he thinks she is even thinking about it, he feels entitled to smash her up a bit—maybe kill her—to make sure she understands who's in control. Admittedly, attitudes are slowly changing. But while public attention to the prevalence of domestic violence in the last twenty-five years has greatly improved, the chances that a battered woman will receive some protection, possibly even justice, from the legal system are not great. Many women in America live in a state of terror, yet one commentator—arguing *against* tougher provisions for men who attack women—called it "as American as apple pie."

A major hurdle in lessening the incidence of domestic violence is that dealing with it through official channels is messy and difficult. Abused women are not the strong champions able to take on their opponents that we would like them to be. They frequently fail to press charges. They want the violence to end, but they are far less likely to want to put their children's father in jail. Without the women's cooperation, police and prosecutors in most jurisdictions are stymied. The batterer walks out to batter again.

While some police officers are being trained in how to respond to domestic violence calls, far more don't have a clue. If it's a "family matter," many cops don't want to intervene. A man's home is his castle, is it not? Cops get tired of the repeated calls to the same house—*Why doesn't she just leave?* they ask, not understanding that leaving is the most dangerous time of all. Prosecutors and judges are not immune to these same biases. Family court, where most of these cases end up, is at the bottom of the barrel in judicial status, and many male judges avoid it like the plague. Officers of the law at every level still tend to be men, and unless they are sensitive to the dynamics of an abusive relationship, they just don't get it.

Change is in the wind, however. A giant step forward was the Violence Against Women Act of 1994 (VAWA), the brainchild of Senator Joseph Biden and his former staffer Victoria Nourse. Among its many provisions, the law attacks the problem with money ($1.6 billion over six years for victims' services, law officers' training, special units of police and prosecutors) and with changes in the criminal law, making it a federal crime, for instance, to cross state lines in pursuit of a spouse when it leads to violence or to violate an order of protection, no matter in what state it was issued. It encourages a pro-arrest policy for suspected batterers and includes a civil rights remedy, allowing victims of gender-related crimes to sue their attackers, seeking damages through federal courts. With cash incentives it encourages training so that prosecutors and judges understand the dynamics of battered women as well as why prosecution should move forward—whether or not the woman cooperates. Under President Clinton the Justice Department set up a special office to oversee the bill's mandate.

But age-old attitudes surfaced as the bill slowly snaked through Congress. The Judicial Conference of the United States, made up of federal judges, declared that its civil rights provisions would so cripple the courts, it would "significantly threaten" their ability to deal with the other provisions of the bill. They were arguing, in effect, that while you can sue a landlord if he evicts you unlawfully, you can't sue him if he rapes you because you are a woman. Jack Greenberg, former director of the NAACP Legal Defense and Education Fund, told the press that while "there is a need for something to be done," such violence is "as American as apple pie" and the tougher laws wouldn't help. Elizabeth Symonds, a legislative counsel for the American Civil Liberties Union, testified that the VAWA "does not make clear the requisite intent or motive that the perpetrator must have had. Is rape per se a crime of violence committed because of gender?" Anyway, she stated, the penalties for sex crimes are already severe, the courts are already crowded, other provisions would restrict individual freedoms. Yes, like making it a crime for anyone named in a restraining order from possessing a firearm. Not surprisingly, the National Association of

Criminal Defense Lawyers argued hotly against it: "The husband who beats his wife is not thinking, I'd better not punch my wife out because I'll have to pay for it," asserted the group's president, Nancy Hollander. "That's crazy." Maybe not, Nancy.

To these organizations, apparently race discrimination and defendants' rights and uncrowded dockets and free speech issues, such as the once every other decade dilemma of flag burning, are more important than a few million women—black and white, rich and poor—getting beaten up every year.

IT STARTS WITH A CALL TO 911

While domestic violence advocates say that some police departments have vastly improved their response to domestic violence calls, the evidence is that we have far to go. As in all these matters, response varies from one jurisdiction to the next.

One of the most chilling examples of what can happen when police look the other way occurred in Torrington, Connecticut, in 1983 when a young mother, Tracy Thurman, was beaten senseless by her estranged husband as a cop stood by; Charles "Buck" Thurman wasn't subdued and manacled until he had kicked her in the face and her neck was broken. The worst of the battering took place while police were at the scene. Tracy Thurman was permanently paralyzed in the melee. Buck Thurman had repeatedly attacked his wife in the past. Once he had even been convicted of breaching the peace. He got a suspended sentence and probation and was ordered to stay away from her. He didn't. On numerous occasions she pleaded with the police to arrest him, for violating both the terms of her protective order and the terms of his suspended sentence. They didn't. When she called the police on June 10, 1983, as her husband ran up the stairs to her apartment, it took twenty-five minutes before someone arrived. The policeman had stopped to relieve himself at the station. Tracy was lying on the ground, suffering from multiple stab wounds, by the time he got there. He took the knife away from Buck and locked it up in the car, leaving him unrestrained. That's when Buck broke Tracy's neck. Even when more police and an ambulance arrived, Buck was still not restrained, and he attacked Tracy again, kicking her several more times in the head. The couple's two-year-old son was watching the whole time. Yes, men beat women, but the odds are that if the police had been witnessing two men in a barroom brawl, Buck would have been restrained before he nearly killed the other man.

But this was just a "family matter." The police had been called many times, and they were exasperated by what they saw as only an ongoing domestic squabble. What they didn't understand is that when men are hell-bent on beating their wives, and possibly killing them, the attacks go on and on and the danger is lethal. If Buck, say, had been locked up in an earlier incident, and if Tracy's protective order had been treated seriously, she might walk without a limp today and have full use of her hands. She sued the Torrington police department and won. Amazingly, a few months after the case ended, the Torrington police were sued again for not responding to a domestic violence call. This time Torrington's insurer settled the case out of court.

Largely in response to the Thurman case, Connecticut passed a Family Violence Prevention and Response Act in 1986 that improved the way the police and criminal courts handled domestic violence. By doing so, Connecticut joined a growing list of states that were either putting new laws on the books or strengthening the ones that were there. Today every state and the District of Columbia have some sort of domestic violence legislation. Over half followed the lead of Oregon, which in 1977 became the first state to enact a mandatory arrest law requiring police to arrest abusers on probable cause that a crime has occurred.

But compliance is another matter. Since 1979 New York City has had a mandatory arrest policy requiring cops to arrest on probable cause in battering cases and report that a crime has been committed. Yet a 1993 study found that reports were filed in only 30 percent of the approximately two hundred thousand annual domestic violence calls* and arrests made only 7 percent of the time. Cops insist they need to use their own judgment, since many times both parties will have calmed down by the time the police arrive and the woman may not want to press charges. Then again, if an arrest is made, the prosecutors may not take the case or the judge may throw the case out, and cops end up wondering why they wasted their time.

"Women learn early on what kind of reception they get when they call the police," says Jeri Woodhouse, director of the Retreat, a woman's shelter on the eastern end of Long Island, New York. "If you have a police force where they don't follow the pro-arrest policy, you are not going to call." For instance, in the five jurisdictions that the Retreat services, which range from the very rich to the poor, police response varies greatly, Woodhouse says, largely because of the response of judges. If they send batterers to jail, the police are more likely

* *Because of inadequate record keeping, a precise count is impossible. Many 911 calls are recorded as an "assault in progress" and do not get rerecorded as a domestic violence call.*

to arrest because they know the case won't be summarily thrown out of court. She says the towns of East Hampton and Southampton do a good job, in contrast with nearby Southold, which "has far to go." It's a pattern repeated across the country. In Colorado a psychotherapist who works with battered women says, "When battered women call the police department, one of the usual responses is no response or they take a long time to come. . . . When they do come, a usual response has been, 'What did you do to provoke this?' 'You haven't been beaten enough,' 'Why don't you just go out and cool off?' " These are quotations from the record.

Consequently a great many victims of domestic violence don't call the police. Nationally only slightly more than half of the women abused by their mates call the police, according to Ronet Bachman, a former Justice Department domestic violence statistician now at the University of Delaware. She coauthored a 1995 study on domestic violence that found that when the women did call the police, arrests were made on the spot in 22 percent of the cases, and another 10 percent were arrested eventually.

One reason women don't call the police is that they run the risk of being arrested themselves. In New York City, for example, largely as a result of the earlier study being publicized, victims' advocates say that there has been a phenomenal increase in the number of women arrested in such cases. "What we are hearing now is that police are saying, 'We are going to arrest both of you or neither of you—which do you want?' " contends Alise Del Tufo, director of the Family Violence Project in New York City, "so women are choosing to be arrested or to have the guy sitting there with her when the cops leave." Del Tufo says that data collected from a variety of sources, including their own hot line, indicate that approximately 16 percent of the women who call the police in New York City are arrested along with the batterer, or no one is. Sometimes, by the time the police arrive, the man will be docile and the battered woman highly agitated, with the guy claiming she started it—*she hit him first*. The cool-headed guy is a lot more credible than the shrieking woman. "The man starts the violence, she defends herself, and then he will rush to claim that she has beaten him up," says Retreat director Woodhouse. "Whoever gets to court first to press charges wins, because the other person cannot press charges." More common is that the police just don't write up a report and don't make an arrest. In California Adrienne Marin* has to deal with an abusive ex-partner every time

* *Names of some battered women were changed for their protection.*

they exchange the children for his court-ordered visitation. She has a restraining order against him. By lying, she says, he was able to get one against her, thereby pretty much rendering both of them ineffective. When he doesn't return the children as scheduled—which is an extremely common tactic of abusive men—she goes to his home and asks for a police standby while she picks up the children. One time she called the Oakland police four times in three hours, and they did not respond. While she was waiting in the street, the man ran up the block and attacked her from behind, choking her. The police arrived at this point, because his new girlfriend had called the police, saying that Marin was violating a restraining order. Follow me? It does get complicated. She's clutching her daughter, he's accusing her, she's accusing him, and the police . . . throw up their hands. Nobody's arrested. Business as usual.

Marin, understandably, is at her wits' end as well as $80,000 in debt to her lawyer. She is appealing his visitation rights to one of the children, a nine-year-old who is not biologically his. Marin says the girl doesn't want to have anything to do with the man. The likelihood that a man who beats his wife will also beat the children is somewhere between 50 and 75 percent. "I see why so many women give up and go back to their batterers," she says. "When the police reports are written up, they are so sarcastic. Or they lose them. Or they won't read the visitation orders carefully and just take his word for it. I have been in court for three years and the state has been on his side for three years. They don't want to listen to me." How, she asks rhetorically, "can I be in a power struggle with the state of California?"

A COMMON THREAD that runs through some of the most egregious examples of a victim being victimized by the system is that the abuser is someone with close ties to the legal system. Or he may be a respected member of the community. Generally speaking, the more prominent the man, the less likely it is that he will be arrested. Although the incidence of battering is highest among the poor, this means wealthier women are the *least likely* to get protection from the legal system. Shelter director Jeri Woodhouse recalls cases of well-connected men—one a policeman, the other a lawyer—who got to court first, claiming that the woman beat him up. Naturally sometimes the policeman/batterer responds to a domestic violence call. "Lo and behold, you find that there was no arrest, the woman didn't press charges, but the next morning the man is in court pressing charges. And there is no proof of any wrongdoing." It couldn't just be that the policeman told him how to deal with the matter, now could it?

When Sheila O'Reilly in Homestead, Florida, began calling the cops for help in the late eighties, they treated her as if she were the crazy one because her husband was their buddy. He treated them regularly to free meals at his restaurant, he played golf with them, he even donated a car to the police force. True, they came when she called, but they didn't record the incidents for years. "From 1986 until 1993, they didn't write them up," she says, "and when they finally began to, they always emphasized that he said that he didn't hit me. Then the reports would mysteriously disappear. I would make complaints against certain officers to the brass, but nothing ever came of it. The PBA [Policemen's Benevolent Association] wouldn't touch him." She says he once broke her tailbone by throwing her off a porch. As I write, the man is at last facing criminal charges for battering.

Incidentally, the man has custody of the children, including their nine-year-old daughter and a teenage son from an earlier marriage of hers. O'Reilly's ex-husband had legally adopted him. O'Reilly is appealing the decision; the son has run away from his adoptive father and now lives with her. The police still aren't being helpful. Recently, when she tried to pick up her daughter in northern Florida for the weekend, she says her ex-husband's brother threw her against a table and chairs. The transfer is made at a rest stop on the highway, and the police are supposed to be there. They were, but they just happened to be—how odd—looking the other way. While they wanted to call paramedics, since she was obviously injured, they wouldn't arrest the man. They said it was an "accident." Hard to know how they knew that, since they were looking the other way.

The most blatant cases of insider justice may be the story of former Bronx acting supreme court justice Frank Diaz. According to the *New York Law Journal,* when the woman he lived with phoned 911 for aid, she said: "I have a maniac over here attacking me . . . I want to keep this quiet because he's a judge." She refused to press charges, but the prosecution went ahead anyway. Two police officers testified that when they arrived they could see into the ground-floor apartment, where they saw a man punching a half-naked woman in the head and chest. Prosecutors testified that she had a black eye and bruising around the other when they interviewed her. She testified that Diaz had never punched her, that the facial swelling was the result of menopause, that her split lip was due to falling into a door. Diaz had waived a jury trial, and the judge who heard the case ruled that the prosecution had not proved the misdemeanor charges. In 1995 Diaz was acquitted and continued to serve out his appointment until the end of 1995.

Failure to arrest can be tragic. In suburban Detroit in 1993 Ray Ponke demolished the inside of the home he and his estranged wife, Jaqueline, owned in Oxford, Michigan. Police told the woman nothing could be done because he was co-owner of the house. Two weeks later she was killed with more than forty blows of a hammer while at work in a dentist's office. Tougher laws in Michigan were ratified that fall.

That same year Caroline Witt in Crystal Lake, Illinois, was besieged by Kristoffer Wendt, her former boyfriend—notes, flowers in her car, repeated phone calls. Although Illinois has one of the toughest antistalking laws in the country, police thought that Witt's case didn't meet the law's requirements. When Witt and her new boyfriend, Brian Woiwode, ran into Wendt at a local gas station, he followed them and bumped their car, and when Woiwode got out to call for help, Wendt made a U-turn and aimed his Mustang at Witt's Toyota. Witt was killed. Authorities said they were hamstrung in enforcing the antistalking law because twice in the previous year Witt had filed reports against Wendt but declined to press charges.

Why didn't she want to press charges? Why didn't she leave? These are the questions everybody who doesn't know anything about domestic violence asks.

"WHY DIDN'T SHE JUST LEAVE?"

Leaving, it turns out, is the hardest part. You have to know something about the cycle of abuse to understand why. The violence doesn't usually begin until the victim is bonded to the batterer, who is often contrite afterward—at least in the beginning—making up with roses and promises to never do it again. Sometimes the abuse does not start until the woman is pregnant or has a child, making it all the more difficult for her to pack up and leave. The violence increases over time. They may have moved to an area where she has no friends or family she can turn to, for batterers are control freaks who isolate the woman from anyone outside the relationship. He typically controls the purse strings, so she has no money of her own. If she does talk about leaving, he is likely to threaten her, the children, and her family, for the abuse almost always escalates when the victim is about to or has actually left him. In short, she is bonded to him, she is penniless, and she is afraid of what will happen if she tries to leave.

Her self-esteem along with her ability for independent action has been crushed. She has no place to go, and she is alone.

Divorced and separated women account for only a tenth of all women in America, but they constitute three-quarters of all battered women—and report being battered fourteen times more often than women still living with their partners. The increased likelihood that women who have left their batterers report the violence can account for only a portion of these increased numbers, for battered women say that virtually all abusive men threaten to kill or injure their victims, as well as the children and members of the woman's family, when they attempt to leave their abusive partners. Researchers contend that women who have been severely battered over a period of time are emotionally equivalent to concentration camp inmates. They see themselves as having no control over their lives or over anything. All the exit ramps have been shut down. The only way to survive is—to survive. In face of threats against them and the children, they drop the charges because they don't believe they have any real choices. They go back to their abusers, who may now be on bended knee, begging forgiveness, for the same reason. Not many police, not many prosecutors, have been through anything like it, and it's not surprising that they get so frustrated. In 1993 a Detroit woman who lost an arm and a leg and miscarried in the fifth month when her boyfriend slammed her into a utility pole with his van begged the court to drop the assault with intent to murder charge against him.

Despite the threats to their (and often their children's) lives, women do leave, but where do they go? Shelters are almost always filled to capacity. In New York State, says Michael Dowd, executive director of the Battered Women's Justice Center at Pace University School of Law, approximately twelve thousand battered women are sheltered each year, but twenty-five thousand more are turned away because of lack of space. "We still live in a country that has three times as many animal shelters as battered women's shelters," he says.

Although horror stories about police indifference or failure to respond abound, experts contend that law enforcement officers are getting better at handling domestic violence calls. Tracy Thurman wasn't the only woman who successfully sued the police in the eighties for failing to protect them, and the suits served as a wake-up call across America. At the same time, more women in the system—as police, prosecutors and judges—has also improved awareness and empathy, if not arrest rates. In New York City each precinct now has a domestic violence specialist who has undergone extra training; the majority of them are women. The Chicago Police Department has a program for victims when the abusers are police officers. The Nashville Police Department has a special division with domestic violence counselors as well as specially trained officers that began offering comprehensive services in August of 1994, and the city has seen a dramatic decrease in spousal murder. At the Department of Justice, Bonnie Campbell, director of the Violence Against Women Office, says anecdotal evidence indicates that law enforcement officers are beginning to work with victims' advocates rather than resist their help.

Miami in the late 1980s was in the midst of a study to see if arrest deterred future family violence, a fact that figured into the escape plan attorney Lorraine Holmes made when she decided to leave her abusive husband. Although he had threatened to kill both her and her parents if she divorced him, with counseling she was realistically able to assess the risk of death. Holmes arranged to take two weeks off from work; she knew the neighbors would be home and she could run there and call the police if he blew up when she told him she wanted out. "The only way to leave would be to make an incident happen so he would be arrested," she says. "I sat him down and told him I wanted a divorce. He responded by throwing me against the wall."

She called the police, they arrested her husband, and she stayed with neighbors for a short time. Although her husband was out of jail in three days, Holmes moved back into her home—this time armed, both with a protection order and a gun. "I slept with a gun under my pillow for eight months," she says. "I never walked from my car to the house without my weapon. To this day, I watch my back. It is a fact of life with me."

WHY VICTIMS DON'T PROSECUTE

Estimates vary on how many women refuse to press charges. Where specialized units handle the cases, the likelihood of vigorous prosecution is greatly enhanced. Nevertheless it appears that 20 to 80 percent of all such cases are dropped, and without the woman's cooperation many prosecutors say their hands are tied. The frustration spills over to all partners in the justice system. Ironically, says Joan Zorza, jurisdictions that prepare cases with enough documentation to go to court without the woman's cooperation have the highest number of women who don't drop charges.

When Seattle's superior court judge Faith Enyeart Ireland heard that prosecutors were filing accessory charges against women who had brought charges but then refused to testify, she wrote to the head of the statewide prosecutors' association. Although the rumor turned out to be unfounded, the response indicated how far we haven't come. "The last paragraph said that the way these women act, you have to waste public funds to do DNA testing," she relates. A woman in Washington had refused to testify that a man had put a gun barrel in her mouth, and the state had to do DNA testing to prove it. "You can imagine why this woman might not go to court to testify against this man who had put a shotgun in her mouth," she reflects. Since 1984 Washington has had one of the toughest domestic violence laws in the country. Police must arrest for any criminal act and violation of court orders if there is probable cause to believe an assault was committed within the last four hours. Failure to do so could result in a civil suit.

As noted earlier, victims' advocates say that women are frequently counseled against making a domestic violence claim when they are seeking child support, because the man could lose his job as a result, which could lead to no support. The advice is baseless, because most abusers don't pay anyway. The women are embarrassed, furthermore, at having been the victim, and they don't want to make the abuse public both for their own sake and that of their children. They are less intent on punishing the abuser than just having it stop, now that they have ended the relationship. But as we have seen, it isn't that simple. Abusers are sick individuals typically intent on punishing . . . until they succeed.

A problem with most current legislation is that it does not take seriously the woman's need to be able to hide her whereabouts. When children are involved, it is especially tricky, according to battered women expert Joan Zorza, since some judges believe that a husband or father has an absolute right to know the address of his wife or children—even if release of a shelter's address may result in that state's losing federal or state funding for domestic violence programs. Batterers often get the home address of their estranged spouse through schools, doctors and the motor vehicle bureau, and while some states have stringent nondisclosure laws, too often judges do not take them seriously.

Headway is being made in some places, notably Seattle, Nashville, Newport News (Virginia), and San Diego, which have instituted a comprehensive approach to domestic violence. It isn't simply a pro-arrest policy, tough prosecutors, and informed judges. It's all three. Some of the jurisdictions that have a pro-arrest policy drop more than 50 percent of the cases, so the batterer is back on the street within a few hours, notes Casey Gwinn, the assistant city attorney who founded and heads San Diego's special domestic violence unit. In San Diego, one of the first cities to adopt such a policy a decade ago, the conviction rate has soared in domestic violence cases while domestic homicide and rearrest rates for family violence have declined dramatically. There were thirty domestic-related homicides in 1985; there were seven in 1994 and 1995. Incidentally, two of the murderers in 1995 came from outside the jurisdiction, so counting them does not accurately reflect what tough policies can do. Nashville has seen a 71 percent drop in the spousal murder rate—from twenty-five in 1993 to two in the first six months of 1995. So much for the contention that getting tough with batterers doesn't stop them.

"Our policy is to go forward with any case we can prove, with or without the victim's participation," says Gwinn, which happens in approximately 70 percent of the cases. When a batterer is arrested, he is held for at least forty-eight hours while prosecutors determine if there is enough evidence to make a case; 20 percent of the batterers cannot make bail and remain incarcerated while the case is pending. "The recidivism rate for these men is zero," he points out. Mention the research that shows that mandatory arrest policies have almost no effect on repeat battering, and Gwinn nearly goes ballistic: "In some of those studies, only a tiny percentage of the cases—in some cases, 1 percent—were ever prosecuted to conviction. You don't have to be very bright to figure out that 99 percent of the batterers were getting away with it. A 'long' arrest was called twelve hours. A short arrest was three hours. That's basically the cops saying, 'You are a bad boy and don't do this again.' "

Gwinn does not believe mandatory arrest policies are the panacea some think they are, since they alone increase the likelihood that the woman will be arrested. "Police will often say something like 'If I have to come back here tonight, somebody is going to be arrested,' and the woman takes that to mean that it could be her," notes Gwinn. "So of course she doesn't call, and that shows up statistically as a 'success.' "

In some jurisdictions counseling programs for batterers amount to little more than a Band-Aid—some of them are only eight hours long. Yet judges routinely order men into them as the only punishment. Estimates as to how many men don't bother showing up or drop out after a few sessions are as high as 50 percent. There is almost never a penalty; if the guy comes before the judge again, he is likely simply to tell him to go back to the program. Period. "Compare this to bank robbery," says Gwinn. "Nobody ever asks the judge to send the bank robber to counseling instead of jail. This is not taking domestic violence seriously. This is paying it lip service."

In contrast, the counseling program in San Diego consists of fifty-two weekly sessions. A warrant for the man's arrest is put out if he misses a session. But, Gwinn adds ruefully, the warrant is not served, and only if the man is picked up for another charge is he jailed. However, the sentence is thirty days the first time he fails to attend, ninety days the second. Then he has to start the battering program all over again. "If battering isn't treated as a serious crime, then what we are doing amounts to nothing," he emphasizes. "You have to have aggressive intervention strategies and the resources to back them up." The city of Chicago recently dropped its comprehensive approach to domestic violence because of lack of funding.

"People in the system still don't understand how serious battering is, so the women are not taken seriously," maintains the Justice Department's Bonnie Campbell. Unless the man uses a weapon of some kind—say, a screwdriver or a frying pan—battering your spouse is usually a misdemeanor, even if the woman is quite obviously banged up. "Say I'm a prosecutor in Chicago, and I've got a dozen felonies that come in overnight—some of them homicides—I weigh them and decide what I'm going to plea-bargain because I only have limited resources," explains Campbell. "So I plead down the domestic violence cases to minor charges, and if he was in jail overnight, he is sentenced to time served, and that gets rid of it. That tells the batterer it isn't so serious to beat up the wife because, he thinks, If it were serious, I'd be in jail." And it tells the police that while they may take the incident seriously—they saw the woman's injuries—the rest of the system doesn't. So why bother arresting the guy in the first place?

"THERE'S NO ACCOUNTING FOR JUDGES"

Campbell maintains that the further up the feeding chain in the legal system one goes, the less likely one is to be knowledgeable about the dynamics of domestic violence. "Prosecutors are doing a better job than they used to, but they are not as well informed as law enforcement officers, and judges are even less well informed than prosecutors," she says. "Judges in many jurisdictions don't have to get mandatory training on these issues." Without training women may encounter rude, nasty and even brutish behavior from the bench. "Judges feel very comfortable allowing the misogyny to show through," asserts attorney Kristian Miccio, who formerly headed a free legal clinic for battered women in Manhattan. "They are disrespectful to the battered women, disrespectful to the lawyers who represent them or the prosecutors who are trying the cases. They still believe that the woman's word is unbelievable as a matter of law, so they require a lot more evidence in these cases than they do in other kinds of cases. Sure, it's changing, but not quickly enough."

While restraining orders are a first step toward the woman's safety, getting them is sometimes more difficult than seeing that they are enforced. Battered women may not be able to afford the fees necessary to get one, a factor that the VAWA should change; sometimes judges are extremely reluctant to order a man to stay away from a house held in his name, which may be where the woman and children are living. The gender bias reports and the media are rife with stories of judges who belittle the women asking for them. In Maryland a woman related the following:

"[The judge] took a few minutes to decide on the matter, and he looked at me and said, 'I don't believe anything that you're saying.' He said, 'The reason I don't believe it is because I don't believe anything like this could happen to me. If I were you and someone had threatened me with a gun, there is no way that I would continue to stay with them. There is no way that I could take that kind of abuse from them. Therefore, since I would not let that happen to me, I can't believe that it happened to you.' "

In New York a few years ago a Queens criminal court judge denied twenty-eight of thirty-one women who were seeking temporary orders of protection from abusive mates in one three-week period. In Central Islip on Long Island, New York, a jury deadlocked in 1992 over whether Suffolk County police violated the civil rights of Cecelia Eagleston by failing to arrest her husband, Thomas Eagleston, after she called them a dozen times in the nine weeks before December 27, 1986. On that day Thomas Eagleston—whom she had recently decided to divorce, against whom she had two restraining orders—stabbed her thirty-three times with a fourteen-inch kitchen knife. Judge Leonard Wexler let the jury consider only three previous incidents at the 1992 trial. In 1995 the U.S. Supreme Court refused to hear her appeal of a lower-court decision, which stated that she had failed to prove that the police had a policy of discriminating against women by not arresting husbands in domestic violence cases. What would proof have been? Thirty-four wounds?

In Georgia in 1989 a judge reported to that state's task force that one of his colleagues, in a case of repeated, severe violence, "mocked . . . ridiculed and humiliated" a woman when she went before him to ask for an extension for a temporary protection order. He then "led the courtroom in laughter as the woman left." The woman, Judith Music, was killed less than a year later by her former partner.

A few days after Christmas 1995 Brooklyn judge Lorin Duckman questioned the severity of a beating that Benito Oliver gave to his ex-companion, Galina Komar. "There is no actual physical injury, is there, other than some bruising?" asked Judge Duckman at a bail hearing for Oliver, who was facing jail time for violating orders of protection. Oliver had a lengthy criminal record. "I am not suggesting that bruising is nice, but there is no disfigurement. There are no broken bones. There are no serious physical injury charges, are there?" Oliver had already been jailed two months earlier for beating Komar and menacing her with a butcher knife. Oliver's lawyer said that he only wanted his dog back. "He has been in jail enough for a person who is charged with these crimes. I want to know about the dog," Duckman said at the hearing before letting Oliver go free. "The return of the dog to him or his family will assure there is no further violence in this case." Oliver tracked her down to the car dealership where she worked and killed her with a .44-caliber revolver in February 1996 before turning the gun on himself.

This year (1996) also saw the novel punishment of a slap on the wrist for spousal abuse. When Stewart Marshall of Vestaburg, Michigan, was convicted for abusing his wife after she had committed adultery, District Court Judge Joel Gehrke ordered Marshall to roll up his sleeve and then punished him with a three-finger slap on the wrist. "In the laws of Israel, if Mr. Marshall had come home and found his wife in this situation, the question would not be, 'Did you strike her?' " said Gehrke. 'It would have been, 'Well, are you ready to publicly be the first one to stone her?' "

In Missouri a witness testified to the gender bias task force that one judge sometimes asks women in court if they like being beaten. It may be the same one who lectures female victims, implying the beating was their fault.

If judges treat spousal abuse lightly, it is not surprising, then, that they sometimes treat the murder of one's spouse as if it were quite different from murdering a stranger. Although only a very small percentage of men who murder their wives and are tried are acquitted, a litany of recent cases attest to how judges forgive murdering a spouse—if she happens to be caught in the act with someone else.

In May of 1994 a Maryland trucker returned home unexpectedly and found his wife in bed with another man. After scaring the wits out of him with his hunting rifle, Kenneth Peacock let the man go. For several hours he continued drinking while he argued with his wife and threatened her with the gun. Ultimately he shot her in the head. At trial he contended that the gun discharged accidentally, while he was toying with it. Under Maryland law a spouse who catches the other in flagrante delicto and kills in the "heat of passion" is eligible to plea-bargain down to manslaughter, which carries a three- to eight-year sentence for a first offense. Judge Robert E. Cahill, sixty-two, gave Peacock the minimum, three years, and suspended half of it, making it possible for Peacock to serve the sentence—eighteen months—in a local detention center. Judge Cahill further recommended that he be made eligible for work release immediately. It is worth noting that Judge Cahill seemed to have been influenced by Peacock's two brothers—both of whom are police officers. At sentencing he likened the case to automobile manslaughter committed by drunk drivers. He also said, "I seriously wonder how many married men would have the strength to walk away . . . without inflicting some corporal punishment. . . . I shudder to think what I would do." So do we. Within two weeks of sentencing Peacock was back at work, hauling cargo between five A.M. and nine P.M.

Sentencing in domestic violence and sexual assault cases often includes "highly misguided requirements that defendants work in battered women's shelters or rape crisis centers," which are not appropriate for these offenders, says Lynn Schafran. "Victim empathy does not come from proximity to victims but from long, intensive, painful treatment in specialized batterers' and sex offenders' programs." Even when they are assigned to rehabilitative programs, a great many of the men just don't show up. Judges rarely do anything about it.

However, even if the men do attend, the programs need to have some substance in them to do any good. In Utah Judge Ronald Kunz sentenced Cameron Clark to an *eight-hour* anger management program—and only after he broke into his ex-wife's home. On several other occasions—from 1991 to 1994—Clark was arrested for threatening his ex-wife, Katrina, with harassing messages on her answering machine and letters in which he called her a bitch and a slut; but he was soon released. On the day Clark finished the program he wrote Kunz a thank-you note. He then went looking for his wife. He found her at her home. Clark broke in and killed her and himself in front of their youngest child. Judge Kunz later said he felt sorry for Clark because he too had been through a painful divorce. When asked why he had not taken the man's threats more seriously, he said: "I knew that he was angry, that he felt alone, that he felt no one cared about him." *This excuses murder?*

These rulings may be exceptional, but they illuminate how some judges trivialize domestic violence—even when it results in murder. Justice Department statistics show that defendants in spousal homicide tend to get shorter sentences than people who murder strangers, although the overall difference is less than two years. In one courtroom a woman will be avenged; in the next her death will be treated as justifiable punishment for her sleeping with another man. Some judges just don't realize that adultery is not a capital crime or that a marriage license is not a license to kill.

And what is one to make of the judge in Palm Beach who in the not so distant past, upon learning that a husband had poured lighter fluid on his wife and set her afire, sang in open court "You light up my wife" to the tune of "You Light up My Life"? In Miami another judge hearing a first-degree murder case, upon learning that the defendant had tried to kill his wife previously, asked in court: "Is that a crime in Florida?"

In 1993 superior court judge William J. O'Neil of Carroll County, New Hampshire, sentenced a man to twenty-eight days to be served on weekends for assaulting his wife, from whom he had been estranged for a year. He had tracked her down on a camping trip and found her in a tent with another man. She required seventeen stitches after he beat her in the face with a flashlight. Because the couple was not yet divorced, the judge said, "I can't conclude that [the attack] was completely unprovoked. I think that would provoke the average man." Obviously Judge O'Neil is in favor of the "reasonable man" standard. He did say the attack went too far: "To have slapped her might have been more normal."

In Ohio that same year a man entered his estranged wife's home and beat her with a crowbar. When her seventeen-year-old daughter tried to call 911, he punched her in the mouth, knocking teeth out and shattering her jaw. Judge William Matthews of the Hamilton County Court of Common Pleas gave Benjamin Blackwell, who had a record for murder, rape and armed robbery, three to fifteen years. Seven months later the judge released Blackwell. "The guy walked into his house with his wife in his bed with another guy," he said. "It's enough to blow any guy's cool if he's any kind of man." Real men obviously beat their wives. With impunity. Sometimes they kill their wives.

Laws on the books are fine, but judges who don't enforce them destroy everybody else's best efforts. *"There's no accounting for judges,"* writes Lynn Schafran. "Sometimes judges' actions are shocking, ignorant, or inexplicable. Often only minimal mechanisms are available to hold them accountable." As we have seen elsewhere, when the behavior is particularly despicable, judges can usually avoid prosecution simply by resigning. Some judicial review committees are notoriously spineless. Judges are not screened for their attitudes about and knowledge of family violence. While acknowledging that long or lifetime tenure and immunity are essential for judicial independence, Schafran says the protections are a two-edged sword. Judges can still get away with belittling domestic violence and treating spousal murder as nearly justifiable if the woman "provokes" the man.

Judicial education in this area has taken modest strides in recent years. Some communities, such as Cook County in Illinois and Dade in Florida, now have special domestic relations courts with judges who have had special training. Women there can count on being treated fairly by sympathetic and knowledgeable judges. But in many states judicial education is sorely lacking. States cite lack of funds. The women who have been abused would not say it is a luxury, nor would the families of the victims who died. And these attitudes are not changing much as new judges are appointed or elected.

A recent textbook case of domestic violence is one with which we are all familiar. Nicole Brown Simpson was an abused woman who called the police, by O. J. Simpson's own reckoning, on nine different occasions. The one time he was arrested, in 1989, he pleaded no contest to a misdemeanor charge and was given a slap-on-the-wrist punishment—$900 in fines, 120 hours of community service, two years of probation, and twice weekly psychological counseling. Some of the counseling was conducted by phone, a provision made to accommodate the demands of O. J. Simpson's television career as a sports announcer and Hertz spokesman. The car rental company said at the time that they had no plans to drop him. The incident, a company spokesman said, was a "private matter between O.J.'s wife and the courts." No problem. We tolerated a smiling O.J. leaping over airport turnstiles after he pleaded no contest to beating up his wife.

Nicole's sister, Denise, says that Nicole had broken off with Simpson for good—this time, she made clear, she meant it—a week and a half before she died. She put up her town house for lease at the same time, just five months after she had bought it. A friend said that she was concerned about safety because she caught O. J. Simpson looking into her windows. Others said that he had stalked her—at gas stations, at restaurants, while she was driving. When an abuser stalks a woman—as the evidence indicates Nicole was—she is at higher risk. "At least 90 percent of battered women who are killed by their past or present lovers were known to have been stalked by them before being murdered," says attorney Joan Zorza. Then Nicole was found dead, brutally stabbed, her head nearly severed, possibly the deed of someone in a rage. Murderer: legally unknown.

Last fall Washington State's sexual predator law, one of the first in the nation to keep sex criminals confined after they serve their prison sentences if they are still thought to be dangerous, was declared unconstitutional, since it has the effect of punishing an offender twice. We accept that a man's right to liberty is a greater good than the possibility of harm he might do to others.

But even this is changing. Reginald Muldrew, a man convicted of four rapes and linked to two hundred others, served his time in a California state prison and was released in 1995—despite a prison psychologist's warning that he's dangerous. However, women's groups publicized the story, and Governor Pete Wilson denounced Muldrew's release. Governor Wilson had signed a "sexual predator" law just months earlier, which would have kept Muldrew in a mental hospital up to another two years, but the law did not take effect in time to affect Muldrew.

Although Muldrew wasn't convicted for battering or raping a mate, the women's outcry against his release indicates that we are in the midst of re-thinking how society responds to violence against women. A decade ago there would have been no notice of Muldrew's release. More than a decade ago Tracy Thurman nearly lost her life in an attack by her husband in front of police. A decade ago special units and courts to handle domestic violence cases were nearly nonexistent. A recent poll indicates that in the year after Nicole Brown Simpson's murder Americans were becoming less tolerant of family violence: 87 percent said they believed outside intervention is necessary if a man hits his wife; a third fewer Americans now believe that reporting domestic violence to the police is pointless; and 57 percent of *men* now agree that abusers should be arrested, up from 49 percent a year earlier. A decade ago the Violence Against Women Act was not even a gleam in Senator Joseph Biden's eye. The act is a comprehensive legal attack on violence against women and includes a provision that allows a woman to bring suit in civil court for any violent crime committed against her that was motivated by gender. It protects battered women across state lines. A little more than a month after it was passed, a man who beat his wife unconscious—soon after she had decided to leave him—and drove through West Virginia and Kentucky for six days with her locked in his trunk became the first person convicted under the new law. Sonya Bailey is in her thirties today, nearly a vegetable, cared for in a nursing home. Christopher Bailey,

thirty-five at the time of sentencing, got life. Under federal sentencing guidelines, he is not eligible for parole until he is seventy.

But all facets of the legal system—the legislators who write the laws, police,
prosecutors, judges, and juries—must work in concert if the system is to mete
out justice fairly for women as well as men. Cities with special prosecutors'
units, and courts devoted to domestic violence cases, do the best job. They have
training. They understand the woman's plight. They "get it." The dramatic drop
in spousal murder rates is the proof that this approach works.

Even when working at top form, however, the legal system alone cannot
eradicate violence against women. When we as a people truly act as if a man
beating up his physically weaker partner is not a "family matter" and "American
as apple pie," we will have taken a step toward creating a society where all
women are as free to live as men.

SEXUAL ASSAULT

Rape

. . . it is the only crime in which the victim becomes the accused.
—**FREDA ADLER,** SISTERS IN CRIME

I DIDN'T CALL the police because it would have been pointless. This was someone I had dated—had even slept with a couple of times—and when he showed up banging at my door at two in the morning a month or so after I had stopped seeing him, I let him in because I didn't want to wake the neighbors. *I didn't want to cause trouble.* I didn't want them complaining about me as a tenant.

I needed to keep that apartment—it was inexpensive and I was just starting out on my own, and you know how hard it is to find a decent place in Manhattan. But the low rent came at a price. The lock on the outside door was broken—and had been for months—so anyone could come right up to my door on the sixth floor. It was one of those tenement buildings on First Avenue in the Sixties.

When he first came to the door, I pretended I wasn't home. But he wouldn't go away, he stayed at the door for about ten to fifteen minutes, saying that he knew I was there, pounding on the door, getting louder and louder. I figured I could talk him into leaving. He had never been abusive, and when I told him I didn't think we should see each other again—over the phone—he didn't argue or anything like that.

So I let him in. But once I did, he said he wasn't leaving until we had sex. It wasn't a question; it was a declaration. It seemed to boil down to the fact that I had no right to break off seeing him. If anybody was going to break off the relationship, *he was.* We argued for about an hour. Understand, he was a big guy, muscular, probably 190–200 pounds of muscle. He looked like a football player. I'm barely five feet five and weigh 115. He could have easily killed me with his bare hands. His grim determination scared me into believing that he was going to beat me up if I didn't let him do what he wanted. I vaguely thought about trying to call the police—the phone was in the next room—but assumed he'd never let me. And even if I was able to, I was afraid that if they came while he was still there, he would come back and get me later. Besides, what would the cops have done? What would I have said? A guy I know is in my apartment at three in the morning and he won't go home? *He's going to make me have sex with him.* Is this, ahh, a rape in progress? And if they came after he left, what would I have said. *What would they have said? They would have laughed at me.*

So, no, he didn't hit me, and, no, I didn't fight. I just let him do what he wanted. I remember the scene leading up to the assault very clearly—the look on his face, the pattern of the fabric I had stapled to my walls, where he sat on the couch, my feelings of utter, complete powerlessness. Of the act itself, I recall nothing. It was as if I hadn't been there. When he was finished, he said nothing and left. I felt used, dirty, numb. I was angry that I had had to submit, angry that I was a woman and subject to this kind of raw male strength.

For months I was scared he would come back. Even today I always look over my shoulder walking down a dark street, peer into the rear seat of my car at night before I get in, sleep with a sharp object next to the bed when my husband is out of town.

I never told anyone about the incident until years later when a girlfriend and I saw *The Accused.* I left the theater upset, hurt, angry, as if the incident had happened two weeks ago, not twenty years earlier. I had told him no in no uncertain terms, and he had given me that smug look that told me I had no choice, but up until I saw *The Accused* it had always seemed like my fault. I shouldn't have let him in. Maybe I should have let him beat me up. Then it would have been easier to deal with, perhaps. Then I could have called the police. But I would have been afraid that he would come back and get me.

As far as I know, our paths had never crossed again.

Unreported sexual assault Number 9,438,796,001 godzillion or something like that. The woman who told me the story stared off into space for what seemed like a long twenty seconds. "I bet he never thinks about that night, what he did."

Was it rape? "Rape is forced sexual intercourse and includes both *psycho-*

logical coercion [emphasis mine] as well as physical force." Forced sexual intercourse means vaginal, anal or oral penetration. This comes from the Justice Department's survey, "Violence Against Women," which says that as sexual assault victims go, she is fairly typical: 45 percent of those women who reported (to the survey takers) that they were raped stated the "self-protective action" they took when a weapon was not involved was "passive/verbal," and another 24 percent said they took no action at all; 52 percent of all nonstranger rapes occur at the victim's home; and 28 percent of the women raped had once been intimate with the rapist. A later Justice Department survey found that nearly 80 percent of all rapes are committed by someone known to the victim, and an independent survey found that 70 percent of the women sustained no injuries other than the rape itself. It may be called rape legally, but what happens in court even today is another matter.

In 1988 a student at East Stroudsburg State University in Pennsylvania forced himself on another student, a nineteen-year-old woman whom he knew slightly. The woman had gone to his room looking for his roommate. When she stayed to talk to Robert Berkowitz, he shoved her on the bed, straddled her and pulled down her sweatpants and underwear, and forced himself into her. She testified that "it was like a dream was happening or something." She couldn't get away because, as she put it, she "couldn't, like, go anywhere" when he was on top of her. Her response mirrors that of many people in circumstances they cannot change: a combination of submission and dissociation. She was terrified and she did not forcibly resist. After he ejaculated on her stomach she jumped up and ran from the room.

Berkowitz told a quite different story, a story of sex that she wanted and later changed her mind about. It was the same defense that rapists have been using, usually successfully, for centuries. He testified that she initiated the sex by talking about penis size, wanting to check out his penis, and that although she was continually "whispering . . . no" she did so "amorously . . . passionately." This time, however, the jurors didn't buy the argument; they found him guilty. The judge sentenced him to one to four years. The decision was hailed as an indicator of how far we have come—it showed that a woman didn't have to be beaten up to be raped, that a woman's testimony alone could be sufficient for a jury to find the man guilty, changes that many rape laws throughout the country had incorporated in the last two decades but that prosecutors, judges, and juries had a hard time successfully adhering to at trial. Five years later, in 1994, the Pennsylvania Supreme Court reversed Berkowitz's conviction. Why?

Because she didn't resist. He was charged only with indecent assault, a misdemeanor. It's a long, long road. We've come only a short way.

"Ask a woman if she has ever been raped, and often she says, 'Well. . . not really,'" writes Catharine MacKinnon. "In that silence between the 'well' and the 'not really,' she just measured what happened to her against every rape case she ever heard about and decided she would lose in court."

ACCORDING TO "RAPE IN AMERICA," a 1992 survey considered to be the most accurate accounting of the incidence of sexual assault in the United States, 683,000 women over eighteen are raped each year. *Only 16 percent of those rapes are ever reported to the police.* That's about one in six.

Rape statistics have always been ambiguous because of the difficulty in collecting them. This survey, conducted by the Crime Victims Research and Treatment Center of the Medical University of South Carolina, was the first national survey in which women's attitudes toward the word "rape" were considered. Instead of using the word itself, four questions about threats of sexual assault and forced sexual intercourse were asked, since if you say "rape," the study's authors say, the number of positive responses goes down by about half, even though the act is forced and falls within the definition of rape. The respondents, 4,008 women who were interviewed annually for three years, could answer yes or no over the telephone, so if the victim was speaking while someone she did not want to know about the assault was in earshot, she could maintain her privacy.

The responses blew previous government statistics on rape and sexual assault out of the water, more than tripling the number of sexual assaults the Justice Department had reported at that time. The "Rape in America" study also found that among women over eighteen, the sample surveyed, *over 60 percent said they were raped before they were eighteen,* leading to the obvious conclusion that the 683,000 figure reflected less than half of all rapes since it did not include the rape of women under eighteen. The number of sexual assaults, the researchers concluded, is at a *minimum 1.5 million.* Others put the number at 2 million. Justice found that women age twelve or older annually sustained almost 5 million violent victimizations (which includes more than rapes) in a two-year period, 1992–93. That these carefully crafted surveys on an explosive subject were not made until the 1990s is a reflection of how deeply our thinking about rape is influenced by the societal myth that the only rape is "stranger" rape.

The huge gap between sexual felonies committed against women and the number reported to the police even today is another indicator of how we as a society tolerate rape. It starts with the police. "Around the country there are still plenty of places where women are not believed," says Beverly Harris Elliott, president of the National Coalition Against Sexual Assault, "so women don't report rapes. Combine that with a fear of being exposed, for if you go through the criminal justice system, you have very little privacy. And there are still places where police ask questions such as 'How come you were out by yourself?' or 'How come you were in that kind of bar?' or 'What did you expect when you were wearing that?' Police in some places are still blaming the victim and not the assailant." As we shall see, even when the police and prosecutors are enlightened and sympathetic, a jury of her peers may not be. Sometimes neither are the judges, who let rapists off with sentences that amount to telling him to go stand in the corner.

According to a 1993 congressional report, bringing a rapist to justice is unlikely:

"Ninety-eight percent of the victims of rape never see their attacker caught, tried, and imprisoned.

"Over half of all rape prosecutions are either dismissed before trial or result in an acquittal.

"Almost a quarter of convicted rapists *never* go to prison; another quarter receive sentences in local jails, *where the average sentence is 11 months*. This means that almost *half* of all convicted rapists can expect to serve an average of *a year or less* behind bars.

"A robber is 30 percent more likely to be convicted than a rapist.

"A convicted rapist is 50 percent more likely to receive probation than a convicted robber."

Remember that handsome quartet of football players in Glen Ridge, New Jersey, who sodomized and sexually assaulted a retarded teenager a few years ago? Yes, they were found guilty by a jury of seven women and five men—two others pleaded down to misdemeanors and did community service—and the judge sentenced three of them to what *sounded* like a tough sentence: indeterminate sentences not to exceed fifteen years. But prison time could end up being as little as a couple of years, and they would serve their time in a prison reserved for youthful offenders. This was in spite of the fact that as the case dragged on through the courts, Christopher Archer, the one prosecutors called the "mastermind" of the crime, went to Boston College, where he allegedly beat and sexually assaulted a young woman. According to the victim's sworn affidavit, the event included Archer's punching her in the crotch. Despite Archer's history, and despite the guilty verdict on the most serious charges, Judge Benjamin Cohen inexplicably let them stay out on bail until they had exhausted their appeals. That was three years ago. None of them has served a day in jail as I write at the end of 1995. Christopher Archer continued his studies at a southern school. Apparently convicted rapists have no trouble meeting the admission standards of some schools.

"When it comes to crime, it seems, there's still nothing like being white, middle-class, and suburban to get you the benefit of the doubt," editorialized *The New York Times.* And there's nothing like committing a violent crime against a woman. Much better than holding up a 7-Eleven. One might assume that Judge Cohen didn't want to "ruin" the lives of the Glen Ridge rapists. Too bad for the young woman, though.

A WOMAN'S WORD WAS NOT ENOUGH

Our attitudes about a woman's right to bodily integrity—and how someone is punished when they violate that right—seem barely better than those of the eighteenth-century English jurist Matthew Hale: "Rape is . . . an accusation easily to be made and hard to be proved and harder to be defended by the party accused though never so innocent."

Although rape has always been recognized as a serious crime, who is raped has a great deal to do with how serious. As we have seen, the penalties for raping propertied virgins were greater than those for raping serving girls, for married women greater than for divorced women, for all virgins greater than for non-virgins. Although the penalties on the books for violent rapes have remained severe through the nineteenth and twentieth centuries, only a few rapists were punished to the full extent of the law. Prosecutors, judges and juries have seen to it that the character of the woman and the color of the rapist are the key factors in deciding how harshly the rapist will be punished. To be deemed a credible victim, Hale wrote, the woman had to be of "good fame." Even into the 1970s courts were instructing juries that evidence of "unchaste character" was relevant in assessing consent as well as credibility.

Historically courts and commentators have distrusted the testimony of the victim, "assuming," in the words of a 1992 court decision, "that women lie about their lack of consent for various reasons: to blackmail men, to explain the discovery of a consensual affair, or because of psychological illness." Considering what one had to go through once a woman has accused someone of rape, and the attendant shame, this assumption is nonsensical. But certainly both the assumption that William Kennedy Smith's accuser, Patricia Bowman, wasn't telling the whole truth, that she had some ulterior motive, and the jury's feeling that she wasn't prim enough to be raped, played into Smith's otherwise improbable acquittal in 1991. Since Bowman was an unmarried mother who was said to have used cocaine, since she was out in a bar at three A.M., she was suspect, not of "good fame."

Not that women don't sometimes falsely accuse someone of rape; it's just that so many judges and juries have relied on this old husbands' tale and let so many rapists free to rape again. We don't know with any certainty what the number of false accusations are, or how many of those ever get to trial, but one study from the Portland, Oregon, police puts the figure at 2 percent, less than false reports of stolen vehicles. Two percent is the same as the percentage of rapists who actually go to prison. That leaves 98 percent unaccounted for.

Our rape laws and their interpretation in court still embody the myths, stereotypes and sexism of the centuries, full of denial, suspicion and disbelief. Even as late as 1988 Lord Hale's prejudicial remark about how easy rape is to charge and how hard to defend was allowed in jury instructions in twenty-six states, convenient for the sex who ran the legal system and perpetrated the crime. A wave of rape reform did sweep the country starting in the mid-1970s, coinciding with the 1975 publication of Susan Brownmiller's seminal book, *Against Our Will: Men, Women and Rape,* and pressure from the women's movement. Rape laws around the country were broadened to (a) include more definitions of what a rape is, (b) eliminate the requirement that the rape be corroborated by a witness other than the victim, and (c) limit, if not outright forbid, the cross-examination of the victim's sexual history, as well as what she was wearing, and so forth, as evidence for the defense. These "rape shield laws" were designed to prevent the victim from being victimized all over again—once by her rapist, twice by the lawyers for the defense and the judge. Yet it would take years before the effects of these laws would be felt in the courts; in some courtrooms they are still ignored. The situation right up until the mid-1980s was so bad that the head of a rape victims citizen's committee, Lorraine Koury of Erie County, was prompted to tell the New York State gender bias commission that in her organization's interaction with criminal justice personnel, "we have heard many attorneys, prosecutors, and even judges state privately to us that if they or a loved one were sexually assaulted, they would not use the criminal justice system." And if they wouldn't, who should?

We are in the midst of a final reform in the laws: eliminating the requirement that there be threatened or actual physical force before a sexual incident can be charged as a rape. As mentioned earlier, Pennsylvania courts in *Berkowitz* decided that "forcible compulsion" must be proved in order to obtain a rape conviction; however, in California that same year, 1994, the state supreme court in *People* v. *Iniguez* reversed a lower court and found that physical force by an attacker is not necessary, nor is verbal or physical resistance from his victim, to secure a rape conviction. As the number of acquaintance rapes by misguided and deluded young men appears to be rising, this distinction is crucial, because women who have been socialized to be "good girls" are far less likely to fight back against someone they previously have known and possibly have trusted. Girls and young women, the group most at risk for rape, are particularly vulnerable, not having the years of experience that teaches them that they do not have to do what men tell them to do.

Without the support of the community and officers of the legal system who deal with sexual assault cases, of course, the reforms are no more than words on paper, symbolic gestures from the state legislatures showing that *something* is being done. Numerous studies have shown that reforms have little impact when officials' attitudes are at odds with reformers' goals.

One state did manage to overhaul the system. Comprehensive reforms in Michigan, the first state to enact sweeping changes in the sexual assault laws, led to a significant increase in the percentage of reported rapes that resulted in indictments in Detroit. The impact of rape reform in Michigan followed soon on the heels of the new laws, according to researchers Julie Horney and Cassia Spohn. But in the five other big-city jurisdictions they studied in other states, the impact of legal rape reform was minimal.

What was different about Detroit? The changes in the law were extensive and accomplished in one major revision of state codes, not done piecemeal. "[I]t may be that only a comprehensive reform package, by sending a strong and unambiguous message to decision makers, can overcome the resistance to change inherent in the system," wrote Horney and Spohn. Detroit also rotates courtroom personnel (assistant prosecuting attorneys, public defenders and the like) to different courtrooms every four months, a factor that discourages "workgroups" from jointly resisting change; and attorneys are assigned to cases rather than courtrooms, increasing their involvement with the victim rather than the "workgroup."

•   •   •

BUT IF THE rape reform laws have been slow to have an impact, what was accomplished outside the legal system has markedly improved the treatment of rape survivors. They are not everywhere required to wait in the emergency room for hours while the doctors treat stab and gunshot wounds and automobile accidents, and then to be examined by a doctor not sympathetic to their trauma. In more counties than not across the country, a rape crisis center will dispatch a victims' advocate—often a volunteer, often a rape survivor—to accompany the individual throughout what can be a humiliating gynecological exam and questioning by police. Many hospitals have streamlined procedures for rape trauma victims to remove them from the pack of emergencies and see that they are examined within a half hour. The Violence Against Women Act encourages states to pay any fees for medical exams of sexual assault victims; in the past the women had the added indignity of having to pay for the test themselves, a fee that could run into the hundreds of dollars. In Georgia the gender bias task force reported that the cost varied from $175 in some areas to $660 in others. If health insurance doesn't cover it, the cost alone will deter some women from pressing their cases. Then there is the exam itself. The woman wants nothing more than a long hot shower to cleanse away the bad feelings and any physical traces of her attacker, but if she doesn't have a gynecological exam almost immediately, the chances that the rapist will be prosecuted fall dramatically.

Rape trauma workers say, furthermore, that police *generally* have become more sensitive to the victim's traumatized state and that they *generally* will take seriously a woman's charge of being raped by an acquaintance. Some police departments have officers who have had special training to work with women who have been raped. And as with domestic violence advocates, the police will often work with the rape crisis center workers. The Nashville Police Department, for instance, has had a victim intervention program within the department for twenty years. It is headed by a social worker, not an officer of the law. But the Nashville program is a beacon in a sea of darkness. In all of Tennessee there are only two rape crisis centers. One is in Nashville, the other Knoxville. If you don't live near either of those two cities, you're on your own.

A VICTIM WHO WASN'T BELIEVED

The reforms are a step in the right direction; they do not mean that the system is not still bounded by myth and stereotype and men and women who don't believe women. Horror stories still abound; they are as common as rats in the ghettos of New York. Many of them come out of Small Town, U.S.A., where victims are routinely asked in all too many places to take a lie detector test, or polygraph, as they are technically called, as part of the investigation. "Asking the victim to take one is like saying 'Prove to me you aren't lying,' " says Brenda Roberson of the Pennsylvania Coalition Against Rape in Harrisburg. In robbery cases the suspect—not the victim—is the one asked to take the test; in rape cases both the victim and the suspect are asked to take the test. Since the results are unreliable, the results cannot be introduced as evidence, and taking it is entirely voluntary. But when a police officer "suggests" that a woman take one, she rightly intuits that the investigation will come to a standstill unless she does. Police use them most frequently in cases when the victim knows the rapist, which, as we have seen, is more likely than not. The letter of the law may mandate prosecuting "acquaintance rape," but to get to that stage the police first have to be convinced. The accused, of course, protests that the sex was consensual: he said, she said. Put the scenario in rural America, where everybody knows everybody else, where the man is an otherwise respectable member of the community, and you have an invitation to a polygraph. "In rural communities, the police officer could be best friends with the rapist, and the police are simply not going to move forward with the prosecution," comments Beverly Elliott of the National Coalition Against Sexual Assault. People just don't want to believe that an otherwise law-abiding man is capable of rape.

There are no national statistics on how often polygraph tests are used in rape cases, and in a handful of states they have been outlawed for use in sexual assault cases. Those who administer the test can be a police officer with minimal training—and it can be someone who starts out with a predisposition not to believe the witness. Then, too, rape victims are highly unreliable subjects. They typically are tested within days or weeks of the assault when they are still severely traumatized. The test requires that you breathe steadily and answer questions about possibly the most painful event that has ever happened to you. The polygraph measures heart rate, blood pressure, breathing. Some women are asked to take them even when they have been severely beaten during the assault and in cases of violent stranger rape. "The polygraph was designed to detect fear and guilt, and those are two of the primary responses rape victims are feeling," explains Roberson. "Many of them feel they have done something to lead the man on, so their responses are likely to skew the results."

When ABC's *PrimeTime* surveyed more than two hundred rape crisis centers around the country, they found that in seventeen states rape victims said that police threatened them with arrest or charges of perjury if they failed the exam.

In 1992 Teresa McHenry of Dayton, Maryland, a college student, was raped by an assailant who entered her home with a gun, tied her up and blindfolded her, and then led her to his car. While she was blindfolded, he drove her to his home, where he had set up a videotape machine. McHenry was able to see certain things through the bottom of the blindfold, such as the color of the car, that it was a hatchback, the tube of lip gloss between the seats. She memorized every turn on the drive to his house, the layout of his house, the color of the walls, even the prints on the walls. The assailant sodomized and raped her, while videotaping it all. He released her in a parking lot, and despite his threats she immediately called the police.

Detective Tom Martin was the lead investigator. Before they drew up a composite sketch of the assailant, he asked her to take a polygraph test.

So a week after the rape occurred, Teresa McHenry was grilled—once again—for four hours on the explicit details of the attack. She failed the test, according to the police, because of her responses to "one or two" of the questions. After the "failed" polygraph, Martin's investigation focused on interviewing neighbors and teachers to find out why the young woman would make this up, according to Dan McHenry, Teresa's father. "You knew that people would begin thinking that the police must know what they are doing, and it put a doubt in their minds about what happened," he says. The chief of the Howard County police, James Robey, told *PrimeTime* that "there were things in her life that caused us to believe that the story itself may not be totally accurate—difficulties with her boyfriend, an exam at college that day." Teresa McHenry was an excellent student.

Six months later a twenty-two-year-old mother who lived fifteen minutes away was assaulted and raped by a man with the same modus operandi. Then they caught the rapist, William Kirk Evans. The sketch drawn from McHenry's description was amazingly accurate. "Her directions to the man's home had only one wrong turn," says Dan McHenry. "Evans's car was as she described. So was the layout of the house." And the one clue that could have led directly to the rapist almost immediately was ignored.

Even though the Howard County police had collected a fingerprint inside the McHenry home, they did not bother to process it through the computer bank that holds fingerprints of all convicted felons in Maryland. If they had, they would have found Evans's prints on file there for previous sex offenses. Later another woman came forward and said she had been raped by Evans, days after police shelved McHenry's case. But the woman lived in another county, and because police had not shared information on the rapist with surrounding counties, her case was not linked to McHenry's. Evans is now serving time, having confessed to McHenry's rape and that of four other women. Although McHenry petitioned the state legislature to ban the use of polygraphs in sexual assault cases, it is still legal in Maryland. McHenry is now married and a student at the University of Maryland.

Tom Martin, the lead detective on the case? He was found guilty last December [1995] of third-degree sexual offenses and assault and battery of an intoxicated college student he drove home while on duty. The incident occurred in August 1995, three years after Teresa McHenry was raped.

After the Florida gender bias report turned up incredible abuses with the use of polygraphs, the state stopped using them, thanks to efforts by Miami attorney Gill Freeman, chair of that state's Gender Bias Implementation Commission. She told a Senate hearing about a woman who was tested for three hours while the officer investigating the case and the polygrapher went over the same sexually explicit territory again and again. "Was it forced? Were you forced?" they asked repeatedly. The assailant was a neighbor at the trailer park where she lived. When he knocked at her door she had invited him in, but then he would not leave. When he dragged her to the back of her trailer, she had pulled off pieces on the door framing. Yet they kept asking if she had been forced. She finally replied, "Well, I don't know whether he understood that I felt I was being forced, and I don't know what was in his mind." Finally, says Freeman, the woman signed a paper stating that she had fabricated the story and that she had not been raped. Case closed. This was a few scant years ago; it sounds like the Inquisition aided by technology.

Freeman says that victims' advocates tell her that although police today are generally sensitive to sexual assault victims, the same cannot be said for district attorney's offices. "They don't like these cases, they get bandied about in the office, and whoever is the lowest on the totem pole gets them," she says, except in places like Dade County [Miami], which has a special unit that deals only with sexual battery.

RAPE SHIELD LAWS DON'T PROTECT THE VICTIM

Rape shield laws, which came into being as a part of rape reform, were designed to protect a victim from character assassination during the trial. While most states have some sort of law on the books, defense attorneys frequently find a way around them, and judges do not enforce them uniformly, believing that a woman's past may be relevant to the defense. Yes, convince the jury she is a slut, and they will not convict.

"The strategy will be to make the woman sorry she ever brought the charges," was Alan Dershowitz's comment to the press regarding Patricia Bowman, the woman who accused William Kennedy Smith of raping her. Even if defense attorney Roy Black could not get all the damaging character inferences into court that he would have liked, she was described in *The New York Times* by an anonymous "friend" as having a "little wild streak" and as liking to drive "fast cars."

Yes, under the rape shield law her alleged cocaine use was kept out of court. But then Judge Mary Lupo also inexplicably kept out the sworn statements of three other women (a doctor, a medical student and a law student) who said Smith had sexually assaulted them, including one who said Smith raped her when she was intoxicated. The judge may have felt constrained by law to not allow in evidence the statements, as they would prejudice the jury against Smith to such a degree that he could not receive a fair trial. But to those of us watching, sworn statements of such prior bad acts, showing a similar MO, most assuredly seemed relevant. But no dice. And Smith got off. Under the Violence Against Women Act, prior bad acts will be allowed in federal courts, but as we got to press that provision of the law is as yet untried.

Judge Lupo had her picture taken with members of the Kennedy family, according to press reports, and it seemed that throughout the trial she was hostile toward the female prosecutor trying the case, Moira Lasch. Indeed, some women have attitudes that are more judgmental of and harsher toward women in trouble than those of men. Perhaps if Bowman had ended up with bruises and cuts, the jury might have taken her side. Incidentally Bowman says she took and passed two polygraph tests and a voice stress analysis test. Before the trial she submitted to a three-day deposition. Smith had to make no statement until he took the stand after he was assured that he could not be questioned about the other women in his life.

THE KIND OF character assassination that *The New York Times* performed for the defense goes on all the time. In New York a few years earlier, defense attorney Jack Litman defended murderer Robert Chambers by putting Jennifer Levin, the young woman he killed, on trial. In court Litman demanded the right to see a diary in which, he said, Levin had chronicled "kinky and aggressive sexual activity." No such diary existed, but the "sex diary" made it into the tabloids.

In his closing argument Litman said: "It was Jennifer who was pursuing Robert for sex . . . that's why we wound up with this terrible tragedy." Not because he overpowered her and killed her. Because Chambers never testified, his cocaine and burglary habits were kept out of the trial.* The previous year model Marla Hanson, who was viciously attacked by men hired by her landlord after she spurned his advances—her face required 150 stitches—was called by defense counsel Alton Maddox a southern bigot who "preyed on men." It was insinuated she was a prostitute because, after all, aren't all models prostitutes? The fact that she was wearing a miniskirt was also somehow allowed into evidence. During her cross-examination Hanson was asked to give a detailed explanation of a part of the female anatomy. Hard to know where her knowledge of anatomy fits into a criminal case that left her permanently disfigured—unless the defense was out to convince the jury that she was a slut. All of this was allowed by New York Supreme Court Justice Jeffrey Atlas, who later whined when Hanson and her attorney criticized him in the press. New York, by the way, had a rape shield law at the time, but it didn't cover Hanson—*she wasn't raped, now was she?*—and it certainly couldn't protect a dead nonwitness like Levin. Three years after Hanson's ordeal, in 1990, the New York law was expanded to cover crimes such as these.

While the "expanded" law was in effect in New York, across the river in New Jersey the retarded young woman at the center of the Glen Ridge trial, who had been assaulted with a small baseball bat, a broom handle and a stick, as well as urged to commit fellatio and masturbate in front of the town's young athlete-heroes, had her sexual history as well as the fact that she took birth control pills paraded for the world to read about. If this childlike victim who couldn't read past the eight-year-old level couldn't be shielded from character assassination by law, couldn't be protected from being portrayed as a seductress, then nobody could.

Under all the laws, judges have some discretion to decide whether a victim's sexual past is relevant to the defense. And they have used that loophole to bring in extraneous evidence of all sorts that do little but prejudice the jury against the victim.

The rape shield laws are under attack for trampling on the right of defendants, according to several gender bias reports, and the statute's protections

---

* *After nine days of jury deliberations without a verdict, Chambers pleaded guilty to first-degree manslaughter. The sentence would be five to fifteen for the murder and an unrelated burglary charge. At press time Chambers was still in prison.*

have eroded in recent years. Defense attorneys often find ways to introduce the victim's sexual conduct: "For example, a defense attorney may say to the victim who testifies that she told her boyfriend about the rape," writes Lynn Schafran. " 'Did you tell him this before or after you moved in with him?' " is the next question, informing the jury that she was not only not a virgin, but someone who lives "in sin." In Missouri an attorney described a proceeding during which a judge allowed questions about diapers the complainant had purchased, which was allowed in ostensibly to establish when she returned home. Mentioning the diapers had the effect of bringing out that the woman was an unmarried mother. Message to the jury: An unmarried mother obviously has no business bringing rape charges.

In the Kentucky gender bias report, Carolyn Smith, director of Rape Victim Services in Paducah, testified at a hearing how victims were denigrated during the opening and closing arguments in rape trials and how, despite the requirement that evidence about a victim's character must be presented before trial for a ruling on its admissibility, a defense lawyer in the middle of a trial announced that he had just found out information about the woman's character that was relevant. It had to do with her first divorce, which had occurred ten years earlier. Questioning her about it in chambers interrupted the trial and undoubtedly made the jury wonder what the defense had on the woman. She emerged from the questioning shaken, not the same witness she was before. Good technique, thinks the defense attorney. Bad justice, thinks the victim. In Broward County, Florida, a man was acquitted because the victim "asked for" the sexual attack with her provocative dress—a lace miniskirt and a green tank top. According to the Florida report, the man in effect admitted that he had raped her, but it was the victim's "enticing dress and cool demeanor on the witness stand that influenced the jury to acquit the defendant." The *Miami Herald* reported that once the trial began, the defense attorney had free rein to attack her character, painting her as a prostitute when there was not a shred of evidence that she was. The judge reportedly stated that he allowed the free-wheeling defense because the prosecutor did not object. Despite the rape shield laws, the judges' lax application of them makes it doubtful that anyone other than Mother Teresa would be protected.

Whether or not the falsely incriminating evidence is allowed in, merely hearing the lawyers squabble over her history can influence the jury. She is a model. She must not be nice. She lives with her boyfriend. She has an illegitimate child. She must be a slut. Defendants' rights unquestionably trample the rights of women who have been raped to survive a trial with their reputations intact.

Sometimes the lawyer for the defense will try to influence the judges with statements that were not allowed in court. Seattle Superior Court judge Faith Enyeart Ireland recalls a defense attorney who tried to libel a rape survivor's credibility at sentencing of his client, who had been found guilty. The attorney told Judge Ireland that the woman couldn't be believed because she had told the police interviewer that she had also been sexually assaulted by a doctor doing a pelvic exam at some time in the past. "His point was that obviously she was exaggerating, as if a woman couldn't be sexually assaulted during a pelvic exam and that that does not occur," says Judge Ireland. "I was so fried by the statement that I had to keep reminding myself that I shouldn't let my anger with him interfere with the sentencing of his client."

ACQUAINTANCE RAPE

Two decades ago nonstranger rape—overwhelmingly the most frequent kind—as a legal entity leading to prosecution and conviction barely existed. Susan Brownmiller devoted only a few pages to it in her book of nearly five hundred pages. Since most rape law at the time required that the victim have corroborating evidence—the woman's word alone was not good enough—rapes of this type were extremely difficult to prosecute: most of them are not committed with a witness looking on. These rapists are not robbers breaking into a home, finding a sleeping woman in bed, and throwing in the rape as part of the crime. These rapists do not jump out of the bushes when a woman is jogging. Relatively speaking, those are easy cases to prosecute.

But in acquaintance rape the men are people the women know, may even trust, and they frequently present clean-cut, nicely dressed images to the public. They are students, they are professionals, they are married men, they are single men with "good" futures ahead of them. They are more often than not sexually active, well-socialized men who have no trouble getting dates. They "don't look like a rapist." They are William Kennedy Smith. "I think he's too charming and too good-looking to have to resort to violence for a night out," said juror Lea Haller after voting to acquit William Kennedy Smith.* (What she was doing on the jury is beyond me.)

---

* This was well before Haller was romantically involved with Smith's attorney, Roy Black, who was married at the time of the trial. Haller and Black are now married.

Linda Fairstein, head of the sex crimes unit in the Manhattan District At-torney's Office and one of the leading prosecutors in the field in America, says that this is one of the most common responses from the friends and family of the women who have been sexually assaulted by a mutual acquaintance. It is one of the reasons jurors have a hard time convicting in nonstranger rapes; studies of jurors' attitudes, particularly in acquaintance rape cases, confirm that jurors are inordinately swayed by the physical appearance of the man on trial. Then, too, the defendant—even if he's Jack the Ripper's cousin—may call people to testify that he is of sound moral character and is the type of person who would never do anything like *that*. "The first thing many victims ask . . . is why we cannot call character witnesses on behalf of the *victims*," laments Fairstein. "It is terribly frustrating to answer that it is not the victim who is on trial, when in fact that is exactly what comes to pass in many acquaintance rape cases." Despite the enormous challenges prosecutors like Fairstein face, the progress to date is impressive, considering where we started from: "We are prosecuting cases that we wouldn't have twenty years ago. The year before I came here [1971], more than 1,800 men were arrested for sexual assaults, and only 18 were convicted," she says, largely because of the corroboration requirement. Now, she notes, hundreds of men each year are either convicted or plead guilty.

Acquaintance rapes often involve the use of alcohol and/or drugs. Fairstein recounted a 1992 case in which both parties had been drinking and using drugs throughout the evening. The man then accompanied the woman to her apart-ment, where he became violent. The evening ended in rape. The woman was examined at Bellevue, a major city-run hospital that had recently disbanded its rape crisis advocacy center because of lack of funding. As a result, no gyne-cologist was on hand at three A.M. to do the examination and take samples of blood, semen and hair. An oral surgeon did it. Because the doctor had never examined a vaginal wall before, he was not qualified to testify about internal injuries. Yet Fairstein's office got a conviction anyway. "If the victim is telling a story we believe, I like to think she will get her day in court," Fairstein says.

It's a welcome sign that even in such circumstances rapists are being pros-ecuted and convicted. But outside the big cities, in rural America, it is a far different story. In Coudersport, Pennsylvania, population two thousand, in the northwestern part of the state, rapes are almost never charged or pros-ecuted. Yet Ann Constantine, executive director of a family crisis center there, says that of the approximately four hundred people a year the center counsels, a third of the cases involve sexual assault of some sort. Yet, she says, "no one who has come through this office in the last three years has chosen to prosecute."

A large part of the county is state forest, and hunters are often passing through. Constantine says she knows of more than one gang rape by hunters. "They say to the women, 'I don't mind telling you my name because no one is ever going to know where we're from and we're out of here tomorrow.' Then the women come here and say, 'I shouldn't have been in that situation, I met them in a bar, I shouldn't have worn that, I shouldn't have accepted that ride home.' " I asked Constantine what the women do. "They move on, they leave the county," she says.

What is perhaps even more disturbing, she says, is that a group of young men—sixteen- and seventeen-year-olds—in the county rape pretty much at will. "The names of the rapists come up again and again," says Constantine. "The young women who are involved in that group think this is a part of life. There is this . . . resignation." The part-time prosecutor for Potter County, Jeff Leber, agrees. He told of a recent incident in which three young teenage girls were molested by the friend of the girls' older brother. He had either passed out or fallen asleep after bringing his friend home. Although school counselors learned of the assault, no one wanted to press charges. "They just accept it as something that is going to happen," he says.

Constantine added that while women could expect sensitive treatment from the county police, prosecutor and judge, the shame of becoming the talk of the county kept them from coming forward. "The guy who did it might be the football coach, or the bus driver, or the doctor," she explains. "If you call the police, everyone will know about it because everyone has a police scanner and hears everything. Now the woman doesn't want to go to the grocery store, to the laundromat, to school." Says Leber, "The likelihood is that in any trial, you are going to know at least one of the jurors or defendants or witnesses or victim." Familiarity buys the women's silence.

Even when someone is willing to come forward, even when the case is a strong one, the probability of a conviction is slim. About five years ago Leber prosecuted a case that had witnesses to back up the young woman's story. Despite her credibility, despite the evidence, despite a fair judge, the trial ended with a hung jury, eleven to one for conviction. Even careful voir dire, Leber says, did not weed out the one man who he later heard said that "a woman couldn't be raped if she didn't want to be." Endings like this, Catharine MacKinnon notes, give women "the message that the law against rape is virtually un-enforceable as it applies to them."

The experience of Krista Absalon in northern New York, twenty miles south of the Canadian border, would confirm any woman's fears. By now many of us know the bare bones of the story. Absalon, a young mother caught in a custody battle with her ex-husband, went on a bender one night in October of 1991 in a bar in her hometown, Gouverneur, New York. Late into the evening she passed out in the women's room. Her date, the son of the Gouverneur police chief, was asleep outside in his pickup truck. Five men in their twenties—all known to her—carried her out to a dining room booth, where four of them raped her while she was unconscious or at best semiconscious. It wasn't until two weeks later, when the men bragged about the assault, that the story got back to her and she went to the police. All five defendants were initially charged with first-degree rape, a felony punishable by eight to twenty-five years. But a year and a half later, in 1993, without Absalon's consent, the charges were reduced to sexual misconduct, a misdemeanor with a maximum one-year sen-tence. These five rapists weren't even ordered to jail. Instead town justice Wallace Sibley fined each of them $750, plus $90 in court fees.

After Absalon and women's groups cried foul, the case was reopened. One of the men, Michael Curcio, stated on national television, "I feel we shouldn't have got anything," and described the rape as just a "gang bang." The men were finally indicted after one of them, Greg Streeter, agreed to testify against the others and plead guilty to first-degree sexual abuse. Even with Streeter's tes-timony and the men's admission of having sexual intercourse with Absalon when she was dead drunk, a jury of six *women* and six men found Mark Hartle, the first of them to come to trial, not guilty earlier this year. She got drunk, she passed out—*what did she expect?* After Curcio was found not guilty in June, charges against the remaining defendants were dropped.

Absalon has since moved to Syracuse. In Gouverneur, folks blame her for the bad press their town got since *she* brought this unwanted notoriety to it. In Gouverneur, Absalon is a woman scorned. Absalon is suing the men for dam-ages in civil court; some in town charge that she is "only in it for the money."

"There is a fundamental assumption that when a woman reports a crime against her, there must be some ulterior motive at work," observes prosecutor Rebecca Roe, head of a special unit in Seattle that handles violent and sexual crimes against women and children. "If a guy gets hit over the head with a baseball bat and reports it to the police, nobody says, 'Why did you report it? Are you out to get the guy?' " she adds. "It's not enough to say this is a crime and it happened to me." Even in Kings County where she has raised the level of sensitivity to gender-related crimes, she says, the police still question a woman's motive. "Just the other day we had a case where an underage victim was abused by a guy in his twenties," she says. "And the cop was making statements about the fact that she must be out to get this guy, that she was involved with him and she liked it and she just changed her mind."

This can hardly be said of Krista Absalon. Rape trauma experts say that survivors of acquaintance rape report more anger, depression and guilt than those raped by strangers. The feeling of trust they once had with the individual intensifies the sense of violation. Women raped by acquaintances may actually have a harder time recovering—they are more likely to keep the rape secret, more likely to blame themselves, more likely to believe they are not worthy of compassion. At the same time, they receive less support from friends and family, who may indeed blame them. While the overwhelming number of rape survivors do recover, and many without treatment, we are coming to understand that trauma has no tidy end to it. The effects of rape are usually long-lasting. In one follow-up study that included one hundred women who had been raped, on the average, nine years earlier, the enduring, destructive effects of the trauma were still apparent. "Rape in America" found that rape survivors were thirteen times more likely than noncrime victims to have actually made a suicide attempt. "Rape survivors reported more 'nervous breakdowns,' more suicidal thoughts, and more suicide attempts than any other group," reports Judith Lewis Herman, author of *Trauma and Recovery*.

"It is hard to know whether to describe our current state in terms of *Pilgrim's Progress* or the myth of Sisyphus," says feminist legal scholar Deborah Rhode. "There have been enormous changes in cultural attitudes and legal norms governing rape proceedings in the last couple of decades, but it is also true that we are still pushing the same rock up the same hill. The problems that have plagued rape laws continue."

To comprehend just how slow we as a culture have been to think of acquaintance rape as a crime, one need only look at the law as it stands in Delaware. That state makes exemptions in the rape law if the victim is a "voluntary social companion" of the attacker. If that is the case, the crime can be prosecuted only as a third-degree offense, which carries slight penalties. Taken to its logical and absurd conclusion, this means that if a woman accepts a date with someone and he rapes her on that first date, or if he walks her home from a party where she has met him, or if she's said hi to him on campus, or if she knows him slightly because they work for the same company or take a class in night school together, she had better end up pretty bloodied and battered if she wants to press charges and get him sentenced to more than probation. Ditto if the victim has slept with her attacker in the last twelve months. If she has, he can't be prosecuted for first-degree sexual assault unless, once again, she suffers serious injury. A few scratches probably aren't enough. Women in Delaware have a great deal to fear, not only from any man they might happen to know, but from the legal system as well.

ONE GROUP that is extremely vulnerable and also far less likely to seek police protection from their attackers are women on campus. Although a public outcry in the last few years has increased campus awareness of date and acquaintance rape, and some schools have put more muscle into their policies and punishments, it is still unquestionably true that if the woman chooses not to go to the police, and the crime is handled solely by the school, the punishment may be not light, but nonexistent. Peggy Reeves Sanday, a University of Pennsylvania anthropologist and author of *A Woman Scorned: Acquaintance Rape on Trial,* says that while most colleges now have sex offense policies, and some expel the student outright, the punishment on other campuses can be as insignificant as twenty hours of community service. At Gettysburg College, when eighteen-year-old Sara Zalewski reported to campus authorities that she had been raped by a fellow student at an off-campus fraternity party, her attacker was suspended. For a semester. That's it, even though he admitted his guilt to school administrators. Zalewski went public with her outrage, noting that "you can be expelled for cheating—but not this?"

Athletes are particularly protected. They are more likely than other students to be arrested and indicted for sexual assault, yet less likely to be convicted, according to new research at Northeastern University. Case in point: The University of Nebraska suspended star running back Lawrence Phillips—convicted of assaulting fellow student and former girlfriend Kate McEwan in the fall of 1995—for six games. His scholarship was not affected. Coach Tom Osborne conveniently allowed Phillips to return to the team in order to lead them to a stunning victory in the Fiesta Bowl just after the New Year. Phillips didn't rape McEwan, at least that we know of. He merely burst into her apartment at four-thirty A.M. and dragged her downstairs as he beat her. He shoved her against a mailbox so hard, she dented it with her head before she was rescued. Coach Osborne insisted that the school had imposed tough sanctions, ordering Phillips to attend counseling—as well as classes—then had the gall to complain that "special interest groups with an agenda" were damaging Phillips's rehabilitation. Other Nebraska Cornhuskers have also been in trouble with the law; Osborne countered that they represented *only 4 percent of his team.* If he has a daughter, one wonders whether he allows her to date members of his team.

"If the young man has a high profile at the school, he is protected," says Sanday. "There is a lot of pressure on the young women not to bring up these cases—not to take them to the police, not to the university administration." The university itself may discourage the woman from pursuing the case, and the harassment from other male students can be quite extreme, including menacing gestures and phone calls threatening, "If you continue with this, I'll get you," she adds.

Even when the woman goes forward, even when the police are involved, there are still other barriers to cross: race, class, the old stereotype that a woman shouldn't be there anyway. All of these came into play in the 1991 acquittal of three athletes at St. John's University in Queens, New York, when it seemed that the prosecution had an unshakable case. The woman said that she had accepted a ride home from a fellow student. Under the pretext of needing money for gas, they stopped at the off-campus home he shared with his buddies on the lacrosse team. He invited her in while he made a phone call. But once inside, she was plied with vodka and orange juice until she was incapacitated, and then the boys had their fun. She was sodomized, they slapped her in the face with their penises, her breasts were fondled. In their plea bargains three of the six defendants admitted that much of what she accused them of was true.

Yet they were acquitted. The victim was black; the white assailants were the sons of middle-class parents. They didn't look like rapists. "We didn't realize that people's attitudes about sex were so ingrained and crossed a wider cross section of the population than we anticipated," one of the prosecutors said. A juror afterward said that while they believed the behavior of the St. John's students was "obnoxious," they felt that it did not violate the letter of the law.

Lynn Schafran observes that black complainants have a harder time being believed than whites, regardless of the race of the rapist. Referring to a case where a black woman accused a white doctor of raping her, a case in which the DNA tests came back positive for the doctor, she writes that a member of the jury, a white-haired gentleman, wrote the prosecutor after his acquittal that the jury thought that "a black woman like that might be flattered by the attention of a white doctor." It sounds like a throwback to the 1800s in the South. This was in 1991, Scarsdale, New York, an upscale suburb of New York.

"My greatest problem is not with the police or the courts," says sex crimes prosecutor Fairstein. "It is with public attitudes. The people who eventually sit on our juries still understand little about sexual assault, the nature of the crime. It is still viewed by many, many people as a victim-precipitated crime because of something the victim has done rather than the offender's conduct. This is nowhere more true than in acquaintance rape. And when you get to date rape, there is tremendous skepticism about the victim's role and her ability to have prevented that crime." The jury in the William Kennedy Smith trial was four *women,* two men.

In Austin, Texas, in 1992 one grand jury refused to indict a man who said a woman had consented to sex because when he threatened her with rape, rather than risk the threat of AIDS, she'd asked him to wear a condom. His lawyer alleged the condom amounted to a show of "consent" on the victim's part. The woman stated she had been assaulted with a kitchen knife for over an hour before she ran from her house *naked,* which apparently this grand jury thought was something that a normal woman would do after consensual sex. After a public outcry in the media, a second grand jury, allowable in Texas, overturned the decision. The man was indicted.

CAN A MAN RAPE HIS WIFE?

"No, I didn't rape my wife," said a defendant a few years ago at his trial. "How can you rape your own wife?" Indeed. That has been the thinking that governed the law for centuries. Married women had no legal rights anyway, and by marriage a wife was considered to have given up the right to say no, whether or not husband and wife were estranged and living apart. This "marital exemption" in our sexual assault laws began eroding in 1975 when South Dakota became the first state to make the rape of a spouse a crime. As of 1993 every state and the District of Columbia had done away with the marital exemption. But only partly. Nearly two-thirds of the states make some sort of allowance for marital rape. Regardless of the statute, attitudes toward a man who rapes his wife have not changed in many places since the days of the cave man. "A woman can go to the police and they will laugh her out of the station," maintains a woman who calls herself Laura X, director of the National Clearinghouse on Marital and Date Rape, a research and consulting organization in Berkeley, California.

This is true despite the fact that the degree of violence involved is often as high as that of stranger rapes, and the couple may have stopped living together months or years earlier. Spousal rape has been found to be no less traumatic, or often not less violent, than sexual attacks from strangers. In fact, rape often accompanies the violent attacks of batterers on women who are trying to leave them, a reality that is only slowly being acknowledged by our legal system.

"The closer the relationship, the more traumatic and long-lasting the effect," contends Laura X. "The rape by someone intimate goes to the heart of the question of whether a woman has the right to control her own body and access to it." Rape is not unusual in abusive relationships, and, as we have learned, separation is the most dangerous time. In the case of the man who wanted to know, "How can you rape your own wife?" the woman testified that he dragged her by the throat into the bedroom, taped her mouth and eyes with duct tape, and put a garter belt and stockings on her legs. He tied her hands and legs with rope. He slapped her genitals and threatened her with a knife, circling her breasts with the knife. This was all videotaped. Her muffled screams were audible on the tape. The jury saw the tape. What they did not hear about were the several police reports for domestic violence that had been filed against him, evidence that was not allowed. When the woman was able to escape, she ran nude from her home to a neighbor's. The defense attorney argued that the videotape portrayed a woman playing a sex game she enjoyed. And the running nude to the neighbor's? In Columbia, South Carolina, the jury of eight *women* and four men acquitted the man. His past record of abuse was not admitted as evidence.

However, there is a light at the end of this tunnel. Laura X notes that the conviction rate for marital rape cases—*when they go to trial*—is nearly 90 percent. The trouble is that so many of them never go to trial. A great many women don't even know that a crime has been committed against them; they are so used to being battered and raped by their husbands that they take it as a condition of life. What we need, what we desperately need, are more judges like state supreme court justice Franklin R. Weissberg. In New York last winter Justice Weissberg tried the case of a man who had threatened his wife with a knife, choked her, raped her and broken her ankle during the assault. He sentenced the man to ten to twenty years. "There are far too many places on this earth where the rape, assault and battering of a wife by her husband is considered acceptable or, at worst, a trivial offense," said Justice Weissberg.

"Unfortunately for the defendant, this state and this courtroom are not such places."

AMAZING EVIDENCE OF JUDGES' PREJUDICES

Unfortunately for us, judges like Justice Weissberg are all too rare. While enormous changes have occurred in rape prosecution and convictions, that we as a nation are still bounded by stereotype and myth is nowhere more evident than in some recent decisions:

In 1994 Vincent Cousin came before Chattanooga Criminal Court judge Doug Meyer after he stopped going to therapy sessions and taking his medication, as he had been ordered to do—after he had been found innocent by reason of insanity in a 1989 rape of a woman in front of her five-year-old daughter. Cousin had stated that voices told him to rape. Mental health experts now urged Meyer to order Cousin to a mental institution. Instead Meyer ordered Cousin back to outpatient therapy sessions, saying: "I think what he needs—he needs a girlfriend, because if he doesn't, he's going to have bad dreams again." Meyer also refused a public defender's plea that Cousin be appointed a guardian until a hearing a month later and suggested that the public defender "arrange a dating service or something" for Cousin. Media attention and a public outcry persuaded Meyer to reconsider three days later, and Cousin was taken into custody.

This wasn't the first time that Meyer thought "dating" was a solution for a rapist. He told twenty-two-year-old Thomas Lee Hopkins, a student at Temple Tennessee University in 1991, much the same. Hopkins had pleaded guilty to raping a fellow student on an elevator. "You need to date," Meyer said at the hearing. "You need to associate with girls. As I say, you're a nice-looking young man and you're just a little mixed up as far as how to deal with your sexual feelings." Meyer gave Hopkins a two-year suspended sentence and ordered counseling. Six months later Hopkins was arrested for rape in his home state of Ohio. Despite an acquittal on that charge, the probation officer in Chattanooga urged Meyer to jail Hopkins. He did. Hopkins served less than a year.

In 1993, in the sentencing of an Ishpeming, Michigan, man for the statutory rape of his thirteen-year-old stepdaughter, Marquette Circuit Court judge Edward Quinnell said that the girl "is not in here with any black eyes or bloody noses." He went on: "She has no broken bones. As far as the act itself, having someone insert a finger in her vagina, that is, I'm told by my wife, part of a routine pelvic examination. So far as the actual physical conduct that took place, that's no worse than being in a doctor's office." After a public outcry, the judge apologized.

The judge had been in the news earlier that year for releasing Steven Woltz after a conviction for raping his ex-wife, pending his appeal. At the trial a witness testified that Woltz had threatened to kill his ex-wife after the trial. "It's not the type of thing that is so alarming," Quinnell said.

In 1993 Judge William Millard of Columbus, Ohio, ruled that the rape charges against Len Barnes, forty-six, accused of attacking an eleven-year-old girl, be dismissed because a prosecution witness was twenty minutes late to court. Millard said that the tardiness infringed on the defendant's right to speedy trial. Barnes, who had previous convictions involving children, was allowed to go free. The *Columbus Dispatch* reported that Millard, a Republican elected to a six-year term, had thirteen complaints filed against him during his first three years on the bench. The complaints accused Millard of harassing and belittling a female lawyer, reversing a jury's guilty verdict for the rape of a twelve-year-old girl, and dismissing criminal charges after a defendant pleaded guilty. Although there was a movement to remove him from the bench, instead the Ohio Supreme Court Disciplinary Counsel ordered that he be suspended for sixty days and spend five hours a month for the next two years discussing with a panel of jurists judicial demeanor and criminal court procedures.

In 1994 Fayette, Kentucky, circuit court judge John Adams granted probation to convicted rapist Clark J. Gross II, the son of a prominent Lexington family. Two years earlier he had broken into his ex-fiancée's apartment. Gross kicked in the door to the bathroom where she was hiding, dragged her to her bed, stuffed part of a comforter in her mouth and raped her. Despite a jury's recommendation that he receive a thirteen-year prison sentence, which Adams initially agreed to, the judge let Gross remain free while his lawyers pursued appeals. After all were denied, powerful supporters and friends of the family besieged Adams with letters asking for leniency. Now deciding that the young man was worth saving as a productive member of society, Adams changed his sentence to five years probation and six months of nights and weekends in prison. He excused Gross's behavior by saying that his girlfriend's leaving him "caused Mr. Gross to snap." Prosecutors appealed, but the Kentucky Court of Appeals upheld the ruling.

In New York in 1992 state supreme court judge Nicholas Figueroa said at the trial of a man convicted of sodomizing a retarded woman, "There are rapes and there are rapes. There are assaults and there are assaults. There was no violence in this case. . . ." The woman, who has an IQ of 51, had been sexually abused by her father and brothers, so Figueroa figured this made the sodomy by Ernesto Garay less heinous. "The impact, I think, on this young woman, given her mental state as it was displayed before this court, was considerably less than you might say the first one was or the second one." Prosecutor Fairstein publicly chastised Figueroa, and after a burst of media coverage Figueroa was persuaded to sentence Garay to eight and one-third years to twenty-four, just shy of the maximum.

In 1990 Judge Kenneth Leffler in Sanford, Florida, who was known primarily for his volunteer efforts on behalf of abused and neglected children, stunned the courtroom when he let an admitted rapist go free. Mark McCulloch had pleaded guilty to sexual battery (the legal term for rape in Florida), false imprisonment and battery of his landlady. State sentencing guidelines called for a prison term of at least three and a half years and ten years probation. Leffler, who had presided over the landlady's divorce three years earlier, said that since he had some experience with the woman he had "a hard time laying all the blame on the gentleman." Other defendants in the courtroom laughed when he urged McCulloch to "more carefully select the women you associate with." Leffler sentenced him to two years probation. Although prosecutor Michele Heller reminded Leffler that the rape and beating had been done with a great deal of violence, he responded by calling it "sort of a mutual thing." He kept bringing up her actions during her divorce proceedings. "She was, perhaps, one of the most pitiful people I have ever known," he said. "I'm almost of the belief that she is a victimizer of men."

In 1992 in California an eighteen-year-old freshman at Humboldt State University named Marie Catchpole sued her former boss, Rudy Brannon, for sexual harassment, including rape. Brannon was her supervisor at the Burger King in Eureka, which was the sponsor of her college scholarship. She testified that Brannon encouraged sexual talk at work and that when she went to his home in December of 1987 to discuss her problems with co-workers, he forcibly removed her clothes and raped her. She added that because Brannon was married, she assumed she would be safe at his house. The case was tried without a jury before superior court judge John Buffington. In his lengthy grilling of her after her testimony and cross-examination, the judge asked, among other things, the following questions: "Is this suit in any way connected with how your father feels about the situation? You want to prove something to him?" and "Can you tell me why you decided to [go forward with the case]?" and "You understand that if Mr. Brannon's opening statement is correct, he has already lost, I guess, quite a bit of money, and been subject to certain trials and tribulations as a result of those allegations, correct?" and "Your testimony is going to be looked at very carefully."

To a rape trauma expert, Buffington suggested that when she sees rape survivors, she should "check and see if they come in with a big 'R' stamped on their forehead in red letters, and then we'll all know." When the expert witness asked if she could remain after her testimony concluded, Buffington said: "If she's excused, she can sit here. If she wants to listen to all of this nonsense, she's welcome." Brannon had admitted the assault in a phone call monitored by the police. Buffington called sexual harassment cases "detrimental to everyone." He said that Catchpole's testimony was "simply not believable." Buffington noted that the young woman had been molested as a child—obviously that had mysteriously slipped through California's rape shield law—and said that he found it "impossible to separate her present condition from the past." In conclusion the judge wrote that the circumstances were unbelievable, the plaintiff was at fault for not resisting, and one might even infer from her actions that she was seeking Brannon's attention. Oh, yes, he added, the suit was a waste of the court's time.

Buffington's ruling for the defendant was reversed in 1995 on the specific ground of gender bias, and a new trial before a different judge was ordered.

Women judges are not exempt from sexist attitudes. Even a judge whose involvement in gender bias programs would indicate that she was born fair-minded and empathetic to women says that she came to the bench with stereotypical convictions. "I didn't know what it meant to be a rape victim," says Judge Faith Ireland. "I had all the same stereotypes that the male judges had—Why would a women let herself get in that position? What was she doing there? At that place at that time of night? Did I really believe this woman, that she couldn't get out of the situation? She went to his apartment, after all. I came through the same male-oriented law schools, I had the same identical socialization." Judge Ireland says that her turnaround came—fortunately, she says, before she "wrecked some sentence"—when another female judge took her aside and she started educating herself about rape and its devastating effects on victims.

THE STORY of the woman who told about being forced to have sex—without physical violence—might have a different ending today. She *might* have called the police, they *might* have taken her seriously, she *might* have been able to convince a prosecutor to take the case, but it is likely that she wouldn't have done anything differently. A young woman in Madison, Wisconsin, had a similar experience just a few years ago—she knew the guy, it happened in her apartment, she didn't resist. He had followed her home after she finished her shift at a fast-food restaurant at two in the morning, then pushed his way into her apartment. The next morning she went to the police. There she learned that her rapist had a lengthy rap sheet that included other incidents of sexual assault. Yet the kindly cop did nothing except tell her what she would face if she actually ended up in court. It did not sound appealing. She decided not to pursue the case. One wonders how many more women the man raped before he was stopped. The evidence is that rapists who get away with it rape repeatedly.

Rape is endemic in America, partly because it's not just the police who question the woman's motives, question whether she was "really raped." Nor is it just judges who treat crime victims with contempt: in 1994 in Norfolk, Virginia, general district court judge Charles Cloud accused the city attorney and the commonwealth's attorney of discriminating against women of any race and African American men by refusing to prosecute violent misdemeanor crimes against them in his court. He sent a two-hundred-page report to the state attorney general, outlining his charges.

Rape is endemic in America, partly because it is not just the prosecutors who don't want to take the cases, particularly the difficult acquaintance rape cases. A new class of prosecutors have been tackling the difficult cases, and despite the odds, despite the ingrained attitudes of the people—including the women— who make up the juries, they are winning many important victories.

Rape is endemic in America, and not just because university administrators and athletic coaches attempt to squelch the woman's accusation of rape and battering and thereby downplay her trauma, her right *not* to be raped, her right to act as if she can go to the library late at night and not worry about walking home alone, to go to a fraternity party and not worry about being assaulted, raped or sodomized if she has a few too many. Some schools do take their punishment to the limit of their ability—they can't send anybody to jail, after all—and expel the rapist, period. Others don't even go so far as to take away the rapists' athletic scholarships. The woman leaves the school instead. There's no question who has more value to the school, to society.

Rape is endemic in America, and not just because if a woman does end up in a courtroom, staring down her rapist, she is likely to face defense attorneys who will have no trouble making her look like a loose woman at best, a slut at worst. Facing a woman who let the man in at two A.M.—a man she had once dated—he will ask: Why did she let him in? Didn't she *know* that he was there only for sex? What was she wearing? Didn't she know that by opening the door she was consenting? Why didn't she live in a safe building, with locks on the downstairs door? To the young woman who was followed home from work at two A.M., he will ask, or at least imply: Didn't she know that she should live in a safer neighborhood? How come she has a job that requires her to walk home at two in the morning? Why did she go up to her apartment if he was following her?

No one would ask guys who were mugged why they were in a certain bar, blame them for being alone, having a job that lasts until two A.M. or criticize their clothes for "leading" a robber on. If you leave your keys in your car, it's possible that it will be stolen rather than the one that has to be broken into; however, if the thief is caught, the police are just as likely to prosecute whether he took the car with the car keys or the one that was locked; it is unlikely they will laugh you out of the station house or submit you to a rigorous lie detector test, then ask whether you are sure you didn't want your car to be stolen or tell you that there's no chance of bringing charges because, well, you had a car stolen in the past. And anyway, are you sure, really sure, that the robber didn't believe that you wanted it to be stolen?

Rape is endemic in America because America lets it happen. The freer women act, the more they skirt convention, in dress, in mobility, in social interactions, the more at risk they are. A friend of mine who was raped early one morning when jogging in Central Park knows this. I barely escaped being raped one night in Mexico by a fellow journalist with whom I had a drink. We women would be safer if we lived in a nunnery, didn't jog, didn't have jobs that required us to walk home at two in the morning, didn't travel. In some not so hidden recess of the American mind, because we do, anything that happens is all our fault. Women should know their place: in the home, the kitchen, at church. Step outside those limits and you get what you deserve.

Rape is endemic in our society. And the legal system, beginning with the police and ending with a jury of our peers, all too often collaborates with the rapist who will rape not only today, but again, and again, and again. He doesn't get punished, why should he stop? Until we stop collaborating with him, one out of every eight women will be raped sometime in her life.

Conclusion:
Still Unequal
After All These Years

If my cup won't hold but a pint, and yours holds a quart, wouldn't you be mean not to let me have my little half-measure full?—SOJOURNER TRUTH

To ITS VERY CORE, the legal system in this country is biased against women—white and black and brown and all the colors between; rich and poor, educated and illiterate. It is true, some women squeeze through the interstices of sexism and find justice when they need it, whether it's from an understanding cop, one who knows the signs and signals of domestic violence, a prosecutor who takes on a difficult acquaintance rape case, or a judge who understands that a fifty-year-old housewife with a degree in English that is two decades old cannot reasonably be expected to compete in the job market, who knows that her contributions to her husband's career were realized in his income.

These things happen, to be sure; women are sometimes treated fairly. Judicial training and education keeps chipping away at age-old biases at the center of our legal system. But judges trained today are often gone tomorrow. And since sexism—raw, unbridled and pervasive, stripped of its more genteel term, *gender bias*—is the norm in our society, the new judges are often no better, or only marginally less biased, than the ones they replace. The trouble is that they often don't even know they are biased and object to being told they are. *They are judges, aren't they?* Aren't they by fiat objective and fair, models of rectitude? Instead of having to abide by the laws, don't they make them? Who dares tell them that they do not dispense justice equally, that they are not open-minded and *just*?

The gender bias reports have pointed out, sometimes quite nakedly, that any assumptions we and the judges might have of their gender impartiality are misguided. Some judges—and from the evidence it is clear that they are not a solitary few—are so prejudiced against women that if a lawyer appears before them with a female client and does not try to have the judge removed from the case, other lawyers condemn it as bad counsel. It is true, some male judges have been immensely helpful in guiding these reports as a first step to eliminating bias from their courts; but others take umbrage at the criticism. Seven judges, in fact, publicly registered their irritation earlier this year of the D.C. circuit report by signing or concurring with a critical memo. And their criticism seems to have directly influenced three Republican senators on the judiciary committee—Charles Grassley of Iowa, Orrin Hatch of Utah, and Phil Gramm of Texas—to urge that money already earmarked for gender bias reports in the federal circuit courts not be spent, that new reports from federal circuits not be written. No matter what's said about how the other circuits may benefit from the work done elsewhere, the "not in my backyard" syndrome is surely to ensue. Yes, the thinking will be, there are a lot of problems in the Ninth Circuit—their report lays it out—but it couldn't possibly be that bad here. Yes, it can. And without this kind of thorough examination and introspection of one's own weaknesses and faults, the stereotypes and prejudices will repeat endlessly, like a tape that loops around and around again.

It starts in how the law is taught. We have heard from women students all over the country just how discriminatory some law professors and thus some law schools are. At Harvard a woman with direct experience in the point of law under discussion, a woman who knew the law inside out, was ignored because she wasn't one of the teacher's pets—they happened to be all men—even though she knew for a fact that *she was right, the "expert" wrong*. She was only a woman, after all. What did she know?

At Emory students who had been sexually harassed by a professor who seemingly couldn't keep his ego or his fondness for attractive female students in check had their law school careers tainted by the school's unwillingness to keep this character under control or boot him out. Abraham P. Ordover brought too much glory to the school; they were only students, female students. They were only temporarily filling the seats. Only after outside intervention from the U.S. Department of Education were their charges of harassment—in all more than a dozen women spoke up—taken seriously. Only when an arm of the federal government told Emory to fix the problem did the school do something besides appoint a committee to investigate. The committee, remember, had found no serious wrongdoing. For the glory of Emory, administrators and faculty simply abandoned its women students to Ordover. This was not an isolated incident. Sexual harassment is common at American law schools. *Caveat mujer.*

It's a fact that women students do better at schools where the faculty is highly integrated with women. Yet at several of the "best" schools in the country, at many of the Ivy League schools, women faculty are stretched thin, given little or no voice in faculty appointments or what the school will emphasize. At the University of Chicago in the 1995–96 school year, *only three women are teaching full-time on the permanent academic law school faculty,* out of a total of twenty-five faculty. When you add in the eight emeritus professors, all male, who sometimes teach a class, and five or six lecturers, mostly male, the odds of finding a woman professor at the head of the class get much worse. At schools where the women are few, each is asked to serve on numerous committees—because they need a woman—and each is asked to oversee an inordinate number of women's papers, and women students naturally flock to them as advisers. Consequently women faculty have less time for the scholarship that really matters in determining who's got clout and who doesn't. Busywork keeps them away from serious scholarship.

Why does what happens in law school matter so much to the rest of us? Because it is there that all our future lawyers and judges are being trained. Teach the white males to think of their position as being first, at the top of the feeding chain, while the law they are being taught is based on biased stereotypes, as well as a monumental lack of understanding of what it means to be female in America, and you have just trained the next generation of officers of the court to be as prejudiced against women as the one preceding it.

As we have also seen, when the female student becomes a lawyer, the biases she encountered in law school are simply translated into her workday world. Law firms will hire her, yes, but there is a lot of busywork at law firms too, and somehow it happens that more of that falls to women. Busywork does not a great lawyer make. Even if she does manage to carve out a niche for herself and establish herself as a rainmaker, we have heard from women how those clients are taken from them, their departments carved up so that they have a small share of the pie, and men brought in over them when they create departments with billings that approach the million-dollar mark. It happened to Johnine Brown in Chicago, and it is happening right now to countless other women in Los Angeles and Boston and Denver and Baton Rouge. We know less about what happens to women in small firms, where the majority of lawyers work, but the evidence is that it is not much different there, and quite possibly much worse.

In terms of sexual harassment, it is absolutely worse. If the boss hits upon a young attorney just starting out, and he's the firm's major rainmaker, is she going to complain or sue? She is either going to put up with it or quit. Whom can she possibly complain to? Some big firms may be better—but not much. Kathleen Frederick, the attorney who said she was pursued by Richard Glanton at Reed Smith Shaw & McClay, one of Philadelphia's white-shoe firms, tried to make Reed Smith pay for their complicity in sexual harassment; but they were found blameless. Glanton, whom the jury found guilty of sexual harassment, is still at Reed Smith. Frederick is not. She is a solo practitioner. She may be happier personally. Professionally, however, Glanton won. How many share-croppers sue Minute Maid? asked Ralph Nader. How many Kathleen Fredericks are willing to sue Reed Smith? More will be like the woman who anonymously called a radio station in Philadelphia and told a talk show host that when she was sexually harassed at Reed Smith, she simply found a new job.

When a woman wants to combine motherhood with the law, she runs smack dab into a system that at most firms makes little or no accommodation to the realities of children. The emphasis is on hours and more billable hours, 1,900 a week, 2,000, 2,100, 2,200, and so on—hours that are impossible to keep if one is to have a life outside the office. Only a few women will be able to pay the quart of blood some firms demand before partnership. The first time a woman has to stay home because her child has a 102-degree fever and she doesn't have child care to cover such emergencies, she will be seen as "not committed." The emphasis on billable hours is one sure way to keep women from ever assuming real power in the profession. It's one way to keep the critical mass of women from becoming meaningful. For the same years that one needs to be making tracks toward partnership at a firm, or tenure at a law school, are the same prime childbearing years.

In the courtroom only men think the ambience for women lawyers has gotten better in the last few decades. Most judges now know not to call female lawyers "young lady" or "little lady." Or to pull their hair playfully. Or to comment on their legs. Or to say outright, as one judge did, that he likes to watch women's tits during oral arguments. Most judges are not chasing their secretaries around desks or forcing themselves on women who come before them asking for, say, a way to collect child support from recalcitrant ex-husbands. But some still are. If the Sixth Circuit has its way, David Lanier, the west Tennessee judge who did just that, will get away with it because a majority of the Sixth Circuit judiciary decided that the right to bodily integrity is not a federally protected right. To use a cliché because the cliché fits so well, the Sixth Circuit decision is a travesty of justice. The Sixth Circuit judiciary itself has become a joke. If you're a woman and a judge sexually assaults you in chambers, don't look for justice from the highest federal court in the states of Tennessee, Kentucky, Ohio and Michigan, the states the Sixth Circuit includes. Try elsewhere.

If you find yourself in the Washington, D.C., circuit, look out for Laurence H. Silberman, who led a charge against the court's gender bias report with a highly critical memorandum. If you are in New York, hope that you won't come before a judge like Lorin Duckman, whose dismissal of domestic violence charges led, in one case, to a woman's death by a convicted rapist. Duckman may no longer be hearing criminal cases, but it is too late for the dead woman. This is not some far-off time we are talking about. This is women's justice circa 1996.

If you are in Florida, try not to have Judge Joseph Tarbuck of Tallahassee hear your plea for increased child support, especially if you are a lesbian. This year Tarbuck awarded custody of an eleven-year-old girl to her father, John Ward, because her mother is a lesbian and her partner lived with her and her daughter. After having served eight years in prison for killing his first wife, John Ward was now living with his fourth wife. Incidentally, Ward was nearly $1,500 in arrears in his child support at the time of the hearing.

In Rhode Island try not to be a healthy housewife looking for an equitable settlement after divorce. The highest court says you had better be sick, either physically or emotionally, to collect any reasonable support. In Chapel Hill, North Carolina, pray that you aren't a professor's wife caught in a custody battle. You will probably lose, no matter what. Those professors have an inordinate amount of sway over Chapel Hill judges. California may not be any better, especially if the man is a smooth-talking type with a good position in the community—women there tried to sue the courts for being discriminatory against battered women caught in custody battles, but the lawyer who brought the case ran out of money and had to drop it. The Ohio courts don't like it, by the way, if you ask for back child support too long or too loud. They are likely to chastise you in their rulings.

And remember, if you get raped in Pennsylvania, it's best to end up badly bruised, or a guilty verdict against your rapist might be overturned. And don't

forget, if you've been raped in Seattle, do not tell the investigator that you had
been raped earlier by a doctor. Some lawyers will tell the judge that obviously
this means you aren't a credible witness. You might not be lucky enough to have
your case heard by a judge like Faith Ireland. And remember in Delaware, if
you've had sex with the guy in the last twelve months, it's not as serious a
crime, so you had better avoid that too. And you had better not be his "voluntary companion," because then, too, it's not as serious a crime. You had
better be extra careful in Delaware whom you associate with. Sure, you can
bring rape charges anywhere in America and sometimes see your attacker go to
jail—but the likelihood of that is two out of a hundred. For no matter how
strong the case against your attacker, you might get one of those idiot judges
who thinks "Boys will be boys" who need to "date" or that the attacker had a
little too much to drink and what's the big deal? If a man drinks, his behavior
is excused; if a woman drinks or wears too short a skirt or is in a place not
deemed "safe," or the hour is too late, she's to blame. What was she doing
there? In that dress? Didn't she know she was asking for it?

It's hard to know where to turn.

While what happens in law school, in the profession, in the courts, is important to women's welfare, they are only part of the story, for laws affect us
in ways we do not always realize. The law intersects with nearly every aspect
of our lives: sex, marriage, reproduction, education, employment, relations
with our bosses and co-workers and even our families. Abortion laws, for instance, are made largely by men because men make our laws. Adoption laws
that seal the original birth certificates, and with them knowledge of one's own
heritage, were promulgated largely under the influence of powerful adoptive
fathers, such as Governor Herbert H. Lehman in New York. The Equal Rights
Amendment didn't become law because there are not enough women lawmakers.

The click! that motivated this book occurred in 1990 when I read about
Donna Carroll, a woman in northern Wisconsin who was being prosecuted for
adultery. In the state code it was a felony punishable up to two years in the
penitentiary and a fine of $10,000. Robert E. Eaton, the district attorney in
Ashland, Wisconsin, a town of 9,500 on the Lake Superior shore, decided to
go after Mrs. Carroll after her estranged husband, with his father in tow, swore
out a civil complaint accusing his wife of adultery in violation of the state code.
This was in the midst of a custody battle over the couple's seven-year-old son.
Donna Carroll's picture was on the front page of Wisconsin newspapers.

Robert Carroll, the husband, admitted to his own extramarital affair, but investigators concluded that it probably occurred over state lines when Carroll, a trucker, was on the road. The man Donna allegedly slept with was not charged because there was "insufficient evidence." Only the woman was being charged.

A *New York Times* story about the incident went on to say that in Massachusetts the police would often use the law against adultery, a felony, as a way of increasing the penalties for prostitution. Massachusetts got away with it as late as 1983, when the state supreme judicial court upheld just such a statute, enforcing it against—you're right—a *woman*.

The story is old news now. Donna Carroll has left town and moved on. But if her story represents the progress we've made, the way to go appears endless. No matter how you define it, for women the law remains profoundly biased and discriminatory and in need of a massive overhaul. Yes, advances are being made. Yes. Yes. Yes. But a mountain of evidence proves beyond doubt that no matter how far we have come, we have not traveled very far at all. Prejudice against women, some of it unconscious, permeates the justice dispensed in our courtrooms. And because any nation's legal system reinforces and shapes cultural attitudes, the shameful inequities in our laws and courtrooms today will be promulgated well into the next century. The scope of the differences in the legal system is so great that in effect we have four different systems operating side by side: one for men, one for women, one for men of color, one for women of color. It is nearly impossible to know how to tackle the problem. The forty-one states, and four federal circuits, that have begun or completed gender bias reports are a beginning—but only if their findings are heeded. So are the numerous conferences, seminars, and sessions at bar meetings and lawyers' organizations on gender bias—but only if attended by the lawyers and judges who need to be woken up to their own biases. Lynn Hecht Schafran's tireless work in educating judges through the National Judicial Education Program is a beacon showing the way—but only two states mandate gender bias training. I can only hope that this book, by virtue of illuminating the overwhelming evidence of the still unequal justice in this country, is another step in the right direction. But, ultimately, the people who run our courts have to cleanse themselves. Unless they do, unless the system changes and rights itself, unless judges and judicial committees do the hard self-critical work, true progress for women will be forever elusive.

Notes

INTRODUCTION

The time to assert a right: Angelina Grimké, quoted in Gerda Lerner, *The Grimké Sisters from South Carolina* (Boston: Houghton Mifflin, 1967), 201.

In 1994, 67 percent of the lecturers/instructors: statistics from the Association of American Law Schools, as reported in "Women in the Law: A Look at the Numbers," Commission on Women in the Profession, American Bar Association, Nov. 1995.

only 5 percent of the women: Cynthia Fuchs Epstein and others, "Glass Ceilings and Open Doors: Women's Advancement in the Legal Profession," 64 *Fordham Law Review* 2, Nov. 1995, 291–449.

THE RISE OF A MORALLY BANKRUPT SYSTEM

Any criticism of the Law School: Duncan Kennedy, "How the Law School Fails: A Polemic," *1 Yale Review of Social Policy* (1970), 11.

Two-thirds of all our presidents: Linda R. Hirshman, "Nobody in Here but Us Chickens: Legal Education and the Virtues of the Ruler," 45 *Stanford Law Review* (1993), 1907.

"How many sharecroppers": Ralph Nader, quoted by Scott Turow in *One L* (New York: G. P. Putnam's Sons, 1977), 147.

study of the country's top law schools in 1970–72: Robert Stevens, *Law School: Legal Education in America from the 1850s to the 1980s* (Chapel Hill: University of North Carolina Press, 1983), 234.

"Intellectual movements": Alfred S. Konefsky and John Henry Schlegel, "Mirror, Mirror on the Wall: Histories of American Law Schools," 95 *Harvard Law Review* (1982), 841.

"There is far too much law": This and the following comments are from Derek Bok, *The President's Report, 1981–82,* Harvard University, 2, 6, 17–20.

"The level of abstraction in most classrooms": Deborah Rhode, "Missing Questions: Feminist Perspectives on Legal Education," 45 *Stanford Law Review* (1993), 1558, quoting from Paul Wice, *Judges and Lawyers* (1991).

that "law is a science": Stevens, 53.

"at some 130 legal texts": Rhode, 1559.

"The student should not be so trained": ABA report quoted by Ian Van Tuyl in the Princeton Review Student Access Guide, *The Best Law Schools* (New York: Villard, 1994), 9.

"freedom to roam in an intellectual cage": Ralph Nader, "Crumbling of the Old Order: Law Schools and Law Firms," *New Republic,* October 11, 1969, 20.

"the law school dialogue": Carrie Menkel-Meadow, "Feminist Legal Theory, Critical Legal Studies, and Legal Education, or The Fem-Crits Go to Law School," 38 *Journal of Legal Education* (1988), 67.

"The present structure of law school": David Margolick, "The Trouble with American Law Schools," *N.Y. Times Magazine,* May 22, 1983, 39.

THE HISTORY OF WOMEN IN LAW SCHOOLS

Mrs. Belva A. Lockwood: quoted in Karen Berger Morello, *The Invisible Bar: The Woman Lawyer in America 1638 to the Present* (New York: Random House, 1986), 71. For the stories of the first women law students I relied on this well-written and informative history, chaps. 2–4; Cynthia Fuchs Epstein's excellent *Women in Law,* 2d ed. (Urbana: University of Illinois Press, 1993), chaps. 3–4; and Stevens's *Law School* throughout the text.

"an honor to her class": Morello, 45.

"mental overexertion": Morello, 46.

"there was a colored woman who read us": Morello, 146.

Gordon "wore a stylish black dress": Morello, 62.

"A woman had better be in almost": Morello, 64.

"distract the attention of the young men": Morello, 71.

"and am entitled to and demand": Morello, 72.

"arouse my indignation by picking out": Morello, 53.

"feminine graces": Morello, 79.

"Married women could better serve": Morello, 81.

"in order to avoid any misunderstanding": Morello, 92.

"The professors had fits": Morello, 85.

In 1926 two black students: J. Clay Smith, *Emancipation: The Making of the Black Lawyer* (Philadelphia: University of Pennsylvania Press, 1993), 39.

"Opportunities for women": Morello, 101.

"one of the legendary Harvard Law professors": Henry Louis Gates Jr., "Hating Hillary," *The New Yorker,* Feb. 26 and March 4, 1996, 116–133, at 126.

"What was the *chose* in question?": Epstein, 67.

"a decline in law school applications": Konefsky and Schlegel, 840.

". . . 'and has brought his girlfriend' ": interview with Suzanne Charle, April 1994. For the remaining text, I follow journalistic style and do not footnote the several hundred interviews I did for this book. If a quote is not footnoted, it indicates that I interviewed the individual quoted personally.

CLASSROOM ATMOSPHERE

the type of student who goes to law school: Robert Stevens, "Law Schools and Law Students," 59 *Virginia Law Review* (1973), 603, 613; Lani Guinier, Michelle Fine, Jane Balin, and others, "Becoming Gentlemen: Women's Experiences at One Ivy League Law School," 143 *University of Pennsylvania Law Review,* Nov. 1994, 1–110. Hereafter cited as *Gentlemen.*

some of her third-year students: Elizabeth Schneider, "Task Force Reports on Women in the Courts," 38 *Journal of Legal Education,* 92.

collected data from nearly two thousand: Taunya Lovell Banks, "Gender Bias in the Classroom," 14 *Southern Illinois Law Journal* (1990), 527–536.

Banks noted that twice the number of women: Taunya Lovell Banks, "Gender Bias in the Classroom," 38 *Journal of Legal Education* (1988), 137–146. All of the data from Banks (and Blocker) come from these sources as well as interviews with Banks and unpublished material.

Studies at Stanford: Janet Taber and others, "Gender, Legal Education, and the Legal Profession," 40 *Stanford Law Review* (1988), 1209–1297; the University of California at Berkeley: Suzanne Homer and Lois Schwartz, "Admitted but Not Accepted," 5 *Berkeley Women's Law Journal* (1989–90), 1–74; University of Pennsylvania: *Gentlemen;* New York University: "Legal Education: Classroom Participation and Greenhouse Effect," *Commentator,* Feb. 3, 1993, 5; Yale: Catherine Weiss and Louise Melling, "The Legal Education of Twenty Women," 40 *Stanford Law Journal* (1988), 1299–1369.

A random sampling of 973 male and female: "The Elephant in Ohio Law Schools: A Study of Perceptions," Joint Task Force on Gender Fairness in the Profession, Final Report, Ohio Supreme Court and Ohio State Bar Association, 1993.

"The women reported significantly higher rates of anxiety": from an interview with Marsha Garrison, author of "Succeeding in Law School: A Comparison of Women's Experiences at Brooklyn Law School and the University of Pennsylvania," in press, *University of North Carolina Law Review.*

with the same aspirations as men: Robert Granfield, *Making Elite Lawyers* (New York: Routledge, 1992), 103.

"By the end of their first year": *Gentlemen,* 3–5.

"[M]any female law students are not performing": Linda Wightman, "Women in Legal Education: A Comparison of the Law School Performance and Law School Experiences of Women and Men," draft copy, Jan. 1996, at 19.

this one from Columbia School of Law: interview with Associate Dean James Milligan and Chiu-Huey Hsia, "Men, women perform equally well, study says," *Columbia Spectator,* March 20, 1995, 1+. When Milligan analyzed a number of female and male Columbia law students between 1992 and 1996 who had won honors, he found that as a group women slightly outdistanced their expectations based on LSAT scores and men did as well as the scores would indicate. Women at Columbia are also winning academic prizes at a greater rate than their makeup in the student body. More than a third of the women have an almost perfect academic record.

"[C]onsider a discussion in Property": Kimberle William Crenshaw, "Toward a Race-Conscious Pedagogy in Legal Education," 1 *National Black Law Journal* (1988–89), 3–5.

Women's undergraduate grade-point: Linda Wightman, "Analysis of LSAT Performance and Patterns of Application for Male and Female Law School Applicants," Law School Admission Council Research Report 94-02, Dec. 1994.

SEXUAL HARASSMENT

"A discriminatorily abusive work environment": Sandra Day O'Connor, quoted in "Excerpts from Supreme Court Ruling on Sexual Harassment," *N.Y. Times,* Nov. 10, 1993, A22.

"by its nature cannot be a mathematically": O'Connor, quoted by Linda Greenhouse in "Court, 9-0, Makes Sex Harassment Easier to Prove," *N.Y. Times,* Nov. 10, 1993, A22.

A 1961 graduate of Yale Law: the biographical data on Ordover comes from a story favorable to him by Bill Schipp, "Fall from Grace," *Atlanta* magazine, June 1991, 23–28; and Letters, Sept. 1991, 7–10.

Except for the interview noted in the text with one of the woman complainants, the information about the climate at Emory Law School leading up to the investigation, and the investigation itself, and statements quoted, comes from the Office for Civil Rights, Region IV, U.S. Department of Education, Investigative Report, Docket Number: 04-91-2127, as well as several Atlanta newspaper (the *Atlanta Journal* and *Constitution*) and magazine articles (*Atlanta* magazine, Sept. 1991, 23), which appeared around the time of the investigation, and press releases and memos issued by law school officials, Abraham O. Ordover and students at the school. A summary of the case prior to the OCR's report may be found in "Emory Professor Takes Leave Amid Charges of Harassment," by Ken Myers in the *National Law Journal,* April 8, 1991, 4.

"[A] major reason that many women": Catharine A. MacKinnon, *Feminism Unmodified* (Cambridge, Mass.: Harvard University Press, 1987), 111.

A TALE OF CASEBOOK CHAUVINISM

Now we are expected to be as wise: Louisa May Alcott in *Jo's Boys,* quoted by Rosalie Maggio, *Quotations by Women* (Boston: Beacon Press, 1992), 347.

"Generations of law students read": Judith Resnick, "Ambivalence: The Resiliency of Legal Culture in the United States," 45 *Stanford Law Review* (1993), 1526–27.

Frug's seminal article: Mary Joe Frug, *Postmodern Legal Feminism* (New York: Routledge, 1992), 53–107.

"[P]art of a lawyer's role includes": MacKinnon, *Feminism Unmodified;* 75.

"a wife should not be paid": Marjorie Maguire Shultz, "The Gendered Curriculum: Of Contracts and Careers," 77 *Iowa Law Review* (1991), 59.

Fuller and Eisenberg: Lon L. Fuller and Melvin Aron Eisenberg, *Basic Contract Law* (St. Paul: West, 1990).

"Are there any types of legal bargain": Shultz, 59.

single case involving a woman: John P. Dawson, William Burnett Harvey, and Stanley D. Henderson, *Cases and Comments on Contracts,* (Westbury, N.Y.: The Foundation Press, 1993), 531–537. *Broemmer* v. *Abortion Services of Phoenix,* in which Broemmer disputes an agreement on the clinic's standardized form to arbitrate any disagreement. Plaintiff suffered a punctured womb as a result of the abortion.

"sex bias continues to be uncritically": Nancy S. Erickson and Nadine Taub, "Final Report: Sex Bias in the Teaching of Criminal Law," 42 *Rutgers Law Review* (1990), 312–608, at 327.

People v. *Berry:* Philip E. Johnson, *Criminal Law, Cases, Materials and Text,* 4th ed. (St. Paul: West, 1990), 150–153.

In 1980 only eight states permitted: James J. Tomkovicz, 102 *Yale Law Journal* (1992), 489 n25.

"[M]uch of the traditional law of rape": Erickson and Taub, 339.

Ronald N. Boyce and Rollin M. Perkins, *Criminal Law and Procedure, Cases and Materials,* 7th ed. (Westbury, N.Y.: Foundation Press, 1989; 5th reprint, 1993).

"manifest the attitudes about women and sex": Joshua Dressler, *Understanding Criminal Law* (New York: Matthew Bender, 1987; 1992 reprint).

"Rape has been almost unique": John Kaplan and Robert Weisberg, *Criminal Law, Cases and Materials,* 2d ed.(Boston: Little, Brown, 1991), 1106.

Feminist casebooks are beginning to appear: Mary Joe Frug, *Women and the Law* (Westbury, N.Y.: Foundation Press, 1992); Herma Hill Kay, *Sex-Based Discrimination, Text, Cases and Materials,* 3rd ed. (St. Paul: West, 1988; 1st reprint, 1990); Katharine T. Bartlett, *Gender and Law, Theory, Doctrine, Commentary* (Boston: Little, Brown, 1993); Mary Becker, Cynthia Grant Bowman, and Morrison Torrey, and Beverly Balos and Mary Louise Fellows, *Feminist, Jurisprudence, Taking Women Seriously, Cases and Materials* (St. Paul: West, 1994).

TEACHING RAPE

Law is shaped by its practice: Nancy S. Erickson and Mary Ann Lamanna, "Sex-Bias Topics in the Criminal Law Course: A Survey of Criminal Law Professors," 24 *University of Michigan Journal of Reform* (1990), 245.

slightly fewer than one out of six women on campus: statistics of Mary Koss and others, "The Scope of Rape," 55 *Journal of Consulting and Clinical Psychology* 2 (1987), 162–170.

"You survive rape": Susan Estrich, "Teaching Rape Law," 102 *Yale Law Journal* (1992), 512.

Regina v. *Morgan:* Sanford H. Kadish and Stephen J. Schulhofer, *Criminal Law and Its Processes, Cases and Materials,* 5th ed. (Boston: Little, Brown, 1989), 249–263. This case, as well as another, *Commonwealth* v. *Sherry,* are included in the discussion of mens rea. Feminist writers quoted here are Estrich, MacKinnon and Robin Weiner. For a different handling of the case, see Kaplan and Weisberg, 159.

nearly 95 percent—said they covered: Erickson and Lamanna, 197–202.

James Tomkovicz: For a discussion of his experience of rape at the University of Michigan, see his paper, "On Teaching Rape: Reasons, Risks, and Rewards," 102 *Yale Law Journal* (1992), 481.

"To silence that debate": Estrich, 515.

Richard O. Lempert and Stephen A. Saltzburg, *A Modern Approach to Evidence,* 2d ed. (St. Paul: West, 1982), 955.

"Teaching rape is . . .": Estrich, 520.

TENURE TRAVAILS

Assistant professors begin their careers: Duncan Kennedy, *Legal Education and the Reproduction of Heirarchy* (Cambridge, Mass.: Afar, 1983), 59.

were less than 6 percent female: Richard H. Chused, "The Hiring and Retention of Minorities and Women on American Law School Faculties," 137 *University of Pennsylvania Law Review* (1988), table 2, 557.

close to 30 percent of full-time law school faculty: Richard A. White, "The Gender and Minority Composition of Law School Faculty," Association of American Law Schools Newsletter, Feb. 1995, 7; and "The Gender and Minority Composition of New Law Teachers and AALS Faculty Appointments Register Candidates," 44 *Journal of Legal Education,* Sept. 1994, 424–433.

third, fourth or even fifth tier. *U.S. News & World Report,* March 21, 1994, 72–74. The magazine publishes its ranking of law schools annually.

at a dinner for Chicago alumnae and women students: Laura Duncan, "U. of C. Pays Tribute to 1st Alumna," *Chicago Daily Law Bulletin,* Oct. 15, 1993, 3. I also interviewed women who attended the dinner.

approximately 20 percent of the women: American Association of Law Schools, Report of the Special Committee on Tenure and the Tenuring Process, Oct. 1992, 2.

"The same work or the same résumé": Deborah Rhode, "Once More with Feeling," *AALS Newsletter,* Feb. 1995, 6–7.

"We are still 'outsiders'": Leslie Bender, "For Mary Joe Frug: Empowering Women Law Professors," 6 *Wisconsin Women's Law Journal* (1991), 7–8.

"[O]ur presence has not correlated": Bender, 4–5.

The queen bee syndrome?: See Marina Angel for this and other issues discussed here, "Women in Legal Education: What It's Like to Be a Part of a Perpetual First Wave, or the Case of the Disappearing Women," 61 *Temple Law Review* (1988), 831.

"[H]ow many of us have": Bender, 8.

"When are we going to lift": "Survey of Ohio Law School Faculty," Joint Task Force on Gender Fairness of the Ohio Supreme Court and the Ohio State Bar Association, 1993, 21.

hired significantly more men: interview with Deborah Jones Merritt and draft of unpublished paper, "Sex, Race, and Credentials: The Truth about Affirmative Action in Law School Hiring," by Deborah Merritt and Barbara Reskin. Their research can also be found in "The Double Standard: Empirical Evidence of a Double Standard in Law School Hiring of Minority Women," 65 *Southern California Law Review* (1992), and also with Michelle Fondell, "Family, Place, and Career: The Gender Paradox in Law School Hiring," 1993, *Wisconsin Law Review* 2, 395–463.

Hirshman is among the most published law professors: James Lindgren and Daniel Seltzer (paper in press), 71 *Chicago-Kent Law Review,* 1996.

"Law Schools and the Construction of Competence": Bryant G. Garth and Joanne Martin, American Bar Foundation Working Paper 9291, 2, 8.

thereby controlled the accreditation process for nearly twenty years: Andrew Blum, "Jim Who?" *National Law Journal,* Nov. 22, 1993, 1, 38+.

four schools were cited for not meeting diversity standards: ABA internal memorandum, Accreditation Chart, Nov. 1992.

cited Penn for lack of diversity: "Report on University of Pennsylvania School of Law," Oct. 25–28, 1992, Office of the Consultant on Legal Education to the ABA, 107.

actually got tenure at a higher rate: "Tenure Practices: Analysis of Data Collected by the American Association of Law Schools," revised Sept. 18, 1991, Table S-1, 70.

sixteen and two-thirds: This figure came from the Harvard Law School public relations office. Current justices who attended Harvard Law School are Anthony Kennedy, Antonin Scalia, David Souter, and, as noted, Ginsburg. Yale, with a student population of less than half of Harvard's, claims eight Supreme Court justices, including Clarence Thomas.

For an overview of feminist scholarship, I am indebted to Carrie Menkel-Meadow, "Feminist Legal Theory, Critical Legal Studies, and Legal Education, or The Fem-Crits Go to Law School," 38 *Journal of Legal Education* (1988), 61–86; and Patricia A. Cain, "Feminist Legal Scholarship," 77 *Iowa Law Review* (1991), 19–39.

"Usually you're told": Eleanor Swift, "Becoming a Plaintiff," 4 *Berkeley Women's Law Journal* (1989–90), 246.

five distinguished academics outside of Berkeley: Swift, "The Battle for Tenure," *Radcliffe Quarterly,* Dec. 1990, 25.

For more on Lucinda Finley's and Drucilla Cornell's tenure stories, see Debra Cassens Moss, "Would This Happen to a Man?" *ABA Journal,* June 1, 1988, 50–55.

"badly photocopied reproduction": Ann Bartow, "Cornell Denied Tenure!" *Penn Law Forum,* April 1, 1988, 1. This same issue discusses sexual harassment by faculty members, including sexually degrading material used in legal writing courses.

Two-thirds of the students queried: "The Elephant in Ohio Law Schools," Executive Summary, 4.

"I get the distinct impression": "The Elephant in Ohio law Schools," 28.

"I was struck by his observations": Kathleen S. Bean, "The Gender Gap in the Law School Classroom—Beyond Survival," 14 *Vermont Law Review* (1989), 31, quoting from *Women Lawyers, Perspectives on Success,* ed. E. Couric, 1984.

"Why does my teaching get labeled": Bender, 17.

five of the top seven schools: Linda Hirshman, "Law schools where women can excel," *Glamour,* Sept. 1995, 122.

"Despite identical entry-level credentials": *Gentlemen,* draft, June 3, 1993. This statement and the next one are not in the final version, which has been toned down considerably.

"What law school does for you": MacKinnon, *Feminism Unmodified,* 205.

HARVARD

"*That peculiar pride*": Scott Turow's *One L* (New York: G. P. Putnam's Sons, 1977), 261. I consulted Scott Turow's *One L* and Richard D. Kahlenberg's *Broken Contract* (New York: Hill and Wang, 1992) throughout the text, particularly chapter 11.

"It is an education in itself": Turow, 259–60.

"paralyzed by spasms of intellectual violence": Peter Collier, "Blood on the Charles," *Vanity Fair,* Oct. 1992, 152.

"the Beirut of legal education": David A. Kaplan, "Battle at Harvard Law over Tenure," *National Law Journal,* June 22, 1987, 3.

"legal rules permit and sometimes mandate" and other quotes from the paper: Mary Joe Frug, "A Postmodern Feminist Legal Manifesto (An Unfinished Draft)," 105 *Harvard Law Review,* March 1992, 1045–1075.

four white men tenured positions: Robert C. Arnold and Steve Yarian, "4 White Men Offered Tenure," *Harvard Law Record,* March 6, 1992, 1. Other articles in the edition also discuss the lack of diversity on Harvard's faculty; and Fox Butterfield, "Harvard Law School Torn by Race Issue," *N.Y. Times,* April 26, 1990, A20.

"Men f**k wom*n every day": Mary Doe, "He-Manifesto of Post-Mortem Legal Feminism (From the Desk of Mary Doe)," 105 *Harvard Law Revue,* April 1992, 13–18.

"deeply regret[ted]" the incident: From Dean Robert Clark's official response, April 13, 1992.

Nine campus organizations: Natasha H. Leland, "Law Student Groups Demand Clark Resign," *Harvard Crimson,* April 17, 1992, 1.

"the hatred of women is a hoax": Caralee E. Caplan, "Tribe Denounces Spoof as Hateful," *Harvard Crimson,* April 13, 1992, 1.

"sophomoric" and "in somewhat poor taste": Alan M. Dershowitz, "Harvard Witch-Hunt Burns the Incorrect at the Stake," *L.A. Times,* April 22, 1992.

"hostile work environment": Elizabeth Bartholet, Memorandum to the faculty, April 23, 1992.

"shows something very scary about male": Fox Butterfield, "Parody Puts Harvard Law Faculty in Sexism Battle," *N.Y. Times,* April 27, 1992, A10.

"the level of arrogance and elitism": Rebecca L. Walkowitz, "15 Faculty Rip Harvard Law Hiring, Climate," *Boston Globe,* April 21, 1992, 1.

butt of an article: "Pat McCrotch: Dersh to Defend Worker," *The Rectum,* April 1, 1993, 1.

"I remember thinking": Robert Granfield, *Making Elite Lawyers* (New York: Routledge, 1992), 114.

"[T]hose who entered": Granfield, 106.

approximately 12 percent: statistics supplied by the Office of Public Interest Advising, Harvard Law School, May 2, 1994.

A third of the men enter: R. Stevens, "Law Schools and Law Students," 59 *Virginia Law Review,* (1973), 613. These figures coincide with other studies at individual schools. The data reflects studies at eight schools, both public and private, national and regional.

THE HISTORY OF WOMEN LAWYERS

Mistress Lockwood, you are a woman: quoted in Morello, 31–32. For information on the first women lawyers in this country, I relied on Morello's history of women lawyers, *The Invisible Bar;* Epstein, *Women in Law;* and Smith, *Emancipation,* noted above.

"By marriage, husband and the wife": Katharine T. Bartlett, *Gender and Law: Theory, Doctrine, Commentary* (Boston: Little, Brown, 1993), 2, quoting from William Blackstone, *Commentaries on the Laws of England.*

"Had I received the education": Grimké quoted in Gerda Lerner, *The Creation of a Feminist Consciousness* (New York: Oxford University Press, 1993), 21.

Brent arrived on these shores: Morello, 2–8.

"female attorneys-at-law were unknown": This and the other quotations from the 1870 Illinois Supreme Court decision noted here are in Morello, 17–18. For an account of Myra Bradwell's legal battle to be recognized as a lawyer, see also Jane Friedman, "Myra Bradwell: On Defying the Creator and Becoming a Lawyer," reprinted from "America's First Woman Lawyer: The Biography of Myra Bradwell," 28 *Valparaiso University Law Review* (Summer 1994), 1287–1304.

The first woman to address: Smith, 70 n74.

"the disability imposed by your condition": Morello, 16. The full quote of the letter from a clerk of the court reads: "The court instructs me to inform you that they are compelled to deny your application for a license to practice as an attorney-at-law in the courts of this State, upon the ground that you would not be bound by the obligations necessary to be assumed where the relation of attorney and client shall exist, by reason of the disability imposed by your married condition—it being assumed that you are a married woman."

"the right to admission to practice": Morello, quoting from the supreme court's majority opinion, written by Justice Samuel F. Miller, 20. That the right to practice law was not a privilege of citizenship was the same argument that would later be used against female voting rights.

"Man is, or should be, woman's protector": quoted in Kenneth L. Karst, *Law's Promise, Law's Expression: Visions of Power in the Politics of Race, Gender, and Religion* (New Haven: Yale University Press, 1994), 38, quoting 83 U.S. at 139; and Joan Hoff, *Law, Gender, and Injustice: A Legal History of U.S. Women* (New York: New York University Press, 1991), 165–166; and Morello, 20.

"not only because she is the first lady": this and Justice Francis Springer's decision, Morello, 12.

"The peculiar qualities": Morello, 25, and Hoff, 164, quoting from *State* v. *Goddell*, 39 Wisc. 323 (1875), at 245–246.

"If her purity is in danger": Morello, 25.

Delaware and Rhode Island finally admit: Hoff, 164.

the first woman lawyer: Smith, 141.

By 1910 census data from Smith, appendix 2.

"housewife and . . . the mother of a young son": Smith, 406, quoting from *Afro-American,* March 5, 1938. Carter's story is also told in Morello, 150–153.

not able to break into the ranks: Smith, 541–546.

Nanette Dembitz: "Political Newcomers, Nanette Dembitz," *N.Y. Times,* June 22, 1972, 46.

"The women in my class": Constance Baker Motley, "My Personal Debt to Thurgood Marshall," 101 *Yale Law Journal* (1991), 19.

"Bring him in": Epstein, 84–85. See also Morello, 184.

Sandra Day O'Connor: "The Brethren's First Sister," *Time,* July 20, 1981, 12.

"would love to hire her": Epstein, 85.

Ruth Bader Ginsburg's dean: "Rejected as Clerk, Now Headed for the Bench," *N.Y. Times,* June 15, 1993, 1.

"to coerce a mismatched or unwanted partnership": "Getting a Piece of the Power," *Time,* June 4, 1984, 63.

reported on a summer picnic: James P. Stewart, "Fairness Issue: Are Women Lawyers Discriminated Against at Large Law Firms?" *Wall Street Journal,* Dec. 20, 1983, A1.

GETTING STARTED

"I had a young girl": "Report of the Florida Supreme Court, Gender Bias Study Commission," 1990, 217.

National Association of Law Placement (NALP): *Diversity in the Legal Community: The Search for Opportunity,* class of 1993.

Earlier data show that when the overall figures for men: Marilyn Tucker and Georgia A. Niedzieklo, *Options and Obstacles, A Survey of the Studies of the Careers of Women Lawyers,* ABA, Commission on Women in the Profession, 1994, 14, and appendix 1, which includes NALP data not included in the above report, which was used to make the comparisons over time.

"I had put down 'golf . . .'": interview with Linda Golden Chatman, plus a copy of her letter to

Baker & McKenzie, Jan. 16, 1989. See also "Dean Suspends Baker & McKenzie from 1989–
'90 Campus Interviews," *National Law Journal,* Feb. 13, 1989.

are interested in some notion of social justice: It has long been believed that *in general* more women
enter law school for different reasons from men—that is, more women are motivated by a
desire to contribute to the social good, and several studies support this. See Paul W. Mattessich and Cheryl W. Heilman, "The Career Paths of Minnesota Law School Graduates: Does
Gender Make a Difference?" 9 *Journal of Law and Inequality* (1990), 59–114; Linda Liefland,
"Career Patterns of Male and Female Lawyers," 35 *Buffalo Law Review* (1986), 601–631;
Taber, 1209–1297; and Stevens, *Law Schools and Law Students,* 551–699. However, other
studies have found no statistical difference between the motivations of men and women. See
Ann Gellis, "Great Expectations: Women in the Legal Profession: A Commentary on State
Studies," 66 *Indiana Law Review* (1991), 941–976; James J. White, "Women in the Law," 65
Michigan Law Review (1967), 1051–1122; and Granfield, chap. 6, "The Contradictions of
Gender, Competing Voices among Women at Harvard Law School," 94–109. Gellis postu-
lates that numerical differences between men and women in where they choose to practice law
(private vs. public) may relate more to job environment and flexibility than the nature of the
work. Granfield notes that more women than men listed both career *and* altruistic reasons for
attending law school. While these findings seem contradictory, they are not, because motives
for life choices are always complex. What is true is that women cannot be considered to have
singular motives for choosing law and that their reasons may be just as varied as men's.
Furthermore, all of the studies manifest age-old cultural differences between the sexes that
may or may not be in the genes: traditionally women have found it more socially acceptable
to go into service professions, and the law can be configured that way, and men, as the
customary breadwinners, choose professions where they can do that well. This doesn't prove
that women aren't essentially more socially motivated than men, and studies of women in the
last few decades argue just that; but it does mean that this assumption should be treated
skeptically.

"almost a suffragette": MacKinnon, *Feminism Unmodified* 75.

A 1990 survey by the Indiana State Bar: Gellis, 946.

White & Case was spared a "finding of discrimination": Ann Davis, "Feds' Audit Checks Bias at
N.Y. Firm," *National Law Journal,* Feb. 27, 1995, A1.

minority women outpaced the national average: Tucker, appendix 1.

unable to find a job in east Tennessee: Project Pamphlet, Commission on Women and Minorities
in the Profession, Young Lawyers Division, ABA, 2.

Since 1983, the first year the NALP: Tucker, appendix 1. For 1990, the figures for minority
women and nonminority women were reversed.

The twenty largest law firms in the country grew fourfold: "Legal Education and Professional
Development—An Educational Continuum," Report of the Task Force on Law Schools and
the Profession, ABA, Section on Legal Education and Admissions to the Bar, 1992, 78, quoting
R. L. Abel in *American Lawyers* (1989).

more than a third of the women interviewed: *The State of the Legal Profession,* ABA Young Lawyers
Division, table 81, 65.

"an enlightened group of male lawyers": *The 1993–94 Insider's Guide to Law Firms,* compiled and
written by Harvard Law students, 124.

PRIVATE PRACTICE

nearly half would not become lawyers: Nancy McCarthy, "Pessimism for the Future: Given a
Second Chance, Half of the State's Attorneys Would Not Become Lawyers," *California Bar
Journal,* Nov. 1994, 1.

widespread discontent: *The State of the Legal Profession,* 52–58.

"Although there is a general crisis of morale": Epstein and others, "Glass Ceilings and Open Doors," 439.

More than 70 percent of women: Klein Associates, Inc. All rights reserved, 1992. These figures and all those from Klein Associates referred to are based on interviews with more than two thousand male and female attorneys at some large law firms (one hundred–plus attorneys). The response rate usually exceeds 90 percent of the male and female associates and partners, and thus the attitudes reported can be generalized to all lawyers in large law firms. They are generally in agreement with other national surveys.

as early as law school: Tucker and Niedzieklo, 21, reporting on the 1986 Harvard Law School Program on the Legal Profession, which looked at the class of 1981, although it provided no gender breakdown. That study found that only half of the class of 1981 respondents remained with the organizations in which they began their careers.

A 1989 Minnesota study: Mattessich and Heilman, 80–87. See also Liefland, 606. She found that a much higher percentage of men leave first jobs for "advancement and salary considerations" and because the work was "not challenging," while a much larger proportion of women left for reasons of "discrimination" and "other."

nearly 60 percent of the women: Thom Weidlich and Charise K. Lawrence, "Sex and the Firms: A Progress Report," *National Law Journal,* Dec. 20, 1993, 1.

lawyer to population ratio halved: Richard Abel quoted in Carrie Menkel-Meadow, "Culture Clash in the Quality of Life in the Law," 44 *Case Western Reserve Law Review* (1994), 626.

Between 1960 and 1985 the average size of New York's: *The 1993–94 Insider's Guide to Law Firms,* 35.

"Litigation is war": quoted by David Margolick, "Rambos Invade the Courtroom, and the Profession, Aghast, Fires back with Etiquette," *At the Bar* (Touchstone: New York, 1995), 114.

claiming that he had been worked to death: "Can't Sue for Overwork," *National Law Journal,* April 18, 1994.

affected white males more than minorities: Claudia MacLachlan and Rita Henley Jensen, "Progress Glacial for Women, Minorities," *National Law Journal,* Jan. 27, 1992, 1.

"But after three years of expensive litigation": Paul Lerner, "Strategic Auditing Is Key to Minimizing Litigation Bills," *Corporate Legal Times,* Nov. 1994, 26.

indicate that he billed 6,022 hours: Stephanie B. Goldberg, "Work Ethics," *Chicago* magazine, Dec. 1994, 86.

Sunoco Atlantic, for example, notified thirty: William A. Brewer III and Dennis J. DuBois, "Law Firms Must Adopt Creative Methods of Billing," and Mike France, "Clock's Running on Billable Hours," *National Law Journal,* Dec. 19, 1994, C1–C5.

one hundred most powerful lawyers: "The 1994 Power List," *National Law Journal,* April 4, 1994, C4–C14.

"power lawyers" in the Windy City: Greg Hinz and Randall Samborn, "Power Lawyers," *Chicago,* July 1994, 60–69.

"I'm at Skadden Arps now": Hinz and Samborn, 63.

"trotted out for clients": "The Burdens of Both, the Privileges of Neither," Report of the Multicultural Women Attorneys Network, ABA, 1994, 18–19.

didn't go to basketball games: Stewart.

reported they had a "mentor": The studies were from Indiana, Wisconsin, and Michigan, as reported in Tucker and Niedzielko, 29. Several states have done studies documenting discrimination against women in the profession. A partial listing: "Report of the Florida Supreme Court Gender Bias Study Commission, Gender Bias in the Legal Profession, 1990," 195–239; "Wisconsin Equal Justice Task Force," 1991, 240–252; "Report of the Kansas Bar Association Task Force on the Status of Women in the Profession," 1992; "1990 Report of the Committee on Women in the Legal Profession," Minnesota State Bar Association; "Sex Discrimination in the Profession," *Texas Bar Journal,* Jan. 1992, 50–51. "Report of the Commission on Women in the Profession," Indiana State Bar Association, 1990; "Kentucky Task Force on Gender Fairness in the Courts," 1992; "Women Lawyers and the Practice of Law in California," 1989, Committee on Women in the Law, State Bar of California in cooperation with the Employment Law Center/Legal Aid Society of San Francisco; "The Women and Minorities Study," *Arkansas Lawyer,* Jan. and April 1992. For an overview, see "Options and Obstacles: A Survey of the Studies of the Careers of Women Lawyers," ABA Commission on Women in the Profession, July 1994; and Gellis.

Ezold's trial caused some commotion: Mary Walton, "Fighting the Firm," *Philadelphia Inquirer Magazine,* July 28, 1991, 11; see also Marcia Chambers, "Partnership: Court Gives Inside Look," *National Law Journal,* Jan. 28, 1991, 13–14.

partner who testified in Ezold's behalf: "Judge Explains Wolf, Block Decision," *National Law Journal,* Dec. 10, 1990, 29.

"Younger male attorneys are just as likely": Diane F. Norwood and Arletter Molina, "Sex Discrimination in the Profession: 1990 Survey Results Reported," *Texas Bar Journal,* Jan. 1992, 50–51.

"People say they don't discriminate": "Women and Minority Lawyers Still Face Stumbling Blocks," *Corporate Legal Times,* Jan. 1994, 40.

BRINGING UP BABY

Even when freshly washed: Fran Liebowitz in *Metropolitan Life,* quoted by Maggio, 49.

62 percent of them were childless: "Women Lawyers and the Practice of Law in California," 11.

bill more than 2,400 hours: "The Report of At the Breaking Point: A National Conference on the Emerging Crisis in the Quality of Lawyers' Health and Lives—Its Impact on Law Firms and Client Services" (ABA:1991), reported by Carrie Menkel-Meadow, in "Culture Clash in the Quality of Life in the Law," 44 *Case Western Reserve Law Review* (Winter 1994), 632.

57 percent of them had access to part-time work: Debra B. Schwartz, "An Examination of the Impact of Family-Friendly Policies on the Glass Ceiling," Families and Work Institute, New York, 1994, 15. Women report higher access to part-time work than men do (66 percent vs. 48 percent), while men report higher access to extended lunch breaks than women do (50 percent vs. 44 percent). Managers and professionals have much higher access than other employees to flexible work arrangements.

5 percent of lawyers in private practice: "The State of the Legal Profession," 26.

not employed full-time outside the home: Weidlich and Lawrence, 1.

less than 2 percent take them: Deborah Rhode, "Gender and Professional Roles," 63 *Fordham Law Review* (1994), 62.

lawyer-fathers ever worked part-time: see below, Wood, Corcoran and Courant.

equals 93 percent of the first-year salary: "Women Stay at Family-Friendly Companies," *Working Woman,* Nov. 1989, 137. The Fortune 500 company statistic is also reported here.

"women with the twenty-four-hour nanny": Quoted in "Report of the Florida Supreme Court, Gender Bias Study Commission," 1990, 223.

quite different from their male counterparts': see also Carrie Menkel-Meadow, "Exploring a Research Agenda of the Feminization of the Legal Profession: Theories of Gender and Social Change," 14 *Law & Social Inquiry* (Spring 1989), 289–319. Also see David L. Chambers, "Accommodation and Satisfaction: Women and Men Lawyers and the Balance of Work and Family," in the same issue, 251–287. Chambers surveyed close to three hundred University of Michigan female law graduates over the course of 1981 to 1986, and he concludes his own study with a cautionary note that the most recent surveys indicate that satisfaction with the balance of family and career is declining. He also notes that his findings may not be replicated for the "graduates of other schools who have different resources, aspirations, and opportunities." It must also be noted that Chambers's studies date from before the downsizing law firms went through in the early 1990s and may represent firms that are family-friendly.

"the earnings given up are": Robert G. Wood, Mary E. Corcoran and Paul N. Courant, "Pay Differences among the Highly Paid: The Male-Female Earnings Gap in Lawyers' Salaries," 11 *Journal of Labor Economics,* no. 3, (1993), 440. The sample consisted of 803 men and 81 women from the graduating classes of 1972–75.

RAINMAKING

and billed only thirty-six hours in 1993: Edward A. Adams, "Some Partners See a 'Cad' in Cadwalader," *National Law Journal,* Nov. 21, 1994, A12.

a 1993 Prentice-Hall survey: J. Stratton Shartel, "Discrimination by Clients Limits Opportunities, Female Litigators Report," *Of Counsel,* March 6, 1993, 1,4+.

could not sit in chairs that have arms: Norma G. Blumenfeld, "Now That Country Clubs Are Admitting Blacks . . . ," *N.Y. Times,* Aug. 29, 1990.

"I know a number of women": Margaret L. Moses, "A Firm-ative Inaction: How Women Fare in Law Firms," *The Compleat Lawyer* (Summer 1994), 37–39.

LAW FIRM LUST

The entrance of sexual harassment into the legal sphere: Drucilla Cornell, *The Imaginary Domain: Abortion, Pornography and Sexual Harassment* (New York: Routledge, 1995), 167.

"I want to take you upstairs . . .": from testimony of Frederick quoted by Lisa De Paulo, *"Frederick v. Glanton:* Now What?" *Philadelphia* magazine, Oct. 1993, 92+.

"I felt that under these circumstances;" quoted by Shannon P. Duffy, "Plaintiff Makes Allegations As Sex-Bias Trial Continues," *Legal Intelligencer,* July 13, 1993, 1+.

"go somewhere": quoted by Duffy, "Plaintiff Makes Allegations."

"too lively": Frederick quoted by Amy S. Rosenberg, "Glanton's Accuser Tells of Seduction," *Philadelphia Inquirer,* July 13, 1993, B1+.

"I want you to be my mistress": quoted by Duffy, "Plaintiff Makes Allegations."

"Mr. Glanton had been very, very good": Rosenberg.

"he hugged me and pressed himself": Rosenberg.

"I told him again": Rosenberg.

"I didn't know how to say no to Mr. Glanton": Rosenberg.

"acting more like his old self": Rosenberg.'

"ashamed, degraded and very depressed": Eugene d'Aquili quoted by Shannon P. Duffy, "Frederick's Former Psychiatrist Testifies in Sex-Bias Trial," *Legal Intelligencer,* July 16, 1993, 1+.

"threatened that if she told": quoted by Joe Slobodzian, "Sex Harassment Suit Is on Trial Against Big Philly Firm," in *National Law Journal,* July 26, 1993, 3.

"extortion": quoted by De Paulo.

"disturbed woman": De Paulo.

"an unspeakable, murderous, just disgusting lie": quoted by Joe Slobodzian, "Glanton Takes Stand, Flatly Denies Affair," *Philadelphia Inquirer,* July 30, 1993, B1+.

"Never, never, never": Slobodzian, "Glanton Takes Stand."

"tends to help people": quoted by Duffy, "Glanton Takes Stand after His Wife Testifies," *Legal Intelligencer,* July 30, 1995.

nineteen times from his car phone: Jim Smith, " 'Predator' vs. the 'Nut,' " *Philadelphia Daily News,* Aug. 5, 1993, 5.

the first he'd heard about the whole nasty business: De Paulo.

"exchange sex for work assignments": quoted by Shannon P. Duffy, "Plaintiff Is Cross-Examined in Sex-Bias Suit," *Legal Intelligencer,* July 14, 1993, 1+.

"Did you bat your eyes?": De Paulo.

"He may be the bottom of the barrel": *Almanac of the Federal Judiciary* (Washington, D.C: Aspen Law & Business, 1995), Third Circuit, 35.

HISTORY OF WOMEN'S PLACE IN OUR LEGAL CODE

If you got the sayso: Ruth Shays, quoted by Maggio, 184.

For this chapter I am particularly indebted to Joan Hoff for her comprehensive study of women's legal history from the War of Independence to the present, *Law, Gender, and Injustice* (New York: New York: University Press, 1991).

"By marriage . . . the husband and wife are one" and "as inferior to him, and acting by his compulsion": William Blackstone, *Commentaries on the Laws of England,* quoted in Katharine T. Bartlett, *Gender and Law: Theory, Doctrine, Commentary* (Boston: Little, Brown, 1993), 2–4.

nearly a fifth of the female servants: Lois Green Carr and Lorena S. Walsh, *The Planter's Wife,* in Nancy F. Cott and Elizabeth H. Pleck, eds., *A Heritage of Her Own* (New York: Touchstone, 1979), 25–58.

"in the new Code of Law" and the following quotes from Abigail Adams's letter and John's response: Hoff, 60–61.

"married women, aliens and negroes": Hoff, 98–103, quote at 102.

"Even were our state a true democracy": Jefferson is quoted by Herma Hill Kay, *Sex-Based Discrimination* (St. Paul: West Publishing, 1988), 1, quoting M. Gruberg, *Women in American Politics* (1968), 4.

"the chief slave of the harem": Gunnar Myrdal, *An American Dilemma: The Negro Problem and Modern Democracy* (New York: Harper & Row, 1962), 1075, quoting Harriet Martineau, *Society in America* (1842).

"Wives and apprentices are slaves": William Fitzhugh, *Sociology for the South,* quoted in Myrdal, 1073.

"took no part in governmental affairs": Myrdal, 1075, quoting Virginius Dabney, *Liberalism in the South* (1932), 361.

"Children got by an Englishman": Paula Giddings, *When and Where I Enter: The Impact of Black Women on Race and Sex in America* (New York: Morrow, 1984), 33–55, quote at 37.

"So, by the early eighteenth century": Giddings, 39.

The rape of a propertied virgin: Deborah L. Rhode, *Justice and Gender* (Cambridge, Mass.: Harvard, 1989), 245.

"There is a great stir": Sojourner Truth in a speech to the Convention of the American Equal Rights Association in New York City, 1867, quoted by Gerda Lerner in *Black Women in White America* (New York: Vintage, 1992; copyright 1972), 569.

"but by forms of law all made by men": Hoff, at 159.

"marital feudalism": Hoff, 137–141, quote at 141.

"Lillian is and will continue to be": Wendy McElroy, "The Roots of Individualist Feminism in 19th-Century America," in *Freedom, Feminism, and the State* (Washington, D.C.: Cato Institute, 1982), this and the other quotes from the marriage vows and subsequent trial, at 16.

beginning in 1835 in Arkansas: Hoff, 120–128, 381. While several other references date the first married women's property act to Mississippi in 1839, Hoff notes that women in Arkansas were able to inherit their husband's estates without incurring his debts in 1835.

"This century-long, tortuous demise": Hoff, at 121.

In Kentucky, for instance, as late as 1921: Mary Joe Frug, *Postmodern Legal Feminism,* 69, 178–179 n58–61.

Hardy v. *Hardy:* For this and several other instances of sexist laws and decisions, I am indebted to Roxanne Barton Conlin, past president of the Association of Trial Lawyers of America. In a speech given at ATLA's annual convention in Washington, D.C., on July 27, 1993, she presented many of the instances given in a talk on "Women and the Law: Protected or Neglected?" *Hardy* v. *Hardy,* 235 F. Supp. 208, 211 (D.D.C. 1964).

"character, habits, education and mental capacity": Conlin, Fla. Sta. Ann. S 62.021 (1969), repealed by Ch 70–4, Sec. 4 [1970] Fla. Laws.

"Plaintiff is in the wrong forum": Roxanne Barton Conlin, "Women, Power, and the Law," *Trial,* Feb. 1990, 22–26, quote at 24.

revoked a woman's license: The U.S. Supreme Court, in *Perez* v. *Campbell,* 402 U.S. 637 (1971), struck down the Arizona statute that revoked a woman's license to operate a motor vehicle if her husband failed to pay a judgment debt for negligent driving.

"The husband is the head of the family": Ga. Code Ann. Sec. 53-501 (1974). Conlin notes that the editor added: "It is well settled in Georgia that where the husband and wife reside together whatever else she may be the head of, he is the head of the family."

"From the time whereof the memory": Senator Sam Ervin quoted in Kay, 11.

"punish the [wife's] body": quoted in Deborah Rhode, *Justice and Gender* (Cambridge, Mass.: Harvard, 1989), 238, 393 n21.

within "reasonable" bounds: Rhode, 238.

"moderate correction": Blackstone quoted in Bartlett, 19.

"administrative inconvenience": Bartlett, 18. *Forbush* v. *Wallace,* 341 F. Supp. 217 (M.D. Ala. 1971).

"No female shall appear in a bathing suit": Conlin.

COURTROOM DEMEANOR

Justice does not depend: Brown v. *Walter,* 62F.2d 798,800 (2d cir. 1933).

"no intention to discriminate": letter from the Hon. Kathryn McDonald to the woman attorney, Sept. 20, 1993. She requested anonymity because she appears before this court.

"So long, kikie" and other notes as noted: Special Supplement, New York State Commission on Judicial Conduct, a Twenty-Year History, 1995 Annual Report.

"little girl" several times: Lynn Hecht Schafran, "Women as Litigators," *Trial,* Aug. 1983, 40–41. Schafran gives a full discussion of this incident and is the source of the further quotes in my account.

"hysterical": transcripts of the O. J. Simpson trial, Feb. 15 and May 24, 1995. The word was actually used several times (sixteen as I write in August 1995) throughout the trial by witnesses referring to other women.

"wins the award for shrillness": Lou Lumenick, "Legal Eagles: Prosecution Did Enough to Convict O.J.," *New York Post,* July 7, 1995, 6.

"the word everybody uses . . .": Jimmy Breslin, "Women We Love . . . Marcia Clark," *Esquire,* Aug. 1995, 48.

"Size small. I guess it is Mr. Bailey's": The Hon. Lance A. Ito, Judge, Case BA097211, *People* v. *Orenthal James Simpson,* Court Order: Attorney Conduct. Judge Ito also included the response of F. Lee Bailey in the conduct code, but it is a rejoinder to her remark. The important factor is that Clark's comment was used as the primary example and not any of the sexist comments directed at her.

"Without exception, we found the same differences": "The Effects of Gender in the Federal Courts: The Final Report of the Ninth Circuit Gender Bias Task Force," July 1993, 71–72.

he deliberately made a sexist remark: Lynn Hecht Schafran, "Overwhelming Evidence: Reports on Gender Bias in the Courts," Trial, Feb. 1990, 28.

nearly 88 percent of the 553 lawyers: J. Stratton Shartel, "Discrimination by Clients Limits Opportunities, Female Litigators Report," 7 Inside Litigation, Feb. 1993, 20.

71 percent of the more than 700 female: Final Report of the Washington State Task Force on Gender and Justice in the Courts, 163, n239. Among the 1,509 respondents were 166 men, 709 women, and 34 unidentified lawyers. Respondents included a random sample of the Washington State Bar Association, the Family Law Section, and the Trial Practice Section. Members of the Defenders' Association, the Prosecuting Attorneys' Association, and Washington Women Lawyers also took part in the survey.

In Louisiana 36 percent of the female attorneys: Louisiana Task Force on Women in the Courts, Final Report (1992), 116.

"whether I am hurting clients": Gender and Justice in the Colorado Courts, Colorado Supreme Court Task Force on Gender Bias in the Courts (1990), 114.

"fairly obvious advantage": Colorado report, 113.

"Should you succeed on your motion": letter from David Cwik to Marilee Clausing. The quote has been repeated in several reports, including Margolick, At the Bar, "Wherein a Lawyer Finds That an Attempt at Humor Can Sometimes Go Very Awry," N.Y. Times, April 19, 1993, B9.

"Tell that little mouse" and "What do you know, little girl?": Daniel Wise, "Attorney Sanctioned for Sexist Insults," N.Y. Law Journal, May 8, 1992. The incident is further discussed in Lorna G. Schofield and Jill A. Lesser, "Depositions and the Gorilla Adversary," in The Woman Advocate 1995 (Englewood Cliffs, N.J.: Prentice-Hall Law and Business, 1995), 185–186.

the Ninth Circuit Court of appeals overturned: "Sexist Letter to Lawyer No Ground for Sanction," National Law Journal, May 22, 1995, B24.

" 'I don't want to hear about it' ": Ninth Circuit Report, 66.

"Disparaging remarks about females": Ninth Circuit Report, 65.

number of women in both the federal and state judiciary: According to the National Association of Women Judges, in 1995 the percentage of judges in the state system who are female is approximately 9.5 percent. The federal system is approximately 12 percent female.

"When women lawyers are evaluated": quote taken from interview with Leslie Abramson in "Gender Bias Highlights," ABA Commission on Women in the Profession, April 7, 1995.

"Minority women are more likely": Gender Bias Study of the Court System in Massachusetts, Supreme Judicial Court (1989), 153.

"You know you don't just get black today": The Burdens of Both, the Privileges of Neither: A Report of the Multicultural Women Attorneys Network, A Joint Project of the ABA Commission on Women in the Profession and the Commission on Opportunities for Minorities in the Profession, 1994, 27.

"partially as a result of exclusion": Report and Recommendations of the Florida Supreme Court Racial and Ethnic Bias Study Commission, Dec. 11, 1991, 55.

"Debate got fairly heated": from the Report of the Florida Supreme Court Gender Bias Study Commission (1990), 202.

"Judges have solicited sexual favors": Marina Angel, "Sexual Harassment by Judges," 45 University of Miami Law Review, March 4, 1991, 817–841.

"untoward propositions to females": Angel, 823.

"district court personnel": Angel, 827–828.

"she was dismayed as to any recourse" and "Although we are willing to share these anecdotes" and ". . . I like to watch women's tits": Kentucky Task Force on Gender Fairness in the Courts, Jan. 13, 1992, 13.

"A woman attorney reported": Final Report of the Equality in the Courts Task Force, State of Iowa, Feb. 1993, 55.

"One of the most offensive things" and "I have had judges stroke my hair" and "surprised her . . .": Gender Bias Task Force of Texas, Final Report, Feb. 1994, 31, 32.

"stood over [her], exposed his penis" and "would do 'anything' for a job" and "willing to perform sexual favors" and "[a]s a result agreed to interview Archie for the job" and "grabbing and squeezing her breasts": U.S. Court of Appeals, 33 F.3d 639 (6th Cir. 1994). The decision, written by circuit judge H. Ted Milburn, is striking for its graphic descriptions of Lanier's actions. Not surprisingly, the trial was followed avidly by people in Dyersburg and nearby.

"Don't worry. I am a judge": Darcy O'Brien, "Trouble in Tennessee Court: Is Rape by Judge a Federal Crime?" *National Law Journal,* July 24, 1995, A10.

Lanier was the first sitting judge: O'Brien. O'Brien is also the author of *Power to Hurt* (New York: HarperCollins, 1996), a compelling account of the Lanier story. See also Scott Minerbrook and Linda L. Creighton, "The Case of the Sexual Predator," *U.S. News & World Report,* April 19, 1993, 31–35.

"What if I went down to Riverfront Stadium": O'Brien, "Trouble."

"We're optimistic and praying for him": Sandy Hodson, "Lanier Released from Jail," *Jackson Sun,* June 16, 1995.

"If Doe has a viable": *Doe v. Taylor Independent School District,* 15 F.3d 443 (5th Cir. 1994).

DIVORCE

Divorce is the one: Brown, quoted by Maggio, 89.

half of all divorcing parties: these and the other statistics quoted here come from Marsha Garrison, "The Economic Consequences of Divorce," 32 *Family and Conciliation Court Review* 1, Jan. 1994, 10–26, at 16.

One study measuring people's responses: George Feifer, *Divorce* (New York: The New Press, 1995), 4–5.

one in ten that actually gets to trial: Marsha Garrison, "How Do Judges Decide Divorce Cases? An Empirical Analysis of Discretionary Decision Making," 74 *North Carolina Law Review,* Jan. 1996, 401–552, 407 n14, citing figures from several sources.

men brought suit in federal court: Patricia Cohen, "Dads File Discrimination Lawsuit," *Newsday,* Jan. 5, 1994, 6.

nearly half said that prejudice: Washington report, 128. See also Lynn Hecht Schafran and Norma J. Wikler, "Integration of Women Minority Judges into the American Judiciary," *The Judge's Book,* 2d edition (Reno: American Bar Association and the National Judicial College), 1994, 61–90.

"[T]he problems of women were more widespread": "Justice for Women," First Report of the Nevada Supreme Court Task Force on Gender Bias in the Courts, 1988, 5.

"We know . . . from our own bitter experience": Former Minnesota Supreme Court justice Rosalie E. Wahl, "Living the Life of a Woman Judge," from a speech delivered at the Chicago-Kent College of Law Women's Legal Studies Institute, July 23, 1994.

"It is common to hear women": Nevada report, 17–18.

"The negotiation process is aborted": "Women in Divorce: Lawyers, Ethics, Fees and Fairness," a study by the City of New York Department of Consumer Affairs, March 1992, 31.

which recommended that the code be revised: The Hon. Lisa Hill Fenning, "An Overview of Gender and Bankruptcy Law," working paper of the Ninth Circuit Gender Bias Task Force, 1993.

"Why do I and other mothers attempt": Gender Bias Study of the Court System in Massachusetts (1989), 20.

two attorneys were retained in only 29 percent: Jessica Pearson, "Ten Myths about Family Law," 27 *Family Law Quarterly* 2 (Summer 1993), 279–299, at 282. The one-third figure for divorcing couples who do not use a lawyer at all is an average of the figures cited here.

"Maintenance is totally dependent": from an interview with Jean Gerval. See also her paper, written with Carelle Muellner Stein, "Spousal Support in Minnesota: Where Are We Going?" 6 *Minnesota Family Law Journal,* March/April 1993 29–39.

these figures have not been duplicated: see Richard R. Petersen, "A Re-Evaluation of the Economic Consequences of Divorce," 6 *American Sociological Review,* June 1996, 528–536. Petersen, using Weitzman's own raw data on 228 women and men following divorce in Los Angeles between 1977 and 1978, reported a standard of living decline of 27 percent for women and a 10 percent increase in men's standard of living after divorce, not the exaggerated figures that Weitzman made headlines with a decade ago. Pamela J. Smock, of the University of Michigan Population Studies Center, reported that when she looked at income data of people in their twenties and thirties from the sixties to the late eighties, she found that per capita income (income divided by number of those in household) for white women and their children declines 21 percent; the drop in actual dollars, however, is substantially larger (43 percent), underscoring the marked disparity between men's and women's salaries. For white men, the increase in actual dollars is much smaller (7 percent) than their increase in per capita income (62 percent). These numbers reflect the income women bring to the joint family unit, as well as the difference between women's and men's value in the job market. The figures for African Americans are somewhat different, pointing up differences in the job market for different races and the fact that in an African American family both spouses are likely to be working: black women's families' per capita income declined after dissolution or divorce by 35 percent, but by 45 percent in actual dollars; black men's per capita income increased by 47 percent but declined in actual dollars by 29 percent. See Smock, "Gender and the Short-Run Economic Consequences of Marital Disruption," 73 *Social Forces* 1, Sept. 1994, 243–262; "The Economic Costs of Marital Disruption for Young Women over the Past Two Decades," 30 *Demography* 3, Aug. 1993, 353–371; and Karen C. Holden and Pamela J. Smock, "The Economic Cost of Marital Dissolution: Why Do Women Bear a Disproportionate Cost?" 17 *Annual Review of Sociology* (1991), 51–78.

"The absence of marriage": Marsha Garrison, "Economic Consequences," 10–26, quote at 10.

No more than 15 percent of divorced wives since 1920: Garrison, citing Census Bureau figures, "Economic Consequences," 14.

In Phyllis Chesler's groundbreaking study of sixty mothers: Chesler, *Mothers on Trial: The Battle for Children and Custody* (New York: McGraw-Hill, 1986), 140–143.

four out of five alimony payments: Garrison, "Economic Consequences," 12.

Today seven states require equal division: Garrison, "How Do Judges Decide Divorce Cases?" n23.

between one and five years: Garrison, "Economic Consequences," 12, 14–15.

"[M]ale perspective on family life": testimony of Harriet Cornell. Report of the New York Task Force on Women in the Courts, 15 *Fordham Urban Law Journal* 1 (1986–1987), 1–198, quote at 73.

"blatantly sexist": *Morrison* v. *Shen,* 21 FLR 1093, N.Y. S.Ct. NYCity (1995).

"a very attractive person": Janell Cole, "N.D. Intends to Weed Out Sexism in Legal System," (Bismarck) *Sunday Tribune,* March 13, 1994, 1A.

In Illinois in 1995: *Toole* v. *Toole,* Ill. AppCt 2dDist, No. 2-94-0858 (1995) 21 *Family Law Reporter* 42, Sept. 5, 1995, 1497, 1504–5.

"ignores the significant wage differentials": Gerval, 36.

39.4 percent of all married women: "Marital and Family Characteristics of the Labor Force from the March 1994 Current Population Survey," U.S. Census Bureau, February 1995. See also U.S. Department of Labor, Bureau of Labor Statistics, "Weekly Earnings of Employed Full-time Wage and Salary Workers by Marital Status, Age, and Sex, 1994 Annual Averages," Table A-4 (unpublished tables; available by phone).

All women whose careers slow down: Cynthia Starnes, "Divorce and the Displaced Homemaker:

A Discourse on Playing with Dolls, Partnership Buyouts and Dissociation under No-Fault," 60 *University of Chicago Review* 1 (Winter 1993), 67–139, at 98, citing research by Jacob Mincer and Solomon Polachek.

The number of women either not working or looking for work: Patricia Braus, "Sorry, Boys— Donna Reed Is Still Dead," *American Demographics,* Sept. 1995, 13–14. See also "Household and Family Characteristics: March: 1994," *Current Population Reports,* P20–483, U.S. Department of Commerce, Economics and Statistics Administration, Bureau of the Census.

Thirty percent of all women with children under eighteen: Bureau of Labor Statistics, above.

two studies demonstrate: Linda Stroh and Jeanne M. Brett, "The Dual-Earner Dad Penalty in Salary Progression," *Human Resource Management Journal,* in press, and Frieda Reitman and Joy Schneer, "The Importance of Family Structure in Mid-Career: A Longitudinal Study of MBAs," symposium presentation, Academy of Management Meeting, Dallas, Aug. 17, 1994.

spousal support awards dropped from 9 percent: Summary of the Report on the Financial Impact of Divorce in Rhode Island, by the Advisory Committee on Women in the Courts, 1992, 1.

Rhode Island Supreme Court rejected: *Stevenson v. Stevenson,* 511 A.2d 961 (RI 1986).

"To prevail on appeal": Starnes, 86–87.

"I don't know my feelings about child support": statement of woman who testified at the Atlanta public hearing, Aug. 3, 1990; "Gender and Justice in the Courts": A Report to the Supreme Court of Georgia by the Commission on Gender Bias in the Judical System, 8 *Georgia State University Law Review* 3, June 1992, 695.

refused to grant women divorces: For a full discussion of the matter, see Bill Martin, "Power of the Press," *Nevada Weekly,* Nov. 23, 1993, 6–7; and Mark Thompson, "Judicial Freefall," *San Francisco Daily Journal,* Sept. 8, 1995.

Massachusetts, Minnesota, Mississippi: *Barron v. Barron,* 556 N.E.2d 111 (Mass. App. Ct. 1990); the trial court erred in limiting alimony to five years where the wife is fifty-six and in poor health, even though the length of the marriage was only twelve years. The husband had sufficient income to meet his needs and help the wife. *Goldman* v. *Goldman,* 554 N.E.2d 860 (Mass. App. Ct. 1990); an award of alimony limited to eight years' duration, following a twenty-year marriage, was reversed. The court could not justify that the husband's standard of living would be maintained, while the wife's would decline substantially. *Boykin* v. *Boykin,* 565 So.2d 1109 (Miss. 1990); permanent alimony was upheld where the result would put the parties in virtually identical positions. And in Minnesota, where earlier appellate decisions in the 1980s pointed to maintenance for rehabilitation purposes only, that trend was reversed in *Nardini* v. *Nardini,* 414 N.W.2d 184 (Minn. 1987), when the court reversed an order of short-term maintenance for a fifty-year-old woman who had been married thirty years and ordered the award changed to permanent maintenance.

Hartog v. *Hartog:* 194 A.D.2d 286, 605 N.Y.S.2d 749 (1st Dept. 1993).

"Statutes in different states": from an interview with M. Garrison; she looked at about nine hundred divorces filed in 1978, two years before enactment of the Equitable Distribution Law, and from the files of approximately nine hundred divorces filed in 1984, four years after the law's passage. Cases were selected from New York City, one from the nearby suburbs and one from an urban/rural area upstate. See also her paper, "Good Intentions Gone Awry: The Impact of New York's Equitable Distribution Law on Divorce Outcomes," 57 *Brooklyn Law Review* 3, Fall 1991, 621–754, at 629–630.

"Often, a couple's only important asset": Starnes, quote at 94.

"In a nutshell, judges": Garrison, "Economic Consequences," 21.

30 percent of the wives: Garrison, "Economic Consequences," 21.

less than half of all divorces: Garrison, "Economic Consequences," 22; see also Jessica Pearson, "Ten Myths about Family Law," 27 *Family Law Quarterly* 2 (Summer 1993), 279–299, at 282.

more than $14 billion goes unpaid: These and the other figures quoted here from Joyce Pitts, program analyst with the Federal Office of Child Support in Washington, D.C. The Urban Institute estimates that $34 billion in back child support is due; the Federal Office of Child Support has a figure of $44 billion for all back due child support, based on figures received from the states, which use different methods of accounting, and not adjusted for deaths of the payers.

35 percent of all mothers with custody: Current Population Reports, Child Support for Custodial Mothers and Fathers: 1991, U.S. Department of Commerce, Bureau of the Census.

"Mrs. Reiner . . . continuously abused": In the matter of Eric Reiner, Common Pleas Crt., Juvenile Ct. Div., 24774. Also see Reiner v. Reiner, Juvenile Ct. No. 247,774, Ct. of Appls. 58121, 58481, 1991.

statute went beyond the jurisdiction: U.S. v. Parker, DC EPa. Crim. no. 95-352, 10/30/95, reported in U.S. Law Week, Nov. 21, 1995, 2314–5.

"the look of a prisoner of war": Florida report, 70.

"Judges seem to be 'bothered' by family law": Texas report, 63.

"They all seem to find their checkbooks": Minnesota Supreme Court Task Force for Gender Fairness in the Courts, Final Report (1989), 21.

criticizing women for anything resembling interference with visitation: Gender and Justice, Report of the Vermont Task Force on Gender Bias in the Legal System (1991), 89.

"The expression 'Justice delayed' ": Nevada report, quoting William Furlong, 53.

child support awards increased almost 56 percent: Summary of the Report on the Financial Impact of Divorce in Rhode Island (1992), 1. The report notes that the guidelines lowered the maximum amount by 50 percent, and thus children of upper-income parents were likely to receive less support than they would have without the guidelines.

By 1995 thirty-eight states and Washington, D.C.: Craig McEwen, Nancy Rogers, and Richard Maiman, "Bring in the Lawyers: Challenging the Dominant Approaches to Ensuring Fairness in Divorce Mediation," 79 Minnesota Law Review 6, June 1995, 1317–1411, appendices A, B.

a resolution rate of between 50 and 70 percent: Nancy Hoennes, Peter Salem, and Jessica Pearson, "Mediation and Domestic Violence, Current Policies and Practices," 33 Family and Conciliation Courts Review 1, Jan. 1995, 6–29, at 6–7.

satisfaction rates of various studies: J. Pearson, "Family Mediation: A Working Paper for the National Symposium on Court-Connected Dispute Resolution Research," Oct. 15–16, 1993, 55–89, at 63.

"women objected to being barred from mediation": Pearson, "Ten Myths," 289.

that they are misleading: the comments here come from an interview, Nov. 1995. See also Robert Levy, "Comment on the Pearson-Thoennes Study and on Mediation," 17 Family Law Quarterly 4 (Winter 1984), 525–533.

"Women usually have some control": from an interview with Penelope Byran, Nov. 1995. See also her paper, "Killing Us Softly: Divorce Mediation and the Politics of Power," 40 Buffalo Law Review 2 (1992), 441–523.

"They tell you not to talk": interview with Trina Grillo, Oct. 1995; see also her paper, "The Mediation Alternative Process: Dangers for Women," 100 Yale Law Journal (1991), 1545–1610.

mothers were providing a home: see Carol Bohmer and Marilyn L. Ray, "Effects of Different Dispute Resolution Methods on Women and Children after Divorce," 28 Family Law Quarterly 2 (Summer 1994), 223–245, figures at 227–228.

"fathers seek custody for leverage": Ohio Joint Task Force on Gender Fairness, A Final Report (1995), 80–81.

CUSTODY

Childhood is only the beautiful: George Eliot, quoted in Maggio, 47.

"You have no idea": Final Report of the Michigan Supreme Court Task Force on Gender Issues in the Courts (1989), 63.

"reverence and respect": Rhode, "Justice and Gender," 154.

"disintegrated with the advent": Lenore Weitzman, *The Divorce Revolution* (New York: The Free Press, 1985), 219, citing attorneys Henry Foster and Doris Freed.

custody more than 80 percent of the time: Rhode, "Justice and Gender," 155.

number of single-father households almost doubled: Deborah Eisel, "Can Fathers Be 'Mothers'?" *Family Advocate* (Winter 1993), 62–67, quoting from *American Demographics Desk Reference,* July 1992.

"In other cases, absentee fathers": Nevada report, 45.

"the deeply held belief that judges": First Year Report of the New Jersey Supreme Court Task Force on Women in the Courts (1984), 97.

when fathers sought custody: Massachusetts study, 62–63, 76 n54. Results of the other Massachusetts study, from Middlesex County, is also reported here. Interestingly, the only longitudinal study of custody disputes—in Utah—found that neither the number of fathers seeking custody, approximately 13 percent, nor the number of fathers who won, change significantly between 1970 and 1993. The study looked at 133 contested custody disputes in those years, in which opposing sides filed court papers. Overall, fathers were awarded custody 21 percent of the time and joint custody 29 percent; mothers won sole custody the remaining 50 percent. A variation in exact numbers of fathers who won custody was noted, but not in the direction expected: "If anything, there was a move against fathers getting custody in the more recent years," says sociologist Stephen Bahr, author of the study and a professor at Brigham Young University. He cautions that the absolute numbers were so small that the finding did not seem statistically significant. See Bahr and others, "Trends in Child Custody Awards: Has the Removal of a Maternal Preference Made a Difference?" 28 *Family Law Quarterly* 2 (Summer 1994), 247–267.

In California, fathers contesting: Eleanor Maccoby and Robert Mnookin, *Dividing the Child* (Cambridge, Mass.: Harvard University Press, 1992), chapter 5, 98–114; chapter 7, 132–161.

"A man with a full-time job": Nancy Polikoff, "Why Are Mothers Losing: A Brief Analysis of Criteria Used in Child Custody Determinations," 7 *Women's Rights Law Reporter* 3 (Spring 1982), 235–243, quote at 239.

"surrogate room mom": testimony of Emily Marvil, in the Prost-Greene custody suit.

"sexually indiscriminate": These and other quotes of circuit court judge Raymond Cashen come from his decision in *Ireland* v. *Smith,* no. 93-385 DS, Macomb County, Mich., June 27, 1994.

because he was going to be living with his parents: Jan Hoffman, "Judge Hayden's Family Values," *N.Y. Times Magazine,* Oct. 15, 1995, 44–49+.

In San Jose last year: Susan Chira, "Custody Case Stirs Debate on Bias against Working Women," *N.Y. Times,* July 1, 1994, 31.

In New York the appellate court awarded custody: Lisa Genasci, "Working Mothers at Risk in Custody Disputes," *L.A. Times,* March 5, 1995, A8.

Tonya Pinkins of *All My Children* lost custody: Thom Weidlich, "Dispute over Custody Gets Really Personal," *National Law Journal,* Sept. 4, 1995, A12.

Jerry Carr Whitehead awarded an infant: interview with Richard Young, Gale Pearson's lawyer, Nov. 13, 1995, and Brendan Riley, "Lawyer Tells Court Reno Judge Broke Law," *Reno Gazette-Journal,* Oct. 18, 1993, 10c.

upheld an Orlando judge's decision: Beth Taylor, "Judge: Custody Ruling Punishes Working Mom," *Orlando Sentinel,* Aug. 12, 1995, A1.

Burchard v. *Garay:* 42 Ca. 3d 531, 229 Cal. Rptr. 800, 724 P2d.486 (1986) in Bartlett, 364–365.

"the children's father could have as many affairs": Iowa report, 133.

"a new girlfriend is often seen as a plus": Texas report, 56.

A 1990 Wisconsin study found that fathers: Daniel Meyer and Steven Garasky, "Custodial Fathers: Myths, Realities and Child Support Policies," Technical Analysis paper no. 42, Office of Human Services Policy, Office of the Assistant Secretary for Planning and Evaluation, U.S. Department of Health and Human Services, July 1991, 15, quoting Judith Seltzer, "Legal and Physical Custody Arrangements in Recent Divorces," *Social Science Quarterly,* vol. 71, no. 2, 250–266.

Committee for Justice for Women: Contested Custody Cases in Orange County, NC Trial Courts 1983–1987: Gender Bias, the Family and the Law, the Committee for Justice for Women, and the Orange County North Carolina Women's Coalition, 2d Rev., 1991.

"being a child of the sixties": Rolland Wrenn, "Sleeping Is an Innocent Act," *Herald,* May 14, 1995. See also Jeffrey McMenemy, "Professor Offered to Help Mistress Find Sex Clients," *Chapel Hill Herald,* May 5, 1995; "Prof Defends Actions in Affair," *Herald,* May 10, 1995, 1.

agreed to pay Ashley $10,000: McMenemy, "Prof's Affair Outside UNC Prohibitions," *Chapel Hill Herald,* April 7, 1995, 1.

"The idea was to put her in jail": J. McMenemy, "Ex-Wife of Embattled Prof Arrested," *Herald-Sun,* June 10, 1995.

"He was ripped from his home": J. McMenemy, "Judge: Son Stays with Ex-Prof," *Herald,* Sept. 14, 1995, 1.

"he's more tentative, tense": J. McMenemy, "Psychologist: William's Son Happier with Mom," *Herald,* Oct. 11, 1995.

"committed to spending appropriate money": press release from National Center for State Courts, 1995.

twice as likely to challenge the mother for custody: Geraldine Butts Stahly, "Surviving Battering: Long-Term Consequences for Women Who Leave: A Review of Three Studies of Domestic Violence and Child Custody," unpublished paper. See also Marsha Liss and Stahly, eds. "Domestic Violence and Child Custody," in *Battering and Family Therapy: A Feminist Perspective* (Newbury Park, Calif.: Sage, 1993).

How else could a known wife batterer, Lonnie Dutton: Mark Potok, "Blue Ribbons Everywhere Show Support," *USA Today,* Aug. 23, 1993, A1.

"weird" and "wicked" and "Trying to unscramble a situation": K. V. Johnson, "Contempt Ruling Called Violation of Girls' Rights," *USA Today,* Oct. 11, 1995, A3.

DOMESTIC VIOLENCE

more than half of the female victims: Maureen Sheeran, "Domestic Violence Affects Courthouse Security," 1 *Courts and Communities: Confronting Violence in the Family,* National Council of Juvenile and Family Court Judges, undated, 3–10, at 3, quoting A. Brown and K. Williams, "Resource Availability for Women at Risk: Its Relationship to Rates of Female-Perpetrated Homicide," presented at the American Society of Criminology, Montreal, Quebec, Nov. 1987.

In 1992 an estimated 1,432 women were murdered: U.S. Department of Justice, "Domestic Violence between Intimates," *Bureau of Justice Statistics,* Selected Findings, Nov. 1992, 2.

"An estimated four million American women": Catherine Klein and Leslye Orloff, "Providing Legal Protection for Battered Women: An Analysis of State Statutes and Case Law," 21 *Hofstra Law Review* 4 (Summer 1993), 801–1189, at 808–809.

"significantly threaten": Naftali Bendavid, "The Surprising Volatility of the Violence Against Women Act," *Legal Times,* June 20, 1994, 16.

"there is a need for something to be done" and "does not make clear the requisite intent or motive": Linda Hirshman, "Making Safety a Civil Right," *Ms.,* Sept./Oct. 1994, 44–47.

"The husband who beats his wife is not thinking": Bendavid, 16.

Tracy Thurman, was beaten senseless: There are many accounts of this attack. Tracy Thurman sued the Torrington Police Department and won nearly $2 million in settlement. In the landmark verdict the jury found that twenty-four officers—nearly half the Torrington police force—were negligent and had violated her civil rights. See *20/20*, "Pushed to the Edge," interview of Tracy Thurman by Tom Jarriel, Aug. 4, 1992; and Sylvia A. Law, "Every 18 Seconds a Woman Is Beaten," *Judges' Journal* (Winter 1991), 12–14.

Oregon, which in 1977 became the first: Joan Zorza, "Mandatory Arrest: A Step toward Ending Domestic Violence," in press, *Criminal Justice* magazine.

reports were filed in only 30 percent: "Behind Closed Doors," Report of the Task Force on Family Violence, New York City, April 1993, 61–63.

"When battered women call the police": Colorado report, 75.

arrests were made on the spot: Ronet Bachman and Ann Coker, "Police Involvement in Domestic Violence," 10 *Violence and Victims* 2 (1995), 91–106, at 95.

"I have a maniac over here attacking me": Daniel Wise, "Bronx Judge Is Acquitted after Assault Bench Trial," *N.Y. Law Journal,* Feb. 14, 1995, 1.

Ray Ponke demolished the inside: Jacquelynn Boyle and L. L. Brasier, "Jury Hears of Death; Domestic Violence Bills Ready," *Detroit Free Press,* Sept. 12, 1994, 1B.

Caroline Witt in Crystal Lake: Michele Ingrassia and others, "Stalked to Death?" *Newsweek,* Nov. 1, 1993, 28–29.

Divorced and separated women account for only a tenth: Joan Zorza, "Recognizing and Protecting the Privacy and Confidentiality Needs of Battered Women," 29 *Family Law Quarterly* 2 (Summer 1995), 273–310, at 274–275.

a Detroit woman who lost an arm: Janet Wilson, "Injured Woman Loses Big to Get Her Boyfriend Freed," *Detroit Free Press,* Nov. 13, 1993.

20 to 80 percent of all such cases are dropped: "Behind Closed Doors," 42.

"[The judge] took a few minutes": Maryland report, 2–3.

a Queens criminal court judge denied: Shaun Assael and J. A. Lobbia, "New York's 10 Worst Judges," *Village Voice,* Sept. 15, 1992, 33.

police violated the civil rights of Cecelia Eagleston: Phil Mintz, "Jury Deadlock in Stab Victim Suit," *Newsday,* June 9, 1992, 25; Timothy M. Phelps, "High Court Backs Suffolk Cops," *Newsday,* Oct. 3, 1995.

"mocked . . . ridiculed and humiliated": Georgia report, 712.

"There is no actual physical injury": Alice McQuillan and others, "He Was Freed to Kill," *N.Y. Daily News,* Feb. 14, 1996, 4–5.

one judge sometimes asks women in court: Report of the Missouri Task Force on Gender and Justice, 58 *Missouri Law Review* 3 (Summer 1993), at 505.

"I seriously wonder how many married men": Bill Hewitt and others, "Heat of Passion," *People,* Nov. 11, 1994, 89; Karl Vick, "Md. Judge Taking Heat in Cuckolded Killer Case," *Washington Post,* Oct. 30, 1994, A1.

"highly misguided requirements": Schafran, "There's No Accounting for Judges," 58 *Albany Law Review* (1995), 101–124, at 102.

"I knew that he was angry": "Day One: Soft on Domestic Violence?" ABC television broadcast transcript, Feb. 2, 1995.

"You Light up My Life" and "Is that a crime in Florida?": Florida report, 121–122.

"I can't conclude that [the attack]": Sheila Weller, "America's Most Sexist Judges," *Redbook,* Feb. 1994, 85.

"It's enough to blow any guy's cool": Weller, "More of America's Most Sexist Judges," *Redbook,* Dec. 1994, 88–91+, at 90–91.

"There's no accounting for judges": Schafran, 106.

"private matter between O.J.'s wife and the courts": Bill Turque and others, "He Could Run . . . But He Couldn't Hide," *Newsweek,* June 27, 1994.

"At least 90 percent of battered women who are killed": Zorza, at 275.

87 percent said they believed outside intervention: Family Violence Prevention Fund poll, San Francisco, Aug. 18, 1995.

SEXUAL ASSAULT

. . . it is the only crime: Maggio, 267.

"Rape is forced sexual intercourse": Ronet Bachman, "Violence Against Women: A National Crime Victimization Survey Report," 1994, U.S. Department of Justice, 14.

80 percent of all rapes: R. Bachman and Linda Saltzman, "Violence Against Women: Estimates from the Redesigned Survey," U.S. Department of Justice (1995), 3.

70 percent of the women sustained no injuries: "Rape in America," National Victims Center, Arlington, Va., and the Crime Victims Research and Treatment Center, Medical University of South Carolina, 1992.

reversed Berkowitz's conviction: *Pennsylvania* v. *Berkowitz,* 641 A2d. 1161 (1994).

"Ask a woman if she has ever been raped": Catharine MacKinnon, *Feminism Unmodified* (Cambridge, Mass.: Harvard University Press, 1987), 105.

2 million: Schafran, "Writing and Reading about Rape: A Primer," 66 *St. John's Law Review* 4 (Fall–Winter 1993), 979–1045, at 994.

"Ninety-eight percent of the victims": Senator Joseph Biden, introduction to "The Response to Rape: Detours on the Road to Equal Justice," Committee on the Judiciary, U.S. Senate, 1993 (III).

"Rape is . . . an accusation easily": Hale quoted in Rhode, "Justice and Gender," 248.

"unchaste character": Rhode, "Justice and Gender," 249.

"assuming . . . that women lie": State in Interest of M.T.S. 609 A.2d 1266 (N.J. 1992).

allowed in jury instructions in twenty-six states: Schrafran, "A Primer," 1010, citing A. Thomas Morris, Book Note, "The Empirical, Historical and Legal Case against the Cautionary Instruction," *Duke Law Journal* 154 (1988), 155 nn12–14.

"we have heard many attorneys": New York report, 51–52.

People v. *Iniguez:* 30 Ca. Rptr. 2d 258 (1994).

"good girls" are far less likely to fight back: Catharine MacKinnon, *Toward a Feminist Theory of the State* (Cambridge, Mass.: Harvard University Press, 1989), 177, 297 n20, referring to Pauline Bart's research, "A Study of Women Who Both Were Raped and Avoided Rape," *Journal of Social Issues* 37 (1981), 132.

reforms have little impact: Julie Horney and Cassia Spohn, "Rape Law Reform and Instrumental Change in Six Urban Jurisdictions," 25 *Law and Society* 1 (1991), 117–153, at 120.

"[I]t may be that only a comprehensive reform": Horney and Spohn, at 147–148.

"there were things in her life": John Quinones, "Testing the Truth," *PrimeTime,* ABC, April 5, 1995.

"Was it forced?": Gill Freeman's testimony, Senate Judiciary Committee, April 9, 1991, 136.

"kinky and aggressive sexual" and "It was Jennifer who was pursuing": James Kunen, "Blaming His Victim: A Killer Cops a Plea," *People,* April 11, 1988, 24–29, at 28.

"For example, a defense attorney": Schafran, "Writing and Reading about Rape," 1036.

a judge allowed questions about diapers: Missouri report, 617.

Carolyn Smith, director of Rape Victim Services in Paducah: Kentucky report, 37.

"enticing dress and cool demeanor": Florida report, 152.

men who have no trouble getting dates: Schafran, "Importance of Voir Dire in Rape Trials," *Trial,* August 1992, 26, on the research by Eugene Kanin of Purdue University, who studied seventy-one self-described date rapists, white, middle-class, undergraduate college students. Schafran notes that he found them "dramatically more [sexually] active" than most male students, and they "pursued a lively and positive interest in women, dating, and sexual activity."

"I think he's too charming": quoted by Schafran, "Importance of Voir Dire," 26.

"The first thing many victims ask": Linda Fairstein, *Sexual Violence* (William Morrow: New York, 1993), 146.

"the message that the law against rape": MacKinnon, *Toward a Feminist Theory,* 179.

"I feel we shouldn't have got anything": *Now,* NBC, interview with Katie Couric, Aug. 25, 1993.

one hundred women who had been raped: Judith Lewis Herman, *Trauma and Recovery* (New York: Basic Books, HarperCollins, 1992).

"Rape survivors reported more 'nervous breakdowns' ": Herman, 49–50.

"voluntary social companion": Jaye Sitton, "Old Wine in New Bottles: The Marital Rape Exemption," 72 *North Carolina Law Review* 1, Nov. 1993, 261–288, at 280, quoting the Delaware statute.

"you can be expelled for cheating": Michael Stetz, "Student: Rape Policy Inadequate," (Harrisburg, Pa.) *Patriot-News,* Dec. 13, 1995, A1.

"special interest groups with an agenda": Robert Lipsyte, "Dr. Tom Practices Spin Control," *N.Y. Times,* Dec. 29, 1995, B12.

"We didn't realize that people's attitudes": Jan Hoffman, "Twelve Angry People," *Village Voice,* Aug. 6, 1991.

"a black woman like that": Schafran, *Writing and Reading about Rape,* 1002.

"No, I didn't rape my wife": AP report, "Marital Rape Acquittal Enrages Women's Groups," *Chicago Tribune,* April 18, 1992.

"There are far too many places": "Man Gets 10–20–Year Term for Raping Wife," *N.Y. Times,* Dec. 21, 1995, B10.

My thanks to Sheila Weller and *Redbook* magazine for bringing several of the following cases to my attention. "America's Most Sexist Judges," Feb. 1994, and "More of America's Most Sexist Judges," Dec. 1994.

"I think what he needs—he needs a girlfriend": compiled from wire services, "Rape Suspect Told to Get a Girlfriend," *St. Petersburg Times,* Feb. 16, 1994, 3A.

"You need to date": AP, "Judge Also Gave Rape Trial 'Advice' in 1991," (Memphis, Tenn.) *Commercial Appeal,* Feb. 25, 1994, A31.

"is not in here with any black eyes": "Judge Apologizes for Remarks in Sexual Assault Case," *Legal Intelligencer,* June 1, 1993, 5.

"It's not the type of thing that is so alarming": Weller, 91.

William Millard . . . ruled that the rape charges: Catherine Candisky, "Witness Late to Court, Rape Defendant Freed," *Columbus Dispatch,* Sept. 22, 1993, 1A; "Judge Not, Lest Ye Be Incompetent," Joe Dirch, Oct. 5, 1993; "Millard Verdict; He Has Another Chance to Do Job Right," Dec. 1, 1993.

"caused Mr. Gross to snap": Weller, 91.

"The impact, I think, on this young woman": Emily Sachar, "Was Rapist Violent? Sentencing Put Off After Judge, Lawyer Duel," *Newsday,* March 14, 1992, 10.

"a hard time laying all the blame": Diane Knox, "The Judge Who Blamed a Rape Victim," *American Lawyer,* Nov. 1990, 21.

"Is this suit in any way connected with how your father": *Catchpole* v. *Brannon,* 42 California Reporter, 2d 440, 1995 WL378854 (C. App. 1 Dist.).

rapists who get away with it: Schafran, "Credibility in the Court: Why Is There a Gender Gap?" noting the work of Gene R. Abel and others, "Self-Reported Sex Crimes of Nonincarcerated Paraphilliacs," 2 *Journal Interpersonal Violence* 3 (1987). The rapists in this study averaged seven victims each. Other studies confirm these findings. This means that like batterers, rapists also rape again and again.

one out of every eight women will be raped: "Rape in America," 2.

CONCLUSION

If my cup won't hold but a pint: Truth, quoted by Maggio, 178.

Donna Carrol, a woman in northern Wisconsin: William E. Schmidt, "Adultery as a Crime: Old Laws Dusted Off in a Wisconsin Case," *N.Y. Times,* April 30, 1990, A1.

Index